The uncanny

Manchester University Press

Leonardo da Vinci, *The Maddona Litta*
The State Hermitage Museum, St Petersburg

The uncanny

Nicholas Royle

Manchester University Press

Published by Manchester University Press
Oxford Road, Manchester M13 9NR, UK
www.manchesteruniversitypress.co.uk

British Library Cataloguing-in-Publication Data
A catalogue record for this book is available from the British Library

ISBN 978 0 7190 5561 4

First published 2003

15 14 13 12 11 10 09 08   10 9 8 7 6 5 4 3

Designed in Dante with Tiffany display
by Max Nettleton FCSD

Typeset by Koinonia, Manchester

Printed in Great Britain
by CPI Antony Rowe Ltd, Chippenham

Contents

Illustrations

Preface

A preface is conventionally signed, dated, placed in a fashion that distinguishes it from the text that follows. Written at the end, it comes at the beginning. It appears to gather everything together, to give an impression of order and mastery over what it prefaces. The genre of the preface is perhaps quite familiar. If so, it is also apt to become strange in the special sense that has interested me in these pages. This is the strangeness of the uncanny, a flickering moment of embroilment in the experience of something at once strange and familiar. Uncanniness entails a sense of uncertainty and suspense, how ever momentary and unstable. As such it is often to be associated with an experience of the threshold, liminality, margins, borders, frontiers. Perceived as being at the threshold of the work, the preface inhabits a peculiar limbo – part of *and* separate from, before *and* after, what follows it.

This is, so far as I am aware, the first book-length study of its topic. The uncanny is an important term for contemporary thinking and debate across a range of disciplines and discourses, including philosophy, literature, film studies, architecture, psychoanalysis and queer theory. Much of this importance can be traced back to Sigmund Freud's essay of 1919, 'Das Unheimliche' ('The Uncanny'). Freud was perhaps the first to foreground the distinctive nature of the uncanny as a feeling of something not simply weird or mysterious but, more specifically, as something strangely familiar. As a ghostly concept and feeling, however, the uncanny has a complex history going back to at least the Enlightenment. I offer a detailed historical account of the emergence of the uncanny, together with a series of close readings of different aspects of the topic. Following the introductory historical and critical overview in Chapter 1, there are chapters on the death drive, *déjà vu*, 'silence, solitude and darkness', the fear of being buried alive, doubles, ghosts, cannibalism, telepathy and madness, as well as more oblique readings concerned, for example, with teaching, politics, film and religion.

The world is uncanny, I suggest in Chapter 1. Notions of the uncanny provide ways of thinking critically about what is happening all around, across the so-called 'western world' and beyond. The date of the present preface is haunted by another date, by what is named 'September 11'. For me, the colossal twin or double towers of the World Trade Center were already rather uncanny: I remember the eerie, vertiginous sensation of standing on top, in October 1982, in the deafening wind, looking across to the adjacent twin tower, weirdly close yet far away, trying to take in not only its immense height but also the fact that that tower, and therefore (I realized) the tower on which I was standing, was swaying visibly from side to side. The events of 11 September 2001 were immediately perceived as having changed the world. The uncanny aspects of what happened can perhaps readily be evoked: on 9.11 (the numerical abbreviation of the month and day, according to US dating convention, but also, by chance, the telephone number of the US emergency services), this extraordinary double-building was destroyed, 'live on television', by hijackers acting out the enormity of a death drive, of a double and more than double death drive. The appalling apparent accident of a plane flying into a skyscraper was followed minutes later by its uncanny repetition, another plane crashing into the other skyscraper, immediately disconfirming (and yet still, in that moment, incredibly) any sense of the merely 'accidental'. As the twin towers collapsed, 'live' on television, and the images of this collapse were repeatedly screened over the hours that followed, a sense of the uncanny seemed all-pervading: Is this real? Is this really happening? Surely it's a film? Is this 'our' apocalypse now?

Thousands of people were murdered in the attacks of that day: at least some of them, an uncountable number, buried alive. As if speaking (impossibly) for all who had lost their lives, there was the terrible prosopopoeia of the voice of someone about to die on one of the hijacked aircraft, left as voice-mail for a loved one and for the world's media. The uncanniness of the telephone, especially the mobile telephone, came across as audible in a new way, whether in the voices of those on board the planes or of those afterwards speaking out of the rubble, effacing and deranging the distinctions between private and public, the living and the ghostly. On 11 September the familiar, so-called 'domestic' security of the United States was evidently wiped out for ever. The first war of the twenty-first century (as the US President boldly termed it) was declared, bizarrely, on an unknown enemy. One of the least popular, most legally questionable presidents in American history experienced an instantaneous rise to a position of overwhelming popularity and authority thanks to this very enemy. Here, very legibly, was the logic of the double and the diabolical. It quickly emerged that the prime suspect responsible for orchestrating the atrocities in the US had, in the past, himself received military training and support from the US.

The spectre of jihad returns. From the US point of view, the fateful, apparently uncircumventable logic of revenge had already imposed itself; hundreds of thousands, even millions of people would suffer for the consequences of the events of a day that, in a sense, has not ended. For the uncanniness of September 11 has to do with what was *already happening* as well as with the fear or dread of what may be to come. Such is the uncanny significance of what it is currently fashionable to call 'blowback': economically, politically, militarily, a strategy proves to have unforeseen and undesirable after-effects. But this strategy was also itself already an after-effect of earlier events. Blowback blows uncannily back down history as well as into the shadowy, tottering projections of the future.

This book has been written, altered and revised, over a number of years. One fragment in particular, the fiction entitled 'A crowded after-life', dates back to 1984. In a sense the un-canny has been my focus of concern for even longer: the first academic paper I ever presented (with Jacqueline Hall, at the University of Oxford in 1979) was on Tennyson and the uncanny, the first university lecture I gave (at Southampton in 1981) was entitled 'Freud's "The Uncanny" and the Later Poetry of Wallace Stevens'. Have I been following this focus of concern or has it been following me? How canny is the uncanny? The preface falls interminably, perhaps, into an autobiographical abyss: as the *OED* suggests, one archaic synonym for the time of birth, giving birth or being born, is 'the canny moment'. A number of the essays published in the present book originally appeared elsewhere, sometimes in quite different form. An earlier and quite different version of Chapter 3 appeared under the title 'Why Teach?' in *Education and Culture at the Dawn of the Third Millennium / Education et culture à l'aube du troisième millénaire*, ed. Issa Asgarally (Réduit: Mauritius Institute of Education / Editions Le Printemps, 1999). An earlier version of 'Exam' (at the end of Chapter 3) was originally published in the *Oxford Literary Review*, vol. 17 (1995). A slightly different version of Chapter 11 appeared as '*Déjà Vu*' in *Post-theory: New Directions in Criticism*, ed. Martin McQuillan, Graeme Macdonald, Robin Purves and Stephen Thomson (Edinburgh: Edinburgh University Press, 1999). A more or less identical version of Chapter 13 was first published as 'Chance Encounter' in *Neon Lit 2*, ed. Nicholas Royle (London: Time Out Books, 1999). A substantially different version of Chapter 14 appeared as

'Starters' in *Verschlungene Grenzen: Anthrophagie in Literatur und Kulturwissenschaften*, ed. Annette Keck, Inka Kording and Anja Prochaska (Tübingen: Gunter-Narr-Verlag, 1999). An earlier version of Chapter 15 originally appeared under the title 'Breathless: Hamsun and Contemporary Scottish Fiction' in *Hamsun in Edinburgh* ed. Peter Graves and Arne Kruse (Hamaroy: Hamsun-Selskapet, 1998). An earlier version of Chapter 17 originally appeared in *The Limits of Death*, ed. Joanne Morra, Mark Robson and Marquard Smith (Manchester: Manchester University Press, 2000). Chapter 18 ('Mole') was first published in French, trans. Ian Maclachlan and Michael Syrotinski, in *L'Animal autobiographique: Autour de Jacques Derrida*, ed. Marie-Louise Mallet (Paris: Galilée, 1999). A slightly different version of Chapter 20 first appeared under the title 'Phantom Review' in *Textual Practice*, vol. 11, no. 2 (Summer 1997), more recently reprinted in Martin McQuillan, ed., *Deconstruction: A Reader* (Edinburgh: Edinburgh University Press, 2000). Chapter 21 ('The private parts of Jesus Christ') first appeared in *The Bodies of Christ: Writing the Church from Thomas Carlyle to Jacques Derrida*, ed. John Schad (Burlington, Vermont: Ashgate Press, 2001). I would like to express my thanks to the various editors and publishers for permission to reprint. And while on the subject of editors and publishers, I would also like to record my gratitude to Matthew Frost, my editor at Manchester University Press. It has been a great pleasure to work with him on this book: he is a fine fellow, as Conrad might say. My thanks go also to others at MUP, especially Kate Fox and Max Nettleton, and to my copy-editor, John Banks.

Many of the pieces in this book were originally delivered as papers at university conferences and seminars. I would like to thank all those who invited me to speak and all those who were willing to listen, in particular at the Universities of Stirling, Glasgow, Edinburgh, Dundee, Aberdeen, Swansea, Cardiff, Sussex, London (Royal Holloway), Staffordshire, York, Leeds, Teesside, Liverpool, Warwick and Oxford, in the UK, as well as at the Gantry Arts Centre, Southampton; the University of Konstanz, Germany; the Institute of Education, Mauritius; the Middle East Technical University of Ankara, Turkey; the University of Jyväskylä, Finland, the State University of New York at Albany; and Cerisy-la-Salle, France. In the course of writing this book I have been inestimably indebted to the love, friendship, support and conversation of many people. Menninkäinen made it possible and kept me going: I could not have done it otherwise. I would also like to thank, as ever, my father and my mother (who is no longer able to read). Some parts of the book were composed while I was teaching at the University of Stirling (1992–99), others (more recently) at the University of Sussex. I would like to express warm thanks and appreciation to all colleagues and students at Stirling who helped shape my thinking on this project, in particular to David Punter (with whom I have had the pleasure of many stimulating conversations on the uncanny as well as of teaching a seminar on the topic), Vance Adair, Valerie Allen, Ares Axiotis, Scott Brewster, Lance Butler, Glennis Byron, Jeremy Carrette, Vic Carroll, Judy Delin, John Drakakis, Alistair Findlay, Nancy Haddow, Asko Kauppinen, Kirsten Kearney, Neil Keeble, Douglas Mack, Alasdair Macrae, Dan McAdam, Sudesh Mishra, Stephen Penn, James Procter, David Reid, Angela Smith, Grahame Smith, Jackie Tasioulas, Margaret Walshe, Rory Watson and Tina Webberley. I should also like to record my gratitude to the University of Stirling for providing me with a research assistant for one semester: Asko Kauppinen was especially helpful in locating some of the older primary material as well as the elusive 'crocodile' story touched upon by Freud in 'The Uncanny' (and discussed below, in Chapter 9). I would also like to express my thanks to all at Sussex who have more recently helped me bring this project to some sort of completion, in particular Geoffrey Bennington (now at the University of Emory, Atlanta), Peter Boxall, Mary Dove, Elena Gualtieri, Margaret Healy, Amber Jacobs, Jeremy Lane, Vicky Lebeau, Laura Marcus, Stephen Medcalf, Peter Nicholls, Vincent Quinn, Minoli Salgado, Alan Sinfield, Jenny Taylor, Sophie Thomas, Evelyn Welch, John Whitley and Marcus Wood. I am very grateful to the University of Sussex for making available some financial assistance towards the production costs of a book that ended up almost twice the length I had initially envisaged. For help with Freud's German I would like to record my indebtedness to Jana Beyreuther, Steffi Boothroyd, Peter Krapp and Julia Lang. (All errors and infelicities, here as elsewhere, I solemnly confess are mine.) For the conversation, thoughts and comments of other friends and colleagues I am especially grateful to Derek Attridge, Andrew Bennett, Leo Bersani, Dave Boothroyd, Julia Borossa, Ron Butlin, Timothy Clark, Yanick Crow, Sarah Dillon, Gerald Doherty, Diane Elam, Maud Ellmann, Rodolphe Gasché, Michael Gasson, Jacqueline Hall, Christopher Johnson, Peggy Kamuf, Ian Maclachlan, Elissa Marder, David Marriott, J. Hillis Miller, Joanna Moore, Pauline Morgan, Forbes Morlock, Robert Penhallurick, Maarit Piipponen, Richard Rand, Alessandro Ricco, Caroline Rooney, Nicholas Royle, Roy Sellars, Robert Smith, Stelarc, Simon Stevenson, Michael Syrotinski, Mikko Tuhkanen, Daniel Watt, Lois Wheller, Heidi and Gary Williamson, David Wills, Sarah Wood, Ann Wordsworth and Robert Young. Finally, I would like to add a word of singular thanks to Jacques Derrida: his writings and his friendship have been especially crucial for my thinking on the uncanny and for the elaboration of this work.

N. W. O. R
Lewes
November 2001

Abbreviations

Chambers   *The Chambers Dictionary* (Edinburgh: Chambers, 1998).

OED   *The Oxford English Dictionary*, 2nd edition, prepared by J. A. Simpson and E. S. C. Weiner, 20 vols (Oxford: Clarendon Press, 1989).

PFL   *The Pelican Freud Library*, trans. James Strachey, Alix Strachey and Alan Tyson, ed. James Strachey, Angela Richards, Alan Tyson and Albert Dickson, 15 vols (Harmondsworth: Penguin, 1973–86). Wherever possible, I refer to this corrected edition of the Standard Edition.

SE   *The Standard Edition of the Complete Psychological Works of Sigmund Freud*, trans. James Strachey et al., 24 vols (London: Hogarth Press and the Institute of Psycho-Analysis, 1953–73).

U   Sigmund Freud, 'The Uncanny', trans. James Strachey, *Pelican Freud Library*, 14 (Harmondsworth: Penguin, 1985), 339–76. References to the German text of this Freud essay are taken from *Gesammelte Werke*, 12 (London: Imago, 1947), 229–68. Where reference is made to the German text, the page number is given after the English translation page reference and preceded by a slash.

Note: unless otherwise stated, all quotations from Shakespeare are based on *The Riverside Shakespeare*, ed. G. Blakemore Evans et al. (Boston: Houghton Mifflin, 1974).

For Sebastian, Alexander and Elena

1

The uncanny: an introduction

When life is over, we are taught to live. (Michel de Montaigne)[1]

We Europeans confront a world of tremendous ruins. A few things are still towering, much looks decayed and uncanny, while most things already lie on the ground. (Friedrich Nietzsche)[2]

An author's words are deeds. (Sigmund Freud)[3]

We are all haunted houses. (H. D.)[4]

The uncanny entails another thinking of beginning: the beginning is already haunted. The uncanny is ghostly. It is concerned with the strange, weird and mysterious, with a flickering sense (but not conviction) of something supernatural. The uncanny involves feelings of uncertainty, in particular regarding the reality of who one is and what is being experienced. Suddenly one's sense of oneself (of one's so-called 'personality' or 'sexuality', for example) seems strangely questionable. The uncanny is a crisis of the proper: it entails a critical disturbance of what is proper (from the Latin *proprius*, 'own'), a disturbance of the very idea of personal or private property including the properness of proper names, one's so-called 'own' name, but also the proper names of others, of places, institutions and events. It is a crisis of the natural, touching upon everything that one might have thought was 'part of nature': one's own nature, human nature, the nature of reality and the world. But the uncanny is not simply an experience of strangeness or alienation. More specifically, it is a peculiar commingling of the familiar and unfamiliar. It can take the form of something familiar unexpectedly arising in a strange and unfamiliar context, or of something strange and unfamiliar unexpectedly arising in a familiar context. It can consist in a sense of homeliness uprooted, the revelation of something unhomely at the heart of hearth and home. It might arise from the seemingly mechanical repetition of a word, such as 'it'. A feeling of uncanniness may come from curious coincidences, a sudden sense that things seem to be fated or 'meant to happen'. It can come in the fear of losing one's eyes or genitals, or in realizing that someone has a missing or prosthetic body-part, in the strange actuality of dismembered, supplementary or phantom limbs. The uncanny can be felt in response to witnessing epileptic or similar fits, manifestations of insanity or other forms of what might appear merely mechanical or automatic life, such as one might associate with trance or hypnosis. And conversely or likewise, it can be felt in response to dolls and other lifelike or mechanical objects. The uncanny can be a matter of something gruesome or terrible, above all death and corpses, cannibalism, live burial, the return of the dead. But it can also be a matter of something strangely beautiful, bordering on ecstasy ('too good to be true'), or eerily reminding us of something, like *déjà vu*. It can involve a feeling of something beautiful but at the same time frightening, as in the figure of the double or telepathy. It comes above all, perhaps, in the uncertainties of silence, solitude and darkness. The uncanny has to do with the sense of a secret encounter: it is perhaps inseparable from an apprehension, however fleeting, of something that should have remained secret and hidden but has come to light. But it is not 'out there', in any simple sense: as a crisis of the proper and natural, it disturbs any straightforward sense of what is inside and what is outside. The uncanny has to do with a strangeness of framing and borders, an experience of liminality. It may be that the uncanny is a feeling that happens only to oneself, within oneself, but it is never one's 'own': its meaning or significance may have to do, most of all, with what is not oneself, with others, with the world 'itself'. It may thus be construed as a foreign body within oneself, even the experience of oneself *as* a foreign body, the very estrangement of inner silence and solitude. It would appear to be indissociably bound up with a sense of repetition or 'coming back'– the return of the repressed, the constant or eternal recurrence of the same thing, a compulsion to repeat. At some level the feeling of the uncanny may be bound up with the most extreme nostalgia or 'homesickness', in other words a compulsion to return to an inorganic state, a desire (perhaps unconscious) to die, a death drive. At the same time, the uncanny is never far from something comic: humour, irony and laughter all have a genuinely 'funny' role in thinking on this topic. Above all, the uncanny is intimately entwined in language, with how we conceive and represent what is happening within ourselves, to ourselves, to the world, when uncanny strangeness is at issue. And it is different (yet strangely the same) every time: its happening is always a kind of un-happening. Its 'un-' unsettles time and space, order and sense.

The uncanny overruns, disordering any field supposedly extraneous to it. Under the heading 'Dawn of a New Millennium', the *Guardian* sets forth its vision of the state of the world on 1 January 2000:

> Attempting to predict the coming century is more than usually foolish. Even 10 years ago we could not have imagined the internet, the speed of computing (currently doubling every eight or nine months), genetic mapping or cloning. While the mystery

of consciousness may elude us for many decades, there are other large areas of our make-up which are about to be revealed. Last month scientists announced the decoding of the first of 23 human chromosomes. It is, as yet, only a rough sketch, but they will be reading the entire genome soon enough, decoding every human characteristic, working out the genes or combinations of genes which are responsible for musicality, schizophrenia, left-handedness, height, athletic prowess and aggression.

It feels uncannily as though human beings are finally getting to the roots of the tree of knowledge.[5]

The world is uncanny. Within the *Guardian*'s tacitly Biblical metaphor of 'finally getting to the roots of the tree of knowledge' is a strong evocation of the uncanny as what should have remained hidden but has come to light: we are taking ourselves, and our world, to pieces; and this is happening in ways and at speeds that are beyond our control.

As this millennial newspaper article goes on to make clear, the central uncanny paradox has to do with what 'has led us to understand ourselves so profoundly and yet still organise our world so badly'. On the one hand we appear to be moving increasingly close to 'know[ing] the innermost secrets of human existence'; on the other we are rendering increasingly uninhabitable the very planet that is our home. If '[t]he geniuses of genetics have opened Pandora's box', if the very identity of the human is increasingly susceptible to uncanny manipulation, transformation and even duplication (gene therapy, genetic engineering, prosthetic body-machines, cloning), this does not prevent us being in a world where there are more poor, suffering and dying people than ever before and where the situation worsens by the week: 'Genetic research may be discovering the secret of making clever babies in London and New York, but in Mali and Malawi children are going blind for lack of basic eye-cream.' The *Guardian* lead-article remains bound up within a Christian discourse and thinking, implicitly subordinating its evocations of the uncanny within this religious framework: 'If the new millennium sees us eating from the tree of knowledge, we need to work out how we can share out the fruit ... We are blessed to live now: let us make this a blessed century and a blessed new millennium.' Lodged within or alongside this religious rhetoric lie possibilities for construing the uncanny differently. As I hope to suggest in the pages that follow, the uncanny can perhaps provide ways of beginning to think in less dogmatic terms about the nature of the world, ourselves and a politics of the future.

The present study is haunted, from before the beginning, by innumerable other texts. The uncanny has been a focus of critical, literary, philosophical and political reflection from at least the mid nineteenth century to the present – from Karl

Marx and Friedrich Nietzsche to Sigmund Freud, Martin Heidegger, Ludwig Wittgenstein and Jacques Derrida. Everything in Marx that speaks of a spectre that is haunting Europe, everything that has to do with notions of alienation, revolution and repetition, comes down to a thinking of the uncanny (or, in German, *das Unheimliche*).[6] It is not by chance that Derrida in 1993 thought to subtitle his long-awaited book on Marxism 'Marx – *das Unheimliche*'.[7] Uncanniness, as we shall see, is as crucial a notion for Derrida and deconstruction as it is for Marxism. Nietzsche's *The Will to Power* (1883–88) opens with his famous announcement concerning European nihilism: 'Nihilism stands at the door: whence comes this uncanniest of all guests?'[8] But everywhere in Nietzsche's texts we can find a more or less explicit engagement with notions of uncanniness.[9]

In the twentieth century, on the other hand, it was Heidegger who, perhaps more intensively than any other modern philosopher, was specifically concerned to explore the notion that 'At bottom, the ordinary is not ordinary; it is extra-ordinary, uncanny'.[10] For Heidegger, the fundamental character of our being in the world is uncanny, unhomely, not-at-home. *Being and Time*, for instance, expounds the view that 'In anxiety one feels "*uncanny*" [*unheimlich*]'. He asserts: 'That kind of Being-in-the-world which is tranquillized and familiar is a mode of Dasein's uncanniness, not the reverse ... [*T*]*he "not-at-home" must be conceived as the more primordial phenomenon.*'[11] At first sight it may appear that the notion of the uncanny has only a small part to play in the philosophy of Wittgenstein. But as Gordon C. F. Bearn has argued, 'the uncanny is the silent shadow of many of Wittgenstein's internal conversations'.[12] Wittgenstein's work is impelled by a desire for security and peace: 'Thoughts that are at peace [*Friede*]. That's what someone who philosophizes yearns for.' But this 'peace' is strange. It is, Wittgenstein says, like 'a gift in a fairy tale: in the magic castle it appears enchanted and if you look at it outside in daylight it is nothing but an ordinary bit of iron (or something of the sort)'.[13] Peace, in effect, becomes uncanny – an estranged ordinariness. As Bearn's account makes clear, the uncanny is a 'philosophically significant form of disquiet' (p. 48) at the heart of Wittgenstein's work.[14] What Heidegger and Wittgenstein perhaps share, in this context, is a preoccupation with what Stanley Cavell has provokingly called 'the surrealism of the habitual'.[15]

Also crucial to an understanding of the twentieth century in this general context of philosophy and literature, culture and politics, is the role and influence of Russian formalism, and in particular the formalists' emphasis on the notion of defamiliarization or 'making strange' (*ostranenie*). Russian formalism (at least as evidenced in the work of its best known practitioner Victor Shklovsky) was impelled not by a desire to domesticate, order and control that strange stuff called literature, but rather by a desire to register and affirm the power of literature (especially poetry) to make strange, to defamiliarize, to make unfamiliar all sorts of familiar perceptions and beliefs. In his most famous essay, 'Art as Technique' (1917), Shklovsky quotes Tolstoy discussing what, in the nineteenth century, was the common practice of punishment by flogging, in other words the act of taking a whip and 'lash[ing someone] about on the naked buttocks'. Tolstoy wonders: 'Just why precisely this stupid, savage means of causing pain and not any other – why not prick the shoulders or any part of the body with needles, squeeze the hands or the feet in a vise, or anything like that?' Shklovsky remarks: 'The familiar act of flogging is made unfamiliar both by the description and by the proposal to change its form without changing its nature. Tolstoy uses this technique of "defamiliarization" constantly.'[16] Shklovsky's example prompts a further related remark here, namely that what seemed familiar to Tolstoy (flogging) is thankfully no longer familiar, at least in the context of western culture. The unfamiliar, in other words, is never fixed, but constantly altering. The uncanny is (the) unsettling (of itself).

A similar point might also be made, especially in the context of theatre in the twentieth century, about the importance of Bertolt Brecht's notion of the alienation effect (or A-effect). The alienation-effect is not to be pinned down and categorized, as if it were an exotic butterfly. Brecht does not specifically name it as uncanny, but the *effect* of the alienation-effect can clearly be construed in this way. The A-effect consists, Brecht argued, 'in turning the object ... from something ordinary, familiar, immediately accessible, into something peculiar, striking and unexpected'. Among the examples that he gives are when '[one sees] one's mother as a man's wife [as a result of the fact that] one acquires a stepfather' and when 'one sees one's teacher hounded by the bailiffs' (both of these examples suggestively to do with an experience of the unhomely or sudden homelessness). Like the Russian formalist concern with defamiliarization, Brecht's interest lay in the political, transformational, indeed revolutionary possibilities of making the familiar strange. As he puts it: 'new alienations are only designed to free socially conditioned phenomena from that stamp of familiarity which protects them against our grasp today'.[17] Brecht's notion of the alienation-effect remains of interest perhaps precisely to the extent that it resists being viewed as a merely mechanical device: rather, it calls to be thought about as constantly engaging with 'new alienations'.

All of these writers – Heidegger, Wittgenstein, Shklovsky and Brecht – allow us to sense in different ways the ineluctable significance of the uncanny as a means of thinking about so-called 'real life', the ordinary, the familiar and everyday. Inextricably bound up with thoughts of home and dispossession, the homely and unhomely, property and alienation, the uncanny becomes, in the words of Anthony Vidler, 'a metaphor for a fundamentally unlivable modern condition'.[18] As he puts it, in his book *The Architectural Uncanny: Essays in the Modern Unhomely*: 'Estrangement and unhomeliness have emerged as the intellectual watchwords of [the twentieth] century, given periodic material and political force by the resurgence of homelessness itself, a homelessness generated sometimes by war, sometimes by the unequal distribution of wealth.'[19]

Of all the texts published on the subject of the uncanny, however, the most indispensable is Sigmund Freud's 1919 essay 'Das Unheimliche', translated into English under the title 'The Uncanny'.[20] In many respects the present study seeks to provide little more than a reading of Freud's short text. The evocations of the uncanny in my opening paragraph are mainly derived from his essay.[21] Judging from his own opening paragraph, Freud seemed to regard the concept of the uncanny as of only peripheral relevance to the peculiar science he had founded, psychoanalysis. 'The Uncanny' begins:

> It is only rarely that a psychoanalyst feels impelled to investigate the subject of aesthetics, even when aesthetics is understood to mean not merely the theory of beauty but the theory of the qualities of feeling. He works in other strata of mental life and has little to do with the subdued emotional impulses which, inhibited in their aims and dependent on a host of concurrent factors, usually furnish the material for the study of aesthetics. But it does occasionally happen that he has to interest himself in some particular province of that subject; and this province usually proves to be a rather remote one, and one which has been neglected in the specialist literature of aesthetics. (U, p. 339)

This opening is so clear yet mysterious, drawing on a feeling of isolation and solitude that will become integral to the subject matter of the essay, conveying a frisson of rarity and remoteness but also confiding intimacy. The uncanny, Freud tells us, is concerned with 'the theory of the qualities of feeling'; it belongs to a 'province' that is 'rather remote', outside the domain of psychoanalysis. There is an unspoken invitation to share, to join Freud in something strange and compelling.

The uncanny is not what Freud (or anyone else) thinks. It has to do with a sense of ourselves as double, split, at odds with ourselves. Let us re-read Freud's opening words: 'It is only rarely that a psychoanalyst feels impelled to investigate the subject of aesthetics, even when aesthetics is understood to mean not merely the theory of beauty but the theory of the qualities of feeling. He works in other strata of mental life' (U, p. 339). The author seems confident and self-assured. He appears to know what it is to be a psychoanalyst and what sort of work he does. But what is happening when someone begins a text by referring to himself in the third person? And what is at stake in this curious reference to being 'impelled' to write on a strange subject? The opening of Freud's essay presents us with someone who has found himself in an unfamiliar place or someone who, apparently without quite knowing why, has chosen to venture into such a place. Do we believe him? 'Him', who? What does believing mean in such a context?

Freud's essay is, perhaps above all, a teaching. It teaches us about psychoanalysis and Freud, about the uncanny and ourselves. It teaches us about teaching. Four remarks might usefully be made in this context.

(1) Freud's account of the uncanny offers new ways of thinking ethics and politics. As Julia Kristeva puts it, in *Strangers to Ourselves*, Freud 'teaches us how to detect foreignness in ourselves'.[22] Exploring the idea that the basis of the concept of universality is 'our own foreignness', Kristeva writes:

> With Freud indeed, foreignness, an uncanny one, creeps into the tranquillity of reason itself, and, without being restricted to madness, beauty, or faith anymore than to ethnicity or race, irrigates our very speaking-being, estranged by other logics, including the heterogeneity of biology ... Henceforth, we know that we are foreigners to ourselves, and it is with the help of that sole support that we can attempt to live with others. (p. 170)

'The Uncanny' is an exemplary work for the analysis and, in many cases, apparently inadvertent demonstration of this foreignness.

(2) The assertions, arguments and beliefs that Freud articulates are not necessarily what is most interesting about the essay. It is a great text for arguing with, for working out what is at stake in its variously problematic, confused, strangely paradoxical lines of argument and demonstration. Freud's essay does not conform to its own specified principles or methodological procedures, it does not keep to the limits it has ostensibly assigned itself. 'The Uncanny' is an extraordinary text for what it does not say, as well as for what it does. It constantly says more or less or other than what it says. In these respects the essay provides an exemplary instance of why it will never be possible to have done with Freud, to finish reading him.

(3) People have very different responses to the essay, not only at first but also on subsequent readings. There is, in short, something strange about the qualities of Freud's text: sometimes a passage or a single sentence can appear to

open up entirely new worlds of thought. At other times it can seem strangely incoherent, curiously repetitive and inconclusive. We may feel, on occasion, that we are 'familiar' with Freud's text, but then something new and unexpected will shift into focus. There may then be a sense of what Slavoj Žižek speaks of as 'the alteration of a small detail in a well-known picture that all of a sudden renders the whole picture strange and uncanny'.[23] More than perhaps any other work by Freud, 'The Uncanny' itself seems uncanny in the sense that it keeps doing different things not only to the reader but also, somehow, *to itself.* As Robert Young puts it: 'Of all Freud's writings, "The Uncanny" is generally recognized as the text in which he most thoroughly finds himself caught up in the very processes he seeks to comprehend'.[24] The uncanny thus consists in what Shoshana Felman has referred to as a 'reading effect', continually open to being re-read but re-read always strangely differently.[25]

(4) Above all, perhaps, Freud's essay teaches us that the uncanny is 'something one does not know one's way about in' (U, p. 341) and that this is where thinking must begin. It is not a question of giving oneself up to a sense of mere aimlessness or alienation, but rather of trying to follow a path as carefully and critically – in a certain sense as *rationally*[26] – as possible, uncertain nevertheless of where it began or appears to end. To write about the uncanny, as Freud's essay makes admirably clear, is to lose one's bearings, to find oneself immersed in the maddening logic of the supplement, to engage with a hydra. This is no reason to give up trying: examples of the uncanny get tangled up with one another, critical distinctions and conclusions become vertiginously difficult, but they are still necessary.[27]

Our concern is with a feeling and a concept, however spectral. The uncanny has a history: this is a fact that Freud scarcely acknowledges, even if its significance is at issue everywhere in his essay. Our concern is with moving beyond his text, not only in terms of considering examples or forms of the uncanny overlooked or only partially dealt with in his work, but also in terms of providing a broader cultural and historical context for thinking about the uncanny in general. The uncanny is inextricably bound up with the history of the Enlightenment and with European and North American Romanticism. As such, it is also characterized by a particular 'take' on things more ancient, archaic, immemorial. Ralph Waldo Emerson recalls a visit with Thomas Carlyle to Stonehenge:

> Stonehenge, in virtue of the simplicity of its plan, and its good preservation, is as if new and recent; and, a thousand years hence, men will thank this age for the accurate

history it will yet eliminate. We walked in and out, and took again and again a fresh look at the uncanny stones. The old sphinx put our petty differences of nationality out of sight. To these conscious stones we two pilgrims were alike known and near.[28]

Stonehenge is uncanny. It seems 'new and recent', but is ancient. It is attributed with a capacity to 'eliminate' time, not only the past but also the future ('a thousand years hence'). Rendering 'differences of nationality' invisible, if only momently, Stonehenge is strangely compelling: its 'uncanny stones' require 'a fresh look' over and over, 'again and again'. The friendship between Emerson and Carlyle (a friendship dating back to their first meeting, in Dumfries, in 1833) had been disintegrating.[29] Stonehenge appears to bring them together again. The stones themselves are 'conscious': Emerson and Carlyle are 'two pilgrims', two foreigners or strangers who are nevertheless 'alike known and near'.[30] There are, in Shakespeare's phrase, 'precious friends hid in death's dateless night'.[31] The night that is death may be dateless, but Emerson's account is quite specifically dated: it describes a visit that took place in July 1848. It would be part of the preciousness to which Shakespeare refers that we cannot know whether the phrase 'uncanny stones' comes from Emerson alone or from his fellow-pilgrim Carlyle: the word 'uncanny' was, in any case, already from elsewhere, a verbal stranger.

What is the history of the word 'uncanny'? As a question of 'what is frightening' (U, p. 339), the uncanny has even one of the boldest thinkers of the twentieth century turning (back) for shelter in a dictionary, indeed in a whole mound of dictionaries. Freud says: 'We will first turn to other languages. But the dictionaries that we consult tell us nothing new ...' (U, p. 341). He makes a lexicological pilgrimage (following in the footsteps of his colleague Theodor Reik: see U, p. 341) looking, supposedly, for the real meaning of 'unheimlich' ('frightening', 'eerie', 'sinister', 'spooky') under the heading of its opposite, 'heimlich' ('intimate', 'friendly', 'familiar', 'not strange'; but also, 'secret', 'secretive', 'kept from sight'). Let us, like Freud, seek cover in dictionaries. The *Oxford English Dictionary* gives the following:

> **Uncanny**, *adj*. [Originally Scottish and northern.] 1. Mischievous, malicious. [*Obsolete.*] 2. Careless, incautious. 3. Unreliable, not to be trusted. [*Obsolete.*] 4. **a**. Of persons: Not quite safe to trust to, or have dealings with, as being associated with supernatural arts or powers. **b**. Partaking of a supernatural character; mysterious, weird, uncomfortably strange or unfamiliar. (Common from *c* 1850.) **c**. In comb. *uncanny-looking* adj. 5. Unpleasantly severe or hard. 6. Dangerous, unsafe.

Chambers Dictionary offers:

> *adj* **uncanny** weird, supernatural; (of eg skill) much greater than one would expect from an ordinary human being; unsafe to associate with; unpleasantly severe (*Scot*); unsafe (*Scot*).

And *Webster's Dictionary*:

> **Uncanny** *adj*. 1. Having or seeming to have a supernatural or inexplicable basis; beyond the ordinary or normal; extraordinary. 2. Mysterious; frightening, as by superstitious dread; uncomfortably strange.

The *OED* and *Webster* definitions are in some respects more precise and helpful than the *Chambers*. That is to say, the uncanny is not simply synonymous with the supernatural (as *Chambers* proposes), but is more accurately *suggestive of* – 'associated with', or 'seeming' to have a basis in – the supernatural. The *OED* and *Webster* also convey the importance not merely of the mysterious or frightening, the strange or alien, but more specifically of the 'uncomfortably strange', the 'uncomfortably strange or unfamiliar'.

All of these dictionary definitions of 'uncanny' are at least implicitly predicated on the so-called positive term, 'canny'. The *OED* traces 'canny', in the sense of 'knowing, sagacious, judicious, prudent; wary, cautious' (sense 1), back to 1637. As an obsolete Scots word, according to the *OED*, 'canny' also means 'cunning, artful, wily' (sense 2), 'supernaturally wise, endowed with occult or magical power' (sense 4, dating back to 1768), 'lucky, fortunate, prosperous' (sense 5). In current usage, 'canny' is principally defined as:

> Careful or cautious in motion or action; *hence*, quiet, gentle, 'soft' of speech; free from commotion, disturbance, or noise. Said of persons or animals, in their action, speech, or disposition; and also applied to things, as running water, the sea, wind, etc. (The usual sense in modern Scotch.) (sense 7)

> Quiet, easy, snug, comfortable, pleasant, cosy. (sense 8)

> Agreeable to the eyes or perception, tidy, seemly, comely; good, worthy, 'nice', very satisfactory. In the north of England (in some parts pronounced *conny*) a general epithet of approbation or satisfaction, as in 'Canny Newcastle', 'the Canny Town'. In N. Lancashire, 'of good size or amount'. (Cf. the vulgar 'a tidy bit of money', and the like.) Not a Scotch sense. (sense 9)

The *OED* also refers 'canny' to a certain humorousness: 'Of humour: Quiet, sly, "pawky"' (sense 7b). *Chambers Dictionary*, on the other hand, has:

> *adj.* Knowing; skilful; shrewd, *esp* in business; sparing in money matters; lucky or fortunate (*Scot*); gentle; innocent; good or nice (*Northern*); sly or pawky.

Webster's offers:

> *adj.* 1. Careful, cautious; prudent. 2. Astute; shrewd; knowing; sagacious. 3. Skilled; expert. 4. *Scot. a.* frugal; thrifty. *b.* safe to deal with, invest in, or work at (usually used with a negative). *c.* gentle; careful; steady. *d.* snug; cozy; comfortable. *e.* pleasing; attractive; pretty. *f. Archaic* having supernatural or occult powers.

Already we confront the oddity of a word with a fateful charge ('lucky' or 'fortunate'), a word with conflicting or even antithetical meanings ('cunning' but 'innocent', 'sly' but 'pleasant', 'knowing' but perhaps *too* knowing). We may also note here the lurking presence of the comic: 'canny' (and therefore, perhaps, 'uncanny') as quietly, slyly humorous.[32] Above all, in its archaic past, 'canny' has already meant its opposite ('uncanny'): 'having or seeming to have supernatural or occult powers'. The similarities between English (or Scottish English) and German, regarding the ways in which 'uncanny' (*unheimlich*) haunts and is haunted by what is 'canny' (*heimlich*), are themselves perhaps uncanny.

Of course the German *unheimlich* is not simply synonymous with the English word 'uncanny'. At the same time, what is uncanny or *unheimlich* is crucially a matter of the strange vicissitudes of translation, including translation effects within what may appear to be a single word: 'unheimlich' *or* 'uncanny'.[33] We have from the beginning been doing something strange with Freud, ventriloquizing him into an English speaker. Strange, but perhaps legitimate. In its James Strachey version, Freud's essay is perhaps as eloquent as any other piece of English prose that came out of what is called 'Bloomsbury'. It is also a work that has, however minimally or subtly, changed the English language. It is with an English 'uncanny' and with an English Freud (as much as a German or a French Freud) that we are concerned in the present study.

In its putatively 'supernatural' sense – as 'associated with supernatural arts or powers', but also as irreducible to 'the supernatural explained'[34] – 'uncanny' dates back to the late eighteenth century: the *OED* cites Robert Fergusson's *Poems* (1773) as its earliest instance. This 'original' context is perhaps worth dwelling on for a moment. The poem, entitled 'An Eclogue, To the Memory of Dr WILLIAM WILKIE, late Professor of Natural Philosophy in the University of St Andrews', is in the form of a dialogue between two shepherds, Geordie and Davie, who are mourning the death of another, called Willy.[35] Davie says of the dead 'Willy':

> They tell me, Geordie, he had sic a gift
> That scarce a starnie blinkit frae the lift,
> But he wou'd some auld warld name for't find,
> As gart him keep it freshly in his mind:
> For this some ca'd him an uncanny wight;
> The clash gaed round, 'he had the second sight;'
> A tale that never fail'd to be the pride
> Of grannies spinnin at the ingle side.[36]

Strikingly, this 'original' usage of the word 'uncanny' as 'associated with super-natural arts or powers' is explicitly concerned with language and storytelling: the 'wight' is 'uncanny' because of his ability to come up with 'some auld warld name' for a star twinkling in the heavens ('frae the lift'), and for this 'auld' word to be (kept) strangely 'fresh'. Aptly too, perhaps, the word in question is not specified: the poem works through an absence or ellipsis of language. Linked to this, we are reading (or hearing) a lament, a sort of elegy: this 'uncanny wight' is dead; death pervades the poem and the very 'freshness' of the language of its mourned protagonist.[37]

The story is passed on, repeated and repeatable, as if endlessly. From 'They tell me, Geordie' to the 'tale' told by 'grannies', the uncanny seems to be bound up with a compulsion to tell, a compulsive storytelling.[38] This new 'uncanny' word, this new sense of the old word 'uncanny', comes out of a poem discussing the very idea of new words and new senses: it constitutes what David Daiches has described as 'something new in eighteenth-century Scottish poetry' while at the same time presenting the English language with the enigmatic origin of a new, ghostly concept.[39] The 'uncanny' comes from Scotland, from that 'auld country' that has so often been represented as 'beyond the borders', liminal, an English foreign body. The 'uncanny' comes out of a language which is neither purely English (as if there could be such a thing) nor foreign. The poetic roots of the modern sense of this word in Scots present a vignette of the uncanny: uncertainties *at the origin* concerning colonization and the foreign body, and a mixing of what is at once old and long-familiar with what is strangely 'fresh' and new; a pervasive linking of death, mourning and spectrality, especially in terms of storytelling, transgenerational inheritance and knowledge; and, last but hardly least, a sense of the strange and irreducibly unsettling 'place' of language in any critical reflection on uncanniness.

Freud's 'The Uncanny' is a crucial text for an understanding of contemporary culture in general, as well as for the unfolding tale of psychoanalysis. It has become a key reference-point in discussions of art and literature, philosophy, film, cultural studies and sexual difference. But its relevance is also more insidious and all-pervasive than such an academic-looking list might suggest. The very idea of a list turns strange, as Freud's essay itself, in some ways no doubt inadvertently, makes clear. Sarah Kofman has captured this in a fine formulation: 'The Uncanny', she says, is 'a text dominated by an investigation which is not, at any moment, complete without being immediately invalidated.'[40] Freud keeps pausing to see if it is now possible to draw up an inventory, an exhaustive list of what is uncanny. It is as if he thinks, or is willing to pretend that we might think, that the uncanny can be collated, classified, taxonomized. But one uncanny thing keeps leading on to another. Every attempt to isolate and analyse a specific case of the uncanny seems to generate an at least minor epidemic. It becomes, at moments, irresistibly comical, verging on the endlessly supplementary 'chief weapons' in Monty Python's 'Nobody Expects the Spanish Inquisition'.[41]

After pages of discussing *other* aspects of the uncanny (above all, literature), Freud opens a fresh paragraph:

> We have now only a few remarks to add – for animism, magic and sorcery, the omnipotence of thoughts, man's attitude to death, involuntary repetition and the castration complex comprise practically all the factors which turn something frightening into something uncanny. (U, p. 365)

And then he goes on for another ten pages, continuing to add to this list that never was, and by definition cannot be, complete. His very next sentence undoes him: 'We can also speak of a living person as uncanny, and we do so when we ascribe evil intentions to him ...' (U, p. 365). Within a page he finds himself adding the case of 'psychoanalysis' itself to his strange conceptual shopping-list. And then he says he 'should like to add, though strictly speaking, it has been included in what has already been said', the fact that 'an uncanny effect is often and easily produced when the distinction between imagination and reality is effaced' (U, p. 367). He knows his 'collection of examples ... is certainly not complete' (U, p. 367) and not least because of the case of literature, exemplary disturber of the distinctions between 'imagination and reality'. On the penultimate page of the essay he admits defeat: 'We have clearly not exhausted the possibilities of poetic licence and the privileges enjoyed by story-writers in evoking or in excluding an uncanny feeling' (U, p. 375). That seemingly parenthetical 'or in excluding' is a formidable supplement, suggesting that Freud himself cannot control the uncanniness of his material or of the very process of writing. He is subject to the subject, at least half under its hypnotic sway: 'We have drifted into this field of research half involuntarily' (U, p. 375).

So what kind of text *is* 'The Uncanny'? Harold Bloom, one of the most important contemporary theorists of the uncanny, has described it as follows:

> The text of 'The Uncanny' is the threshold to the major phase of Freud's canon, which begins the next year with *Beyond the Pleasure Principle* [1920]. But quite aside from its crucial place in Freud's writings, the essay is of enormous importance to literary criticism because it is the only major contribution that the twentieth century has made to the aesthetics of the Sublime. It may seem curious to regard Freud as the culmination of a literary and philosophical tradition that held no particular interest for him, but I would correct my own statement by the modification, no *conscious* interest for him. The Sublime, as I read Freud, is one of his major *repressed* concerns, and this literary repression on his part is a clue to what I take to be a gap in his theory of repression.[42]

Bloom's account of Freud calls for comment in its own right. For him, Freud is not a scientist but a writer. As he puts it elsewhere: '[Freud] will survive as a great essayist like Montaigne or Emerson, not as the founder of a therapy.'[43] There are clearly problems with the aestheticization implied here, even if the founder of psychoanalysis in a sense asks for it: 'The Uncanny' opens, as we have seen, with an explicit invocation of 'the subject of aesthetics' (U, p. 339). Freud is indeed a great essayist, but psychoanalysis is not merely an 'aesthetic discourse' (whatever that might be). To recall Michel Foucault's phrase, Freud is a 'founder of discursivity'.[44] Above all perhaps, the power of psychoanalysis consists in its uncanny character as a humble but invasive metadiscourse, providing forms of questioning and conceptual displacement, constantly capable of grafting itself on to, and thus transforming, other discourses. Thus, for example, a literary critic, such as Bloom, can deploy the language of psychoanalysis (in particular the notions of conscious and unconscious motivation and the workings of repression) in order to 'analyse' what Freud is or is not doing: 'The Uncanny' can thus have both a 'crucial place in Freud's writings' and at the same time be 'of enormous importance to literary criticism because it is the only major contribution that the twentieth century has made to the aesthetics of the Sublime'.

Freud's essay is and is not psychoanalytical, is and is not literary criticism, is and is not literary. Rather it broaches a new kind of writing, even if *in spite of itself*, indeed without apparently 'knowing' what it is saying or doing. In Bloomian terms, Freud's 'The Uncanny' offers a powerful, self-reflexive model of 'great writing'. What makes a work canonical or 'great' is its uncanniness. This is, in fact, precisely how Bloom theorizes canonicity. Harold Bloom has achieved a certain canonical status of his own, it might be suggested, thanks to his many dazzling demonstrations of the thesis that 'the authentically daemonic or uncanny always achieves canonical status'.[45] He has consistently and compellingly

argued that what makes a particular work or author canonical has to do with a
certain 'strangeness, a mode of originality that either cannot be assimilated, or
that so assimilates us that we cease to see it as strange ... When you read a
canonical work for the first time you encounter a stranger, an uncanny
startlement rather than a fulfilment of expectations.'[46] Great works come to us as
if composed in a foreign yet strangely recognizable language. What makes 'The
Uncanny' uncanny is that it seems to show us, more acutely than any other text
by Freud, things about psychoanalysis that perhaps ought to have remained
hidden and secret. In particular it presents us with an extraordinary, seemingly
inexhaustible demonstration of psychoanalysis succumbing to madness or more
precisely to literature. In these respects a strange turn might be glimpsed: psychoanalysis is thus posed as a theory of the uncanny.[47] We are led to the sense that
the uncanny is not so much an aspect of psychoanalysis, as psychoanalysis is an
aspect of the uncanny.

Harold Bloom stresses the importance of Freud's essay in relation to
aesthetics, literary criticism and theory, but, above all, in relation to the resistant
strangeness of literature. Literature is uncanny; the resistance of literature to
psychoanalytical and philosophical accountability is what we, like Bloom and so
many others, will keep coming back to, or keep coming to, as if for the first time.
Freud's realization that the uncanny is especially liable to arise 'when the
distinction between imagination and reality is effaced' (U, p. 367) is decisive here:
the literary does not permit a settling on one side or the other ('imagination'
versus 'reality'). Discussing this sort of 'art versus real life' distinction in Freud's
work, Adam Bresnick has commented: 'the moments of greatest heuristic power
in the Freudian practice of reading, whether it be the interpretation of dreams or
the interpretation of literature, militate against this distinction, which amounts
to little more than a chimerical *idée reçue*'.[48] Unsettling the ground of both poles
(imagination/reality), literature entails the experience of a *suspended* relation.[49]
Samuel Weber makes a similar point in his essay 'The Sideshow, or: Remarks on
a Canny Moment':

> Constitutive for the uncanny is not the alternative: reality-imagination, for this
> alternative presupposes the identity and meaning of whatever it thus questions, and
> seeks only to fix its ontological status. Uncanny is a certain indecidability which affects
> and infects representations, motifs, themes and situations, which ... always mean
> something other than what they are.[50]

Freud's essay demonstrates, with unstinting energy and at moments comical
lucidity, that the uncanny is destined to elude mastery, it is what cannot be

pinned down or controlled. The uncanny is never simply a question of a statement, description or definition, but always engages a performative dimension, a
maddening supplement, something unpredictable and *additionally strange*
happening in and to what is being stated, described or defined. To quote Freud in
another context: 'an author's words are deeds'.[51] They are deeds, we might say,
precisely to the extent that they can produce unpredictable and strange effects.

In Hélène Cixous's celebrated phrase, Freud's 'The Uncanny' is less a
psychoanalytic discourse than 'a strange theoretical novel'. She goes on:

> Nothing turns out less reassuring for the reader than this niggling, cautious, yet wily
> and interminable pursuit (of 'something' – be it a domain, an emotional movement, a
> concept, impossible to determine yet variable in its form, intensity, quality, and
> content). Nor does anything prove to be more fleeting than this search whose
> movement constitutes the labyrinth which instigates it; the sense of strangeness
> imposes its secret necessity everywhere.[52]

As Freud's essay shows, and as Cixous's account beautifully brings out, the uncanny is – even (or especially) if *inter alia* – an experience of *writing*. And
conversely of reading. One tries to keep oneself out, but one cannot. One tries to
put oneself in: same result. The uncanny is an experience of being *after oneself*, in
various senses of that phrase. It is the experience of something duplicitous,
diplopic, being double. It calls for diplomacy, the regulation of a strange
economy, an art of negotiation which presupposes a kind of double talk, double
reading, double writing. Freud's essay is a ghost-work in which we never
encounter a sense of 'Freud himself' as anything other than double. As Cixous
summarizes it: 'Everything takes place as if the Unheimliche went back to Freud
himself in a vicious interchange between pursued and pursuer.'[53]

It is impossible to think about the uncanny without this involving a sense
of what is autobiographical, self-centred, based in one's own experience. But it is
also impossible to conceive of the uncanny without a sense of ghostliness, a sense
of strangeness given to dissolving all assurances about the identity of a self. As
Adam Bresnick has put it: 'The uncanny ... would not merely be something a
given subject experiences, but the experience that momentarily undoes the
factitious monological unity of the ego.'[54] The uncanny is thus perhaps the most
and least subjective experience, the most and least autobiographical 'event'.
Near the beginning of 'The Uncanny' Freud declares, in what is at once a
paradoxical and highly significant passage:

> The writer of the present contribution, indeed, must plead guilty to a special
> obtuseness in the matter [of sensitivity to the feeling of uncanniness], where extreme

delicacy of perception would be more in place. It is long since he has experienced or
heard of anything which has given him an uncanny impression, and he must thus start
by translating himself into that state of feeling, by awakening in himself the possibility
of experiencing it. (U, p. 340)

The statement seems to be intended to distance Freud himself from any direct,
personal experience of his subject; but of course it also has the opposite effect.
We are invited to read everything that follows as an essay in what Vaihinger
called the 'as if':[55] I, Sigmund Freud, have had no uncanny experiences, at least
not for a long time, and therefore in what follows I am not really present, not
really talking about my own experience (or if I am, it is only in a dim and
dreamlike world of memory), in short I am my own double, a sort of ghost, a
fiction-writer who will be concerned with auto-translation, 'translating [my]self'
into the uncanny.

Freud's weird (no-)escape-clause is compounded, or confounded, in at
least two respects. First, if his biographer Ernest Jones is to be believed, Freud is
being at least a little bit fraudulent here. Jones vividly recalls late-night talks with
him as follows:

In the years before the great war I had several talks with Freud on occultism and
kindred topics. He was fond, especially after midnight, of regaling me with strange or
uncanny experiences with patients, characteristically about misfortunes or deaths
supervening many years after a wish or prediction. He had a particular relish for such
stories and was evidently impressed by their more mysterious aspects. When I would
protest at some of the taller stories Freud was wont to reply with his favourite
quotation: 'There are more things in heaven and earth than are dreamt of in your
philosophy.'[56]

If in 'The Uncanny' Freud wishes to distance himself from first-hand experience
of his topic, it is clear from Jones that he took considerable pleasure and interest
in, as it were, dealing in second-hand goods. More strikingly and perhaps more
comically, however, Freud's 1919 essay does indeed go on to furnish a number of
directly personal, autobiographical anecdotes about having uncanny feelings or
experiences. There is, for example, his experience of reading 'The Sandman' and
the uncanny story he comes across in a wartime issue of the English *Strand
Magazine*,[57] as well as the ostensibly less 'literary', more 'everyday', 'real', 'actual'
experience of being lost in a provincial town in Italy and repeatedly finding
himself returning to a quarter where 'Nothing but painted women were to be
seen at the windows of the small houses' (about which he says 'a feeling
overcame me which I can only describe as uncanny': p. 359).

Freud is storytelling in ways that make his essay irreducibly literary, touched and energized by the fictional. Towards the end he declares: 'The uncanny as it is depicted in *literature*, in stories and imaginative productions, merits in truth a separate discussion' (U, p. 372). Again, it becomes difficult to know how (seriously) to take him. Yes, he is right: in which case, why has he spent so much of his text focusing on literature? No, he is wrong: he has demonstrated very well that the question of literature, fictionality and 'imaginative productions' *cannot* be dissociated from any attempt (including his own) to elaborate a theory or critical account of the uncanny. Taking Freud, or half of Freud, or one Freud, at his word, it is necessary to acknowledge the importance of the question of literature, not only in a thematic or argumentational sense but also in a formal, stylistic, performative sense. Working through digressions, fictional insertions, autobiothanatoheterographical supplements and the subterranean passageways of so-called footnotes, we must try to reckon with the ways in which *a text does not belong*. There are mixings, deformations and transformations of genre. What is the uncanny? Does it belong to philosophy or literature or psychoanalysis? *If* it belongs, it is no longer a question of the uncanny. Rather, the uncanny calls for a different thinking of genre and text, and of the distinctions between the literary and non-literary, academic and non-academic writing.

In his chapter on 'The Uncanny and the Marvellous' in *The Fantastic: A Structural Approach to a Literary Genre* (1970), Tzvetan Todorov works his way into a strange corner over his general thesis that 'the fantastic', as a literary genre, has to do with 'ambiguity' and 'hesitation'.[58] Todorov's study demonstrates, in some respects quite cannily, the folly of attempting to provide a structuralist 'explanation' of the topic. At one moment 'the uncanny' is a genre, at another it isn't. He declares that 'we cannot exclude from a scrutiny of the fantastic either the marvellous or the uncanny, genres which it overlaps': the uncanny is 'a neighbour' (p. 44).[59] But then within two pages we find him saying that, 'unlike the fantastic', 'the uncanny is not a clearly delimited genre' (p. 46). He goes on: 'More precisely, it is limited on just one side, that of the fantastic; on the other, it dissolves into the general field of literature (Dostoevsky's novels, for example, may be included in the category of the uncanny)' (p. 46). A little later he suggests that 'the uncanny is … linked … to what we might call "an experience of limits", which characterizes the whole of Poe's *oeuvre* [as well as the work of] Dostoevsky' (p. 48). The case of Poe, indeed, leads Todorov to postulate the telling notion of the 'meta-uncanny' (p. 48).[60] What is the meta-uncanny? Every allegedly uncanny text is always a text *about* the uncanny. The uncanny is always 'meta-uncanny'. And at the same time, there can be no 'meta-uncanny', since we can never fix the place or borders of where the alleged discourse of the uncanny ends and the putatively 'meta-' discourse begins. As with the notion of meta-language in general, it is a question of what is at once necessary and impossible. We cannot do *without* a notion of meta-language, but there is no meta-language that is purely detached or distinct from its so-called 'object' language. As a figure and experience of what is at once inside and added on, always already at home yet an outsider, constitutive yet supplementary, the 'meta-' 'itself' may be uncanny. The uncanny overflows. As Rosemary Jackson has put it, the uncanny 'is not a literary category'.[61] Against Todorov, and some of his commentators, it is necessary to spell out what *The Fantastic* itself shows (even if this runs counter to the central argument and aspirations of his book), namely that the uncanny is essentially to do with hesitation and uncertainty. The uncanny is not a literary genre. But nor is it a non-literary genre. It overflows the very institution of literature.[62] It inhabits, haunts, parasitizes the allegedly non-literary. It makes 'genre' blink.[63]

Never begun and said already: 'We will first turn to other languages. But the dictionaries that we consult tell us nothing new, perhaps only because we ourselves speak a language that is foreign' (U, p. 341). Freud says 'We will *first* turn', but – as we have seen – he had already begun. We 'first' turn to dictionaries only after the essay has been under way for a couple of pages. 'We ourselves speak a language that is foreign' (U, p. 341). So much that we might try to think about the uncanny is condensed into this remarkable, cryptic and perhaps rigorously unreadable observation that Freud seems simply to throw off in passing. In what language should we read and seek to understand this statement? In German? In English? It would appear to make little difference, at least at one level: no matter what language we speak (or write or think through), Freud seems to be suggesting, it is foreign. Freud's statement has a certain lapidary beauty and strangeness all of its own, as if it were itself written in a foreign language, foreign to any and every reader, a chiselling away at the very principle of a Rosetta Stone. It recalls Gilles Deleuze's definition of 'style' as 'the foreign language within language'.[64] The statement, we might say, is an example of Freud's signature or singularity. It appears in a revised version in the work of Jacques Derrida: 'One never writes [or speaks] either in one's own language or in a foreign language.'[65] 'We ourselves speak a language that is foreign', says Freud: who is this 'we'? 'We' psychoanalysts? Or 'we' non-psychoanalysts? Should the statement be taken as suggesting that psychoanalysis is foreign to the language of everyday life? Unconscious thoughts, memories, desires and fears make our consciousness a kind of text in translation: the language of everyday life is subject to forms of editing, distortion, censorship, slippage, misinformation, translation, transposition and wordplay of which we are necessarily unaware. Or is the foreignness in question equally foreign to the language of everyday life as to that of psychoanalysis? In which case psychoanalysis will always have been speaking a language uncanny to itself. Doubtless it is not a question of *choosing* between these two.

Let us recall another suggestive, comparatively early use of the word 'uncanny', also Scottish, cited by the *OED*. This is in Sir Walter Scott's *Guy Mannering* (1815): 'I wish she binna uncanny! Her words dinna seem to come in God's name, or like other folk's.'[66] What this usage makes clear is a sort of dehiscence within the uncanny as regards the religious. What is 'uncanny' is what does not 'seem to come in God's name'. Freud does not say so in as many words, in the text entitled 'The Uncanny'; but the strangeness of the uncanny offers, demands or presupposes a new way of thinking about religion. It is, in fact, one of the unstated assumptions of Freud's essay that the uncanny is to be theorized in non-religious terms. The experience of the uncanny, as he seeks to theorize it, is not available or appropriate to, say, a Jewish or Christian 'believer'.

Freud makes this clear in another context, in a passage in his most celebrated essay on religion, 'The Future of an Illusion' (1927). In the context of 'the terrors of nature' (earthquakes, floods, storms, diseases), 'the cruelty of Fate, particularly as it is shown in death', and 'the sufferings and privations which a civilized life in common has imposed on [people]' (*PFL*, 12: 197), Freud highlights the advantages of having a god or gods to believe in:

> But if the elements have passions that rage as they do in our own souls, if death itself is not something spontaneous but the violent act of an evil Will, if everywhere in nature there are Beings around us of a kind that we know in our own society, then we can breathe freely, can feel at home in the uncanny and can deal by psychical means with our senseless anxiety. We are still defenceless, perhaps, but we are no longer helplessly paralysed; we can at least react. Perhaps, indeed, we are not even defenceless. We can apply the same methods against these supermen outside that we employ in our own society; we can try to adjure them, to appease them, to bribe them, and, by so influencing them, we may rob them of a part of their power. ('The Future of an Illusion', *PFL*, 12: 196)

With a belief in God or some 'evil Will' or a variety of divine 'Beings', the uncanny does not even rear its eerie head: there is no need for 'senseless anxiety', we 'can feel at home in the uncanny' without indeed even being aware that that is what we are doing.[67]

The uncanny will always have posed a challenge or threat to religious belief.[68] Repeatedly, in the first half of the nineteenth century, texts dealing with the supernatural and superstition come to the same stumbling block. In his *Inquiries Concerning the Intellectual Powers and the Investigation of Truth* (first published in 1830), for example, John Abercrombie evokes what for him would be madness itself and what for Freud would be everyday life:

> And surely if there is among human beings, an affecting representation of a mind lost to every function of a healthy understanding, incapable of rising from effects to causes, or of tracing the relations of things, – a mind deserted by its rightful guardian, and left the unprotected victim of every wild delusion that flutters by, – it is to be found in him, who, possessed of the senses of a living man, can stand before the fair face of creation, and say in his heart – 'there is no God.'[69]

Tempered by reason, Christian religious belief is the basis of everything. Such is the condition of what is known as the European Enlightenment. In a work first published in 1845, Brierre de Broismont puts this in a seemingly unambiguous way:

> The necessity of believing is characteristic of our species. When this impulse is guided by faith and reason combined it conducts us safely to the goal towards which we all tend … Faith apart from reason leads to superstition, and reason without faith almost always results in pride.[70]

The author does not pause to reflect on what is 'unsafe' (or, in English perhaps, *uncanny*), on why or how death ('the goal') could ever be conceived as a place of safety. Religious belief or 'religious sentiment' precedes and effectively rules over any possible meditation on what we might today call the uncanny. As he goes on to state:

> the feeling of the unknown to which man attaches himself, and from which arises the want of something in which to believe, a love of the marvellous, a desire for knowledge, and a craving after excitement, is itself only a weakened condition of the religious sentiment.[71]

In short, the first half of the nineteenth century witnesses the emergence of a sense of strangeness that ought to remain secret and hidden, subsumed within a Christian understanding, including a Christian understanding of mystery. David Brewster's *Letters on Natural Magic* (1832) offers a neat example of this. Referring to Eusèbe Salverte's recently published *Sciences occultes* as bringing 'scientific knowledge' to bear on 'ancient superstitions', Brewster warns in a footnote:

> We must caution the young reader against some of the views given in M. Salverte's work. In his anxiety to account for everything miraculous by natural causes, he has ascribed to the same origin some of those events in sacred history which Christians cannot but regard as the result of divine agency.[72]

It is perhaps not surprising, then, that a sense of what we call the 'uncanny' should have taken time to establish itself, even though its haunting presence defines the very project of the Enlightenment. As Mladen Dolar has put it:

> There is a specific dimension of the uncanny that emerges with modernity ... [I]n premodern societies the dimension of the uncanny was largely covered (and veiled) by the area of the sacred and untouchable. It was assigned to a religiously and socially sanctioned place ... With the triumph of the Enlightenment, this privileged and excluded place (the exclusion that founded society) was no more. That is to say that the uncanny became unplaceable; it became uncanny in the strict sense.[73]

The ghostliness of the uncanny creeps, slowly but irrepressibly, into the common light of day. As the *OED* suggests, it is only around 1850 that the sense of the word 'uncanny' as 'Partaking of a supernatural character; mysterious, weird, uncomfortably strange or unfamiliar' becomes 'common'.

In *The Female Thermometer: Eighteenth-century Culture and the Invention of the Uncanny*, Terry Castle writes:

> the eighteenth century in a sense 'invented the uncanny'... the very psychic and cultural transformations that led to the subsequent glorification of the period as an age of reason or enlightenment – the aggressively rationalist imperatives of the epoch – also produced, like a kind of toxic side effect, a new human experience of strangeness, anxiety, bafflement, and intellectual impasse.[74]

What she calls 'the "enlightening" turn from magic to reason' creates the uncanny in its wake, brings it to light in the process.[75] *The Female Thermometer* is specifically focused on the eighteenth century. Our own concern is with a broader historical context, and perhaps above all with attempting to elucidate and argue for the importance of notions of the uncanny as a way of beginning to think about culture, philosophy, religion, literature, science, politics *in the present*. In the course of the nineteenth century, particularly in Britain, uncanniness begins to manifest itself across a range of social and political issues. Freud's 'The Uncanny' does a strange violence to its subject, not least in appearing to deny it a history and in seeking to situate it simply as a 'province' of 'aesthetics'. As Allan Lloyd Smith has remarked, in the context of Victorian Britain, the uncanny

> is linked both psychologically and politically to wider issues. Male and female interactions involving power and sexual desire are determinants; so also may be the historical and political experiences of class, race, or age, and certain specific features of culture, such as imperialism and the fear of what is brought back from colonial adventures.[76]

All of these nineteenth-century issues are still with us, in some respects more subtle and attenuated perhaps, in others more widespread, indeed 'global', and profound.

The uncanny, then, is not merely an 'aesthetic' or 'psychological' matter (whatever that might mean): its critical elaboration is necessarily bound up with analysing, questioning and even transforming what is called 'everyday life'. This applies not only in relation to issues of sexuality, class, race, age, imperialism and colonialism – so many issues of potentially uncanny 'otherness' already evident in the nineteenth century – but also, for example, in relation to notions of automation, technology and programming. There seems to be general acknowledgement that our lives, our experiences, the comings and goings within and all around us are increasingly *programmed*. Such is in part the very meaning of 'globalization'. As Christopher Johnson has described it, in an essay on the uncanny and technology: 'we are animated and agitated by a power or program that seems to violate our most intuitive sense of self-determination'.[77] He goes on:

> Freud's essay on the uncanny – beyond and in spite of its psychoanalytical bias – helps us understand what might be our affective response to the regime of the program. Not that the program is unconscious, as Freud would have it, but that with the increasing relief of human motion, memory, calculation and communication, with the increasing delegation of the vital to the programmatic, it becomes increasingly impossible to locate the program.[78]

Johnson's account draws attention to a frequently overlooked or underestimated aspect of this 'new world' of the program, namely the importance of feeling, affect and belief. A critical focus on the nature of the uncanny provides a means of exploring what may after all be one of the most interesting dimensions of the coming decades, the future of human feelings. In this respect there is something strangely singular and, perhaps, valuable and instructive about the uncanny. Above all as a theory of the ghostly (the ghostliness of machines but also of feelings, concepts and beliefs), the uncanny is as much concerned with the question of computers and 'new technology' as it is with questions of religion.[79] Spectrally affective and conceptual, demanding rationalization yet uncertainly exceeding or falling short of it, the uncanny offers new ways of thinking about the contemporary 'return of the religious' and the world war of religions that continues to rage all around, for example, as well as about the strangeness of 'programming' in general.[80]

As a term for what might be called the critical spectralization of feeling and belief, the uncanny is a key to understanding both modernity and so-called postmodernity.[81] Crucial to such an understanding are psychoanalysis and deconstruction, together constituting arguably the most significant 'philosophical revolutions' of the twentieth century. Both can be described as uncanny modes of thinking, uncanny discourses. And both, uncannily, overlap; and overlap *in* and *as* the uncanny. Psychoanalysis is uncanny on account of what Freud himself calls its capacity for 'laying bare … hidden forces' (U, p. 366): for many people, at least, it brings to light things that perhaps should have remained hidden or repressed. It makes the familiar (the self, desire, memory, sexuality, everyday language and behaviour) uncomfortably, even frighteningly unfamiliar. Freud's work (and 'The Uncanny' is perhaps exemplary in this respect) teaches us to be uncertain, to question, to experience, in strangely new ways. But if the world becomes uncannily different in the light of psychoanalysis, this uncanniness is perhaps to be derived as much from our differences *with* Freud's work or our sense of differences *within* it, as from Freud's explicit arguments and observations in relation to the authority of consciousness, dreams, art and literature, memory, desire, language, and so on. As suggested earlier, it is perhaps now becoming possible to see psychoanalysis as a branch of the uncanny, rather than vice versa. As Mikkel Borch-Jacobsen has put it: 'Psychoanalysis is a mystery to itself – foreign to itself, *unheimlich.*'[82] The uncanny overflows psychoanalysis.

Another name for uncanny overflow might be deconstruction.[83] Deconstruction makes the most apparently familiar texts strange, it renders the most apparently unequivocal and self-assured statements uncertain. With a persistence or consistency that can itself seem uncanny, it shows how difference operates at the heart of identity, how the strange and even unthinkable is a necessary condition of what is conventional, familiar and taken-for-granted. Deconstruction involves explorations of the surprising, indeed incalculable effects of all kinds of virus and parasite, foreign body, supplement, borders and margins, spectrality and haunting. Two short quotations from Derrida may be helpful here. First, as a sort of watchword, early on in *Of Grammatology* (1967), he declares: 'One always inhabits, and all the more when one does not suspect it'.[84] Second, in the context of an essay commemorating the death of Roland Barthes in 1981, Derrida remarks: '[Barthes's] texts are familiar to me but I don't yet know them – this is my certainty – and this is true of all writing that matters to me.'[85] With both of these quotations we are explicitly engaged in the economy of a strange familiarity.

A characteristic deconstructive strategy is to write not about the ostensibly 'central' texts in an oeuvre but rather to pick up on a seemingly marginal text. Freud's essay 'The Uncanny' would be exemplary here. In part despite – in part because of – its apparent lack of importance to a more 'mainstream' understanding of psychoanalysis, Derrida comes back to 'The Uncanny' again and again. As he remarks in a footnote in 'The Double Session' (1970):

> We find ourselves constantly being brought back to that text by the paradoxes of the double and of repetition, the blurring of the boundary lines between 'imagination' and 'reality', between the 'symbol' and the 'thing it symbolizes' ..., the references to Hoffmann and the literature of the fantastic, the considerations on the *double meanings* of words ... (to be continued). [*sic*][86]

Freud's essay is for Derrida, above all perhaps, concerned with 'the inexhaustible resistance of the "literary" to the schemas of *Das Unheimliche*' or what he elsewhere refers to as 'literary fiction's eternally renewed resistance to the general law of psychoanalytic knowledge'.[87] Derrida attributes the awareness of such 'resistance' to Freud himself: Freud's writing is thus, for Derrida, at once humbler and more powerful, less 'dogmatic' than the work of Jacques Lacan, which seeks to subordinate literary writing to a merely 'illustrative' function in the service of psychoanalytic 'truth'.[88]

If psychoanalysis and deconstruction have one thing to teach, it would be about how and why we must not simply give ourselves up or over to the uncanny. There has to be an abiding attachment to the familiar, even if it is one that requires ceaseless suspicion. There has to be a grounding in the rational in order to experience its trembling and break-up.[89] There has to be a sense of home and homeliness within and beyond which to think the unhomely.[90] It is a question of *economy*, a Greek word etymologically signifying 'law' (*nomos*) of the 'house' (*oikos*). There must be laws of the house, home economics, the regulation of an economy of one's own. As Derrida has described this, in the context of how he conceives his own writing:

> It is less a question of ... trying to master the *Unheimliche* or the uncanny so that it
> becomes simply the familiar, than it is of the opposite movement. But this is not to say
> that one has to turn oneself over, bound hand and foot, to the *Unheimliche*, because I
> don't believe in that. In other words, I don't believe in seeking out absolute risk,
> absolute nonreappropriation, alienation and madness for their own sake, and, besides, I
> don't want to have anything to do with that. I'm too afraid of it. [What I have been]
> trying to do [is] work out a kind of economy with the means at hand, an economy that
> would not be one of a maniacal and 'self-centred' autotranslation ... [I have been trying
> to work with texts as] things that don't come down to me or come back to me. A text,
> I believe, does not come back ... One regulates an economy with one's texts, with other
> subjects, with one's family, children, desire.[91]

At issue is something like uncanny economy: an economics of the uncanny.
Everyone's relation with the uncanny is in some sense their own and no one
else's. But the attempt to regulate an economy in this context is neither simply
narcissistic and 'self-centred', nor a blank submission to otherness and alienation.
Derrida's initial emphasis in the above quotation remains crucial to what we are
concerned with exploring here: 'It is less a question of ... trying to master the
Unheimliche or the uncanny so that it becomes simply the familiar, than it is of the
opposite movement.'

Everyone perhaps has a different story or stories to tell concerning the uncanny.
In the closing paragraphs of 'The Uncanny' Freud writes:

> the storyteller has a *peculiarly* directive power over us; by means of the moods he can
> put us into, he is able to guide the current of our emotions, to dam it up in one direction
> and make it flow in another, and he often obtains a great variety of effects from the
> same material. All this is nothing new, and has doubtless long since been fully taken
> into account by students of aesthetics. We have drifted into this field of research half
> involuntarily, through the temptation to explain certain instances which contradicted
> our theory of the causes of the uncanny. (U, p. 375)

Freud's text is more literary, more a work of story telling, than his rhetoric of
analytic detachment might suggest. His royal 'we' is already strange enough, but
it is also to be distinguished from the at least equally strange third-person 'he'
with which, as we have seen, the essay begins. Like 'the storyteller' to whom he
refers, 'Freud' is multiple, split and proliferating. But he is also very much alone,
writing a text with an uncertain addressee (the implied reader, after all, is neither
a student of aesthetics nor a student of psychoanalysis). He is writing a letter of
sorts, despatched from 'a rather remote province' (U, p. 339), with all the curious
senses of isolation and solitude that such a scene may evoke. 'The Uncanny'

might be thought of as a strange piece of 'private correspondence' that has come into our hands. Every reader may experience it differently, and each time with a different sense of what is familiar and unfamiliar, surprising and strange. As a 'field of research' that calls for new ways of combining and transforming the concerns of art, literature, film, psychoanalysis, philosophy, science and technology, religion, history, politics, economics, autobiography and teaching, the uncanny is a 'province' still before us, awaiting our examination.

NOTES

1   Michel de Montaigne, 'On the Education of Children', *Essays*, trans. J.M. Cohen (Harmondsworth: Penguin, 1958), p. 70.

2   Friedrich Nietzsche, *The Gay Science*, trans. Walter Kaufmann (New York: Vintage, 1974), section 358.

3   Sigmund Freud, letter to Thomas Mann, *SE*, XXII: 255.

4   H. D. [Hilda Doolittle], *Tribute to Freud*, revised edition (Manchester: Carcanet, 1985), p. 146.

5   *Guardian*, no. 47696 (1 January 2000), pp. 1 and 19: here, p. 19. Further references are to page 19 of the article.

6   For a provoking study of Marx in this context see Jeffrey Mehlman, *Revolution and Repetition: Marx / Hugo / Balzac* (Berkeley: University of California Press, 1977). Mehlman is concerned with a revisitation of Marx through psychoanalysis, whereby 'rediscovering a certain Freud within Marx is itself *unheimlich*' (p. 8).

7   See Jacques Derrida, *Spectres of Marx: The State of the Debt, the Work of Mourning, and the New International*, trans. Peggy Kamuf (New York: Routledge, 1994), p. 174. I discuss Derrida's book in more detail below: see, in particular, Chapters 8, 11, 18, 20.

8   Friedrich Nietzsche, *The Will to Power*, trans. Walter Kaufmann and R. J. Hollingdale (New York: Vintage, 1968), p. 7.

9   I explore Nietzsche and the uncanny in further detail below, especially in Chapter 3.

10 Martin Heidegger, 'The Origin of the Work of Art', in *Poetry, Language, Thought*, trans. Albert Hofstadter (New York: Harper Colophon Books, 1975), p. 54.

11 See Martin Heidegger, *Being and Time*, trans. John Macquarrie and Edward Robinson (Oxford: Blackwell, 1967), pp. 233–4. As David Farrell Krell puts it: 'Our being in the world, the world that is our only home, is marked by the uncanny discovery that we are *not* at home in the world' (David Farrell Krell, '*Das Unheimliche*: Architectural Sections of Heidegger and Freud', *Research in Phenomenology*, 22 (1992), 43–61: here, p. 44). Krell's essay provides a thought-provoking and well-informed account of Heidegger and Freud on the uncanny. Also of interest here is Mark Wigley's work on Heidegger in relation to Derrida and architecture: see his *The Architecture of Deconstruction: Derrida's Haunt* (Cambridge, Mass.: MIT Press, 1993), esp. pp. 106–18.

12 Gordon C. F. Bearn, 'Wittgenstein and the Uncanny', *Soundings: An Interdisciplinary Journal*, vol. 76, no. 1 (1993), 29–58: here, p. 48.

13 Ludwig Wittgenstein, *Culture and Value* (Chicago: University of Chicago Press, 1980), sections 43, 11; quoted in Bearn, 'Wittgenstein and the Uncanny', p. 50.

14 Bearn, 'Wittgenstein and the Uncanny', p. 48.

15   See Stanley Cavell's essay on 'The Uncanniness of the Ordinary', in his *In Quest of the Ordinary: Lines of Skepticism and Romanticism* (Chicago: Chicago University Press, 1988), pp. 153–78: here, p. 154. Cavell's essay is concerned to argue that 'the uncanniness of the ordinary is epitomized by the possibility or threat of what philosophy has called skepticism' (p. 154). Bearn offers a gloss on Cavell and Wittgenstein in this context: 'the disappearance of the world which is one of the traditional fears of epistemological skepticism appears in Wittgenstein as the world's becoming uncanny': see 'Wittgenstein and the Uncanny', p. 30.

16   See Victor Shklovsky, 'Art as Technique' (1917), in *Russian Formalist Criticism: Four Essays*, trans. Lee T. Lemon and Marion J. Reis (Lincoln, Nebraska: University of Nebraska, 1965). p. 13.

17   See Bertolt Brecht, *Brecht on Theatre: The Development of an Aesthetic*, trans. and ed. John Willett (London: Methuen, 1978), pp. 143–4, 192. As Willett points out (p. 99), Brecht's term 'alienation-effect' (*Verfremdungseffekt*) is specifically derived from Shklovsky's notion of the 'device for making strange' (*Priem Ostrannenija*).

18   Anthony Vidler, *The Architectural Uncanny: Essays in the Modern Unhomely* (Cambridge, Mass: MIT Press, 1992), p. x.

19   Vidler, *The Architectural Uncanny*, p. 9.

20   We should no doubt already have made it clear: an introduction to the uncanny is impossible. This was perhaps apparent with the first word of our title: the 'the'. The title of Freud's essay presents the ghostly model. The 'the' (or das 'das') turns 'uncanny' into something different, a sort of stranger to itself. It becomes a (strangely insubstantial) substantivised adjective. The title-phrase 'the uncanny' is a kind of oxymoron: there is no 'the' for 'the uncanny'. There is then already an oddity, oddly supplementary, in the decision of Freud's English-language translator, James Strachey, to put the word 'uncanny' in quotation marks: 'The "Uncanny"'. If we have chosen to leave the 'scare' quotes out, it is not because they seem unimportant, but rather because of a more preliminary and perhaps far-reaching uncertainty about where to stop, in other words to begin. At the very least, additional quotes would need to surround the 'The': ' " "The" "Uncanny"'', or (more precisely no doubt) ' " ' " "The" ' " " ' "Uncanny" ' " ' ... and so on. In writing 'das' – 'das Unheimliche' – Freud is doubtless in some sense seeking (impossibly) to appropriate the uncanny, to make it his own. This ambition, desire or fear is in play, perhaps, whenever anyone uses the phrase 'the uncanny'.

21   To wonder about how far they are derived from Freud is to engage with the notion of ghosts, with the question of intellectual debt and originality, legacy and inheritance. Cf. Philip Rieff's use of the word 'uncanny' in relation to the biography of Freud by Ernest Jones, in the Preface to his first edition of *Freud: The Mind of the Moralist* (1959): 'I have used the Jones volumes even though I cannot entirely believe them. Clearly, master and disciple grow to resemble each other. In the process of writing, the portrait of the master may be transformed into an uncanny likeness of the disciple.' Philip Rieff, *Freud: The Mind of the Moralist*, 3rd edn (Chicago: Chicago University Press, 1979), p. xiv.

22   Julia Kristeva, *Strangers to Ourselves*, trans. Leon S. Roudiez (New York: Columbia University Press, 1991), p. 191. See, more generally, Chapter 8 ('Might Not Universality Be ... Our Own Foreignness?'), pp. 169–92. Further page references will appear in the text.

23   Slavoj Žižek, *Looking Awry: An Introduction to Jacques Lacan through Popular Culture* (Cambridge, Mass.: MIT Press, 1991), p. 53.

24   Robert Young, 'Psychoanalytic Criticism: Has It Got Beyond a Joke?', *Paragraph*, vol. 4 (1984), 93.

25   As Felman puts it: 'The scene of the critical debate is thus a *repetition* of the scene dramatized in the text. The critical interpretation, in other words, not only elucidates the text but reproduces it dramatically, unwittingly *participates in it*.' See Shoshana Felman, 'Turning the

Screw of Interpretation', *Yale French Studies*, vol. 55/56 (1977), pp. 94–207: here, p. 101. It is striking that, while Freud's essay is a key point of reference in Felman's account, the immediate context of her remarks is in fact Henry James's horror story *The Turn of the Screw*. That they should seem equally apt in relation to Freud's essay, bears out the characterization of 'The Uncanny' as itself a kind of ghost story or fairy tale. Cf. Robert Young, who talks about 'The Uncanny' as a 'mystery tale' in his essay 'Psychoanalytic Criticism: Has It Got Beyond a Joke?' (p. 95), and who, in a related and more recent move, explores Freud's *The Interpretation of Dreams* as a 'gothic novel' (see Robert J. C. Young, 'Freud's Secret: *The Interpretation of Dreams* Was a Gothic Novel', in *Sigmund Freud's* The Interpretation of Dreams: *New Interdisciplinary Essays*, ed. Laura Marcus (Manchester: Manchester University Press, 1999), pp. 206–31).

26   Following Freud, the uncanny is perhaps inseparable from a new kind of rationalism, a new kind of enquiry into and engagement with rationalism and rationality. As Jacques Derrida has put it: 'In Freud, an old positivist rationalism, a sentimental *Aufklärung* and precritical philosophemes cohabited with a quite other logic which, vigilantly driving back all the demons of irrationalism or obscurantism, ought to correspond, if not to a new figure of reason, at least to a new interpretation of the very history of reason, perhaps even of the principle of reason, and with it the responsibility which follows from it.' See Jacques Derrida, 'Let Us Not Forget – Psychoanalysis', trans. Geoffrey Bennington and Rachel Bowlby, *Oxford Literary Review*, vol. 12 (1990), 5.

27   This sense of entanglement or 'not knowing one's way' might be illustrated by reference to a striking instance of the 'uncanny' that occurs in a letter Freud wrote to Martha Bernays, his future wife, in October 1882. In it he declares: 'I always find it uncanny when I can't understand someone in terms of myself' (Sigmund Freud, letter to Martha Bernays (29 October 1882), quoted in Ernest Jones, *Sigmund Freud: Life and Work* (London: Hogarth Press, 1953), vol. 1, p. 352). Everything Freud has to say, in all his writings, might be read as a meditation on this statement. What on earth does he mean or think he means? What should the addressee (Bernays, but also by extension you and I, ghostly readers of Freud's future) make of it? Is the statement tautological – in other words, is the uncanny not indeed just this otherness to oneself, but somehow within oneself? If Freud is suggesting that it is his usual, familiar experience to find that he can and does understand others in terms of himself, what kind of understanding would that be? It is in any case an experience of familiarity that is repeatedly disturbed, defamiliarized: the 'always' already indicates a sort of uncanny repetitiveness. To reiterate: the uncanny has to do with what is not ourselves, not assimilable to ourselves, despite being something that is only experienced by ourselves.

28   Ralph Waldo Emerson, *The Collected Works*, V, *English Traits* [1856] (Cambridge, Mass. and London: Harvard University Press, 1994), p. 157.

29   On the importance of the friendship between Emerson and Carlyle for an understanding of the cultural, philosophical and political history of 'America' and 'England' in the nineteenth century – indeed, for an understanding of the very forging of the term 'Anglo-American' – see Philip Nicoloff's Historical Introduction to the Harvard edition of *English Traits*, pp. xiii–l; on the 'Anglo-American', see in particular pp. xliii-xliv. As Nicholoff puts it: 'In the years since their first encounter in 1833 the two men had maintained a cordial and mutually beneficial relationship, Emerson assisting generously with the American publication of *Sartor Resartus*, *The French Revolution*, *Miscellanies*, *Past and Present*, and *The life of Cromwell* while Carlyle was providing "tit for tat" with Emerson's British publications' (p. xxxviii).

30   The word 'pilgrim' probably 'comes to us', as the saying goes, on an etymological pilgrimage through old French *pelegrin* from the Latin *peregrinus*, meaning 'foreigner' or 'stranger'.

31   William Shakespeare, Sonnet 30, l. 6.

32   For two more detailed explorations of the relations between the canny, the uncanny and the comic, see Elizabeth Wright, *Psychoanalytic Criticism: A Reappraisal*, 2nd edn (Cambridge: Polity Press, 1998), esp. 'The Return of Freud: Jokes and the Uncanny', pp. 124–34; and Kalpana Seshadri-Crooks, *Desiring Whiteness: A Lacanian Analysis of Race* (London: Routledge, 2000), esp. p. 82 ff. On 'The Antithetical Meaning of Primal Words', see Freud, *SE*, 11: 153–61.

33   The uncanny has to do with strangenesses within and between words and languages. In German one speaks of 'das Unheimliche', in English 'the uncanny', in French 'l'inquiétante étrangeté' (disquieting strangeness). Derrida, for example, often uses the German or English term in the midst of his 'own' French text. Jacques Lacan, on the other hand, invents a new word, *extimité* (at once 'intimate' and 'exterior'). See, for example, *The Ethics of Psychoanalysis 1959–1960: The Seminar of Jacques Lacan*, Book VII, ed. Jacques-Alain Miller, trans. Dennis Porter (London: Routledge, 1992), p. 139. In his essay ' "I Shall Be with You on Your Wedding-night": Lacan and the Uncanny' (in *October*, vol. 58 (Autumn 1991), 5–23), Mladen Dolar glosses Lacan's neologism as follows: '[*Extimité*] points neither to the interior nor to the exterior, but is located there where the most intimate interiority coincides with the exterior and becomes threatening, provoking horror and anxiety. The extimate is simultaneously the intimate kernel and the foreign body: in a word, it is *unheimlich*' (p. 6).

34   On 'the supernatural explained' see E. J. Clery, *The Rise of Supernatural Fiction, 1762–1800* (Cambridge: Cambridge University Press, 1995), esp. Chapter 7, pp. 106–14. The uncanny is quite different from the gothic scenario in which (to quote Clery) 'apparently supernatural occurrences are spine-chillingly evoked only to be explained away in the end as the product of natural causes' (p. 106). As I have been trying to suggest, the uncanny entails a sort of trembling of what is 'natural': it is an involuntary querying, the experience of a hesitation and suspension concerning the very nature of the explicable.

35   Robert Fergusson, *Poems* (Edinburgh, 1773), pp. 92–6.

36   Fergusson, *Poems*, pp. 95–6.

37   In a recent poem, Les Murray aptly evokes the idea of Fergusson being given a 'writership-in-revenance'. See 'Robert Fergusson Night (for the commemoration at St Andrews University, October 2000)', in *London Review of Books*, 4 January 2001, p. 28.

38   On the 'archetypal storyteller' as 'an old woman sitting by the fireside, spinning', see Angela Carter, Introduction, *The Virago Book of Fairy Tales*, ed. Carter (London: Virago, 1990), p. x. 'Storytelling' here would have an inevitable association with fairy tales. As Walter Benjamin remarked: 'The first true storyteller is, and will continue to be, the teller of fairytales': see 'The Storyteller', in *Illuminations: Essays and Reflections*, ed. and with an Introduction by Hannah Arendt, trans. Harry Zohn (New York: Schocken Books, 1969), p. 102.

39   As Daiches goes on to say: 'Fergusson uses heroic couplets with gravity and flexibility (though the lines are as a rule end-stopped) and the Scots appears completely at home in this verse form … The pastoral convention had really had its day by this time, and to lament Wilkie by having two shepherds mourn the death of a poetic and astronomically minded fellow shepherd is hardly the most effective way of writing a Scots elegy.' Daiches's account thus intimates its own uncanny logic: a poem that is a mixture of the new and long-familiar presents a language (Scots) that is said to be 'completely at home'. See David Daiches, *Robert Fergusson* (Edinburgh: Scottish Academic Press, 1982), pp. 60–2.

40   Sarah Kofman, *Freud and Fiction*, trans. Sarah Wykes (Cambridge: Polity Press, 1991), p. 121.

41   The setting is 'a mill-owner's opulent sitting-room' in Jarrow, 1912, featuring Lady Mount-bank and a mill-worker who has come to say there's 'Trouble at mill'. Then 'The door flies

open and Cardinal Ximinez of Spain [Michael Palin] enters flanked by two junior cardinals.' Ximinez shocks the mill-owner and mill-worker with: 'Nobody expects the Spanish Inquisition. Our chief weapon is surprise ... surprise and fear ... fear and surprise ... our two weapons are fear and surprise ... and ruthless efficiency. Our *three* weapons are fear and surprise and ruthless efficiency and an almost fanatical devotion to the Pope ... Our *four* ... no ... *amongst* our weapons ... amongst our weaponry are such elements as fear, surprise ... I'll come in again. *(exit and exeunt)*.' See *Monty Python's Flying Circus: Just the Words*, vol. 2 (London: Methuen, 1989), pp. 192–3. This note may also be an appropriate place to say a little more about the question of the uncanny in relation to notions of humour, comedy and laughter. If the writings of Sigmund Freud and Jacques Derrida have provided consistent points of reference in the present study, this is where something like a sense of humour has helped to dictate my trajectory. It perhaps helps to explain, for example, why I have preferred to work with the texts of Freud and Derrida rather than those of Heidegger. To put the matter in a doubtless rather idiosyncratic nutshell, reading Heidegger does not make me laugh. Here I can only plead a certain perversity. My interest in the uncanny is intimately bound up with humour, laughter and the threat or promise of non-seriousness. I realize I am not alone in my feeling about Heidegger. Jacques Derrida makes a similar point when he declares: 'There is little room for laughter in Heidegger': see *Politics of Friendship*, trans. George Collins (London: Verso, 1997), p. 57. Perhaps not by chance the context of this remark is the question of the uncanny and how it can be seen to be surreptitiously at work in Heidegger's writings. Derrida's concern is with what 'destabilizes all the conceptual distinctions that seem to structure the existential analytic, dooming its logic to an *Unheimlichkeit* marking each of its decisive moments' (p. 58). Heidegger's solemn shadow thus no doubt haunts the present study, along with the shadows of so many others. The texts of Freud and Derrida, on the other hand, haunt and move me in part precisely because they demonstrate a certain openness to laughter, an unexpected lightness. They evince and take pleasure in a sense of what Freud calls the 'irresistibly comic' (U, p. 359). I have elsewhere attempted to begin an exploration of laughter in Freud and Derrida: see, in particular, 'The Remains of Psychoanalysis' (Chapters 4 and 5), *After Derrida* (Manchester: Manchester University Press, 1995), pp. 61–123. In the case of Freud in particular, I confess that I find many of his writings charming, delightful, marvellously funny, even if on occasion in spite of themselves. In this respect my reading of him on the uncanny is perhaps closer to Wittgenstein than to Heidegger. Wittgenstein is reported as saying of psychoanalysis that 'explanations are adopted because they have a peculiar charm. The picture of people having subconscious thoughts has a charm. The idea of an underworld, a secret cellar. Something hidden, uncanny ... A lot of things one is ready to believe because they are uncanny.' See Ludwig Wittgenstein, *Lectures and Conversations on Aesthetics, Psychology and Religious Belief*, Compiled from Notes taken by Yorick Smythies, Rush Rhees and James Taylor, ed. Cyril Barrett (Oxford: Basil Blackwell, 1966), p. 25. A moment or so earlier he is reported as saying of Freud: 'The connections he makes [in dream interpretations etc.] interest people immensely. They have a charm. It is charming to destroy prejudice' (p. 24). As Asko Kauppinen has put it: from Wittgenstein's perspective, 'the charm of the uncanny is what makes Freud's psychoanalysis make sense at all, and it is what gives Freud's writing its peculiar persuasiveness.' See Asko Kauppinen, *The Doll: The Figure of the Doll in Culture and Theory* (PhD diss., University of Stirling, 2000), p. 191.

42   Harold Bloom, 'Freud and the Sublime: A Catastrophe Theory of Creativity', in Maud Ellmann, ed., *Psychoanalytic Literary Criticism* (London: Longman, 1994), p. 182.

43 Harold Bloom, *The Western Canon* (London: Macmillan, 1994), p. 3. For a fuller 'literary' reading of Freud as essayist see Mark Edmundson, *Towards Reading Freud: Self-creation in Milton, Wordsworth, Emerson, and Sigmund Freud* (Princeton, NJ: Princeton University Press, 1990).

44 Michel Foucault, 'What Is an Author?', in *Textual Strategies: Perspectives in Post-structuralist Criticism*, ed. Josué V. Harari (London: Methuen, 1979), p. 154. Foucault puts Freud with Marx in this category: 'they both have established endless possibilities of discourse' (ibid.).

45 Harold Bloom, *The Western Canon*, p. 458.

46 Ibid., p. 3. For a reading of Bloom's preoccupation with the uncanny see Catherine Belsey, 'English Studies in the Postmodern Condition: Towards a Place for the Signifier', in *Post-theory: New Directions in Criticism*, ed. Martin McQuillan, Graeme MacDonald, Robin Purves and Stephen Thomson (Edinburgh: Edinburgh University Press, 1999), pp. 123–38. Belsey admires Bloom's emphasis on literature's 'strangeness', but finds reductive the way he elaborates his provoking and in many ways potentially uncanny thesis that Shakespeare 'largely invented us' (*The Western Canon*, p. 40, quoted by Belsey, p. 132). Bloom, she says, 'backs away from his own recognition' (p. 133) of the importance of the uncanny in so far as he puts the extraordinary 'weirdness' of Shakespeare's writing down to powers of characteriza-tion: while Shakespeare's writing may often reach 'the limits of language', argues Bloom, his 'greatest originality is in representation of character' (*The Western Canon*, p. 47). She then upbraids: 'But there is nothing uncanny in Bloom's account of Shakespeare's characters, and the gap between what he says about the limits of language and his character sketches might be read psychoanalytically as itself a mark of repression' (p. 133). Belsey is perhaps a little hasty: the formulation 'there is nothing uncanny' (in such and such a text or context) recalls Freud's own assertion that there is nothing uncanny about the ghosts that appear in *Hamlet*, *Macbeth* or *Julius Caesar* (see U, p. 373). The uncanny cannot be confined, acknowledged as something present or absent in this fashion: it is a question of *reading*. And 'reading' here need not be understood as narrowly referring to books, films, paintings, and other 'aesthetic objects'. (Jeffrey Mehlman has suggested an apt generalization in this context: 'what is *unheim-lich* about the *unheimlich* is that absolutely *anything* can be *unheimlich*': see his *Revolution and Repetition*, p. 6.) Correspondingly, Bloom's account of Shakespeare is perhaps cannier, and thus more open to the uncanny, than Belsey allows. For example, the passage from *The Western Canon* that she quotes (on the issue of 'the limits of language') ends with the following assertion: 'Bottom is a wistful triumph; Shylock, a permanently equivocal trouble to all of us; but Sir John Falstaff is so original and so overwhelming that with him Shakes-peare changes the entire meaning of what it is to have created a man made out of words' (*The Western Canon*, p. 47). Bloom's final phrase would seem to comport with Belsey's own allegedly contrasting emphasis on language or what she likes to call 'the signifier'. The phrase 'man made out of words' is of course not Bloom's at all, but rather the title of a poem by Wallace Stevens: Bloom's discourse is a canny hosting, evocalized out of the uncanny spaces of Stevens's poetry. In 'English Studies in the Postmodern Condition', Belsey foregrounds a striking continuity between the writings of Matthew Arnold and Harold Bloom. Both, for her, remain 'confined within the discipline of literary criticism'. By contrast, she concludes, 'English studies in the postmodern condition ... has no excuse for evading the implications of the uncanny power of the signifier that both Arnold and Bloom ... have brought to our attention ... [Their work serves to remind us of] our own linguistic constitution as subjects, and our consequent vulnerability to the meanings and values in circulation in our culture. Whether our motive in reading is solitary self-cultivation or a struggle against social injustice, we ... do well to remember what we are, and the relativity of the place we speak from' (p.

136). This account raises fresh difficulties of its own: there is a danger, for example, perhaps implicit in the very title of the essay ('English Studies in the Postmodern Condition'), that Belsey's argument in turn appears to confine itself within the discipline of 'English Studies'. We may wonder, too, if the notion of 'our motive in reading' is not more equivocal, multiple and heterogeneous than her description, with its division of 'motive' into 'solitary self-cultivation or a struggle against social injustice', may suggest. What kind of division is this, in any case? Can or must 'solitary self-cultivation' and the 'struggle against social injustice' be mutually exclusive? In these respects, Belsey's conclusion seems to recapitulate problems she highlights in the work of those 'conservatives' (p. 126) she discusses. [Perhaps a final word here should be given over to the language of dreams or to what might be called the dream of Kate Belsey. During the night of 22–3 August 2000, asleep in the heart of the Finnish countryside, I dreamt that I was in the company of Professor Belsey, someone whom, in waking life, I scarcely know. The setting of the dream was quite formal, as if for a radio programme recording, and we were supposed to be in conversation. Although I was (apparently, or so I imagined) present, Catherine Belsey referred to me only in the third person. She declared (and these are the only words of the dream I recall): 'Nicholas Royle is a little too interested in growing strange orchids on the moon.']

47 This is not to deny the so-called 'clinical' or 'practical' dimensions of psychoanalysis as a therapy. On the contrary: psychoanalysis would be very much a theory of the uncanny with 'practical applications'. But then any theory of the uncanny should have 'practical applications', starting from the fact that the uncanny is above all, I would argue, about education and learning to live. I explore this issue in more detail in Chapter 3.

48 See Adam Bresnick, 'Prosopoetic Compulsion: Reading the Uncanny in Freud and Hoffmann', *Germanic Review*, vol. 71, no. 2 (1996), 114–32: here, p. 116.

49 Cf. Derrida's proposal that 'There is no literature without a *suspended* relation to meaning and reference'. See Jacques Derrida, 'This Strange Institution Called Literature', in *Acts of Literature*, ed. Derek Attridge (New York: Routledge, 1992), p. 48.

50 Samuel Weber, 'The Sideshow, or: Remarks on a Canny Moment', *Modern Language Notes*, vol. 88, no. 6 (1973), 1102–33: here, p. 1132.

51 As cited in note 3, above.

52 Hélène Cixous, 'Fiction and Its Phantoms: A Reading of Freud's *Das Unheimliche* (The "Uncanny")', trans. Robert Dennomé, *New Literary History*, vol. 7, no. 3 (1976), 525–48: here, p. 525.

53 Cixous, 'Fiction and Its Phantoms', p. 526.

54 Bresnick, 'Prosopoetic Compulsion', p. 117.

55 H. Vaihinger, *The Philosophy of 'As if': A System of the Theoretical, Practical and Religious Fictions of Mankind*, trans. C. K. Ogden (London: Kegan Paul, Trench, Trubner, 1924).

56 Jones, *Freud*, 3: 408.

57 E. T. A. Hoffmann, 'The Sandman', in *Tales of Hoffmann*, trans. R.J. Hollingdale (Harmondsworth: Penguin, 1982), pp. 85–125. For more detailed discussion of 'The Sandman' and the *Strand* story see below, Chapters 2 and 9.

58 Tzvetan Todorov, *The Fantastic: A Structural Approach to a Literary Genre* (1970), trans. Richard Howard (Ithaca: Cornell University Press, 1975), p. 44. Both 'the fantastic' and 'the uncanny' have to do with the question of response to apparently supernatural occurrences. 'The *fantastic*', Todorov notes, 'refers to an ambiguous perception shared by the reader and one of the characters' (p. 46). But there are cases of the uncanny ('uncanny in the pure state'), he contends, in which 'events are related which may be readily accounted for by the laws of reason, but which are, in one way or another, incredible, extraordinary, shocking, singular, disturbing or

unexpected' (p. 46). In this very attempt to distinguish the uncanny from the fantastic, however, it becomes clear that both terms have to do with what Todorov calls 'ambiguity' and 'hesitation'. How else could 'events' be construed as 'readily accounted for' *and* 'incredible'? Further page references to Todorov are given in parentheses in the main body of the text.

59   In the original French, in the context of the fantastic, Todorov speaks of the marvellous and the uncanny as '*deux voisins*', constituting '*deux domaines voisins*': see Todorov, *Introduction à la littérature fantastique* (Paris: Éditions du Seuil, 1970), p. 49.

60   The example Todorov gives is Poe's story 'The Angel of the Odd': see *The Fantastic*, p. 48. It is difficult to see why this tale should be categorized 'meta-uncanny' rather than, or as distinct from, any other Poe tale. (For further discussion of the 'uncanny' and 'meta-uncanny' in the context of Poe, see Chapter 10, below.) This may also be an apposite moment to comment on a related point raised by Todorov's account. Poe figures for Todorov as an example of the 'pure uncanny' (p. 48), and indeed for many other critics as well Poe's work epitomizes 'the uncanny in literature'. Yet, as far as I am aware, Poe's texts themselves do not contain the word 'uncanny'. As far as I am aware, this is also something that critics have not considered worthy of discussion. The uncanny need not be named as such, in order for there to be a sense of uncanniness. Indeed, the uncanniness of a text can even be linked to the non-appearance of the word itself. To give two other brief examples. E. M. Forster's *Howards End* (1910; Harmondsworth: Penguin, 1975) contains only one instance of the word 'uncanny', at the very end of the text (p. 331), yet as I have argued elsewhere (*E. M. Forster* (Plymouth: Northcote House, 1999), pp. 58–9), uncanniness may be on that very account a more pervasive factor in our reading of the novel. In a rather different way, the singularity and strangeness of Angela Carter's fiction is promoted in part by its tendency to deploy the word 'eldritch' rather than its perhaps better-known 'uncanny' accomplice. Thus, in her story 'The Bloody Chamber', we may read: 'The first grey streamers of the dawn now flew in the sky and an eldritch half-light seeped into the railway carriage'; and in another story, 'The Erl-King', we are told that this eponymous creature 'knows which of the frilled, blotched, rotted fungi are fit to eat; he understands their eldritch ways, how they spring up overnight in lightless places and thrive on dead things'. See Angela Carter, *Burning Your Boats: Collected Short Stories* (London: Vintage, 1996), pp. 116, 188.

61   Rosemary Jackson, *Fantasy: The Literature of Subversion* (London: Methuen, 1981), p. 32.

62   Linda Ruth Williams, for example, follows James Donald's account of Todorov in seeing 'the fantastic' as involving 'a moment of uncertainty' that can be distinguished from the 'neighbouring genre' of the marvellous (wherein something 'is truly realized as supernatural') and the uncanny (wherein 'the disquieting thing can be finally explained rationally, as with Freud's uncanny'). On the contrary, I would argue that the uncanny is 'disquieting' only to the extent that it entails 'uncertainty'. The uncanny is no more uncanny when 'explained rationally' than it is when explained supernaturally. The liminal, uncertain, but persistently uncanny sense we are concerned with here is indeed tacitly inscribed in the strangeness of Todorov's (and Donald's and Williams's) characterization of the uncanny as a 'neighbouring genre' (at once apart from and linked to, familiar yet unfamiliar, a genre of the *para-*, the border and bordering). See Linda Ruth Williams, *Critical Desire: Psychoanalysis and the Literary Subject* (London: Edward Arnold, 1995), p. 95, and James Donald, Introduction, *Fantasy and the Cinema*, ed. Donald (London: British Film Institute, 1989), pp. 10–21; here, p. 11. It should be noted that Donald's essay is principally concerned with film, not literature, and indeed that he goes on to explore other ways of thinking about the uncanny, for example in terms that are 'less formal, more social and psychoanalytic' (p. 19).

63   I am thinking here of Jacques Derrida's analysis of the blink, for example, that at once allows a genre to be identified and remains heterogeneous to the genre. See 'The Law of Genre', trans. Avital Ronell, in *Acts of Literature*, ed. Derek Attridge (London and New York: Routledge, 1992), pp. 231, 251.

64   See Gilles Deleuze, 'He Stuttered', in *Essays Critical and Clinical*, trans. Daniel W. Smith and Michael A. Greco (London: Verso, 1998), p. 113.

65   Jacques Derrida, 'Border Lines', trans. James Hulbert, in *Deconstruction and Criticism*, ed. Harold Bloom et al. (New York: Seabury Press, 1979), p. 101. I discuss this formulation in greater detail in Chapter 8 below.

66   Sir Walter Scott, *Guy Mannering or The Astrologer*, with Introductory Essay and Notes by Andrew Lang (London: Macmillan, 1912), p. 554.

67   In fact the uncanniness of what Freud is here evoking has become perhaps doubly strange for us today. 'Global warming', 'the greenhouse effect', 'climate change' or whatever in English we decide to call what we apparently do not know quite how to name (and this very uncertainty perhaps already gestures towards uncanniness) means that nature's raging passions are no longer simply discrete, autonomous, dissociated from ourselves. It is *our* planetary pollution coming 'home' to us.

68   I recall an occasion some years ago, when I was conducting a seminar on the uncanny at the Summer University of Seinäjoki in Finland and had been talking for some time about the various ways in which it might be appropriate to think about the topic. A very attentive and articulate student finally put up her hand in sheer frustration: she was a Christian, she said, and had no idea what I was going on about. Nothing, she said, was uncanny for her. Her frustration made clear to me the importance of this largely implicit aspect of Freud's essay on the uncanny. What she was also – perhaps unintentionally – doing was revealing something taboo in the university classroom. For the question of God or gods remains at the foundation of what is going on in teaching, even if (or precisely in so far as) this remains a question generally deemed inappropriate for discussion. This is not to say that discussion could or should end at that point. No doubt from different perspectives religion may be uncanny for a so-called non-believer (such as Freud claimed to be), just as non-belief may be uncanny for a so-called believer. At issue in any case is something like the experience of uncanniness as a trembling of belief: I discuss this in further detail in Chapters 11 and 21 below.

69   John Abercrombie, *Inquiries Concerning the Intellectual Powers and the investigation of Truth*, 3rd edn (Edinburgh: Waugh and Innes, 1832), p. 178.

70   A. Brierre de Broismont, *On Hallucinations: A History and Explanation of Apparitions, Visions, Dreams, Ecstasy, Magnetism, and Somnambulism*, trans. Robert T. Hulme (London: Henry Renshaw, 1859; based on the 3rd edn), p. 7.

71   Brierre de Broismont, *On Hallucinations*, p. 9.

72   David Brewster, *Letters on Natural Magic, Addressed to Sir Walter Scott* (London: John Murray, 1832), p. 6.

73   Dolar, ' "I Shall Be with You on Your Wedding-night" ', p. 7.

74   Terry Castle, *The Female Thermometer: Eighteenth-century Culture and the Invention of the Uncanny* (Oxford: Oxford University Press, 1995), p. 8. Castle provides fascinating material concerning what she regards as a 'new', 'darker' view of the eighteenth century: 'The "new" eighteenth century is not so much an age of reason, but one of paranoia, repression and incipient madness, for which Jeremy Bentham's malign, all-seeing Panopticon, grimly refurbished by Foucault, might stand as a fitting, nightmarish emblem' (p. 7). Castle models her book on Freud's essay: her argument that 'it is precisely the historic internalisation of

rationalist protocols that produces the uncanny' is explicitly acknowledged as being Freud's own 'central insight' (p. 15). Freud's essay allows her to 'tell a similar Freudian story: the more we seek enlightenment, the more alienating our world becomes; the more we seek to free ourselves, Houdini-like, from the coils of superstition, mystery, and magic, the more tightly, paradoxically, the uncanny holds us in its grip' (p. 15). Two remarks may be added here regarding Castle's project. First, it seems to me that there is a danger in this 'similar Freudian story' in so far as it implies a kind of recurrent dead-end, a double-bind that leads nowhere: it is perhaps not so much a fact of the uncanny 'hold[ing] us in its grip', as Castle argues, but rather a *question* of the uncanny as *the continuing experience of an uncertainty*, or as *a decisive suspension of experience*, as something in relation to which one must still (to borrow a phrase from Derrida to which we will return) regulate an economy. Second, and linked to this, it may be appropriate to hesitate as regards Castle's attempt at historicizing the uncanny in terms of *invention*. The subtitle of her book (*Eighteenth-century Culture and the Invention of the Uncanny*) is indicative of how she conceives history and historiography. To speak of the 'invention' of the uncanny seems to presuppose (if only in principle) an inventor or inventors, in other words to presuppose that the invention is human, and that it is something firm and fixed, invented once and for all, neatly stowed away in 'the eighteenth century'. Is it not possible to think that invention itself may be uncanny, neither fixed nor in the past? Isn't that in a sense what 'invention' means?

75   Castle, *The Female Thermometer*, p. 14. Linked to this is the emergence of what is called 'the gothic'. As Fred Botting has described it: 'The new concern inflected in Gothic forms emerged as the darker side to Romantic ideals of individuality, imaginative consciousness and creation. Gothic became part of an internalised world of guilt, anxiety, despair, a world of individual transgression interrogating the uncertain bounds of imaginative freedom and human knowledge. Romantic ideals were shadowed by Gothic passions and extravagance. External forms were signs of psychological disturbance, of increasingly uncertain subjective states dominated by fantasy, hallucination and madness. The internalisation of Gothic forms reflected wider anxieties which, centring on the individual, concerned the nature of reality and society and its relation to individual freedom and imagination. Terror became secondary to horror, the sublime ceded to the uncanny, the latter an effect of uncertainty, of the irruption of fantasies, suppressed wishes and emotional and sexual conflicts.' See Fred Botting, *Gothic* (London: Routledge, 1996), pp. 10–11.

76   Allan Lloyd Smith, 'The Phantoms of *Drood* and *Rebecca*: The Uncanny Reencountered through Abraham and Torok's "Cryptonymy"', *Poetics Today*, vol. 13, no. 2 (Summer 1992), 285–308: here, p. 285. Smith is concerned with the idea that 'the weakness of [Freud's] model [of the uncanny] is its failure to articulate adequately the social and political aspects of the uncanny' (p. 288). He sees the uncanny as arising out of the 'loss of faith' and increasing secularity of society in Britain: 'The shadow at the edge of Victorian consciousness was the "other" of social, sexual, or racial out-groups: the anarchist, the gypsy, the sexual transgressor, the colonial subject, the past' (p. 290).

77   Christopher Johnson, 'Ambient Technologies, Uncanny Signs', *Oxford Literary Review*, vol. 21 (1999), 131–2.

78   Johnson, 'Ambient Technologies, Uncanny Signs', p. 132. Terry Castle makes a similar point about the uncanniness of contemporary electronic technology: 'Just about anything electronic has its uncanny aspect: telephones, cameras, television, personal computers, ATM machines, X-ray machines, answering machines, bar-code sensors, compact disks, laser disks, beepers, and on and on. Whenever something non-human can move on its own, respond to

our movements, signal to us, answer questions, or image our bodies or voices back to us in some luminous or resonant fashion, we confront, I think, a kind of cognitive *mise-en-abyme*. We assent to such devices rationally (after all, everyone else seems to, too) but in some atavistic part of us they remain magical and inexplicable.' See 'Interview with Terry Castle', conducted by Michael Arnzen, in *The Return of the Uncanny*, special issue of *Paradoxa: Studies in World Literary Genres*, vol. 3, no. 3–4 (1997), 521.

79 If, as we will argue in the course of the chapters that follow, telepathy (literally 'feeling', 'mind' or 'suffering', 'at a distance') has a privileged place in an understanding of the uncanny, this is to be witnessed no less in literature and the arts than in, for example, computers and 'new technology'. More rapidly than can be comprehended or controlled, 'we humans' are becoming decentred, invaded, mixed up with the strange reality and effects of 'new technology'. More than ever, what seems to be coming to light is the uncanny 'shared thinking', for example, already inscribed in the etymological matrix of the 'computer', the 'com-' from the Latin 'cum', meaning 'with', and the verb 'putare', to think, suppose, calculate, reckon. In 'our' world of computers, who or what is thinking, and for whom?

80 That 'religion' and 'programming' can belong together – easily and uneasily, naturally but strangely – will be one focus of discussion below: see in particular Chapters 20 and 21.

81 As Mladen Dolar has described it: 'What is currently called postmodernism ... is a new consciousness about the uncanny as a fundamental dimension of modernity' (' "I Shall Be with You on Your Wedding-night"', p. 23). From a Lacanian-cum-Žižekish perspective, this means that, for Dolar, 'ideology' itself might be rethought in terms of the uncanny. He remarks: 'ideology perhaps basically consists of a social attempt to integrate the uncanny, to make it bearable, to assign it a place, and the criticism of ideology is caught in the same framework if it tries to reduce it to another kind of content or to make the content conscious and explicit ... Psychoanalysis doesn't provide a new and better interpretation of the uncanny; it maintains it as a *limit to interpretation*' (p. 19). In his Introduction to the *Paradoxa* special issue on the uncanny, Michael Arnzen also remarks on the concepts of modernity and postmodernity: 'Modernity and postmodernity share similar, yet different anxieties – the uncanny gives us a way of thinking about the interrelationship of both; the *dopplegänger* and the automaton haunted the moderns, for example, while clones and techno-human cyborgs haunt us today.' See Michael Arnzen, Introduction to *The Return of the Uncanny*, special issue of *Paradoxa: Studies in World Literary Genres*, vol. 3, no. 3–4 (1997), 316.

82 Mikkel Borch-Jacobsen, *The Freudian Subject*, trans. Catherine Porter (London: Macmillan, 1989), p. 227.

83 By 'deconstruction' I am referring, in particular, to work by or related to Jacques Derrida. Sarah Kofman was perhaps the first to write at length about Derrida as 'uncanny philosopher'. See 'Un philosophe "unheimlich"' in Kofman, *Lectures de Derrida* (Paris: Galilée, 1984), pp. 11–114.

84 Jacques Derrida, *Of Grammatology*, trans. Gayatri Chakravorty Spivak (Baltimore: Johns Hopkins University Press, 1976), p. 24.

85 Jacques Derrida, 'The Deaths of Roland Barthes', trans. Pascale-Anne Brault and Michael Naas, in *Continental Philosophy I: Philosophy and Non-philosophy since Merleau-Ponty*, ed. Hugh Silverman (London: Routledge, 1988), p. 264.

86 Jacques Derrida, 'The Double Session' (orig. pub. 1970), in *Dissemination*, trans. Barbara Johnson (Chicago University Press, 1981), p. 220 n. 32 (translation slightly modified).

87 Jacques Derrida, *The Post Card: From Socrates to Freud and Beyond*, trans. Alan Bass (Chicago: Chicago University Press, 1987), pp. 342, 426–7.

88   See, for example, *The Post Card*, pp. 426–7, and 'My Chances/*Mes Chances*: A Rendezvous with Some Epicurean Stereophonies', trans. Irene Harvey and Avital Ronell, in *Taking Chances: Derrida, Psychoanalysis, and Literature*, eds Joseph H. Smith and William Kerrigan (Baltimore and London: Johns Hopkins University Press, 1984), p. 10.

89   C. St John Sprigg (aka Christopher Caudwell) makes a similar point in his introduction to a collection of uncanny short stories: 'People must be rational to be thrilled by the irrational. If you believe whole-heartedly in the world of matter-of-fact events, then, when for a moment all this concrete reality seems to quiver and the Impossible peeps through, the effect is shattering.' See *Uncanny Stories*, ed. with an Introduction by C. St John Sprigg (London: Thomas Nelson, 1936), p. x. (My thanks to Robert Young for bringing this text to my attention.)

90   As Ken Gelder and Jane M. Jacobs put it, in a discussion of land ownership and Aboriginal land claims in postcolonial Australia: 'An "uncanny" experience may occur when one's home – one's place – is rendered somehow and in some sense unfamiliar; one has the experience, in other words, of being in place and "out of place" *simultaneously*'. See Gelder and Jacobs, 'The Postcolonial Ghost Story', in *Ghosts: Deconstruction, Psychoanalysis, History*, eds Peter Buse and Andrew Stott (Basingstoke: Macmillan, 1999), p. 181. Gelder and Jacobs explore these issues more fully in their book *Uncanny Australia: Sacredness and Identity in a Postcolonial Nation* (Melbourne: Melbourne University Press, 1998).

91   Jacques Derrida, *The Ear of the Other: Otobiography, Transference, Translation*, trans. Peggy Kamuf, ed. Christie V. McDonald (New York: Schocken Books, 1985), pp. 156–7.

2

Supplement: 'The Sandman'

There is nothing more marvellous or madder than real life. ('The Sandman')

In a paragraph added to *The Psychopathology of Everyday Life* (1901) in 1919, Freud speaks of 'how hard it is for a psychoanalyst to discover anything new that has not been known before by some creative writer' (*PFL*, 5: 262). Nowhere is this perhaps more evident than in the case of E. T. A. Hoffmann's 'The Sandman' (*Der Sandmann*) (1816).[1] Much has been written on the importance for Freud's 'The Uncanny' of this story about a young man called Nathaniel who is engaged to a young woman called Clara but disastrously haunted by childhood memories of the sandman coming to tear out children's eyes and who compounds the disaster by falling fatally in love with the beautiful Olympia, an automaton.[2] 'The Sandman' employs a series of narrators, switches back and forth in time, and presents a number of characters whose features seem weirdly to blend into one another: the sandman ('no longer that bogeyman of the nursery tale who took children's eyes as food to his owl's nest in the moon: no! he was now a repellent spectral monster bringing misery, distress and earthly and eternal ruination wherever he went': p. 90); the most obvious embodiment of 'the terrible sandman', in other words the 'loathsome and repellent' old advocate Coppelius (pp. 89–90); Nathaniel's father (pictured wearing 'a repulsive devil-mask' and 'look[ing] like Coppelius': p. 91); and 'the repulsive barometer-dealer' (p. 103) Coppola (his very name indicating some sort of mingling with 'Coppelius', or with what Clara at one point calls 'the advocate sandman and the barometer-dealer Coppelius': p. 97).

Reading or re-reading 'The Sandman' after reading 'The Uncanny', one cannot help feeling rather sorry for the founder of psychoanalysis. It is easy to see why Freud gets himself so discombobulated over this text and why he should have felt at a loss 'to discover anything new'. Acknowledging Hoffmann as 'the unrivalled master of the uncanny in literature' (U, p. 355), Freud begins his account of 'The Sandman' by recalling what his more immediate precursor, Ernst Jentsch, says in his 1906 essay 'On the Psychology of the Uncanny'. Writing with specific reference to the work of Hoffmann, Jentsch remarks: 'In story-telling, one of the most reliable artistic devices for producing uncanny effects easily is to leave the reader in uncertainty as to whether he [*sic*] has a human person or rather an automaton before him in the case of a particular character.'[3] Freud's account in this respect merely supplements Jentsch's; both Freud and

Jentsch are in turn merely supplements to 'The Sandman'. At the same time, as we will try to demonstrate, Hoffmann's story is itself a text *about* supplements. 'The Sandman' supplements itself. It figures the uncanny as the experience of the supplementary.

What Freud particularly wants to do is refute Jentsch's argument that the uncanny has to do with a sense of 'intellectual uncertainty'. Having earlier pronounced Jentsch's account 'fertile but not exhaustive' (U, p. 340), Freud now notes his indebtedness to him for 'remind[ing] us of a writer [Hoffmann] who has succeeded in producing uncanny effects better than anyone else' (U, p. 347). He then sets off on his strangely laborious, normativizing summary of 'what happens in "The Sandman"'.[4] After almost three pages (U, pp. 348–51), he provides us with perhaps the most amusing litotes in the essay, referring to all of this as a 'short' summary:

> This short summary leaves no doubt, I think, that the feeling of something uncanny is directly attached to the figure of the Sandman, that is, to the idea of being robbed of one's eyes, and that Jentsch's point of an intellectual uncertainty has nothing to do with the effect. (U, p. 351)

Quite apart from the sense of a gentleman protesting too much, and from the trembling fragility of that 'I think' ('This short summary leaves no doubt, *I think* …'), what is bizarre is that Freud seems completely oblivious to the fact that his 'short summary' is fundamentally *his own* 'short story': he recounts the story as if it were an objective, disinterested, merely 'factual' summing up. In highlighting what he sees as the central importance of the idea of blindness or 'being robbed of one's eyes' in Hoffmann's story, Freud himself seems robbed of the sense that telling or retelling a story is always, in some sense, something new, another story.[5] His summary inevitably differs in various ways from Jentsch's or indeed anyone else's.[6]

Freud's summary does not simply describe (accurately or inaccurately) the contents of Hoffmann's narrative; it reveals what it is in or about the narrative that most affects, intrigues, haunts Freud. This suggests the uncanny power of Freud's essay in a more general way: that is to say, it suggests that there is always some 'blindness', there is no reading that is not uncannily blind to its own procedures, presuppositions, effects or discoveries.[7] Freud contends that the uncanniness of 'The Sandman' has to do, above all, with a fear of blindness, and that this fear is itself 'a substitute for the dread of being castrated' (U, p. 352). Hoffmann's story thus provides corroboration of a 'substitutive relation between the eye and the male organ which is seen to exist in dreams and myths and phantasies' (U, p. 352). Even if we grant that there is some truth in Freud's symbolically equating these two fears (a concession a good deal less obvious, perhaps, to a female reader than to a male), there is nothing to prevent us from supposing that what Freud is 'really' saying here has to do with the explanatory power of the concept of substitution rather than or as much as with the explanatory power of 'castration anxiety'. And what are we thus being confronted with here if not 'intellectual uncertainty'? In a way that seems to go beyond the control of Freud or indeed any other reader, 'The Uncanny' suggests an uncanny strangeness in the notion of substitution or substitutability as such.[8]

Freud's reading of 'The Sandman' is a violent attempt to reduce or eliminate the significance of Jentsch's work on the uncanny, and in particular the importance of the figures of the doll and automaton for an understanding of the uncanny.[9] It is also a violent attempt to reduce or eliminate the place and importance of women. As Jane Marie Todd has argued, in an essay entitled 'The Veiled Woman in Freud's "Das Unheimliche"', 'in disregarding the theme of the doll Olympia, Freud failed to see that the question of woman is inextricably connected to Nathaniel's fear of castration'.[10] This, for Todd, is part of a more pervasive sense that '[i]t is women who are *unheimlich*' (p. 527): the ghostly presence of 'the strangely familiar woman' in Freud's various examples of the uncanny, she suggests, 'tell[s] a story about men's fear of women and the social consequences of that fear' (p. 528).

Todd perhaps makes too easy or smooth a move from Freud's text to what she calls the 'social':

> Olympia's 'castration' signifies nothing other than [the] social oppression of women. She is denied life, power, and autonomy, all symbolized by the eye/penis. By passing over the theme of the doll Olympia, Freud failed to see the social meaning of castration. (p. 525)

Kaja Silverman provides what is in some respects a sharper sense of this aspect of Freud's reading of 'The Sandman'. She picks up on a passing reference that Freud makes to uncanniness in his 1927 essay on 'Fetishism' (*PFL*, 7: 345–57), where he argues that 'Probably no male human being is spared the fright of castration at the sight of a female genital'. Freud describes the 'impression' made by such a sight as 'uncanny and traumatic' (*PFL*, 7: 354). Recalling his definition of the uncanny as 'that class of the frightening which leads back to what is known of old and long familiar' (U, p. 340), Silverman writes:

> According to the terms of Freud's own argument, if the spectacle of female castration strikes the male viewer as 'uncanny', he himself must already have experienced

castration; far from functioning merely as an 'innocent' (albeit horrified) onlooker, he too inhabits the frame of the unpleasurable image. In other words, the recurrence of the word *uncanny* in the essay on fetishism reminds us that even before the so-called castration-crisis, the male subject has an intimate knowledge of loss – that he undergoes numerous divisions or splittings prior to the moment at which he is made to fear the loss of his sexual organ.[11]

Silverman's account foregrounds a sense of the uncanny in terms of what Freud's text itself calls (in the context of a brief discussion of another work by Hoffmann, *The Devil's Elixir*) the 'doubling, dividing and interchanging of the self' (U, p. 356).[12] Like Todd, she argues that 'at the heart of woman's otherness there remains something strangely familiar, something which impinges dangerously upon male subjectivity'; but Silverman is more careful to avoid translating this simply into a realm of implicitly fixed and pre-established 'social meaning'.[13] Her concern is with 'dislodging woman from the obligatory acting out of absence and lack'.[14] Her account of the flickering apparition of the word 'uncanny' in Freud's 'Fetishism' evokes a disseminatory sense of what uncannily 'precedes' the apparent fixings of sexual identity and difference, a space of polysexual possibilities.

Such is the space of Hélène Cixous's great essay 'Fiction and Its Phantoms' (first published in English in 1976). What Freud's reading of 'The Sandman' tries but fails to repress is homosexuality, along with the uncanny nature of animism (a living doll) affirmed by Jentsch. Freud's account of Hoffmann's story 'minimizes the uncertainty revolving around Olympia' (p. 533), says Cixous: in this way Freud struggles to render 'The Sandman' *less uncanny*. Cixous focuses on how the doll Olympia is 'relegated' to a footnote or to what she calls a 'typographical metaphor of repression' (p. 537). In this footnote Freud declares: 'This automatic doll [Olympia] can be nothing else than a materialization of Nathaniel's feminine attitude towards his father in his infancy' (U, p. 354 n. 1). Cixous then specifies what Freud's essay keeps typographically low profile, that is to say 'homosexuality' (p. 538). Nathaniel, as Freud's footnote goes on to assert, is 'incapable of loving a woman' (U, p. 354 n. 1).

Cixous's essay brings out the queerness of Freud's text. 'Queer' here does not just signify 'homosexual' (a sense which, according to the *OED*, has been in use since at least 1922) but more generally refers to what Eve Kosofsky Sedgwick has described as 'the open mesh of possibilities, gaps, overlaps, dissonances and resonances, lapses and excesses of meaning when the constituent elements of anyone's gender, of anyone's sexuality aren't made (or *can't be* made) to signify monolithically'.[15] The emergence of 'queer' as a cultural, philosophical, social and political phenomenon, at the end of the twentieth century, figures as a formidable example of the contemporary 'place' and significance of the uncanny. The uncanny *is* queer. And the queer is uncanny.[16] The shared, secret history of the uncanny and the queer goes back some way before the *OED*'s proposed date of 1922. But their explicit conjunction might be another way of theorising the emergence of what is called modernism. In the context of literature in English, powerful effects of overlap, resonance and substitution between the 'queer' and the 'uncanny' appear across a wide range of texts, including the writings of Henry James, Virginia Woolf, D. H. Lawrence, Joseph Conrad, E. M. Forster and Elizabeth Bowen.[17]

In Cixous's reading of 'The Uncanny' the words 'heimlich' and 'unheimlich' themselves come to life, as an androgyne. They form a strange disidentity, joining together, joining themselves, homo- and hetero-, canny and uncanny. Their coupling is evident even in the 'polymorphic perversity' of dictionary extracts that Freud sets before us, though only later does this become a 'sexual threat' (p. 530). It is, as Schelling says, a question of 'what should have remained hidden': Freud's essay will go on, reductively, to construe this in terms of 'the fear of castration'. But, as Cixous puts it, this sexual threat

> had always been there latently, in the coupling itself and in the proliferation of the *Heimliche* and of the *Unheimliche*; when one makes contact with the other, it closes again and closes the history of meaning upon itself, delineating through this gesture the figure of the androgyne. The word joins itself again, and *Heimliche* and *Unheimliche* pair off. (p. 530)

Her reading uncannily brings to light a sense of how the uncanny is bound up with generative, creative uncertainties about sexual identity. Above all, her own compelling, unpredictable, seemingly haphazard account can be read as a response or countersignature to what can be called the blindly, unconsciously, inadvertently, chancily performative power and strangeness of Freud's text. For Cixous, 'The Uncanny' is a text about Freud being spookily 'after himself', hunter and hunted, as a writer. This is why Hoffmann, and the example of 'The Sandman', is so important to him. As she puts it:

> 'Better than anyone else', says Freud, it is the [creative] writer who consents to give birth to the *Unheimliche*. The writer is also what Freud wants to be. Freud sees in himself the writer, the one whom the analyst must question concerning the literature which psychoanalysis must understand in order to know itself. He is, in his relationship to the writer, as the *Unheimliche* is in its relationship to the *Heimliche*. In his strangeness with respect to 'creation', he feels himself 'a case'. (p. 532)

Hoffmann and Jentsch play midwives in a polymorphously perverse, andro-gynous 'case', as they give birth to Freud 'himself'.

What 'The Sandman' shows, above all perhaps, is that the uncanny is a reading-effect. It is not simply *in* the Hoffmann text, as a theme ('spot the uncanny object in this text') that can be noted and analysed accordingly. The uncanny is a ghostly feeling that arises (or doesn't arise), an experience that comes about (or doesn't), as an effect of reading. The uncanny figures as the very impossibility of a so-called thematic reading. As Sarah Kofman observes: '[Freud's] aim being to prove the existence of themes capable of producing a universal feeling of uncanniness, he makes a strictly thematic reading of the [literary fictional] texts he cites as proof of his hypothesis.'[18] But 'it is really the form of the narrative and not the theme in itself which plays the decisive role in the production of [uncanny] effects'.[19]

The most obvious dimension of 'form' to be noted in the context of 'The Sandman' is that the text mixes genres, in particular it mixes an epistolary form with a first-person omniscient (or, perhaps more accurately, telepathic) narrator. Hoffmann's text begins with a letter from Nathaniel to Clara's brother Lothario, then a letter from Clara to Nathaniel, then another letter from Nathaniel to Lothario, the remainder of the text being narrated in the first person by an unnamed 'friend' (p. 99) of Nathaniel. In other words, 'The Sandman' is from the very outset explicitly, self-remarkingly concerned with the performative nature of (its own) language. A letter – not least a love letter or letter between friends or 'within the family' – is always capable of generating unanticipated effects. The letters that constitute the early sections of 'The Sandman' do not simply describe a situation, they bring it into existence, and they do so in ways that are not subject to the conscious control of their authors.

Take the case of Clara's response to the first letter, from Nathaniel to Lothario:

> It is true you have not written to me for a long time, but I believe nonetheless that I am present in your thoughts. For you were certainly thinking of me when you intended to send off your last letter to brother Lothario but addressed it to me instead. I joyfully opened the letter and first became aware of the mistake at the words 'Ah, my dear Lothario'. I ought to have read no further but given the letter to my brother. (p. 94)

It is a multiple instance of uncanniness. Nathaniel's is not only a letter about the uncanny, about 'something terrible', 'dark presentiments' (p. 85) and above all 'the uncanny ghost' of the sandman (p. 88): its very address and despatch make it uncanny, as it comes to be read by someone other (familiar but strange) than the 'intended' recipient. The very sense of what is 'intended' – of so-called authorial intention or narratorial intention – becomes strange. And the letter is supposed to be private, something that ought to have remained that way: as Clara says, 'I ought to have read no further but given the letter to my brother'. Freud appears simply to ignore all of this. He remarks that the tale 'opens with the childhood recollections of the student Nathaniel' (U, p. 348), but says nothing about the structure of multiple narration, the mixed epistolary and omniscient (or, rather, telepathic) third-person form of the text. From its very beginning 'The Sandman' is a text concerned with the supplementary and substitutive: the figure of the sandman as a substitute, the supplementary or substitutive roles of the author-narrators of the letters, the telepathic narrator of the text as a supplement to or substitute for the author-figure, the figure of Nathaniel himself as a writer and thus a supplement or substitute for the writer of 'The Sandman', the figure of the sandman as the spectral figure of the author of what happens *in* the text, the text itself *as* the sandman, and so on. We might illustrate this, most succinctly, in terms of the word 'uncanny' itself. As Rosemary Jackson has observed apropos of a 'literature of the uncanny': '["uncanny"] is a term both to describe and to create unease'.[20] Strangely supplementary, describing and creating, the word 'uncanny' (*unheimlich* and its related forms) recurs over and over again in Hoffmann's story: it would be difficult enough to try to do justice simply to these repeated appearances.[21] Almost, we might think, too obvious to point out: Freud nowhere draws explicit attention to the fact that 'The Sandman' keeps using the word.

'The Sandman' is inexhaustible. Its uncanny concerns and characteristics will all come back, up to their revenantics, in the chapters that follow. Supplementing the issues of doll and automaton, the figure of the woman, queerness, ghosts, strange presentiments, the figure of the sandman and writing itself, let us for the moment simply specify four further Hoffmanniacal supplements.

(1) Freud's essay 'The Uncanny' may appear to be pervasively concerned with the visual. Its ocularcentrism is perhaps nowhere more marked than in its *focus* on castration and the fear of blindness. Sexual identity (having or not having a penis) is a matter of visual revelation and perception. No doubt uncanny feelings are very often generated by strange sights, unveilings, revelations, by what should have remained out of sight; and 'The Sandman' is a magnificent, relentless exploration of the uncanniness of seeing and not seeing, of the optical imagination. As Freud's supplementary study makes clear, ghostly apparitions, dismembered limbs, the 'evil eye' (U, p. 362), the double and '*déjà* vu' are all most immediately associated with seeing. But the uncanny can also involve other senses. Like Poe's 'The Fall of the House of Usher' (with its strange, repeated

stress on 'cracking' sounds) or M. R. James's 'Oh, Whistle, and I'll Come to You, My Lad' (with its hearkening to the bizarre power of an old bronze whistle) or Conrad's 'The Secret Sharer' (with its weird attentiveness to the nature of whispering), Hoffmann's story suggests uncanniness in the experience of sound, ear and voice. Freud makes no mention of this dimension of 'The Sandman'. Again, it is a question of something neither simply thematic nor formal, but rather an eerie, performative twisting. There is repeated emphasis on the frightening *sound* of the sandman. Thus Nathaniel recalls the evenings when

> our mother became very gloomy, and the clock had hardly struck nine before she said: 'Now, children, to bed, to bed! The sandman is coming.' On these occasions I really did hear something come clumping up the stairs with slow, heavy tread, and knew it must be the sandman. (p. 86)

The coming of the sandman is first of all something to be experienced *in the ear*.[22] Its force consists above all, perhaps, in the unsettling strangeness of what is 'to come': 'The sandman is coming' can be heard as at once a statement of what is already happening and as promise and/or threat; it is undecidably constative and performative. The sandman is to come, through the ear, still.

(2) In Hoffmann's story we encounter a letter from Clara in which she writes: 'Ah, my beloved Nathaniel, do you not then believe that in cheerful, unaffected, careless hearts too there may not dwell the presentiment of a dark power which strives to ruin us within our own selves?' (p. 96). This, she goes on to specify, is an 'uncanny power' (p. 96). Freud doesn't quote any of this in his essay. Hoffmann's story, in other words, is explicitly concerned with what Freud will call the 'death drive' or 'death instincts' (*Todestriebe*). Freud does not name it as such in 'The Uncanny': it is only a year later, in *Beyond the Pleasure Principle* (1920), that he finds himself compelled to repeat, in effect, what Hoffmann's text was saying a hundred years earlier.[23]

(3) 'The Sandman' is mad. It is a work of madness. In this respect it is perhaps exemplary of the literary as such. As Shoshana Felman has observed of literature in general and of 'The Sandman' in particular: 'there is no safe spot assuredly outside of madness, from which one might demystify and judge it'.[24] By way of illustration, Felman focuses on what she sees as 'the most revealing moment' in Freud's 'The Uncanny', where he is talking about how 'The Sandman' dissolves distinctions between what is real and what is not, to the point that 'we perceive that [Hoffmann] intends to make us, too, look through the demon optician's spectacles or spy-glass' (U, p. 351). It is not a matter of our 'looking on at the products of a madman's imagination' (U, p. 352): we as readers

are 'rhetorically placed *within* that madness', as Felman puts it; 'madness is uncanny, *unheimlich*, to the precise extent that it *cannot be situated*, coinciding, as it does, with the very space of reading'.[25]

(4) Freud acknowledges a comic or satirical element in 'The Sandman': Hoffmann 'treats ... Olympia with a faint touch of satire and uses it to poke fun at [Nathaniel's] idealization of his mistress' (U, p. 348). But he claims that this has nothing to do with 'the quite unparalleled atmosphere of uncanniness evoked by the story' (p. 348). Freud thus appears very serious; he likewise conveys a sense of 'The Sandman' as very serious. But Hoffmann's story is funny, in more than one sense, or rather, perhaps, it is 'funny' in a multiple, undecidable sense. As Freud's fleeting allusion indicates, the story satirizes a certain idealization of women:

> To be quite convinced they were not in love with a wooden doll, many enamoured young men demanded that their young ladies should sing and dance in a less than perfect manner ... [and] above all that they should not merely listen but sometimes speak too, and in such a way that what they said gave evidence of some real thinking and feeling behind it. (pp. 121–2)

But Hoffmann's text also satirizes the supernatural and 'mystical', for example in its account of Nathaniel's composing 'an exposition of ... mystical theory and cruel powers' and Clara's reaction:

> Early in the morning, as Clara was helping to prepare breakfast, he stood beside her and read to her out of his mystical books, so that Clara asked: 'But, dear Nathaniel, suppose I were to call *you* the evil force which is having a bad influence on my coffee ...?' (p. 104)

Cunningly, cannily sending up the 'mystical' and 'mystical theory', 'The Sandman' perhaps becomes *more* uncanny. Its recurrent moments of laughter, comedy and satire are not to be separated out in the way that Freud appears to assume is possible.[26] They too play a part in 'the unparalleled atmosphere of uncanniness evoked by the story'.

NOTES

1   E. T. A. Hoffmann, 'The Sandman', in *Tales of Hoffmann*, trans. R. J. Hollingdale (Harmonds-worth: Penguin, 1982), pp. 85–125. Further page references to this story will appear in the main body of the text.

2   For some particularly thought-provoking critical readings of Freud and Hoffmann, see Sarah Kofman, 'The Double is/and the Devil: The Uncanniness of *The Sandman (Der Sandmann)*', in her *Freud and Fiction*, trans. Sarah Wykes (Cambridge: Polity Press, 1991), pp. 121–62;

Hélène Cixous, 'Fiction and Its Phantoms: A Reading of Freud's *Das Unheimliche* (The "Uncanny")', trans. Robert Dennomé, *New Literary History*, vol. 7, no. 3 (1976), 525–48; Jane Marie Todd, 'The Veiled Woman in Freud's "Das Unheimliche"', *Signs: Journal of Women in Culture and Society*, vol. 11, no. 3 (1986), 519–28; Neil Hertz, 'Freud and the Sandman', in *The End of the Line* (New York: Columbia University Press, 1985), pp. 97–121; Nicholas Rand and Maria Torok, '*The Sandman* Looks at "The Uncanny": The Return of the Repressed or of the Secret; Hoffmann's Question to Freud', in *Speculations after Freud: Psychoanalysis, Philosophy and Culture*, eds Sonu Shamdasani and Michael Munchow (London: Routledge, 1994), pp. 185–203; Phillip McCaffrey, 'Freud's Uncanny Woman', in *Reading Freud's Reading*, eds Sander L. Gilman, Jutta Birmele, Jay Geller and Valerie D. Greenberg (New York: New York University Press, 1994), pp. 91–108; Adam Bresnick, 'Prosopoetic Compulsion: Reading the Uncanny in Freud and Hoffmann', *Germanic Review*, vol. 71, no. 2 (1996), 114–32; Christopher Johnson, 'Ambient Technologies, Uncanny Signs', *Oxford Literary Review*, vol. 21 (1999), 117–34.

3   Ernst Jentsch, 'On the Psychology of the Uncanny', trans. Roy Sellars, *Angelaki*, vol. 2, no. 1 (1995), ed. Sarah Wood, pp. 7–16: here, p. 13. Quoted in Freud, 'The Uncanny', p. 347.

4   As Cixous notes, for example: 'As a condensed narrative, Freud's story is singularly altered in the direction of a linear, logical account of Nathaniel and strongly articulated as a kind of "case history", going from childhood remembrances to the delirium and the ultimate tragic end.' She also rightly remarks that one gets from Freud's account the sense of 'a confrontation between the Sandman and Nathaniel which is much more sustained and obsessive but also less surprising [in other words, less unfamiliar, unsettling, uncanny] than in the original version'. See 'Fiction and Its Phantoms', p. 533. Further page references to Cixous's essay will appear in the main body of the text.

5   Cf. Cixous: '" This short summary leaves, I think, no doubt ..." Do we understand by that, Hoffmann's story or the story that is quickly recounted? But it is precisely the short summary that displaces and engenders doubt' (pp. 534–5). At once supplementing and displacing 'The Sandman', Freud's reading provokes, above all perhaps, doubt or intellectual uncertainty about what a supplement 'is'.

6   This is most obvious in the case of Freud's misreadings or misrememberings of Hoffmann's text. Thus he claims, for example, that 'it was [the] approach [of Coppelius], seen through the spy-glass, which threw Nathaniel into his fit of madness' (U, p. 351), whereas it is clear from the text of 'The Sandman' itself that it was 'Clara [who] was standing before the glass' (p. 123). In his book *Uncanny American Fiction: Medusa's Face* (London: Macmillan, 1989), Allan Lloyd Smith compares such misreadings to 'negative hallucinations' (p. 2). Freud's 'misreading' of Clara for Coppelius, however, is perhaps more complex than Lloyd Smith allows. Freud prefaces his claim with a canny 'We may suppose' ('We may suppose that it was [the] approach [of Coppelius] ... ' (U, p. 351)): *we may suppose*, for example, that Freud is thinking of an earlier passage in Hoffmann's story in which we read of a poem in which 'Clara's lovely eyes' are connected with the appearance of 'the terrible Coppelius' ('The Sandman', p. 105). Such a supposition would not, of course, contradict the point that Freud's reading seems Coppeliusly intent on blinding the woman, eliminating her together with the confrontation with death that (as numerous critics, including Lloyd Smith, have noted) Clara explicitly figures in Hoffmann's story. As the seemingly telepathic narrator of the second half of 'The Sandman' puts it: 'Nathaniel looked into Clara's eyes, but it was death which gazed at him mildly out of them' (p. 105).

7   This formulation perhaps inevitably evokes the work of Paul de Man, especially his book *Blindness and Insight*, 2nd edn (London: Methuen, 1983): I discuss this in more detail in

relation to 'darkness', in Chapter 7 below. As will also become evident, I hope, 'blindness' need not be privileged here over other sorts of sensory deprivation or deprivation of sense.

8   This is what Derrida seeks to do with the quasi-concept of dissemination as that which *'affirms the always already divided generation of meaning'*. See Jacques Derrida, 'The Double Session', in *Dissemination*, trans. Barbara Johnson (Chicago: Chicago University Press, 1981), p. 268. In a footnote he makes clear that he has Freud and the uncanny in mind here: castration is not the origin of or explanation for dissemination; rather, dissemination 'entails, entrains, "inscribes" and relaunches castration'. Derrida writes: 'No more than castration, dissemination – which entails, entrains, "inscribes" and relaunches castration – can never become an originary, central, or ultimate signified, the place proper to truth. On the contrary, dissemination represents the affirmation of this non-origin, the remarkable empty locus of a hundred blanks no meaning can be ascribed to, in which mark supplements and substitution games are multiplied *ad infinitum*. In "The Uncanny", Freud – here more than ever attentive to undecidable ambivalence, to the play of the double, to the endless exchange between the fantastic and the real, the "symbolized" and the "symbolizer", to the process of interminable substitution – can, without contradicting this play, have recourse both to castration anxiety, behind which no deeper secret (*kein tieferes Geheimnis*), no other meaning (*keine andere Bedeutung*) would lie hidden, and to the substitutive relation (*Ersatzbeziehung*) itself, for example between the eye and the male member': see *Dissemination*, p. 268, n. 67. Or as he puts it elsewhere: 'Lapidarily: dissemination figures that which *cannot be* the father's. Neither in germination nor in castration ... Dissemination ... is neither truth (adequation or unveiling) nor veil. It ... can no longer be measured by the opposition veil/nonveil.' See Jacques Derrida, *Positions*, trans. Alan Bass (Chicago: Chicago University Press, 1981), pp. 86–7.

9   On dolls and automata, see in particular Asko Kauppinen, *The Doll: The Figure of the Doll in Culture and Theory* (PhD diss., University of Stirling, 2000); Eva-Maria Simms, 'Uncanny Dolls: Images of Death in Rilke and Freud', *New Literary History*, vol. 27 (1996), 663–77; and Hal Foster, *Compulsive Beauty* (Cambridge, Mass.: MIT Press, 1993).

10   Jane Marie Todd, 'The Veiled Woman in Freud's "Das Unheimliche"', p. 523. Further page references appear in parentheses in the main body of the text.

11   Kaja Silverman, *The Acoustic Mirror: The Female Voice in Psychoanalysis and Cinema* (Bloomington: Indiana University Press, 1988), p. 17.

12   Quoted by Silverman, *The Acoustic Mirror*, p. 18.

13   *The Acoustic Mirror*, p. 17. It should be noted that Todd also quotes Freud's essay on 'Fetishism' but her reading of what is uncanny or *unheimlich* here is perhaps less subtle and analytical, seeming to assume in advance the meaning of 'the reality of castration' and its value as a theoretical bedrock: 'Female genitals are *unheimlich* for precisely this reason: they seem to confirm what the male has wished to deny – the reality of castration' ('The Veiled Woman in Freud's "Das Unheimliche"', p. 524).

14   Silverman, *The Acoustic Mirror*, p. 14.

15   See Eve Kosofsky Sedgwick, *Tendencies* (London: Routledge, 1994), p. 8. For a brief account of the queer philology of this word and especially its 'official' 'first' usage see Andrew Bennett and Nicholas Royle, 'Queer', in *An Introduction to Literature, Criticism and Theory* (London: Prentice Hall, 1999), pp. 178–9.

16   On the queer as 'the taboo-breaker, the monstrous, the uncanny' specifically in the context of vampire literature, for example, see Sue-Ellen Case, 'Tracking the Vampire', *Differences*, vol. 3 (1991), 1–20; here, p. 3. Ken Gelder discusses this also in his essay 'Vampires and the Uncanny', in *Reading the Vampire* (London: Routledge, 1994), esp. pp. 58 ff.

17   From within the discourse of the 'Freud camp', as it were, we may recall Ernest Jones's phrasing on the subject of 'The Uncanny': 'Freud considered the essay ["The Uncanny"] as being a contribution to aesthetics, using that word in its broad sense of "the psychology of feeling". He remarked that he himself had for long not experienced the feeling of uncanniness. This was doubtless true [how did Jones know this? was he telepathic?], if he meant intense fear, but he had at times experienced milder forms of the same feeling of the kind to which the word "queer" might be applied.' See Ernest Jones, *Sigmund Freud: Life and Work*, 3 (London: Hogarth Press, 1957), 427.

18   Kofman, *Freud and Fiction*, p. 128.

19   Kofman, *Freud and Fiction*, p. 137.

20   Jackson, *Fantasy: The Literature of Subversion*, p. 64.

21   For appearances of the word 'uncanny' in the English translation, see pp. 88, 95, 96, 99, 109, 115, 116, 117.

22   Cf. other references to Nathaniel 'continu[ing] to hear him coming up the stairs' (p. 87), the 'creak[ing]' of 'the housedoor' and the 'slow, heavy, thudding steps' and the 'strange coughing, rasping and growling outside' (p. 89), and again 'the housedoor creak[ing] on its hinges, and slow, leaden footsteps' coming 'up the stairs' (p. 93). Hoffmann's stress on sound also explicitly incorporates the uncanniness of voice in relation to *reading*. The text thus provides an account of writing a poem and the demonic strangeness of reading aloud: 'While Nathaniel was composing this poem he was very quiet and self-possessed: he polished and improved every line, and the constraint of metre made it possible for him not to rest until everything was clear and harmonious. Yet when he had finished the poem and read it aloud to himself, he was seized with horror and exclaimed: "Whose dreadful voice is this?"' (p. 105).

23   For a further discussion on the death drive, see esp. Chapter 5 below.

24   Shoshana Felman, 'Turning the Screw of Interpretation', *Yale French Studies*, vol. 55/56 (1977), 200.

25   Felman, pp. 200–1.

26   Diabolical or affirmative, laughter can be uncanny. It can become all the more uncomfortable and peculiar for being made a subject of discussion or analysis. For examples of strange laughter in 'The Sandman', see for example pp. 85–6, 110–11, 119 and 123.

3

Literature, teaching, psychoanalysis

The *Unheimliche*, as estrangement, is the estrangement of the human ... It follows that the *Unheimliche* is essentially a matter of language, or that language is the site of the *Unheimliche* – if the latter can be said to have a site. (Philippe Lacoue-Labarthe)[1]

Most of the time we forget the strangeness of reading. (Peter Schwenger)[2]

There is a peculiar moment (one of so many), quite late on in 'The Uncanny', when Freud speaks of where he 'might indeed have begun [his] investigation', namely with the phrase *es spukt* ('it haunts', 'it spooks', 'it comes back', 'it apparitions' or, in more neologistic fashion perhaps, 'it spuks'). He observes: 'some languages in use to-day can only render the German expression "an *unheimlich* house" by "a haunted house" (*ein Haus, in dem es spukt*). We might indeed have begun our investigation with this example, perhaps the most striking of all, of something uncanny' (U, pp. 364/255). The most striking example of the uncanny has to do with ghosts and haunting, and Freud might have started with that but apparently didn't, didn't want to, forgot to, or couldn't. The passage in question suggests that the reason for not starting there has to do with 'what is purely gruesome', with the strange reality of death, with dead bodies and the frightening persistence across the centuries of belief in the 'return of the dead', including modern-day 'spiritualism' with its proclamations about being able telepathically 'to get into touch with the souls of the departed' (U, pp. 364–5).

Ghosts from the start, ghosts at the origin: such will have been the primary concern of the present study, a concern reflective of what can be described as perhaps the two greatest philosophical upheavals or 'events' of the twentieth century, that is to say psychoanalysis and deconstruction. *Es spukt* is also a matter of language and the untranslatable: in English we say 'a haunted house', unable to catch the strangely anonymous, subjectless-objectless *es spukt*.[3]

As we have already seen, Freud's 'The Uncanny' is a peculiarly uncertain, wavering and eccentric text. It is also one of his most thought-provoking and – in the strongest senses of the word – haunting works. It keeps trying to lay certain ghosts to rest, but they keep coming back. In the following pages I want to elaborate on his essay as what might be called *haunted teaching*. The uncanny is about 'everything that ought to have remained secret and hidden but has come to light' (U, p. 345); but it is also, at the same time, about what is elusive, cryptic, still to come (back). We will attempt to track three ghosts, or ghost-effects, that are indissociably linked: intellectual uncertainty, literature and psychoanalysis. Let me try, at the outset, briefly to describe them:

(1) *Intellectual uncertainty.* Freud is, by his own admission in the opening paragraph of the essay, in a strange place, in the 'remote ... province' of what he calls 'aesthetics' (and what we might today, too easily and too quickly, call literary or cultural theory) (U, p. 339), where his only precursor (Ernst Jentsch, author of 'On the Psychology of the Uncanny' (1906)) came and saw and proposed that the uncanny is about intellectual uncertainty or insecurity (*der intellektual Unsicherheit*).[4] Freud wants to lay the ghost of his precursor and the ghost of intellectual uncertainty (the two become ghosts for one another: what is a precursor if not a ghost, a source of intellectual uncertainty?), but the ghosts keep coming back. As he asks (himself or us, it's difficult to tell, to tell whether it's himself or us or someone or something else) near the end of his essay: 'are we after all justified in entirely ignoring intellectual uncertainty ...?' (U, p. 370). Roy Sellars remarks: 'Jentsch emphasizes that the uncanny arises from a certain experience of the uncertain or undecidable, and this seems to be intolerable for Freud. Freud decides, in other words, that the undecidable cannot be tolerated as a theoretical explanation, but it nonetheless recurs in his own essay, undecidably.'[5] Intellectual uncertainty is not necessarily or simply a *negative* experience, a dead-end sense of not knowing or of indeterminacy. It is just as well an experience of something open, generative, exhilarating (the trembling of what remains undecidable). I wish to suggest that 'intellectual uncertainty' is in part what Freud's essay has to teach and, indeed, that this is a crucial dimension of any teaching worthy of the name.

(2) *Literature.* As numerous commentators have made powerfully clear, Freud's 'The Uncanny' is haunted by literature – not simply in so far as his examples are literary, but also, and more disturbingly, in so far as his ostensibly *non*-literary examples keep turning, in the very moment of his handling them, Midas-like, into literature. As David Farrell Krell has put it: 'What is uncanny about Freud's efforts is that *all* his sources for the uncanny are literary; for even what he claims to be autobiographical lived experiences are of course marvellously narrated and beautifully crafted pieces of writing.'[6] Freud needs to distinguish what he is doing from literature: there has to be the protective headgear of a metadiscourse ('aesthetics', 'psychoanalysis', etc.). Literature must be kept in its place: the ghostly figures emanating out of the writings of Dante and Shakespeare, for example, are just fine, for Freud, so long as they remain within their literary confines. Yet Freud's very phrasing in this matter seems strangely to dissolve the position he is trying to occupy: 'So long as they remain

within their setting of poetic reality, such figures *lose any uncanniness* which they might possess' (U, p. 373, emphasis added). Uncanniness will have been there, from the start; but it gets (apparently) 'lost'.[7] The point here is not so much to catch Freud out – to show, for instance, how he flatly 'misreads' the literary texts he is talking about[8] – but rather to suggest that his essay lets all sorts of unexpected things come to light with respect to the uncanniness of literature. The 'unexpected' here includes things that Freud would not necessarily regard as 'his' or would not regard as belonging to psychoanalysis. I want to explore at least some of the ways in which the uncanniness of literature might be important for thinking about the ostensibly non-literary, in particular the University.

(3) *Psychoanalysis.* As a counter to any impression I may have given of Freud's essay as of 'merely literary interest' (whatever that would mean), I want to emphasize that its import (and export) carries far beyond the question of aesthetics or literary or cultural studies. Psychoanalysis retains great power and specificity as a discourse and as a teaching. If literature turns out to have been 'teaching psychoanalysis', psychoanalysis is itself a ghostly teaching, one with resources (I want to suggest) that have to date remained in some ways quite untapped. Psychoanalysis is itself uncanny: Freud's admission of this idea is one of the ways in which his essay on 'The Uncanny' gets most cunningly (and cannily) tangled up in itself: 'psychoanalysis … has itself become uncanny to many people', he says, on account of its capacity for bringing to light what should have remained secret and hidden, for 'laying bare … hidden forces' (U, p. 366).

One might imagine omitting the commas from the title of this chapter: 'literature [is and has been] teaching psychoanalysis' – literature teaching us psychoanalysis, letting its uncanny truths come to light in the discussion of literary works, but also literature teaching psychoanalysis what psychoanalysis is or might be. With or without commas, the phrase is also intended to suggest that the three terms belong, strangely, together. At the heart of this strange belonging would be a logic of haunting and ghosts. To be haunted, to be in the company of ghosts is not necessarily a cause for fear or panic. It is something to affirm: it is the very condition of thinking and feeling. There is no teaching without memory (however unconscious or cryptic) of the dead, without a logic of mourning that haunts or can always come back to haunt, without an encounter with questions of inheritance (Who or what is a teacher? Who or what has taught the teacher? How did this scene of teaching come about? Am I thinking my own thoughts? Where does a thought, an idea, a teaching begin?). To affirm the uncanny 'presence' and power of ghosts is not to give oneself up to some gothic fantasy or lugubrious nostalgia: it is the very basis of trying to think about the future. In this respect a remark by Derrida might indicate the drift of what follows: 'The future belongs to ghosts, and modern image technology, cinema, telecommunications, etc., are only increasing the power of ghosts.'[9] If, as Derrida has also suggested, 'everyone reads, acts, writes with *his or her* ghosts' (*SM*, p. 139), this is perhaps most crucially the case with the experience of teaching or of being taught.

How might we construe the possible force and value of a thinking of the uncanny in relation to the University? The University is, increasingly, a ghostly institution. It is haunted not only by questions concerning the nature of teaching, but also by a sense of its relationship to itself and to its own past. There is also a kind of dismemberment in operation that recalls Freud's remark about '[d]ismembered limbs, a severed head, a hand cut off at the wrist [and] feet which dance by themselves': 'all these have something peculiarly uncanny about them' (U, p. 366). If the University is a body, it is strangely headless, estranged and disconnected from itself. Directives come from the phantom of 'the centre' – and here we might recall Derrida's provoking contention that the centre, as 'the absence of play and difference', is 'another name for death'.[10] In British universities all teaching is judged (by a sort of spectral, invisible or scarcely visible body of authorities) in terms of 'learning outcomes'. As a teacher one is obliged to act and feel like a sort of automaton, someone concerned with 'delivering a unit' (rather than 'teaching a course') the 'outcome' of which should be specifiable in advance. Teaching is becoming mechanized in a way that makes caricature seem improbably realistic: Dickens's Mr Gradgrind would have found it difficult to believe. It is not only the teacher who becomes an automaton, but also the student, for he or she too is obliged to live up to the 'learning outcomes' set down in advance, in other words in a sense not to *live* at all, merely to 'receive delivery'. Research in British universities too has for years now been subject to the eerie power and disquieting effects of what is called the Research Assessment Exercise – a ghostly mechanism that insinuates itself into all academic writing, including the writing of a book like this.[11]

The University is in ruins. For me, in spectral fashion, these words call up the remarkable work of Bill Readings, in particular his book entitled *The University in Ruins* (published posthumously in 1996).[12] Readings provides an exhilarating account of what teaching could be, of how to think about a future for the University and for teaching that would not simply sign up for an automatist program. He organizes his book around the name of 'thought', to which he gives an ironic capital letter. Like 'feeling' (to which it cannot simply be opposed), 'thought' is a familiar, straightforward word. 'Thought' might be a one-word answer to the question 'Why teach?', so long as we recognize that it is an answer that still (in Readings's words) 'waits upon our response' (p. 161). 'Thought' seems promising as a name around which to teach, and around which to articulate the desire to teach. Readings's book concludes with an invocation of 'the freedom and the enormous responsibility of Thought at the end of the twentieth century, which is also the end of what has been the epoch of the nation-state' (p. 193). His argument is that the history of the modern University and of its *raison d'être* can be divided into three phases: the University as founded on the concept of reason (this is the version deriving from Kant and post-Kantian German philosophy), the University as founded on a concept of culture (this is the version that became prominent in the twentieth century), and finally (what we have today) the University as founded on the concept of excellence. In a chapter called 'The Scene of Teaching', Readings writes about 'Thought' as a means of 'decentring' (p. 153) teaching:

> In the classroom, Thought intervenes as a third term alongside speaker and addressee that undoes the presumption to autonomy, be it the autonomy of professors, of students, or of a body of knowledge (a tradition or a science) … [T]his third term [i.e. Thought] does not resolve arguments; it does not provide a metalanguage that can translate all other idioms into its own so that their dispute can be settled, their claims arranged and evaluated on a homogeneous scale. As a name, Thought does not *circulate*; it waits upon our response. What is drawn out in education is not the hidden meaning of Thought, not the true identity of students, not the true identity of the professor (replicated in the student). (p. 161)

The notion of higher education as founded on the concept of culture is, in Readings's view, essentially bound up with the concept of the nation-state itself: the University has for a long time served the interests of the nation-state by promoting and protecting the idea of a national culture. Readings sees the emergence of 'the University of Excellence' as signalling the erosion and even disappearance of the governing importance of the idea of the nation-state: institutions of higher education are increasingly becoming transnational corporations.

The notion of excellence is a cipher that covers up for the fact that the University, the concept of the University, has disintegrated. As Readings puts it: 'there is no longer any Idea of the University, or rather … the Idea has lost all content'. 'Excellence' is a tautological, non-referential term. The excellent University is excellent at being excellent. As such it is a nihilistic institution, the very institution of nihilism. There is perhaps something uncanny about the capacity a word ('excellence') has for becoming quite empty, devoid of any sense or familiarity – the object or subject of a blind, eerie repetition ('words, words, words', as Hamlet reiterates).

'In the University of Excellence', Readings says, 'the problem of value is bracketed, and statistical evaluation (of the measure of excellence) is presumed to provide definitive answers that then feed into funding, resources, and salary decisions' (pp. 150–1). Readings proposes a shift away from the idea of the University of Excellence towards a University of Thought. To think in terms of a University of Thought is no longer, in fact, to be thinking in terms of a governing idea at all. 'Thought, unlike excellence, does not masquerade as an idea' (p. 160), he asserts. 'Thought differs from excellence in that it does not bracket the question of value' (p. 159). 'Thought' is just a name. He writes:

> Thought does not function as an answer but as a *question*. Excellence works because no one has to do ask what it means. Thought demands that we ask what it means, because its status as mere name – radically detached from truth – enforces that question. Keeping the question of what Thought names open requires a constant vigilance to prevent the name of Thought from slipping back into an idea, from founding a mystical ideology of truth. We can only seek to do justice to a name, not to find its truth … The meaning-effects of a name are structurally incapable of final determination, are always open to discussion. (p. 160)

What goes for the name of 'Thought' goes also for that of 'teacher'. As he then makes clear: 'these reflections [he says] are written from the point of view of someone who is, professionally, a teacher, though he does not know in any absolute sense what is the signification of the name of teacher' (p. 160). 'Thought' and 'being-a-teacher' would entail a certain affirmation of intellectual or psychical uncertainty, a certain 'lack of orientation' (to recall a term used by Jentsch).[13] We might illustrate this in two ways, first in terms of the identity of addressee, and second in terms of the experience of time. Who is speaking and to whom is one speaking when one teaches? One of the most 'obvious' yet still perhaps incomprehensible truths of psychoanalysis becomes evident as soon as one questions, in the classroom, who is present and who is not: am I not, as a teacher, inseparable from those who have taught me? And does the classroom contain only those who are 'literally' present? Are there not mothers and fathers, friends and others, alive and dead, and even not yet born, known and unknown, also in the classroom? There is no teaching, it may be said, without this experience of radical uncertainty about whom one is addressing and, by extension, who is teaching whom. The experience of such uncertainty is not a negative thing: it is rather the condition of teaching and learning. To love teaching, to love certain texts, to love certain ways of thinking: this is possible only in a context of mortal uncertainty. There can be no love without the uncanny, without the strangely unsettling promise of address ('I love you'). As Peggy Kamuf has formulated it: '"I love" always brushes up against the uncanny.'[14]

In so far as teaching entails public discourse (and the preceding remarks, like any critical reflections on psychoanalysis and the uncanny more generally, suggest that it is in precisely this uncertainty of what is public and what is private that teaching happens), Thought has to do with a sense of what Kamuf, in another context, has referred to as 'the absence of any figure who can stand in for the final destination of public discourse'.[15] Intellectual uncertainty about identity-in-the-classroom has its counterpart in the experience of time. Thought (in Readings's terms) would have to do with a different experience of time, an experience no doubt in some ways inimical to the University of Excellence. Two or three aphorisms might clarify this sense of time. The first is from Pascal: 'When one reads too quickly or too slowly one understands nothing.'[16] It is impossible to know how quickly or slowly to read; reading entails something unreadable, in reserve, something that resists being understood *now*. Put in different terms, any reading or teaching worthy of the name does not happen when it happens: it is bound up with a strange experience (which may be the very impossibility of an experience) of deferral, of ghostly time. The most familiar words, texts, ideas, thoughts or feelings are those that are capable of becoming most uncanny. The second aphorism is from Kafka: 'All human errors are impatience, a premature breaking-off of methodical procedure, an apparent fencing-in of what is apparently at issue.'[17] Kafka's statement points towards an uncanny experience of the interminable, an affirmation of the importance of being patient and methodical, accompanied by an acknowledgement that there are really no boundaries: all fencing-in of time and space is ghost-work. With such patience in mind, we might also here recall Lyn Hejinian's watchword, in her poem entitled *My Life*: 'One cannot be afraid to watch too long to render the world uncanny.'[18]

With respect to the scene of teaching, Readings observes: 'the transgressive force of teaching does not lie so much in matters of content as in the way pedagogy can hold open the temporality of questioning so as to resist being characterized as a transaction that can be concluded, either with the giving of grades or the granting of degrees' (p. 19). The vision of the future of education and culture that Readings's book ends up with is that of the University (or other institution of education) as the place 'where thought takes place beside thought, where thinking is a shared process without identity or unity. Thought beside itself perhaps' (p. 192). It is in exploring this notion of 'thought beside itself' that we can perhaps most helpfully get a sense of what may be uncanny about literature, teaching and psychoanalysis.

There are three impossible professions: teaching, psychoanalysis (or healing) and governing. Freud said this at least twice.[19] On both occasions, he puts the impossibility of educating first. Teaching is impossible, perhaps even more than psychoanalysis or the art of government. This is what Freud, with characteristic dryness, calls a *bon mot*.[20] But within any implied hierarchy of these impossible professions, psychoanalysis itself has a double role, for it itself teaches. More precisely, psychoanalysis teaches something about the impossibility of thinking about teaching without engaging with the thinking that, perhaps paradoxically, psychoanalysis makes possible. This is where we encounter the compelling and ceaselessly generative differences and slippages within what is called Freud's thought, in other words (in the wake of Freud's teaching) within the very notion of such-and-such a person's 'thought'. Freud's thought here would be thought beside itself. It is necessarily at least double. On the one hand there is a Freud that everyone may feel they are familiar with, even to the point of feeling they don't actually need to read Freud: they already know what he is on about. On the other there is a Freud who is a stranger to himself, someone whose 'thought' makes all of us (in Julia Kristeva's phrase) 'strangers to ourselves'.[21] On the one hand there is a Freud passionately committed to rationalism and scientific thought ('methodical procedure' in Kafka's phrase); on the other, there is a Freud who says more or other than he thinks.

We can see these two dimensions of Freud's thought at work in a short text written a year before the publication of 'The Uncanny', entitled 'On the Teaching of Psychoanalysis in Universities' (1918).[22] Here he weighs up the pros and cons of introducing a 'general psychoanalytic course' that would be designed for all students, not only those training to acquire expertise in 'the field of psychological disorders' but in all 'the branches of learning which lie within the sphere of philosophy and the arts' (p. 173). He concludes that such a general course would be worthwhile: 'for the purposes we have in view it will be enough if [the student] learns something *about* psychoanalysis and something *from* it' (p. 173). As Shoshana Felman has noted, in her fine discussion of Freud's short essay: 'To learn something *from* psychoanalysis is a very different thing than to learn something *about* it: it means that psychoanalysis is not a simple object of the teaching, but its subject.'[23] To learn *about* psychoanalysis might be no different from learning something by rote; to learn something *from* psychoanalysis might constitute the basis for revolutionizing learning and institutions of learning in general. Freud's little essay does and does not say this. Felman is thus led to argue that – as regards 'the implication of psychoanalysis in pedagogy and of pedagogy in psychoanalysis' – 'psychoanalysis has shifted pedagogy by radically displacing our very modes of intelligibility' (p. 75). Psychoanalysis alters the ways in which we are obliged to conceive of thought, identity and teaching.

There is another short Freud text which Felman discusses from this period, called 'A Difficulty in the Path of Psychoanalysis' (1917), which can be read as a sort of ghost-text within 'The Uncanny' itself. It shows Freud thinking about uncanniness specifically in relation to psychoanalysis and teaching. He thus formulates what makes psychoanalysis a kind of uncanny pedagogy:

> Psychoanalysis sets out to explain … uncanny disorders; it engages in careful and laborious investigations, devises hypotheses and scientific constructions, until at length it can speak thus to the ego:
> '… Come, let yourself be taught something on this one point! What is in your mind does not coincide with what you are conscious of; whether something is going on in your mind and whether you hear of it, are two different things … In every case … the news that reaches your consciousness is incomplete and often not to be relied on. Often enough, too, it happens that you get news of events only when they are over and when you can no longer do anything to change them. Even if you are not ill, who can tell all that is stirring in your mind of which you know nothing or are falsely informed? You behave like an absolute ruler who is content with the information supplied him by his highest officials and never goes among the people to hear their voice. Turn your eyes inward, look into your own depths, learn first to know yourself! … '
> It is thus that psychoanalysis has sought to educate the ego.[24]

To learn something from, as well as about, psychoanalysis means getting involved in this extraordinary scene of teaching. It is, Freud says, 'uncanny'. There are 'thoughts', he says, that are 'alien guests' in the 'house' of the mind, guests more powerful than the emperor: *the ego is not master in its own house*.[25] Freud translates the Greek dictum, 'Know thyself', into something irreducibly strange. To recall from 'The Uncanny' what, for thought and for teaching, forms the basis of an interminable, implacable demand: 'we ourselves speak a language that is foreign' (U, p. 341). You may think you are on the throne, there where news reaches your consciousness; but the news is neither complete nor reliable, and in any case the topography is all askew, the place of the throne is thrown completely. 'Turn your eyes inward, look into your own depths' – a visual metaphor, but metaphor in an abyss. The form of Freud's remarks is striking: it is literary, specifically in that he is personifying psychoanalysis and (in a silent, ghostly fashion) attributing to it a fictional power of enunciation. '"Turn your eyes inward … learn first to know yourself! … " It is thus that psychoanalysis has sought to educate the ego.' The abyssal visual metaphor is contained within an extended metaphor of voice, a fiction, a prosopopoeia of psychoanalysis.

Alongside this, but disordering and altering everything, there is strangeness in the experience of time: often, psychoanalysis says, 'you get news of events only when they are over', you hear things that make sense only later. This is an example of what Derrida has described as Freud's greatest discovery,[26] the discovery of *Nachträglichkeit*, deferred or belated action, after-effect, *après-coup*. In the temporal logic of this fictional prosopopoeia, you hear and recognize the voice of psychoanalysis (it is like the voice of the people), which tells you (as if you have not yet learnt anything, including the ability to recognize the voice of psychoanalysis or the voice of the people) that you must 'learn first to know yourself'. More generally – and in ways that perhaps resist thought, resist the thinking of Freud or of anyone else – the logic of deferred action or after-effect must diffract back upon and indeed make up the logic of the present moment and all thought concerning the time of psychoanalysis and the time of teaching. Freud does not put it in that way: indeed his wording ('you get news of events only when they are over') suggests an only partial realization of the logic of what he is saying – as if the 'news' and the 'events' still arrive, intact and 'the same', it's just that they arrive late. The more uncanny, because in some strange sense 'truer' turn here (articulated most notably by Derrida), entails an acknowledgement that this logic of the 'late news and events' constitutes the very condition of the present, setting it aside from itself. The ghostly effects of delay and deferral are what make the present and presence possible.[27] Psychoanalysis teaches, then, that the time of teaching is irreducibly strange: what passes does not pass when it passes. The meaning of an experience, the experience of a teaching, does not belong to the present. Nor does it belong to any other time. It is never at home in time. Perhaps this will have been one of the most uncanny lessons of psychoanalysis. The time of the classroom is beside itself, haunted, in deferral. Nothing of this is available for translation into the demented language of 'learning outcomes'. If, to borrow Freud's phrase in the *Introductory Lectures on Psychoanalysis*, psychoanalysis is a sort of 'after-education' (*Nacherziehung*),[28] it entails an experience of the *after* that belongs to no present.

I have begun to indicate, I hope, some of the ways in which psychoanalysis, especially in the words of its so-called founder, may be uncanny not only by its own account but also in ways that Freud himself may not have considered. Psychoanalysis is attentive to the faultiness of news reports reaching consciousness and to the effects of what it reveals as being the foreign language of the self; at the same time, it is susceptible to being heard otherwise, construed as being stranger than it appears – both in terms of being, for example, more literary, *and* in terms of being more educative. Psychoanalysis is a precursor to deconstruction as the twentieth- and twenty-first-century philosophy of 'thought beside itself'. In other words, like deconstruction, psychoanalysis is neither simply philosophy nor science nor just a 'way of thinking'. To recall a remark made by Paul de Man, on the occasion of Jacques Lacan's giving a lecture in New Haven in 1975: 'I would say that we have not yet begun to suspect the extent to which this teaching [the teaching of psychoanalysis, what psychoanalysis has to teach] partakes of literature. Like Freud, like Nietzsche, Jacques Lacan is one of those who know language's uncanny power to refuse the truth that nonetheless it never stops demanding.'[29] De Man's observation is valuable not only for its claim regarding the literariness of psychoanalysis, but also for its emphasis on the question of teaching. If a great deal of attention has been given to psychoanalysis as a 'talking cure', as a clinical practice, and as a means of reflecting on society, religion, literature and culture, comparatively little has been given to it as a theory of teaching. Or to be more exact: a lot has been said and done in the name of teaching and psychoanalysis (the work of Lacan being one among numerous examples); but relatively little has been said or done about teaching and psychoanalysis outside the psychoanalytic institution itself. Psychoanalysis remains a kind of foreign body to and within higher education: the University in general does not admit it, even in the form of that 'general course' Freud so conservatively welcomed in 1918. And yet at the same time psychoanalysis is self-evidently *within* the University, for example in the teaching of literature departments and in ways that would no doubt have seemed quite foreign to what Freud may himself have thought was his thought.

In the remainder of this chapter I want to explore the hypothesis that there are areas of psychoanalysis still to be thought, in particular concerning the distinctiveness and productiveness of psychoanalysis as a haunted theory of teaching or theory of haunted teaching, starting out as a theory of teaching oneself. Commentators have stressed the ironies of the fact that the first analysis was a self-analysis (Freud's auto-analysis), but we have perhaps hardly begun to explore the resources of Freud's work as uncanny auto-didactics, as a self-teaching on the subject of thought-beside-itself, an interminable *after*-education that cannot but be heterogeneous to itself, a kind of auto-hetero-didactics.

Why teach? Teaching, and indeed even talking about teaching, can seem quite disgusting. So-called 'theories of education' have perhaps taken insufficient account of such disgust. There is something disgusting, incipiently uncanny perhaps, about the experience of repetition in talking to students, in memorizing or trying to memorize their names, in finding oneself seeming to say or being on the verge of saying exactly the same thing as one did an hour, or a day, or a year before. In her preface to a special issue of *Yale French Studies* devoted to the question 'what does literature have to teach us about the act of teaching?', Barbara Johnson attempts to read, or to allow herself to be read by, S. T. Coleridge's uncanny mariner: 'I pass, like night, from land to land; / I have strange power of speech; / That moment that his face I see, / I know the man that must hear me: / To him my tale I teach.'[30] Johnson argues that what tends to get repressed in teaching is 'the very stuff that literature is made of' and that 'a reading of the mariner himself would suggest that teaching is a compulsion: a compulsion to repeat what one has not yet understood'.[31] We may recall here what Freud refers to as 'the uncanny effect' produced by 'the impression of automatic, mechanical processes at work behind the ordinary appearance of mental activity' (U, p. 347). The immediate context of his remark is that of 'epileptic fits' and 'manifestations of insanity' (U, p. 347), but it would seem to hold strangely true for teaching as well. 'Whatever reminds us of this inner "compulsion to repeat" is perceived as uncanny' (U, p. 361), says Freud: in an ironic, even abyssal way, this suggests that teaching is least uncanny when it is most uncanny, or that when it is not uncanny in a conscious way (where we are 'reminded' and able to perceive things as uncanny) it is all the more uncanny in an unconscious way (where we become mere mechanico-pedagogical dolls, marionettes of the lecture theatre, plastic components in the teaching machine).

But if teaching is uncanny in these respects, this also has to do with a sense that the haunted university, the university in ruins, is not new, perhaps, but strangely familiar. Let us consider, for example, the case of Friedrich Nietzsche's 1872 lectures 'On the Future of Our Educational Institutions'.[32] These lectures seem to suggest that disgust is the very condition of teaching. Nietzsche (or one of the fictitious speakers he has mouth much of the text: the literary dimensions of these lectures, too, are inextricably part of their strangeness and power) speaks of 'two seemingly antagonistic tendencies, equally deleterious in their action, and ultimately combining to produce their results: a striving to achieve the greatest possible *expansion* of education on the one hand, and a tendency to *minimise and weaken* it on the other' (pp. 35–6). Modern culture is 'barbaric' and 'revolting' (p. 42), 'unbearable' and 'repulsive' (p. 134). The figurative language of marionette, puppet or mechanical doll seems to pervade every level of Nietzsche's account. The lectures are largely structured around 'the solitary, remote, and at times abusive duologue of [a] philosopher and his companion':

Nietzsche speaks of these as 'marionettes' featuring in 'the puppet-play' (p. 91) of his lectures. At the same time, however, he seems mechanically, compulsively to resort to the same figurative language at the very end of the lectures when he wishes to evoke the possibility of 'a true educational institution' (p. 142). Here he imagines the 'pseudo-culture of the present' (p. 140) as an orchestra full of 'mechanical, lifeless bodies' (p. 142) that might – if 'your musical sense ... returned' and 'your ears ... opened' – produce the sort of 'impassioned feeling of rapture' (p. 141) that 'a true educational institution' would be about.

In a recent essay, Valerie Allen and Ares Axiotis argue for the relevance of Nietzsche's 1872 lectures for thinking about the future of education now, especially in the context of a University of Thought. They take as seminal the Nietzschean exclamation: 'One should not have points of view, but thoughts!'[33] They see Nietzsche's lectures as having a specific message: 'if thought is to be the ultimate aim of education, then the structure of thinking must itself be embodied in the structure of educational institutions themselves'.[34] Nietzsche's lectures are in turn the subject of an intriguing lecture by Derrida, entitled 'Otobiographies', given in 1976.[35] Against Nietzsche, Derrida seeks to explore the role, not of disgust, but of pleasure in teaching. He declares:

> I do not teach truth as such; I do not transform myself into a diaphanous mouthpiece of eternal pedagogy. I settle accounts, however I can, on a certain number of problems: with you and with me or me, and through you, me and me, with a certain number of authorities [*instances*: proceedings] represented here. I understand that the place I am now occupying will not be left out of the exhibit or withdrawn from the scene. Nor do I intend to withhold even that which I shall call, to save time, an *autobiographical* demonstration, although I must ask you to shift its sense a little and to listen to it with another ear. I wish to take a certain pleasure in this, so that *you may learn this pleasure from me*. (p. 4)

This passage might serve as a basis for exploring what Derrida's work suggests about the nature of teaching and the future of institutions of education, as well as about what might be called the legacies of psychoanalysis as a teaching and in particular as a hetero-didactics. Two brief preliminary remarks may be made regarding the passage just cited. First, the autobiographical is always inscribed in the context of teaching but it is inscribed, as Derrida goes on to argue, in ways that do not come back to a me, that do not belong to an 'I'. If teaching always involves a sort of 'auto-translation' (translating oneself at a particular moment for a particular audience, with particular 'aims and objectives' or 'learning outcomes', however transparent or secretive, conventional or transgressive, conscious or unconscious), it should be stressed that, in Derrida's phrase, 'it is less a question of auto-translation turned back in on itself, trying to master the

Unheimliche or the uncanny, than it is of the opposite movement'.[36] Second, and contrary to the apparent conviction of a great number of commentators that Derrida's work is preoccupied above all with writing, and in particular with privileging writing over speech, the passage I have just cited may serve to suggest the opposite – or at least to give some intimation of the importance he attaches to the figure of the voice and, here, the ear. As in so many of his texts, in fact, the explicitly oral, the audile or acoustic dimension is fundamental.

In its etymology the word 'teach' seems to foreground the visual: it comes from the Old English *taecan*. Thus in the *OED* the first definition of 'teach' is '1. *v.t.* Show, present or offer to view. Only in OE [i.e. Old English]'. The second (Old English–Late Middle English) is '2. *v.t.* Show or point out (a thing, the way, etc.) to a person'. For Derrida, however, teaching is perhaps above all a matter of the voice and ear. Derrida '[does] not teach truth as such' – or as he puts it, more peremptorily, in another context: 'I do not seek to establish any kind of authenticity.'[37] And truth and authenticity here apply to the autobiographical, to narcissism in general, to the most intimate self-relation, including the experience of hearing-oneself-speak. He is interested in how Nietzsche's lectures on the future of education focus on the importance of the ear, and in particular on the idea of hearing otherwise. The figure of the ear becomes a way of describing, accentuating and analysing the fact that texts (specifically Nietzsche's, but it could also be Freud's or Derrida's own writings) are capable of a 'double interpretation' (p. 32). Thinking in particular of the disturbingly different political appropriations of Nietzsche's work, Derrida asks:

> Is there anything 'in' the Nietzschean corpus that could help us comprehend the double interpretation and the so-called perversion of the text? The Fifth Lecture tells us that there must be something unheimlich – uncanny – about the enforced repression [*Unterdrückung*] of the least degenerate needs. Why 'unheimlich'? This is another form of the same question.
> The ear is uncanny. Uncanny is what it is; double is what it can become; large or small is what it can make or let happen (as in laissser-faire, since the ear is the most tendered and most open organ, the one that, as Freud reminds us, the infant cannot close); large or small as well the manner in which one may offer or lend an ear. (pp. 32–3)

The ear is an unspoken key to the future of education. The ear is uncanny, for example, because it is double: it can be at once open and closed; receptive and unresponsive; source and destination. The ear is the ear of the other. The ear of the other is an 'eerily' dismembered ear. The ear is that from which the very possibility of speaking (or writing) comes, it is the one that does not answer, for example when Derrida asks, and I now ask in turn: 'Who is listening to whom right here?' (p. 35).

Derrida says that his lecture can be called 'an *autobiographical* demonstration' on condition that we 'shift its sense a little and ... listen to it with another ear'. And he adds: 'I wish to take a certain pleasure in this, so that *you may learn this pleasure from me.*' Teaching is about pleasure, and in particular as a way of trying to account for the fact that what or who I am, the very possibility of my being able to tell my own thoughts or feelings, is an effect of the ear of the other: autobiography becomes otobiography (from *otic*, 'of or relating to the ear'). Rather than a thinking of teaching in terms of a kind of Gradgrindingly mechanical repetition compulsion, Derrida proposes an affirmation of what conditions such a repetition compulsion, namely the notion that 'every other is altogether other' (*tout autre est tout autre*, 'every other is every (bit) other').[38] In the context of his reading of Nietzsche on the future of education, it is a matter of what Derrida calls '*the difference in the ear*'. As he then goes on to make clear, one of the names for such difference is 'death':

Stelarc's Third Ear Project

AN EXTRA EAR WOULD BE CONSTRUCTED AS A SOFT PROSTHESIS
BY STRETCHING, GRAFTING AND AUGMENTATION
IT WOULD MIMICK THE SHAPE AND STRUCTURE OF AN EAR
BUT WITH AN IMPLANTED SOUND CHIP AND PROXIMITY SENSOR
IT WOULD SPEAK TO ANYONE WHO WOULD GET CLOSE
OR CONNECTED TO A MODEM AND WEARABLE COMPUTER
IT WOULD AMPLIFY REALAUDIO SOUNDS TO AUGMENT THE LOCAL SOUNDS
HEARD BY THE ACTUAL EARS – THE EXTRA EAR AS AN INTERNET ANTENNA

> The most important thing about the ear's difference ... is that the signature becomes effective – performed and performing – not at the moment it apparently takes place, but only later, when ears will have managed to receive the message. In some way the signature will take place on the addressee's side, that is, on the side of him or her whose ear will be keen enough to hear my name, for example, or to understand my signature, that with which I sign ... Nietzsche's signature does not take place when he writes. He says clearly that it will take place posthumously ... it is the ear of the other that signs ... Every text answers to this structure ... A text is signed only much later by the other.[39]

Here, then, is the uncanny, ghostly logic of deferred action or *après coup* as inscribed by 'death': a proper name and a signature carry death; the meaning of a text (or of a teaching) comes later, from the other. Death, then, is strangely at the heart of life, of writing and of teaching. This affirmation is linked to pleasure, the sort of experience of pleasure suggested elsewhere when Derrida says: 'no deconstruction without pleasure and no pleasure without deconstruction'.[40]

Not only does Derrida angle his account of the future of education in terms of pleasure rather than of that disgust which he says, in Nietzsche's lectures, 'controls everything' ('Oto', p. 23), but he also insists on a thinking that would, unlike Nietzsche's, seek to accommodate and give way to the place of woman. Derrida concludes his lecture by emphatically suggesting that woman, in Nietzsche's account, 'never appears at any point ... either to study or to teach' (38). What Derrida is doing here with Nietzsche's *Lectures on the Future of Our Educational Institutions* is similar to a certain reading of Freud's 'The Uncanny': the figure of woman may indeed appear in Freud's essay but does so with consequences and effects to which Freud himself seems blind.[41] Nietzsche's text is haunted and defined by this absence. If there is pleasure in teaching, it would have to do with a different thinking of 'man' and 'woman' alike. If, as has been suggested elsewhere, one of the most common forms of the uncanny concerns 'a sense of radical uncertainty about sexuality', in particular about whether a person is male or female, or what the terms 'man' and 'woman' mean, this is for Derrida not a matter of neutering or neutralizing sexual difference but of proliferation.[42] Pleasure, one is tempted to suppose, is here linked to the possibilities of what he elsewhere calls 'a choreographic text with polysexual signatures', an experience of teaching, of the voice and of the ear, that

> perhaps goes beyond known or coded marks, beyond the grammar and spelling ... of sexuality ... beyond the binary difference that governs the decorum of all codes, beyond the opposition feminine/masculine, beyond bisexuality as well, beyond homosexuality and heterosexuality which come to the same thing.[43]

This, a dreaming of new institutions, is perhaps Derrida's version of the 'populist' metaphor of hearing the voice of the people that we observed in Freud. As Derrida puts it: 'I would like to believe in the masses, this indeterminable number of blended voices, this mobile of non-identitifed sexual marks whose choreography can carry, divide, multiply the body of each "individual", whether he be classified as "man" or "woman" according to the criteria of usage.'[44]

Derrida's *Spectres of Marx* (1993) has to date made its impact, primarily, as a reading of Marx and Marxism following the disintegration of the Soviet Union and, secondarily, as an account of spectrality, ghosts and spirits. The future, as Derrida says, belongs to ghosts. Ghosts don't belong to the past, they come from the future. The same goes for communism and democracy. But *Spectres of Marx* is also an astonishing work about teaching, about the relations between education and spectres. At the centre of the book is the blackboard on which Derrida writes how badly the world is going, inscribing what he calls the ten plagues of the so-called '"new world order"' (*SM*, p. 81). Framing the book is a rethinking of the concept of the scholar or intellectual as someone who would 'learn ... from the ghost' (p. 176). Derrida looks towards a new notion of scholarship, other spaces of intellectual thinking, spaces that can be called affirmatively spectral or phantomistic.

The pedagogical dimension of *Spectres of Marx* is made clear in the 'exordium' with which it begins. The whole of the book can be summarized, he says, in this exordium, in the form of this strange tutorial: 'learn to live finally' (p. xvii). Derrida writes:

> But to learn to live, to learn it *from oneself and by oneself*, all alone, to teach *oneself* to live ('I would like to learn to live finally'), is that not impossible for a living being? Is it not what logic itself forbids? To live, by definition, is not something one learns. Not from oneself, it is not learned from life, taught by life. Only from the other and by death. In any case from the other at the edge of life. At the internal border or the external border, it is a heterodidactics between life and death. (p. xviii)

The time of this tutorial is strange because in a sense it never takes place: it is structured by that logic of deferral that Derrida sees as so important in Freud, it is structured (like every legacy, inheritance or teaching) as a trembling, as the radically uncertain experience of a promise. Derrida writes: 'The time of the "learning to live", a time without tutelary present [*un temps sans présent tuteur*], would amount to this ... to learn to live *with* ghosts' (p. xviii/15). Derrida concludes *Spectres of Marx* with an evocation of this ghostly tutorial in terms of what Freud had designated as the uncanny. He gives a different, ghostly turn to Freud's characterization of the psychoanalytic imperative to 'look first inside yourself'. The uncanny, Derrida suggests, entails the sense of

> a stranger who is already found within (*das Heimliche-Unheimliche*), more intimate with one than one is oneself, the absolute proximity of a stranger whose power is singular *and* anonymous (*es spukt*), an unnameable and neutral power, that is, undecidable, neither active nor passive, an an-identity that, *without doing anything*, invisibly occupies places belonging finally neither to us nor to it. (172)

To talk or write about teaching is doubtless what Derrida calls 'a theatrical infraction of the laws of genre and academicism' ('Oto', pp. 25–6), and thus to some degree like all the texts I have been discussing here. In keeping with this theatricality, I propose to conclude by setting an examination – or more precisely by trying to sketch a possible reading of a short text entitled 'Exam'. By conventional accounts 'Exam' may be judged a short story, a short work of narrative fiction. In choosing to end with such a text we return to the motif of literature which, in however tacit a fashion, has been weaving away in the background. Any consideration of the future of insitutions of education will have to reckon with the ghostly power of literature. 'Literature' here may be described as the discourse that effects an undecidability about the status of its own language. It generates an undecidable turbulence, a strange trembling. It is, perhaps, the experience of intellectual uncertainty *par excellence*. As Derrida puts it: literature 'always is, says, does something other, something other than itself, an itself which moreover is only that, something other than itself'.[45] This is what makes the study of literature, the passion of and for teaching literature, distinctive and resistant to assimilation within any broader area of education, such as 'cultural studies'; but it is also what contaminates any and every other area. As Timothy Clark has observed:

> Part of the force of literature … is to be transgressive of institutional boundaries and values … [literary studies] cannot define itself (or its object) without consideration of the way its legitimacy as a field is bound up with that of the university as a whole and the very possibility of disciplinarity.[46]

Literature overflows the institution. In Peggy Kamuf's phrase, it figures 'the university in deconstruction'.[47] In this sense – though (as I have been trying to suggest) it is not a sense we have perhaps really begun to think – teaching is a literary genre. What Catherine Belsey has observed in relation to English Studies pertains above all perhaps to the study of literature: 'No other discipline confronts the strangeness of language in a way which enables us to glimpse the corresponding strangeness of the [human] subject to itself.'[48]

Published anonymously in 1995, 'Exam' is, among other things, a text *about* anonymity.[49] If the name has a capacity for generating uncanny effects, so does its absence.[50] We expect a work of literature to have an author, to be identifiable with an authorial name; and yet the link between a work and an authorial name is never absolutely certain (witness the interminability of the so-called Bacon-Shakespeare controversy). There is, perhaps, some quasi-essential link between anonymity and literature, between fiction and 'the absolute proximity of a stranger whose power is singular *and* anonymous'. As E. M. Forster suggested, in a fascinating essay called 'Anonymity: An Enquiry' (published in 1925), literature 'wants not to be signed'.[51] The anonymity of 'Exam' immediately draws attention to the peculiarity of an examination paper, the way in which the student sitting an exam becomes at once subject *to* and subject *of* a strangely anonymous, disembodied and disembodying experience. Is 'Exam' an exam, or something else? In what ways is the literary text in general an exam? Conversely, in what ways is the exam in general an irreducibly literary experience? Can there be a university without exams? The generality of the title, 'Exam', suggests its interdisciplinary or transdisciplinary nature. It might be an exam in any subject or discipline. How 'seriously' should we 'take' exams, for example *this* exam? 'Exam' is ghostly in various respects: its very title seems to effect a sort of flickering, an uncertainty about the status of *this* title and therefore of titles in general, an uncertainty along the lines, or rather within the line, of what Freud refers to as the time and space in which 'the distinction between imagination and reality is effaced' (U, p. 367). What is an exam? Is this an exam? Is it a 'real' exam? When and where will it have begun? We are invited, here and now, to read 'to ourselves', in silence, subvocalizing the words in the so-called silence of our own heads. 'Exam' is a test-case, a work about repetition and compulsion, a test-drive and death drive, *déjà vu*, an out-of-body experience linked up to a recording of and listening to one's own voice. In what sense is it one's 'own'? In what sense is it *one* voice at all? What is the sexual identity of the speaker? Is there one, or might there not be *more than one*? Might this 'exam' offer a way of exploring the possibilities of a University of Thought? What is going on when we find ourselves suspended in the voice of someone, apparently, returning from the dead?

EXAM

The exam starts at nine and I'm on the motorway. It's one of those muggy early June mornings you don't know if it's going to be asphyxiating or a gift. I get up extra early to be sure I'm on the road in plenty of time. I decide against breakfast, or my stomach does. I pack a banana in my bag for the car, just in case. But I don't want to think about that. The idea makes me queasy. I've already spent an hour in the bathroom, getting myself ready. In the kitchen I drink a cup of coffee to wake up, and then another in the hope it will have me wishing to pay a visit before I set out. But instead I find myself back in the bathroom picking as clean as possible a hairbrush I haven't so much as looked at in twelve months. I have several hairbrushes. I ought to be checking I've memorized all my quotations properly, but there I am plucking dead hair and bits of grey fluff from an old hairbrush, like some demented harp-player. It's funny isn't it, the way you choose to do the most practical of things at the most impractical of times. I stupidly imagine it's going to take sixty seconds at most, but the operation sends me into a trance. Ten minutes later I'm still at it. It reminds me of the fairy tale about the boy and girl who must set an impossible task for a giant, otherwise he's going to eat them, and in the end, in desperation, they ask him to straighten out a single curly hair, not a pubic hair needless to say, but a single strand of that kind of curly hair that children have in fairy tales. Somehow I manage to drag myself out of it. I put the brush back on the shelf and get going. I've lost valuable time but haven't we all?

The car starts like a dream, and I'm off. It's 7.50. As it's rush-hour I'm allowing myself forty minutes to get into the city and find a space in one of the student car-parks, then another five minutes to get across to the main building. Déjà vu for a moment, just thinking about that. But I'm on the motorway. I'm on the motorway and it's a beautiful, bright but hazy June morning. The road seems unusually clear, I'm sailing along at such a rate I can feel myself making up time. There's hardly another car in sight. Keep this up, I tell myself, and I'll be there with minutes to spare. Perhaps even long enough to grab another cup of coffee. But the thought of that has my innards churning and I realize a third cup would be out of the question. One moment I'm as calm as one of those S.O.S orange call-boxes that punctuate the hard-shoulder, the next I'm overtaken by nerves. I'm one of those people who take exams really seriously. I can't help it. I find myself taking exams really seriously, I mean taking the idea of taking exams, really seriously, even when I'm trying my best not to take them seriously at all. Anyway this is the last one, my final finals, and a lot's at stake. My life, the works, if you really have to know. Or that's how it feels. I'm not a confident person, even at the best of times. I'm speeding along but then I'm overtaken by nerves. I switch on the radio and it's a classical music station playing something peaceful and sad, but then the voice of the guy in between gets me going again. I don't even take in what he's saying but the way he intones the composer's name and title, it's as if he were announcing a nuclear accident. Panic stations. I lurch forwards and kill it, suddenly quite ready to be sick. I run my hand quickly through my hair. Calm down, I tell myself. But running a hand through my hair reminds me of my neurotic behaviour with the hairbrush and the disgusting tufts of grey. I try to focus my attention on something else. I'm in the middle lane, travelling at the legal limit, but still cars overtake me. For a while I concentrate on timing it so that I turn my head to look at the driver in the outside lane at precisely the moment of overtaking. But it seems, no matter how many times I do this, the other driver simply ignores me. It's as if I didn't exist. I fumble in my bag and eventually extricate my all-important cassette. I stick it in the machine, press play and wait, as I drive, eyes on the road straight ahead. Shut up, Heathcliff! (That's me, talking to the dog.) The exam starts at nine and I'm on the motorway. (I listen to the tape, which is a recording of my own voice, recounting all the significant facts and reading out all the key quotations.) And there I am, sailing along at top speed, when it happens. I come over the brow of a gentle upward incline and spread out before me, dazzling and glittering in the June morning sun, is a great sea of frozen traffic. It's like being unexpectedly face to face with a shimmering corpse. The way the sound of screeching brakes and smell of burning rubber fill the air is appalling. It's impossible to tell who's going to hit who, or up ahead, who's already hit and already dead. This is the moment, I know, in which the whole of your life supposedly passes in front of you. The whole story, in one fell swoop, a single polaroid snapshot. It's the split second in which you see the light streaming at the end of the tunnel. It's the time, it's said, that a person is most susceptible to having an out-of-body experience. All that happens with me is that I hear a voice. I hear myself saying: What's an exam if it's not an out-of-body experience?

Write an essay about this story, giving particular attention to tone, imagery and narrative perspective. Time allowed: forty-five minutes.

NOTES

1   Philippe Lacoue-Labarthe, 'Catastrophe: A Reading of Celan's "The Meridian"', trans. Timothy Clark and Sylvia Gautheron, *Oxford Literary Review* (special issue, *Experiencing the Impossible*), vol. 15 (1993), 12.

2   Peter Schwenger, 'Uncanny Reading', *English Studies in Canada*, vol. 21, no. 3 (1995), 340.

3   As we shall see, Jacques Derrida picks up on the *es spukt* in his *Spectres of Marx: The State of the Debt, the Work of Mourning, and the New International*, trans. Peggy Kamuf (London: Routledge, 1994). See his discussion (p. 133) of the difficulties of translating the phrase, as well as his remark in the penultimate footnote of the book: 'In truth, "unheimliche" is just as

untranslatable as "es spukt"' (p. 195, n. 38). Further page references to *Spectres of Marx* are given in the main body of the essay, with the abbreviation 'SM' where clarity dictates. Where appropriate, references to the French text, *Spectres de Marx: L'État de la dette, le travail du deuil et la nouvelle Internationale* (Paris: Galilée, 1993), are given in parentheses, following the English translation page number and a slash.

4   Ernst Jentsch, 'On the Psychology of the Uncanny' (1906), trans. Roy Sellars, *Angelaki*, vol. 2, no. 1 (1995), *Home and Family* special issue, ed. Sarah Wood, pp. 7–16.

5   Roy Sellars, Preface to Jentsch, in *Home and Family*, p. 7.

6   See David Farrell Krell, '*Das Unheimliche*: Architectural Sections of Heidegger and Freud', *Research in Phenomenology*, vol. 22 (1992), 43–61: here, p. 60. It should be added that the literariness of Freud's account is not simply formal (as Krell's description here might imply). The uncanniness of the literary, as I hope will become evident, is more slippery, ghostly and strangely pervasive than this.

7   Cf. Marjorie Garber, whose book *Shakespeare's Ghost Writers: Literature as Uncanny Causality* (London: Routledge, 1987) offers an extended questioning and unsettling of Freud's claims regarding the *non*-uncanniness of Shakespeare's ghosts. See, for example, Garber, pp. xiv, 62–3, 103, 127. A similar point applies in the context of fairy tales. Freud seems quite happy to categorize fairy tales as not being uncanny, as containing 'no trace of uncanniness', as being altogether quite 'remote from the uncanny' (U, pp. 368–9); but this confidence has decidedly dodgy foundations, for as I have suggested earlier (see Chapter 1, note 46, for example) uncanniness is crucially a question of reading, not simply a matter of content or theme. For a study of fairy tales that seeks to explore such uncanny possibilities of reading, see Jack Zipes, *Fairy Tales and the Art of Subversion: The Classical Genre for Children and the Process of Civilization* (London: Methuen, 1988). Zipes writes: 'Using and modifying Freud's category of the uncanny, I want to argue that *the very act of reading a fairy tale is an uncanny experience in that it separates the reader from the restrictions of reality from the onset and makes the repressed unfamiliar familiar again*' (p. 174).

8   This is perhaps a danger in the case of an essay such as Nicholas Rand's and Maria Torok's '*The Sandman* Looks at "The Uncanny": The Return of the Repressed or of the Secret; Hoffmann's Question to Freud', in *Speculations after Freud: Psychoanalysis, Philosophy and Culture*, eds Sonu Shamdasani and Michael Munchow (London: Routledge, 1994), pp. 185–203. They are concerned with why 'Freud may have selected *The Sandman* for a reason different from the one he stated or even intended' (p. 186). Hoffmann's story, for Rand and Torok, is not about castration (as Freud claimed) but rather about an encrypted secret which, nevertheless, the authors are able to locate and describe: 'we will question the relevance of substituting the penis for the eyes in *The Sandman*. The eyes do in fact play a major role, but for a different reason. They symbolize the hero's thwarted attempt to see, to inquire, to discover' (p. 188). This specification of *the* (symbolic) meaning of eyes in Hoffmann's story is reductive, it seems to me, not only of the force and possibilities of Hoffmann's text but of the literary more generally. Literature is more resistantly cryptic, more elusively ghostly than Rand's and Torok's reading here may suggest. I explore the notions of crypt, resistance and the elusive supplementarity of phantoms in greater detail elsewhere: see *Telepathy and Literature* (Oxford: Blackwell, 1990), esp. Chapter 3, 'Cryptaesthesia: The Case of *Wuthering Heights*', and 'This is Not a Book Review: Esther Rashkin, *Family Secrets and the Psychoanalysis of Narrative*', *Angelaki*, vol. 2, no. 1 (1995), *Home and Family*, ed. Sarah Wood, pp. 31–5.

9   Quoted in *Jacques Derrida*, by Geoffrey Bennington and Jacques Derrida, trans. Bennington (London: University of Chicago Press, 1993), p. 349.

10   Jacques Derrida, 'Ellipsis', in *Writing and Difference*, trans. Alan Bass (London: Routledge and Kegan Paul, 1978), p. 297.

11   I discuss the RAE in more detail in Chapter 8 below.

12   Bill Readings, *The University in Ruins* (Cambridge, Mass.: Harvard University Press, 1996). Further references to the text are given in brackets in the main body of the text.

13   Jentsch, 'On the Psychology of the Uncanny', p. 9.

14   Peggy Kamuf, 'Deconstruction and Love', in *Deconstructions: A User's Guide*, ed. Nicholas Royle (Basingstoke and New York: Palgrave, 2000), p. 156.

15   Peggy Kamuf, 'Going Public: The University in Deconstruction', in *Deconstruction is/in America: A New Sense of the Political*, ed. Anselm Haverkamp (New York: New York University Press, 1995), p. 110.

16   Cited by Paul de Man as epigraph to his *Allegories of Reading: Figural Language in Rousseau, Nietzsche, Rilke, and Proust* (New Haven: Yale University Press, 1979). See Pascal, *Pensées*, trans. A. J. Krailsheimer (Harmondsworth: Penguin, 1966), no. 723, p. 251.

17   Franz Kafka, *The Collected Aphorisms* (London: Syrens, 1994), p. 3.

18   Lyn Hejinian, *My Life (The Nineties)*, in *Out of Everywhere: Linguistically Innovative Poetry by Women in North America & the UK*, ed. Maggie O'Sullivan (London: Reality Street Editions, 1996), p. 64.

19   See *SE*, 19: 273, and 23: 248.

20   *SE*, 19: 273.

21   Julia Kristeva, *Strangers to Ourselves*, trans. Leon S. Roudiez (New York: Columbia University Press, 1991).

22   *SE*, 17: 171–3. Further page references to this text are given in brackets in the main body of the text.

23   Shoshana Felman, 'Psychoanalysis and Education', in her *Jacques Lacan and the Adventure of Insight: Psychoanalysis in Contemporary Culture* (Cambridge, Mass.: Harvard University Press, 1987), p. 74. Further page references to Felman are given in brackets in the main body of the text.

24   'A Difficulty in the Path of Psychoanalysis', *SE*, 17: 142–3.

25   'A Difficulty in the Path of Psychoanalysis', *SE*, 17: 141, 143.

26   See Jacques Derrida, *Writing and Difference*, trans Alan Bass (London: RKP. 1978), p. 203; cf. *Archive Fever: A Freudian Impression*, trans. Eric Prenowitz (Chicago: University of Chicago Press, 1996), p. 80. I discuss this further in Chapter 18 below.

27   See, in particular, Jacques Derrida, 'Freud and the Scene of Writing', in *Writing and Difference*, trans. Alan Bass (London: Routledge and Kegan Paul, 1978), pp. 202–3.

28   See Lecture 28, in *Introductory Lectures to Psychoanalysis*, PFL, 1: 504; cf. *SE*, 19: 274.

29   Paul de Man, cited by Felman, in *The Lesson of Paul de Man, Yale French Studies*, vol. 69 (1985), 51.

30   Barbara Johnson, 'Teaching as a Literary Genre', Preface to a special issue of *Yale French Studies* (no. 63, 1982), entitled *The Pedagogical Imperative: Teaching as a Literary Genre*, pp. iii–vii.

31   Johnson, 'Teaching as a Literary Genre', pp. vi–vii.

32   *On the Future of Our Educational Institutions*, trans. J. M. Kennedy (London, 1909). Further page references will be given in parentheses in the main body of the text.

33   Cited by Valerie Allen and Ares Axiotis, p. 121, in their 'Nietzsche on the Future of Education', *Telos*, vol. 111 (Spring 1998), pp. 107–21.

34   Allen and Axiotis, p. 121.

35   See Jacques Derrida, *The Ear of the Other: Otobiography, Transference, Translation*, trans. Peggy Kamuf, ed. Christie V. McDonald (New York: Schocken Books, 1985), pp. 3–38. Further page references to 'Otobiographies' will be given in the main body of this essay, abbreviated 'Oto' where clarity dictates.

36   Derrida, *The Ear of the Other*, p. 156.

37   'Limited Inc a, b, c … ', trans. Samuel Weber and Jeffrey Mehlman, in *Limited Inc* (Evanston, Illinois: Northwestern University Press, 1988), p. 55.

38   See Derrida, *Spectres of Marx*, p. 173, and p. 195, n.37. The reference is to the French text, p. 273.

39   See Derrida, *The Ear of the Other*, pp. 50–1.

40   'This Strange Institution Called Literature', trans. Geoffrey Bennington and Rachel Bowlby, in *Acts of Literature*, ed. Derek Attridge (London and New York: Routledge, 1992), p. 57.

41   See, for example, Jane Marie Todd, 'The Veiled Woman in Freud's "Das Unheimliche"', *Signs: Journal of Women in Culture and Society*, vol. 2, no. 3 (1986), 519–28. I discuss this and related readings of Freud's essay in Chapter 2 above.

42   See Andrew Bennett and Nicholas Royle, 'The Uncanny', in *An Introduction to Literature, Criticism and Theory*, 2nd edn (London: Prentice Hall Europe, 1999), p. 38.

43   Jacques Derrida, 'Choreographies', trans. Christie V. McDonald, in *Points … Interviews, 1974–1994*, ed. Elisabeth Weber, trans. Peggy Kamuf et al. (London: Routledge, 1995), pp. 107–8.

44   'Choreographies', p. 108.

45   Jacques Derrida, 'Passions: "An Oblique Offering"', trans. David Wood, in *On the Name*, ed. Thomas Dutoit (Stanford: Stanford University Press, 1995), p. 144.

46   Timothy Clark, 'Literary Force, Institutional Values', *Culture Machine*, vol. 2 (2000): http://culturemachine.tees.ac.uk

47   Peggy Kamuf, *The Division of Literature, or The University in Deconstruction* (Chicago: Chicago University Press, 1997).

48   See Catherine Belsey, 'English Studies in the Postmodern Condition: Towards a Place for the Signifier', in *Post-theory: New Directions in Criticism*, ed. Martin McQuillan, Graeme MacDonald, Robin Purves and Stephen Thomson (Edinburgh: Edinburgh University Press, 1999), p. 136.

49   'Exam', *Oxford Literary Review*, vol. 17 (1995), 158–60. 'Exam' (reprinted with the kind permission of the editors) appears here in a slightly modified version.

50   I explore the question of the uncanniness of the name in greater detail below, in particular in Chapters 8 and 12.

51   E. M. Forster, 'Anonymity: An Enquiry', in *Two Cheers for Democracy* (London: Edward Arnold, 1951), p. 92.

4
Film

Witness explode in the face a detonated bullfrog or similar, its viscid FX 'film' embodied.

Has 'writing on film' ever really begun?

The caul of film.

The entire 'industry' might be defined as a palliative working to repress the uncanniness of film.

Think of these remarks as a series of surreal subtitles. Keep looking up for the visive remains.

Distended as a bullfrog, dream of a discourse in the dark, out of the cinematographic Hansard of Charles Dickens, Emily Dickinson's unspeakable home-videos.

I'm not going to watch that film again, *The Reflecting Skin* (dir. Philip Ridley, 1991).

I'm still watching. It is still watching me.

Flicker-writing: slipping, spilling, splicing – at once 'spoof', 'spook' and 'spool'.

Still.

First, the hallucinatory reality of the photograph. As Tom Gunning observes: 'if photography emerged as the material support for a new positivism, it was also experienced as an uncanny phenomenon, one which seemed to undermine the unique identity of objects and people, endlessly reproducing the appearances of objects, creating a parallel world of phantasmatic doubles alongside the concrete world of the senses verified by positivism' (pp. 42–3).

The photographic image is doubly uncanny: a question of the double and of what Barthes termed 'that rather terrible thing which is there in every photograph: the return of the dead' (p. 9).

And then it will have started to move. As if the still were not already a motion picture.

The frame is never still.

Forming a film over the senses.

As Robert Smith has framed it: 'Early viewers of film were amazed and moved by this miraculous gift dispensed by film, that of reanimating what had gone ... Like Christ calling Lazarus, film seemed to bring back to life what had been irrevocably lost; it blurred uncannily the distinction between life and death' (p. 121). To adapt Freud's phrase to this world of cinematic spectralisation: 'So the dead *do* live on ... ' (U, p. 371).

That strange projector or 'projection-machine' called psychoanalysis.

Film haunts Freud's work. It is there in the essay on the uncanny, for example, flickering allusively, elusively, illusively at the edge of the textual screen, in particular in the footnote on the double and the reference to Otto Rank: 'In [Hanns Heinz] Ewers's *Der Student von Prag* [*The Student of Prague*, 1913], which serves as the starting-point of Rank's study on the "double", the hero has promised his beloved not to kill his antagonist in a duel. But on his way to the duelling-ground he meets his "double", who has already killed his rival' (U, p. 358, n. 1). Neither here nor anywhere else in the text does Freud spell out the point that Rank's 'starting-point' is in fact film, or what Rank terms a 'film-drama' (Rank, p. 4).

Imagine Freud adding a final sentence to his account of the double as follows: 'The theme of the "double" has been very thoroughly treated by Otto Rank (1914). He has gone into the connections which the double has with reflections in mirrors, with shadows, with guardian spirits, with the belief in the soul and with the fear of death; but he also lets in a flood of light on the surprising evolution of the idea. *Significantly, however, it is with film that Rank begins*' (U, p. 356).

Film in a flood of light.

Rank takes as his 'point of departure', then, a film that 'not long ago made the rounds of our cinemas' (p. 3). He is struck by the potential links between psycho-analysis and the cinema: 'It may perhaps turn out that cinematography, which in numerous ways reminds us of the dream-work, can also express certain psychological facts and relationships – which the writer often is unable to describe with verbal clarity – in such clear and conspicuous imagery that it facilitates our understanding of them' (p. 4).

Very much as Freud does with Hoffmann's 'The Sandman', Rank offers a suspiciously long, seemingly exhaustive description of what happens in *The Student of Prague* (see *The Double*, pp. 4–6). He prefaces this with the words: 'First of all, let us try to capture the shadowy, fleeting, but impressive scenes of [this] film-drama' (p. 4). The coherence and 'verbal clarity' of Rank's *The Double* has already dissolved. If, as Ian Christie has put it, *The Student of Prague* is 'cinema's first demonstration of its ability to conjure a complete, eerily credible world of horror' (p. 130), this eeriness entails an experience of the incommensurable: the capture to which Rank refers is not possible.

Rank concludes his description of Ewers's silent film with a denial of doubt similar to Freud's regarding his own description of 'The Sandman': 'This short summary leaves no doubt, I think, that the feeling of the uncanny is directly attached to the figure of the Sand-Man, that is, to the idea of being robbed of one's eyes' (U, p. 351), says Freud; 'The scenario does not leave us long in doubt about the intention and meaning of these uncanny happenings' (p. 6), says Rank.

The Student of Prague presents us with a sense that everyone is haunted by the past: 'a person's past inescapably clings to him and ... it becomes his fate as soon as he tries to get rid of it' (Rank, p. 6). Rank writes: 'An obscure but unavoidable feeling takes hold of the spectator and seems to betray that deep human problems are being dealt with here. The uniqueness of cinematography in visibly portraying psychological events calls our attention, with exaggerated clarity, to the fact that the interesting and meaningful problems of man's relation to himself – and the fateful disturbance of this relation – finds here an imaginative representation' (p. 7). Or as Friedrich Kittler describes it: 'Silent films implement with technological positivity what psychoanalysis can only conceive of: an unconscious that has no words and is not recognised by His Majesty the Ego' (p. 92).

Each one of us has an 'eerie double' (Rank, p. 6). Ewers's film is uncanny, because *film* is uncanny.

'Exaggerated clarity': as if film let something be seen too clearly.

On the one hand, the figure of the double in the silent film of *The Student of Prague* is already a writing-effect, in so far as it 'belongs' to a literary history of the double and more specifically to a Romantic tradition in which the double is the figure of the writer. As Kittler declares: '[T]he Double turns up at the writing desk ... It can hardly be more clearly stated that the Double of classical Romanticism essentially emerges from books' (pp. 88–9).

On the other, film is in its essence a world of doubles. As Kittler notes, in the context of early cinema such as Ewers's: 'In order to catch sight of Doubles, people need no longer be either educated or drunk. Even illiterates, or especially they, see the student of Prague, his lover and his mistress – all of Rank's "shadowy, fleeting scenes", which as such are already Doubles – as celluloid ghosts of the actors' bodies' (p. 96).

Starting out from what Gunning refers to as 'the fundamentally uncanny quality of photography, its capture of a spectre-like double' (p. 47), film will have captured us.

'Writing on film': who is it that writes on film? *As whom* does s/he (pretend to) write?

Subtitles always mean polyphony, silent as the grave.

Supposedly creating a bigger sensation in New York than *The Interpretation of Dreams* is the occasion in 1925 when, as Ernest Jones recalls, Freud sends Samuel Goldwyn a telegram refusing Goldwyn's offer of $100,000 for co-operating in 'making a film depicting scenes from the famous love stories of history, beginning with Antony and Cleopatra' (Jones, 3, 121). Another bid is more successful: 'In June [1925]', Jones informs us, 'Neumann, on behalf of the Ufa Film Company, suggested that a film be made illustrating some of the mechanisms of psychoanalysis. [Karl] Abraham, who had been approached, asked Freud for his opinion, and thought himself it would be better to have one produced under authentic supervision than assisted by some "wild" analyst. Freud refused to give his own authorization, but did not actively discourage Abraham's making the attempt. His main objection was his disbelief in the possibility of his abstract theories being presented in the plastic manner of a film' (Jones, 3, 121).

What kind of film might one envisage produced under the 'authentic super-vision' of psychoanalysis?

Perhaps a Freud 'home movie'? See the 'authentic ghost' of Freud at home, right now, in the 'private videos' collection of the Media Library of the Freud Museum, Vienna, at: *http://freud.to.or.at*

To contemplate a film produced under 'authentic' psychoanalytic 'supervision': does that not just as readily evoke the uncanny 'rigour' of Hitchcock?

Always the swamp.

Doubtless a logic of transference imposes itself. No 'authentic supervision' of a film by a ('tame') psychoanalyst without a transferential return of the filmic gaze. Suffice to state what would have been staring Freud in the face in any case: film and psychoanalysis are locked up together. To borrow Cleopatra's phrase, they 'die with looking on [their] life' (1.5.33–4). They are interlocking effects of the same machinery: to recall Jones's mechanistic words, 'a film ... illustrating some of the mechanisms of psychoanalysis'. Freud does not simply reject it as impossible. Indeed, as Jones goes on to say, 'If ... it proved to be feasible, [Freud] would reconsider giving his own authorization' (Jones 3, 121). Freud, in short, is already on the transfer market, suspended somewhere between considering and reconsidering, caught up in the transferential possibilities of 'illustrating some of the mechanisms of psychoanalysis'.

The film, *Secrets of a Soul* (dir. G. W. Pabst, 1926), was duly made. Contrary to media reports (for example the claim in *Time* magazine (27 October 1925) that 'every foot of the film ... will be planned and scrutinized by Dr. Freud': see Jones, 3: 122), Abraham remained at least nominally in the role of supervisor. But Abraham was ill. Indeed his illness, Jones tells us, 'went on and on and the doctors were unable to find out why. Freud found this uncanny and became more and more anxious about the outcome' (Jones, 3: 122): he died on Christmas Day 1925. Jones saw the film shortly after that, in Berlin in January 1926.

Friends, popcorn, buffs and guides aside, you are in the dark and 'on your own'.

No one walks out of *The Truman Show*.

Death: such might be the most 'familiar' and least readable subtitle for 'authentic supervision'.

Stephen Heath remarks: 'There is something absolutely right and wrong in Goldwyn's approach to Freud [...]: film and psychoanalysis join and disjoin in the image, the subject, the reality of their positions' (p. 3). Their relations are usually, and perhaps hardly surprisingly, construed in terms of the visual. Hence the preponderance of attention to the image, the spectator, the gaze, voyeurism, fetishism, objectification of the woman, the flashback and so on, all or any of which may give rise to feelings of uncanniness, even if the film industry is generally concerned to *contain* such feelings, to tame, in the name let us say of so-called 'domestic audiences'.

Take, for example, 'recreational terror'. As Isabel Pinedo describes it: 'The fan audience encounters the horror genre with the expectation of experiencing recreational terror, a bounded experience of fear that includes elements of the uncanny' (p. 415). Imagine an experience of film that was not 'bounded'. That is perhaps where writing on film would begin.

Screen memory: isn't that the point of the Lumière train crashing into the station, into the audience? There is no station.

If Freudian discourse is no talkie when it comes to the cinema, this silence is still telling in all sorts of ways. The shared or sutured relations between psycho-analysis and film are also an affair of the ear, of the 'talking ear'.

Witness the explosion of Film Studies as an academic discourse, a discourse, at least in recent decades, bizarrely dominated by a species of cinematographic anamorphosis, a regime of hallucination that could be called the Lacan Effect. Might Freud's wariness of film be construed not only from the visual angle of how film inevitably interferes with psychoanalysis in 'illustrating', or failing to illustrate, 'the mechanisms of psychoanalysis', but also in terms of the eerie compulsions generated by talking about film, trying to remember, recapture or capture film, discourse and analysis interminable? Doesn't the peculiar solitude of witnessing, and thus being blind, when it comes to film, render it strangely similar to the fragile darkness of the couch?

What did I see then? Did she say what I thought she said? Am I following this properly or not?

Don't listen now.

Déjà vu for a moment, just thinking about that.

Every day is Groundhog Day in a movie.

Picture yourself, 'writing on film': you become an *extra*. To be an extra is to be in some sense *outside* (from the Latin preposition *extra*, 'outside'), an outsider or foreign body, an apparently unnecessary addition. Critical writing on film will always be a supplement, coming from outside, leaving the film untouched and untouchable. Which is doubtless what drives the desire to write 'on' it: the desire of the impossible.

And yet the extra is also within, a part of film: not only in the sense that there is no film without a language or languages, no film without script, however 'abstract' that script may be (for example, Samuel Beckett's 'Film', its 'climate' so 'comic and unreal' (p. 323)), but also perhaps in the sense that there is no writing on film unless it be *on* film in a sort of ghostly double sense, a writing that is impelled by the fantasy or dream of identification, of being part of the film, participating in it. That is to say, like an 'extra', 'a person temporarily engaged for a minor part in a film, etc, eg to be one of a crowd' (*Chambers*).

As Hitchcock understood, a great director (perhaps more than anyone else) desires to be an extra.

The extra is always double, from the beginning, in 'itself'.

To write on film is to engage with the irreducible strangeness of the extra. Given its uncanny early history or prehistory in phanstasmagoria and magic lantern shows, given its essential spectrality, duplicity and eerie 'ontology' (to recall André Bazin's terminology) as the animation of what is at once 'hallucination' and 'fact' (p. 16), film might be felt to call for a kind of writing akin to spirit photography. Tom Gunning writes: 'The images that appear in these photographs were generally described with the noncommittal, but provocative, term *extras*. They were defined as presences that had not been visible, at least to the sitters, at the time the photographs were made and whose appearance first on the negative and then on the print were a surprise to the sitters and sometimes to the photographers' (p. 51).

To write on film is to dream of a writing that responds and aligns itself to the uncanniness of cinematic magic. As Lesley Stern remarks of early cinema (but perhaps there is no 'early cinema', at least not without trying to reckon with the haunting, compulsive returns of 'early' in the latest, for instance in the apocalyptic lateness of so many end-of-the-world, end-of-photography films): 'At its most representational the cinema could bring into focus the unseen or previously unseeable, but the wonder of it was that in addition to representational prowess it possessed magical powers, could make things appear and disappear, could conjure ghosts, could mutilate and multiply and reconstitute bodies – could mess with time and matter' (p. 357).

Flashbacks of a writing attuned to such vanishings and conjurations.

Freeze with Cleopatra: 'You laugh when boys or women tell their dreams; / Is't not your trick?' (5.2.73–4)

CLOSING CREDITS

Barthes, Roland, *Camera Lucida: Reflections on Photography*, trans. Richard Howard (London: Fontana, 1984)

Bazin, André, *What Is Cinema?*, 1, trans. Hugh Gray (Berkeley: University of California Press, 1967)

Beckett, Samuel, 'Film', in *Complete Dramatic Works* (London: Faber and Faber, 1986), pp. 321–9

Brunette, Peter, and David Wills, *Screen/Play: Derrida and Film Theory* (Princeton, NJ: Princeton University Press, 1989)

Christie, Ian, *The Last Machine: Early Cinema and the Birth of the Modern World* (London: British Film Institute, 1994)

Gunning, Tom, 'Phantom Images and Modern Manifestations: Spirit Photography, Magic Theater, Trick Films, and Photography's Uncanny', in *Fugitive Images: From Photography to Video*, ed. Patrice Petro (Bloomington: Indiana University Press, 1995), pp. 42–71

Heath, Stephen, *Questions of Cinema* (Basingstoke: Macmillan, 1981)

Jones, Ernest, *Sigmund Freud: Life and Work*, 3 (London: Hogarth Press, 1957)

Kittler, Friedrich, 'Romanticism–Psychoanalysis–Film: A History of the Double', in *Literature, Media, Information Systems*, ed. John Johnston (Amsterdam: G + B Arts International, 1997), pp. 85–100

Paul, William, 'Uncanny Theater: The Twin Inheritances of the Movies', *Paradoxa: Studies in World Literary Genres*, vol. 3, no. 3–4 (1997), 321–47

Pinedo, Isabel, 'Wet Death and the Uncanny', *Paradoxa: Studies in World Literary Genres*, vol. 3, no. 3–4 (1997), 407–16.

Rank, Otto, *The Double: A Psychoanalytic Study* (1914), trans. Harry Tucker, Jr (Chapel Hill, NC: University of North Carolina Press, 1971)

Shakespeare, William, *Antony and Cleopatra*, ed. M. R. Ridley (London: Methuen, 1954)

Smith, Robert, 'Deconstruction and Film', in *Deconstructions: A User's Guide*, ed. Nicholas Royle (Basingstoke and New York: Palgrave, 2000), pp. 119–36

Stern, Lesley, 'I Think Sebastian, Therefore I … Somersault: Film and the Uncanny', in *The Return of the Uncanny*, special issue of *Paradoxa: Studies in World Literary Genres*, vol. 3, no. 3–4 (1997), 348–66

5
The death drive

There is no having, only a being, only a state of being that craves the last breath, craves suffocation. (Franz Kafka)[1]

And can a man his own quietus make
with a bare bodkin?
With daggers, bodkins, bullets, man can make
a bruise or break of exit for his life;
but is that a quietus, O tell me, is it quietus?
          (D. H. Lawrence)[2]

Suggestibility; hypnosis; entrancement; possession; inspiration; telepathy; transference; affective identification; repetition compulsions and the so-called 'death drive'. These are the kind of things that criticism usually tries to ward off or else control, not without reason. (Caroline Rooney)[3]

I hereby promise to try to make this as smooth and speedy as possible. I intend to organize my discourse by way of a series of bullet points, accompanied by passages of brief commentary. I will do my utmost not to digress or, at least, to keep my digressions under control. Where did the desire for 'bullet points' come from? Why do we speak of bullet points rather than, say, nutshells or propositions or simply points? Who is shooting whom?

● Something comes back because in some sense it was never properly there in the first place.

To repeat: the uncanny seems to be about a strange repetitiveness. It has to do with the return of something repressed, something no longer familiar, the return of the dead, the 'constant recurrence of the same thing' (U, p. 356), a 'compulsion to repeat' (U, p. 360). It is this notion of constant recurrence or compulsive repetition that leads Freud to his theory of the death drive. (*Todestriebe* is sometimes translated as 'death instinct' or 'death instincts', though we might also think of it in terms of a current or flow, in other words as a 'death drift'.)

● *The aim of all life is death.*

This is the bullet point that Freud proposes in 1920, in the extraordinary text called *Beyond the Pleasure Principle*.[4] In some respects the proposition is not especially original. Jonathan Dollimore elaborates on this idea, in a recent book entitled *Death, Desire and Loss in Western Culture*.[5]

● Death is right inside us, working away busy as a mole, all the time.

Dollimore contends that 'death is not simply the termination of life (that being the mystifying banality by which we live) but life's driving force, its animating, dynamic principle'.[6] In particular, he emphasizes how extensive some sort of 'death drive' is in so-called premodern writing:

> Well before Freud, there were those who entertained the attraction of death almost as scandalously as he did ... As Hamlet famously meditated, to die is a consummation devoutly to be wished. From the earliest times, death has held out the promise of a release not just from desire but from something inseparable from it, namely the pain of being individuated (separate, differentiated, alone) and the form of self-consciousness which goes with that.[7]

Thus, for example, Dollimore cites Michel de Montaigne's proposition that 'the goal of our career is death. It is the necessary object of our aim', and describes this as 'an uncanny anticipation of Freud's death drive'.[8] Indeed, in a manner ineluctably suggestive of the repetition compulsion, Dollimore keeps coming up with examples of such 'uncanny anticipation'.[9] In doing so, he alerts us not only to the strange insistence, repression and disavowal of the 'death drive' in the history of western culture, but also to the peculiar power of naming itself, of re-deploying the specificity of Freud's term back down the centuries, of calling it (again and again) 'death drive'.

● The death drive is irreducibly bound up with the performative, in particular with the act of naming. In putting forward the name 'death drive', Freud changes everything.

Freud's importance lies in the fact that, as Jonathan Dollimore puts it, he 'evolved a new language ... to express the conviction that death is absolutely interior to life': he takes the old idea of a desire for death and 'implant[s]' it 'into the "new" world of interiority created by psychoanalysis'.[10] In the rest of this chapter I try to explore some of the uncanny ways in which Freud's account of the death drive is 'new' and different.

● The death drive works in silence.

Freud doesn't explicitly name the death drive in 'The Uncanny' – that doesn't happen till the following year, with the publication of *Beyond the Pleasure Principle*. But the death drive lurks, as if forbidden to speak its name, everywhere in the 1919 essay. This silence is at once appropriate and strange, for it is a crucial attribute of Freud's theory of the death drive that it works in silence, imperceptibly, without being noticed. 'The death instincts seem to do their work unobtrusively' (*BPP*, p. 338); or as he puts it in *The Ego and the Id* (1923): 'The death instincts are by their nature mute ... the clamour of life proceeds for the most part from Eros' (*PFL*, 11: 387). The instincts identified with Eros or life (the life instincts, the life drive, *Lebenstriebe*) are noisy, bustling, all a-chatter. The death drive is shtoom.

There are many silences in 'The Uncanny'. In part, no doubt, it is a question of what Jacques Derrida has in another context called the 'silence that is walled up in the violent structure of the founding act'.[11] There is always silence or silences within institutions (within psychoanalysis, the university, social, political or religious organizations, and so on) and within the texts that found or define them. Exploring the tacit or unspoken elements of a text or institution can alter our understanding of its structure, transform its meaning and effects. But as Derrida has also remarked, 'silence is not exterior to language'.[12] In other words, it cannot simply be a matter of talking things out, as if it would be possible to exhaust Freud's essay and get everything out into the open, before some imaginary tribunal. 'The Uncanny' is a great text about how to do things with silence, as much as 'how to do things with words'.[13] Indeed, Freud's theory of the death drive could be said to change the very idea of silence. It prompts a quite different sense of the workings of silence, not only in social, political and religious organizations, for example, but also in works of art (above all, in literature, film and music). If silence is golden, there will have been something deadly about its glitter. Freud's essay on 'The Uncanny', then, seems strangely silent concerning the (as yet unnamed) death drive. For example, as we noted in Chapter 2, Hoffmann's story 'The Sandman' – to which Freud devotes so much attention in his essay – is explicitly concerned with the idea of a drive towards death and destruction, with what it calls 'the presentiment of a dark power which strives to ruin us within our own selves'.[14] But Freud makes no mention of this 'drive towards death' in his seemingly exhaustive account of Hoffmann's story. Why? And why, more generally perhaps, does he appear to feel uneasy about introducing the concept of the death drive in 'The Uncanny'?

● The death drive has to do with the figure of woman.

Such is the explanation proposed by Sarah Kofman:

> Everything takes place as if Freud could not bear the importance of his discovery concerning the death drive and as if 'The Uncanny' with its successive invalidations, its tortuous procedure, is a last effort to conceal 'the return of the repressed' which emerges in the theory: an effort which once again proves the unacceptable nature of the theory of the death instincts.[15]

The theory of the death drive is 'unbearable and *unheimlich*' to Freud, Kofman argues, in so far as it is linked to 'the prohibition on incest', in other words to an 'identification with the mother and the death which she threatens': the death drive is to be understood in terms of an 'internalization of the forbidden mother'.[16]

Kofman's reading is consonant with others that stress the mostly silent, cryptic connections made in Freud's essay between death and what has been called 'the uncanny woman'.[17] As Elisabeth Bronfen puts it:

> Though issues of femininity are not directly at stake in his formulation of [the] concept [of the death drive], one implicit connection emerges from the fact that both 'death' and 'woman' function as Western culture's privileged tropes for the enigmatic and for alterity.[18]

In Freud's writing, she proposes, 'woman functions as privileged trope for the uncanniness of unity and loss, of independent identity and self-dissolution, of the pleasure of the body and its decay' (p. 56). More specifically, Bronfen suggests that an earlier essay by Freud, entitled 'The Theme of the Three Caskets' (1913) (*PFL*, 14: 235–47), 'significantly connects femininity with the need to acknowledge mortality', offering a sort of ghostly prototype or forerunner, a 'gender-oriented commentary' (p. 55) on *Beyond the Pleasure Principle*. Though Bronfen does not say so, it is striking that 'The Theme of the Three Caskets' not only aligns the desirability of 'death' with the 'most beautiful' woman, but also identifies this figure with silence. The resolve of Cordelia, in Shakespeare's *King Lear*, to 'Love, and be silent' (I.i.54), for example, is for Freud characteristic of various mythological and literary figurations of the most beautiful of three women, and in all such cases, he contends, the 'peculiarities' of this woman are 'concentrated in her "dumbness"' (*PFL*, 14: 239). He then adds: 'psychoanalysis will tell us that in dreams dumbness is a common representation of death' (p. 239). In other words, the uncanny commingling of silence, woman and the desirableness of death is quite explicit in the 1913 essay, even if it appears to fall silent in 'The Uncanny' and *Beyond the Pleasure Principle*.

● The death drive is eerily uncanny, uncannily eerie.

'The Uncanny' keeps mum. The power of Freud's 1919 essay can perhaps be located in this curious impression: it is a text that seems to call out for its silences to be described, explained, theorized. It is not that Freud does not think that the death drive is uncanny: he specifically refers to 'the mute and uncanny activity' of the death drive, for example, in one of the *New Introductory Lectures on Psychoanalysis* in 1933.[19] There is an important further point here, regarding the 'absence' of the death drive in the text of 'The Uncanny'. In a way that may itself seem eerie or uncanny, the death drive comes to figure uncanniness better than anything that is actually discussed in Freud's essay. The most uncanny example of uncanniness is eerily *not in* 'The Uncanny'. 'Eerie' *or* 'uncanny'? What is the difference? The death drive seems to prompt a clarification of these two terms. Gordon Bearn has suggested the following helpful formulation: 'The absence of what ought to be present is eerie', whereas '*the presence of what ought to be absent* is uncanny'.[20] But the death drive seems to confound this distinction: it is eerie and uncanny, eerily uncanny and uncannily eerie. It ought to be present in 'The Uncanny', it ought to be absent; it is neither present nor absent.

● The death drive is demonic and diabolical.

In bringing to light what should perhaps have remained concealed in Freud's text, readings such as Sarah Kofman's also illustrate the strangeness of the intertextual links, the encryptings, mirrorings, repetitions and doublings that characterize the relationship between these two overlapping works of 1919, 'The Uncanny' and *Beyond the Pleasure Principle*. What Jean Laplanche says of *Beyond the Pleasure Principle* might also be said of 'The Uncanny': 'the holes in the reasoning constitute so many traps; the sliding of concepts results in blurring terminological points of reference; the most far-reaching discussions are suddenly resolved in the most arbitrary manner'.[21] But the relationship between the two texts is also more disturbing and profound than this. As Derrida has suggested, in the course of his brilliant and exhaustive reading of *Beyond the Pleasure Principle*, 'the systematic and kinship ties between these two essays' are nothing short of devilish.[22] In unfolding his tale of the death drive in *Beyond the Pleasure Principle*, Freud testifies to having thrown himself into the role of '*advocatus diaboli*' (BPP, p. 332). Derrida suggests that 'the one who ... calls himself the "*advocatus diaboli*" of the death drive' is necessarily a double, Freud's double, Freud as double, and that this entails an 'effect of duplicity without an original, which is perhaps is what the diabolical consists of, its very inconsistency'.[23] This diabolism is the very stuff of the death drive 'itself'. The 1920 text becomes, in Derrida's account, a work of uncanny *literary possession*. The figure of 'literary fiction', he contends, is 'like a fairy or a demon' that 'already watches over' the scene of writing in *Beyond the Pleasure Principle*.[24] Everything that 'The Uncanny' has to say about the double, the demonic and the literary comes back in *Beyond the Pleasure Principle*. 'The Uncanny' spells out the demonic rhythm to which the discourse of *Beyond the Pleasure Principle* is being beaten.

● The death drive manifests itself in a 'compulsion to repeat'.

The ghostly presence of the silent, as yet unbaptized 'death drive' in Freud's essay of 1919 is evident above all perhaps in his focus on the notion of a 'compulsion to repeat' (U, p. 360). Freud himself contends that 'the constant recurrence of the same thing' (U, p. 356) is a powerful element in many literary texts and is what can help to give them their uncanny character. He specifies 'the repetition of the same features or character-traits or vicissitudes, of the same crimes, or even the same names through several consecutive generations' (U, p. 356); and he refers to works of literature, specifically Hoffmann's novel *The Devil's Elixir*. (In English the most obvious, intricate and powerful example might be Emily Brontë's *Wuthering Heights*).[25] But Freud's remarks are equally pertinent for thinking about so-called 'real-life' cases of strange recurrence in family and culture, in naming and behaviour across the generations. Once again, it is a matter of 'literary fiction' and 'real life' caught strangely in league. Sometimes there are just coincidences, like the same number (for example, 66) cropping up repeatedly. And sometimes these repetitions take on a sort of demonic element. Freud tries to steer clear of too detailed a discussion of all this in 'The Uncanny'. He declares:

> How exactly we can trace back to infantile psychology the uncanny effect of such similar recurrences is a question I can only lightly touch on in these pages; and I must refer the reader instead to another work [i.e. *Beyond the Pleasure Principle*, which he was writing at the same time]. For it is possible to recognize the dominance in the unconscious mind of a 'compulsion to repeat' proceeding from the instinctual impulses and probably inherent in the very nature of the instincts – a compulsion powerful enough to overrule the pleasure principle, lending to certain aspects of the mind their demonic character, and still very clearly expressed in the impulses of small children; a compulsion, too, which is responsible for a part of the course taken by the analyses of neurotic patients. All these considerations prepare us for the discovery that whatever reminds us of this inner 'compulsion to repeat' is perceived as uncanny. (U, pp. 360–1)

Freud turns away at this point (his English translator, James Strachey, even marks this in a manner not present in the German text, by skipping a line and leaving a gap on the page: see U, p. 361): 'Now, however, it is time to turn from these aspects of the matter, which are in any case difficult to judge' (U, p. 361).[26] All of these are aspects that he can 'only lightly touch on': he is trembling on the threshold of letting *Beyond the Pleasure Principle* invade 'The Uncanny', and 'The Uncanny' invade *Beyond the Pleasure Principle*. But the double invasion has already occurred. All of these aspects are 'difficult to judge': they give rise to intellectual uncertainty or insecurity *(der intellektuellen Unsicherheit)*. The feeling of uncanniness lies in this uncertainty, an uncertainty that opens onto the space of the demonic and diabolical. It is that strange feeling again. In a sense, the devil is precisely *not* in the detail. (Indeed, one is led to wonder what else that cliché is *about*, if not a certain negation of this uncanny detaillessness.) It is not a matter of discovering something 'behind' the repetition. As Neil Hertz has acutely remarked: 'The feeling of the uncanny would seem to be generated by being reminded of the repetition compulsion, not by being reminded of whatever it is that is repeated.'[27]

● The death drive manifests itself in a 'compulsion to repeat'.

The repetition compulsion is something, Freud says, that we encounter for example in people 'all of whose human relationships have the same outcome'; and he gives among his examples 'the man whose friendships all end in betrayal by his friend' and 'the lover each of whose love affairs with a woman passes through the same phases and reaches the same conclusion'. These are instances, Freud says, of the '"perpetual recurrence of the same thing" ' (BPP, p. 292). According to James Strachey, this last phrase is in quotation marks because it 'seems to be an echo from Nietzsche' (see U, p. 356, n. 1).[28] There is something strange, at once repetitive and compulsive, about this 'quotation': Freud does not attribute it, it is a repetition, it is not his wording apparently, and yet it encapsulates his thinking. He is apparently compelled to use this phrase, a phrase from elsewhere, from somewhere beyond. At one moment in *Beyond the Pleasure Principle* Freud suggests that 'when people unfamiliar with analysis feel an obscure fear – a dread of rousing something that, so they feel, is better left sleeping – what they are afraid of at bottom is the emergence of this compulsion with its hint of possession by some "demonic" power' (BPP, p. 308). Here, again, one might feel the demonic, interleaving presence of 'The Uncanny'. When does anyone become 'familiar' with the writings of Nietzsche or Freud or, let us say,

D. H. Lawrence?[29] With all of these writers, such 'demonic power' is not only a so-called thematic focus of their writing: it is what *drives* the writing.

● The death drive is uncanny *for* psychoanalysis. It is a foreign body within psychoanalysis itself.

In 1919, the same year that 'The Uncanny' was published, another work appeared in German, which was translated and published two years later in English as *Psychoanalysis and the War Neuroses*. Freud's short Introduction to this book appears in the *Standard Edition*, in fact, immediately before 'The Uncanny' itself.[30] *Psychoanalysis and the War Neuroses* was important because it brought to light something at once apparently new and old, something uncanny for the very theory of psychoanalysis. Maud Ellmann has described it as follows:

> In *The Interpretation of Dreams*, Freud insists upon the principle that the dream is a fulfilment of a wish, and leaves no loophole for dissension: even when a patient presents him with a dream that seems to contradict this axiom, he argues slyly that the dream fulfils her wish to invalidate his theory that the dream is the fulfilment of a wish [see *PFL*, 4: 234]. Freud maintained this doctrine stubbornly until the First World War, when the dreams of shell-shock victims finally forced him to rethink the pleasure principle. These dreams, he found, compulsively returned to the traumatic moments of the victims' lives; and it was clear that no pleasure, in any ordinary sense of the word, could be derived from these horrendous nightmares.[31]

The death drive figures as something uncanny 'for' psychoanalysis in that it would seem to disturb some of the most basic and familiar psychoanalytic tenets, in particular the argument that dreams are wish-fulfilments and that we are all basically driven by a desire for pleasure. Thinking about the nature of 'war neuroses' enables Freud to develop a fuller understanding of trauma more generally. As he remarks in 1920, in *Beyond the Pleasure Principle*: 'it is impossible to classify as wish-fulfilments the dreams … which occur in traumatic neuroses, or the dreams [during a patient's analysis] which bring to memory the psychical traumas of childhood. [These dreams] arise, rather, in obedience to the compulsion to repeat' (*PFL*, 11: 304). Freud's speculations take him back to a very bizarre 'time', a time in which, we are invited to imagine, dreams were merely 'scenes' of compulsive repetition: 'If there is a "beyond the pleasure principle", it is only consistent to grant that there was also a time before the purpose of dreams was the fulfilment of wishes' (*PFL*, 11: 305).

The notion of the death drive is also uncanny 'for' psychoanalysis, however, in that it poses as a sort of foreign body within the institution and history, the development, theory and practice of psychoanalysis. As Jean Laplanche and J.-B. Pontalis comment in *The Language of Psycho-analysis*: 'The notion of a death instinct ... has not managed to gain the acceptance of [Freud's] disciples and successors in the way that the majority of his conceptual contributions have done – and it is still one of the most controversial of psychoanalytic concepts.'[32] As Laplanche notes elsewhere:

> The introduction of the death drive could only provoke on the part of Freud's heirs every conceivable variety of defence: a deliberate refusal on the part of some; a purely scholastic acceptance of the notion and of the dualism: Eros-Thanatos on the part of others; a qualified acceptance, cutting the notion off from its philosophical bases, by an author like Melanie Klein; and, most frequently of all, a passing allusion to or a total forgetting of the notion.[33]

Once announced, the death drive becomes a permanent resident, a stranger in the 'house of Freud'. Freud puts forward the theory of the death drive in *Beyond the Pleasure Principle* seemingly with a kind of reluctance, with a 'limping' hesitation.[34] But once he has committed himself, as it were, you cannot see him for dust. As he acknowledges ten years later, in *Civilization and Its Discontents* (1930):

> The assumption of the existence of an instinct of death or destruction has met with resistance even in analytic circles ... To begin with, it was only tentatively that I put forward [these] views ... but in the course of time they have gained such a hold upon me that I can no longer think in any other way. (*PFL*, 12: 310–11)

● The death drive cannot be confined to a distant wing or isolation ward.

Freud does not simply see the death drive as one drive among others. The death drive is, to adapt a phrase from Laplanche and Pontalis, the drive *par excellence*: it 'typif[ies] the repetitive nature of instinct [or drive] in general ... [I]n so far as it is "the essence of the instinctual", [the death drive] binds every wish, whether aggressive or sexual, to the wish for death'.[35] The death drive is in the driving seat. But the driving seat is impossible to locate. It is never possible to find, let alone put the death drive in its place. It is always different. Precisely in so far as it underlies all other structures and logics, the death drive is not to be isolated. As Laplanche has remarked, 'the death drive does not possess its own energy'.[36] It is essentially alien, not-at-home, unowned, unownable. Rather it inhabits, affects, impels everything, above all its supposed opposite, in other words life or Eros. The death instincts (Thanatos) are not the opposite of the life instincts (Eros). As Freud puts it in *Civilization and Its Discontents*:

the two kinds of instinct seldom – perhaps never – appear in isolation from each other, but are alloyed with each other in varying and very different proportions and so become unrecognisable to our judgement. In sadism, long since known to us as a component instinct of sexuality, we should have before us a particularly strong alloy of this kind between trends of love and the destructive instinct; while its counterpart, masochism, would be a union between destructiveness directed inwards and sexuality ... I know that in sadism and masochism we have always seen before us manifestations of the destructive instinct ... but I can no longer understand how we can have overlooked the ubiquity of non-erotic aggressivity and destructiveness and can have failed to give it its due place in our interpretation of life. (The desire for destruction when it is directed *inwards* mostly eludes our perception, of course, unless it is tinged with erotism.) (*PFL*, 12: 310–11)

As Elisabeth Bronfen has summarized it: 'The challenge posed by Freud's formulation of a death drive resides in the fact that he ultimately binds all desire, whether sexual, aggressive or melancholic, to a desire for death.'[37] All our desires bear the tinge or trace of the death drive. What Freud elsewhere calls 'the sadistic urges which are a part of erotic life' (*PFL*, 7: 258) are a turning outwards, a turning towards or upon the exterior world, of urges that are originally self-directed, self-destructive. At its most generalized, all forms of aggression conform to this thanatological model. The death drive is inextricably entangled, for example, with 'the instinct for mastery' and 'the will to power' (*PFL*, 11: 418). But in principle every desire, however benevolent and apparently 'non-erotic', can be susceptible to a sort of uncanny metamorphosis, an exposure of strange innards.

● 'The organism wishes to die only in its own fashion' (*BPP*, p. 312).

This is the other famous bullet point at the heart of *Beyond the Pleasure Principle*. It is in effect what Frank Sinatra was trying to say in that impossible retrospective: 'I did it my way.' It is not just that deep down inside – whether we realise it or not, whether we like it or not – we all want to die. More precisely, we all want to die in our own way, on our own terms, according to our own trajectory, in accordance with 'detours' of our own devising, in keeping with a certain 'rhythm' (see *BPP*, pp. 311–13). One can here perhaps pick up some sense of the uncanniness of the notion of the death drive: everyone has their own, the death drive is a matter of what makes everyone of us different and tick differently. The death drive is thinkable only on the basis of a weird solitude: a solitude within you, a solitude that is no one else's but still is not your own. Freud's contention that 'the organism wishes to die only in its own fashion' implies a law of the proper, of what is the organism's 'own fashion', only and solely that of a particular organism.

Derrida describes it very well, in his essay 'To Speculate – on "Freud"'. The organism, he writes,

> is nothing other outside this demand and this order: let me die properly, I am living so that I may die properly, and so that my death is my own … [Freud is here] pronouncing the law of life-death as the law of the proper. Life *and* death are opposed only in order to serve [this law]. Beyond all oppositions, without any possible identification or synthesis, it is indeed a question of an *economy* of death, of a law of the proper (*oikos, oikonomia*) which governs the detour and indefatigably seeks the proper event, its own, proper propriation (*Ereignis*) rather than life *and* death, life *or* death.[38]

This law is uncanny. Uncanniness will have been the law. As Freud puts it, in one of the most provocative claims in *Beyond the Pleasure Principle*: the 'self-preservative instincts' or 'guardians of life … were originally the myrmidons of death' (pp. 311–12). My way is not *straightaway*. We are each driven in our own idiosyncratic, perverse but deadly fashion:

> It is as though the life of the organism moved with a vacillating rhythm. One group of instincts rushes forward so as to reach the final aim of life as swiftly as possible; but when a particular stage in the advance has been reached, the other group jerks back to a certain point to make a fresh start and so prolong the journey. (*BPP*, p. 313)

But the original sentinel or guardians of life were in any case already just carrying out orders from elsewhere. Derrida comments on this uncanny 'vacillation' as follows:

> The sentinel of life having to become that which it 'originally' will have been, the courier of death, everything changes sign at every moment. This vacillation is set forth more obviously, more thematically in 'Das Unheimliche'. Nothing surprising about this. *Heimlichkeit* is also the German name of what we have in mind here as the 'economic law of the proper' or of the 'house', of domesticity, along with its genealogy of the properly familial, of its 'patronage' and its 'parentage'.[39]

● The death drive is inextricably bound up with writing, narrative and autobiography.

This has been perhaps most sharply demonstrated by Derrida, in the essay to which I have been referring, 'To Speculate – on "Freud"', and by Peter Brooks, in an essay entitled 'Freud's Masterplot'.[40] What both Derrida and Brooks highlight in relation to Freud's account of the death drive is its self-reflexivity: *Beyond the Pleasure Principle*, in other words, is a text about itself, about its own writing, about the nature of writing and narrative. Just as 'the organism wishes to die only in its own fashion' (*BPP*, p. 312), so Freud wishes to relate what he calls the 'interpretation of life' (*PFL*, 12: 311), to tell the story of life, in his own fashion. Indeed, as Derrida and Brooks in their own different fashions show, it is not clear how one could separate out the movements of 'life' and 'writing' or 'storytelling' here. Thus every bullet point may tell a story, even if it is a story about the end of the story, the impossibility of stories. Brooks remarks of what he calls 'Freud's masterplot', *Beyond the Pleasure Principle*:

> It is indeed so difficult to say what Freud is talking about in this essay – and especially, what he is *not* talking about – that we are almost forced to acknowledge that ultimately he is talking about the very possibility of talking about life – about its very 'narratability'. (p. 97)

Or, as Derrida puts it, what *Beyond the Pleasure Principle* presents us with is '[n]ot simply an autobiography confiding [Freud's] life to his own more or less testamentary writing, but a more or less living description of his own writing, of his way of writing what he writes, most notably [*Beyond the Pleasure Principle*]'.[41] It is necessary to reckon with the oddity of *the example* as such: when it comes to the death drive, every writer, indeed every fictional text, and every reading, will figure its workings differently. What Brooks calls 'Freud's masterplot', then, is indeed a plot, a strange conspiracy that is at once a narrative and a theory of narrative. And it is, uncannily, unownably, Freud's. When it comes to a good story (whether it's a short story, a novel, a film, even perhaps a critical essay or a scientific account of something), we all want the end, but we don't want it right away: we want a story that holds itself up, takes certain kinds of detours, creates certain digressions and postponements. A good story is one that knows that it has to end, but insists on not ending too quickly, on going on a journey that ends in its own fashion, on its own terms. It has to have 'the right death, the correct end' (p. 103). As Brooks puts it: 'One must have the arabesque of plot in order to reach the end' (p. 107). A strong narrative (and Freud's *Beyond the Pleasure Principle* is in many respects a great narrative text) is one that conveys a strong sense of wanting to end in its own fashion and, having returned finally to 'the quiescence of … the unnarratable' (p. 103), of wanting still to 'recapture us in its doomed energies' (p. 110).

● Just because the death drive isn't popular doesn't mean the death drive isn't popular.

In a letter to Albert Einstein in 1932, published as 'Why War?', Freud wryly notes that the 'popularity' of his theory of the death drive 'is by no means equal to its importance' (*PFL*, 12: 357). He knows he is on to a winner. How could the notion of the death drive be 'popular'?[42] A similar point might be made in relation to the 'place' and 'significance' of the death drive in the context of literary criticism. Despite being 'thick with literary significance and potential', Linda Ruth Williams remarks, 'the death drive has itself received comparatively little attention from critics and readers'.[43] This claim can seem at once apt and absurd. On the one hand, Williams is surely right: there is a striking reluctance to consider the strange workings of the death drive, not only in the context of literature, film, music and other arts, but also in broader and more fundamental social and political contexts. No doubt this has to do with rather obvious kinds of defensiveness and resistance. The death drive, in short, is never going to be a great crowd-pleaser. On the other hand, however, as we have seen, the death drive is itself strangely *possessed* by the activities and effects of literary fiction. The workings of the death drive are always already enmeshed in literature, fiction and storytelling. Moreover, Williams's claim can easily be misleading: to say that 'the death drive has itself received comparatively little attention from critics and readers' is not to say that it has not been at work. On the contrary, it may be that the 'attention' of 'critics and readers', indeed the very discourses of literature, literary, film or music criticism, are 'possessed' by the demonic strangeness of the death drive even, or most of all, when they least appear to be. This is the uncanny strangeness suggested by Freud's insight that 'the death instincts seem to do their work unobtrusively' (*BPP*, p. 338). And of course what goes for literary critics goes for the 'general public'. The death drive is everywhere (even when it appears not to be) and nowhere (even when it appears to be). This is its diabolical (in)consistency, its duplicitous consistency-as-inconsistent, as Derrida has argued. In this way the death drive might even be described as the crowd-pleaser *par excellence*, albeit perhaps unbeknownst to the crowd.

Some such suggestion flickers in another text from 1921, 'Group Psychology and the Analysis of the Ego' (*PFL*, 12: 91–178), where Freud explores what he calls 'the uncanny and coercive characteristics of group-formation' (p. 160) in terms of hypnosis. If 'hypnosis has something positively uncanny about it' (p. 157), as he contends, and if there is something hypnotic about the nature of crowd-pleasing, about the way in which group psychology works, this is perhaps not unrelated to the death drive. As Paul Hirst and Penny Woolley have argued, what is involved in cases of hypnosis and related forms of trance is 'a state of self-obliteration which corresponds to the "wishes" Freud considers to be at the heart of the Death Instinct'.[44] Again, however, we should note the beautiful seductiveness of Freud's account: its appeal is singular, an appeal to uncanny singularity. The suggestion (and suggestibility is perhaps the hallmark of all these Freudian bullet points) is that, if the death drive is bound up with hypnosis, it is a question of everyone being hypnotized differently, hypnotized 'in their own fashion'.

● There is a shade of the surreal about the death drive and a shade of the death drive about surrealism.

We might try to elucidate the death drive's capacity to be everywhere and no-where in terms of what is called surrealism. As Hal Foster has persuasively argued in his book *Compulsive Beauty*, the early twentieth-century artistic and cultural phenomenon known as surrealism was above all concerned with the uncanny.[45] He explores an uncanny double-bind at the heart of surrealist projects:

> The death drive theory seems anathema to the surrealist affirmation of love, liberation, and revolution, at least as conventionally thought. And yet if the surreal is bound up with the uncanny, then so too is it bound up with the death drive. In short, just as surrealist automatism [automatic writing and automata of all sorts] suggests not libera-tion but compulsion, so surrealism in general may celebrate desire only, in the register of the uncanny, to proclaim death.[46]

Foster's study is concerned with the uncanny relations between Freud's work and that of the surrealists, and with investigating the logic of the death drive in surrealist writing and art. He writes:

> certain surrealist practices intuit the uncanny discoveries of psychoanalysis, sometimes to resist them, sometimes to work through them, sometimes even to exploit them: i.e. to use the uncanniness of the return of the repressed, the compulsion to repeat, the immanence of death for disruptive purposes – to produce out of this psychic ambivalence a provocative ambiguity in artistic practice and cultural politics alike.[47]

If, as Foster argues, surrealism is essentially bound up with the uncanniness of the death drive, we might ask ourselves where it is located today. People can always think of it as an 'artistic movement' which has 'had its day', or suppose that (in Jean Baudrillard's words) 'surrealism can only survive as folklore'.[48] But is it so certain that there has *ever been* surrealism? Rather than consider it as a cultural and aesthetic 'phenomenon' of the earlier twentieth century, and indeed rather than consider it a *still active* 'movement' (to be witnessed, for example, in the television series *Twin Peaks* or in the fiction of J. G. Ballard), could we not suppose that surrealism remains a strange 'non-event' that has no proper place, but still *haunts*? In reflecting on what is happening today, in terms of politics (above all, perhaps, as regards so many spectral figures of nationalism and religion), the environment (above all, perhaps, as regards the strange 'reality' of 'climate change'), literature, film, television, advertising and the internet (so many virtual, interactive and other 'special FX'), could we not suppose that surrealism is, precisely, everywhere and nowhere? Is that not, perhaps, what surrealism essentially 'is'? And might this not also be a way of thinking about the strangely placeless place of the death drive?

● Psychoanalysis and surrealism are not alone in elaborating the uncanny logic of a death drive in the shattered Europe left in the wake of the so-called Great War.

Composed around the same time as *Beyond the Pleasure Principle*, but explicitly drawing on classical and ancient sources, T. S. Eliot's *The Waste Land* (1922) is one of innumerable literary texts that provide correspondences with Freud's theory.[49] Pervasively characterized by articulations of the desire to be still, to have it all over and done with, Eliot's poem starts with an epigraph taken from the first-century writer Petronius: 'For once I myself saw with my own eyes the Sibyl at Cumae hanging in a cage, and when the boys said to her, "Sibyl, what do you want?" she replied, "I want to die".' Such a desire is still resonating in the seemingly compulsive repetitiveness of the final words of Eliot's poem, 'Shantih shantih shantih': the poet's own note for this Hindu citation is 'the Peace which passeth understanding'.[50] It is difficult to think of a more concentrated instance of the death drive as the essential *mechanism* of religion (here in the deathly Christian appropriation of the Hindu). Let us all right now, in short, rest in peace. Let me end, let this be my end. Let this poem rest in peace.

'Why do you never speak. Speak. / What are you thinking of?'[51] Quick, now: think of a few more examples of literary works in English at the wake of the First World War. Think of W. B. Yeats's poem, 'The Wheel', written in September 1921, with its dark affirmation that, through the course of all the changing seasons and all human desire, 'what disturbs our blood / Is but its longing for the tomb'.[52] Think of D. H. Lawrence's 1921 novel *Women in Love*, perhaps his most famous statement of apocalyptic longing, of couples compelled to 'fight to the death', of 'pleasure in self-destruction', of the 'uncanny and inhuman', and the compulsion to repeat.[53] Think of the maddening suicidal drift of Virginia Woolf's *Mrs Dalloway* (1925); or of Elizabeth Bowen's *To the North* (1932) with its focus on a romantic but fatal attraction between a man and woman, Markie and Emmeline, who are carried along by the sense that they '*are* riding for a fall' and end everything in a final deadly car-drive together.[54] Think of that celebrated other, seemingly 'literal' death drive from 1925: F. Scott Fitzgerald's *The Great Gatsby*.

● Freud's theory of the death drive will have been haunted by D. H. Lawrence.

In terms of writers publishing in English around the same time as Freud, the example of Lawrence must constitute a privileged case. Indeed, we might have based our entire account of the death drive on his writings. Gilles Deleuze and Félix Guattari make a forceful assertion in their *Anti-Oedipus*: 'Let us keep D. H. Lawrence's reaction to psychoanalysis in mind, and never forget it.'[55] But it is not only a matter of Lawrence's 'reaction to psychoanalysis': it is also a question of the ways in which his writing strangely anticipates, doubles, repeats, amplifies but at the same time divides and unsettles Freud's. Harold Bloom has devoted extensive attention to the concept of the precursor, the 'strong' poet or other writer who figures as a crucial, even uncanny predecessor or harbinger (Milton for Wordsworth, Keats for Tennyson, Shelley for Hardy, Shakespeare for Freud, and so on). The example of Lawrence prompts us to formulate a somewhat different notion, namely that of the concursor. The concursor would be the strange contemporary.[56] He or she might be completely or largely unknown to the writer or thinker in question. Close yet distant, familiar but unfamiliar, concursors can have strangely similar concerns. In the case of Freud, he can even look like Lawrence's uncanny double.[57]

Lawrence's work is shot through with all the characterizations of the death drive that we have bullet-pointed here: the uncanny links with silence, woman, compulsive repetition, the demonic and diabolical, ghostly ubiquity and placelessness, solitude and singularity, writing and storytelling. So articulately *and* inarticulately ambivalent about Freud's work, Lawrence's extraordinary writings are at once explorations *and* performances of uncanny repetition.[58] It is not only in novels such as *Women in Love* that we find explicit attention to the connections between repetition and death, death and desire, or what Leo Bersani has called 'a longing to die disguised as a formula for life'.[59] It is everywhere in Lawrence, from his poetry to his critical essays. Let us confine ourselves for the moment, however, to consideration of a brief extract from one of his critical essays, 'The Reality of Peace' (1917): 'For there are ultimately only two desires, the desire of life and the desire of death. Beyond these is pure being, where I am absolved and made perfect.'[60] Characteristically oppositional, conflictual, repetitive, provocatively incoherent, and Christian in language and tone, the first of these two sentences asserts what is 'ultimately' the case – only for this, in the very next sentence, to be superseded by something else, 'beyond'. What could such a 'beyond' be if not death, the ultimate absolution, the absolute release? Or equally, *and conversely*, what is Lawrence talking about here if not the 'pure being' of 'life' as 'absolute presence'?[61] Lawrence's prose keeps relentlessly hammering on, a single sentence again and again seemingly repeating *but* overturning, contradicting *and* complementing the sentence that went before. As he goes on to assert, in the same passage of 'The Reality of Peace':

> We, we are all desire and understanding, only these two. And desire is twofold, desire of life and desire of death. All the time we are active in these two great powers, which are for ever contrary and complementary. Except in understanding, and there we are immune and perfect, there the two are one. Yet even understanding is twofold in its appearance. (p. 681)

Compulsively repetitive, maddening and maddened: such is the effect of what we might call Lawrence's signature, marked here in his characteristic rhetorical strategy of starting sentences with prepositions such as 'For', 'And', 'Except' or 'Yet'. At moments 'The Reality of Peace' can sound like a corroboration or even an eerie prequel of Freud's *Beyond the Pleasure Principle*. Like Freud, Lawrence speaks of deathly, ghostly or ghastly 'myrmidons' (pp. 684, 686). Like Freud, he suggests that the devilish is part of the 'proper': 'It is no good casting out devils. They belong to us ... They are of us ... in our own proper person' (p. 677). Like Freud, he argues that a death drive is not something of which we are ever necessarily conscious: 'We cannot admit the desire of death in ourselves', says Lawrence, 'even when it is single and dominant. We must still deceive ourselves with the name of life' (p. 682). And then almost immediately Lawrence can sound demonically, deliriously different: 'I want to kill, I want violent sensationalism, I want to break down, I want to put asunder, I want anarchic revolution – it is all the same, the single desire for death' (p. 682). For Freud in the course of a 'scientific' text such as *Beyond the Pleasure Principle* explicitly, lyrically, ecstatically to express his desire to die: that would indeed be strange. Nowhere in his work could we expect to find such an articulation of longing to die in one's own fashion: 'Release me from the debased social body, O death, release me at last; let me be by myself, let me be myself' (p. 687).

● The death drive is intimately linked with the question of telepathy.

Let us conclude by returning to the question of silence in Freud's work and note one further, enigmatic linkage arising in relation to the uncanny and the death drive. As we saw, in 'The Theme of the Three Caskets' Freud points up a correspondence between the beauty of woman, the desirability of death and silence. He concludes, or at least appears to conclude, with the remark that 'psycho-analysis will tell us that in dreams dumbness is a common representation of death' (*PFL*, 14: 239). He then begins a new paragraph:

> More than ten years ago a highly intelligent man told me a dream which he wanted to use as evidence of the telepathic nature of dreams. In it he saw an absent friend from whom he had received no news for a very long time, and reproached him energetically for his silence. The friend made no reply. It afterwards turned out that he had met his death by suicide at about the time of the dream. Let us leave the problem of telepathy on one side: there seems, however, not to be any doubt that here the dumbness in the dream represented death. (*PFL* 14: 239–40)

Freud then goes on to discuss two of Grimms' *Fairy Tales* ('The Twelve Brothers' and 'The Six Swans') in order further to substantiate the links between death and silence. But there is something quite bizarre about this appearance, this incursion or interposing of the question of telepathy in the text. Freud seems to summon it up, only in order to send it away again: 'Let us leave the problem of telepathy on one side.' We might set this alongside a brief consideration of a short story by Lawrence, 'The Rocking-horse Winner' (1926).[62] Uncertainly parodic, gothic, surreal, Lawrence's text generates an extraordinary fusion of elements concerned with the death drive, the figure of the mother, the compulsion to repeat, silence and telepathy (or the 'omnipotence of thoughts'). It centres on an uncanny, apparently telepathic rapport between a woman and her young son Paul. They live in a house dominated by silence, by the need to 'read [things] in each other's eyes' (p. 734). The house 'came to be haunted by the unspoken phrase: *There must be more money! There must be more money!*' (pp. 734–5). By riding his rocking-horse and going into a silent but frenzied kind of trance, Paul is able to '"know"' (p. 743) which horse is going to win at the races and thus bring in the money for which his mother yearns. The mother–son relationship is characterized not only by Paul's telepathic, magical 'knowledge', but also by the mother's strangely telepathic 'rushes of anxiety' (p. 745) about him. And throughout all of this there is the over-whelming sense of a death drive. There is the automatism of the rocking-horse and Paul's riding itself; the 'compulsion to repeat' not only in his acts of riding but in the gambling itself; Paul's eyes which are specifically described as being 'uncanny' (pp. 744, 745), and as having a hypnotic, 'staring', 'glass-bright' (p. 736), stony intensity; and, finally, the characterization of Paul as a 'poor devil', the childish but diabolical embodiment of a death drive, someone (in his uncle's words) 'best gone out of a life where he rides his rocking-horse to find a winner'

(p. 747). Lawrence's text suggests that there is a crucial relation between the death drive and what, in Freud's 'The Theme of the Three Caskets', interposes as the apparent red herring called 'telepathy'. This is something to which we will return.

NOTES

1   Franz Kafka, *The Collected Aphorisms* (London: Syrens, 1994), p. 9.
2   D. H. Lawrence, 'The Ship of Death', in *The Complete Poems of D. H. Lawrence*, ed. Vivian de Sola Pinta and Warren Roberts (London: Heinemann, 1972), p. 717.
3   Caroline Rooney, *African Literature, Animism and Politics* (London: Routledge, 2000), p. 56.
4   See *PFL*, 11: 269–338: here, p. 311. Further page references to *Beyond the Pleasure Principle* will be given in the main body of the text, abbreviated '*BPP*' where appropriate.
5   Jonathan Dollimore, *Death, Desire and Loss in Western Culture* (London: Allen Lane the Penguin Press, 1998).
6   Dollimore, *Death, Desire and Loss in Western Culture*, p. 192. Dollimore makes no mention of the work of Derrida, either here or elsewhere in his book, though such an argument is central to an understanding of how Derrida's work (for example, the notion of differance) makes the familiar radically unfamiliar, introducing uncanniness into 'familiarity itself'. As he writes in *Of Grammatology*: 'The outside, "spatial" and "objective" exteriority which we believe we know as the most familiar thing in the world, as familiarity itself, would not appear without the gramme, without differance as temporalization, without the nonpresence of the other inscribed within the sense of the present, without the relationship with death as the concrete structure of the living present.' See Jacques Derrida, *Of Grammatology*, trans. Gayatri Chakravorty Spivak (Baltimore: Johns Hopkins University Press, 1976), pp. 70–1.
7   Dollimore, *Death, Desire and Loss in Western Culture*, p. xx. For an account of these 'earliest times', see Dollimore's opening chapter, 'Eros and Thanatos, Change and Loss in the Ancient World', pp. 3–35.
8   Dollimore, *Death, Desire and Loss in Western Culture*, p. 61.
9   See also, for example, *Death, Desire and Loss in Western Culture*, pp. 5, 72, 75, 132–3, 134, 143, 150, 173, 178–9.
10   See Dollimore, *Death, Desire and Loss in Western Culture*, pp. 180, 193.
11   Jacques Derrida, 'Force of Law: The "Mystical Foundation of Authority"', trans. Mary Quaintance, *Cardozo Law Review*, vol. 11, no. 5/6 (1990), 921–1045: here, p. 943.
12   Ibid.
13   See J. L. Austin, *How to do Things with Words* (Oxford: Clarendon Press, 1962). In a fine passage in his book *The Legend of Freud* (Minneapolis: University of Minnesota, 1982), Samuel Weber has commented on the silence (or *Stummheit*) of the death drive as follows: 'the very *Stummheit* of the death drive precludes it from ever speaking for itself; it is inevitably dependent on another discourse to be seen or heard. And that discourse, however much it may seek to efface itself before the "silence" it seeks to articulate, is anything but innocent or neutral. The death drive may be dumb, but its articulation in a theoretical or speculative discourse is not' (p. 129).
14   E. T. A. Hoffmann, 'The Sandman', in *Tales of Hoffmann*, trans. R. J. Hollingdale (Harmondsworth: Penguin, 1982), p. 96.

15   Sarah Kofman, *Freud and Fiction*, trans. Sarah Wykes (Cambridge: Polity Press, 1991), pp. 160–1.

16   Kofman, *Freud and Fiction*, pp. 161–2.

17   See Phillip McCaffrey, 'Freud's Uncanny Woman', in *Reading Freud's Reading*, eds Sander L. Gilman, Jutta Birmele, Jay Geller and Valerie D. Greenberg (New York: New York University Press, 1994) pp. 91–108. Although he refers to the work of Sarah Kofman and Allan Gardner Lloyd Smith, McCaffrey curiously makes no reference to important earlier work on the spectral presence and power of the 'Uncanny Woman', such as Hélène Cixous's 'Fiction and Its Phantoms: A Reading of Freud's *Das Unheimliche*', *New Literary History*, vol. 7, no. 3 (1976), 525–48, or Jane Marie Todd's 'The Veiled Woman in Freud's "Das Unheimliche"', *Signs*, vol. 2, no. 3 (1986), 519–28.

18   See Bronfen's short essay, 'The death drive (Freud)', in *Feminism and Psychoanalysis: A Critical Dictionary*, ed. Elizabeth Wright (Cambridge, Mass., and Oxford: Blackwell, 1992), pp. 52–7. Further page references are given in the main body of the text. Bronfen discusses the uncanny interrelations of death and the feminine at greater length in *Over Her Dead Body: Death, Femininity and the Aesthetic* (Manchester: Manchester University Press, 1992).

19   See 'Anxiety and Instinctual Life', *PFL*, 2: 143.

20   Gordon C. F. Bearn, 'Wittgenstein and the Uncanny', *Soundings: An Interdisciplinary Journal*, vol. 76, no. 1 (1993), 33 (Bearn's emphasis).

21   Jean Laplanche, 'Why the Death Drive?', in *Life and Death in Psychoanalysis* (1970), trans. Jeffrey Mehlman (Baltimore: Johns Hopkins University Press, 1976), pp. 103–24: here, p. 107.

22   Jacques Derrida, 'To Speculate – on "Freud"', in *The Post Card: From Socrates to Freud and Beyond*, trans. Alan Bass (Chicago: Chicago University Press, 1987), pp. 259–409: here, p. 270.

23   See 'To Speculate – on "Freud"', pp. 269–71.

24   'To Speculate – on "Freud"', p. 343. Here and elsewhere in this chapter I have chosen to conform to a 'demonic' rather than 'daemonic' orthography. For a rather different reading of the demonic character of the death drive see Caroline Rooney's account of 'the death drive and spirit possession' in her *African Literature, Animism and Politics*, pp. 135–49. Concerned to explore the ways in which 'Freud's thinking of the death drive is mystical', Rooney contends that 'the death drive derives its energy from a warding off of being possessed by other forces – "be gone, leave me be" – or, as Freud says, the organism only wants to die in its own fashion' (p. 137).

25   Cf. J. Hillis Miller, '*Wuthering Heights*: Repetition and the "Uncanny"', in his *Fiction and Repetition* (Oxford: Blackwell, 1982), pp. 42–72. Idiosyncratically and perhaps a little mysteriously, Miller identifies the uncanny with a feeling of guilt on the part of the reader: 'the narration in *Wuthering Heights* somehow involves the reader's innocence or guilt … Any repetitive structure of the "uncanny" sort, whether in real life or in words, tends to generate an irrational sense of guilt in the one who experiences it. I have not done anything (or have I?), and yet what I witness makes demands on me which I cannot fulfill. The mere fact of passive looking or reading may make one guilty of the crime of seeing what ought not to have been seen. What I see or what I read repeats or seems to repeat something earlier, something deeper in' (p. 69).

26   Ironically but perhaps predictably, in other words in a fateful spirit, he turns in the direction of literature once more, quickly moving on to discuss Schiller's 'The Ring of Polycrates': see U, p. 361.

27   Neil Hertz, 'Freud and the Sandman', in *The End of the Line: Essays on Psychoanalysis and the Sublime* (New York: Columbia University Press, 1985), p. 101. Cf. Derrida's discussion of the passage in *Beyond the Pleasure Principle* where Freud speaks of the compulsion to repeat in terms of 'the impression' that some people ('neurotic' or 'normal') give 'of being pursued by

a malignant fate or possessed by some "demonic" power' (*BPP*, p. 292). The 'most moving' example of such demonization, Freud goes on to suggest, is to be found in the fateful repetitions that characterize Tancred's relationship with his beloved Clorinda in Tasso's *Gerusalemme Liberata* (*BPP*, p. 293). Derrida counters and radicalizes this: 'No, what is "*most* moving" … is the repetition … of these *unheimlich* repetitions of repetitions': see 'To Speculate – on "Freud"', p. 343.

28   Besides the Nietzschean 'eternal recurrence of the same' itself, there are obvious resonances between Freud and Nietzsche on the notion of the death drive as a desire to 'return to the inanimate state' (*PFL*, 11: 311). In an essay entitled 'The Death Drive Does Not Think' (in *Post-theory: New Directions in Criticism*, eds Martin McQuillan, Graeme MacDonald, Robin Purves and Stephen Thomson (Edinburgh: Edinburgh University Press, 1999), pp. 161–75), Robert Smith recalls Nietzsche's corresponding concern with 'the attempt to win for man an approximation to what in certain animals is *hibernation*, in many tropical plants *estivation*, the minimum metabolism at which life will still subsist without really entering consciousness'. See Friedrich Nietzsche, *On the Genealogy of Morals*, trans. Walter Kaufmann and R. J. Hollingale (New York: Vintage, 1969), p. 131. (Quoted by Smith, p. 162.)

29   For an account of the importance of the 'demon' who writes Lawrence's work, see for example his Preface to *The Collected Poems*, reprinted in *Phoenix: The Posthumous Papers of D. H. Lawrence*, ed. Edward D. McDonald (New York: The Viking Press, 1972), pp. 251–4.

30   Sigmund Freud, 'Introduction to *Psycho-analysis and the War Neuroses*' (1919; London: International Psycho-Analytic Press, 1921); reprinted *SE*, 17: 205–10.

31   Maud Ellmann, Introduction to *Psychoanalytic Literary Criticism* (London: Longman, 1994), p. 7.

32   J. Laplanche and J.-B. Pontalis, *The Language of Psycho-analysis*, trans. Donald Nicholson-Smith (London: Hogarth Press and the Institute of Psychoanalysis, 1973), p. 97.

33   Laplanche, 'Why the Death Drive?', p. 107.

34   *Beyond the Pleasure Principle* ends with 'the words of the poet', Rückert: 'What we cannot reach flying we must reach limping … ' (*BPP*, p. 338). Derrida discusses this figure of limping at length, relating it to the notions of rhythm and 'vacillation': see, in particular, 'To Speculate – on "Freud" ', pp. 405 ff.

35   See *The Language of Psycho-analysis*, pp. 98, 103.

36   Laplanche, 'Why the Death Drive?', p. 124.

37   Bronfen, 'Death drive (Freud)', p. 56.

38   Derrida, 'To Speculate – on "Freud" ', pp. 358–9.

39   Derrida, 'To Speculate – on "Freud" ', p. 361.

40   Peter Brooks, 'Freud's Masterplot', in *Reading for the Plot: Design and Intention in Narrative* (Cambridge, Mass.: Harvard University Press, 1984), pp. 90–112. Further page references are given parenthetically in the main body of the text.

41   'To Speculate – on "Freud"', p. 303. It is in this way, Derrida goes on to suggest, that the death drive 'is not opposed to the [pleasure principle], but hollows it out with a testamentary writing "*en abyme*" originally, at the origin of the origin' (p. 304).

42   There is something here too, perhaps, of Wittgenstein's sense of the 'uncanny charm' of Freud's arguments consisting in the 'repellent' and 'ugly' nature of his explanations for things. See Ludwig Wittgenstein, *Lectures and Conversations on Aesthetics, Psychology and Religious Belief*, Compiled from Notes taken by Yorick Smythies, Rush Rhees and James Taylor, ed. Cyril Barrett (Oxford: Basil Blackwell, 1966), pp. 24–5. As Stephen Mulhall has put it: for Wittgenstein, the 'very popularity [of Freudian theorizing] may be a function of the repellent nature of its conclusions'. See Mulhall, *On Being in the World: Wittgenstein and Heidegger on*

Seeing Aspects (London: Routledge, 1990), p. 202.

43   See Linda Ruth Williams, 'Writing the Death Drive', in her *Critical Desire: Psychoanalysis and the Literary Subject* (London: Edward Arnold, 1995), pp. 160–1.

44   Paul Hirst and Penny Woolley, *Social Relations and Human Attributes* (London: Tavistock, 1982), p. 116, n. 2.

45   Hal Foster, *Compulsive Beauty* (Cambridge, Mass.: MIT Press, 1993).

46   Foster, *Compulsive Beauty*, p. 11.

47   Foster, *Compulsive Beauty*, p. 17.

48   Jean Baudrillard, *For a Critique of the Political Economy of the Sign*, trans. Charles Levin (St Louis, Mo.: Telos Press, 1981), p. 194. Quoted by Foster, p. 212. *Compulsive Beauty* concludes with a short chapter entitled 'Beyond the Surrealism Principle?' (pp. 209–13), concerned with a series of questions about the supposed stability and 'pastness' of the concept and practice of surrealism. Foster foregrounds the surreal's uncanny, spectral capacity to return. Thus he proposes that if there is a case for thinking that there is a 'contemporary eclipse of the uncanny', 'as long as there is repression there will be its uncanny return' (p. 211). If, in other words, 'There will be other revolutions' (p. 213), they will always have something uncanny about them.

49   T.S. Eliot, *The Waste Land*, in *The Norton Anthology of English Literature*, 6th edn, 2, ed. M. H. Abrams (New York: Norton, 1993), pp. 2147–60. The translation of Petronius is from the Norton, p. 2147, n. 1.

50   Eliot's note to *The Waste Land*: see *The Norton Anthology*, p. 2160, n. 2.

51   Eliot, *The Waste Land*, ll. 112–13.

52   *The Collected Poems of W. B. Yeats* (London: Macmillan, 1977), p. 237.

53   D. H. Lawrence, *Women in Love* (1921; Harmondsworth: Penguin, 1960), pp. 159, 348, 298.

54   Elizabeth Bowen, *To the North* (1932; Harmondsworth: Penguin, 1984), p. 184. For an account of Bowen's novel in terms of what they call the 'auto-thanato-mobile', see Andrew Bennett and Nicholas Royle, *Elizabeth Bowen and the Dissolution of the Novel* (London: Macmillan, 1995), pp. 23–41.

55   Gilles Deleuze and Félix Guattari, *Anti-Oedipus: Capitalism and Schizophrenia*, trans. Robert Hurley, Mark Seem and Helen R. Lane (London: Athlone Press, 1984), p. 49.

56   The concursor is a figure of the strange contemporary and the strangeness *of* the contemporary. Hence the peculiar future anterior of the bullet point: Freud *will have been haunted* by Lawrence.

57   H. D. (Hilda Doolittle) recalls meeting Freud: 'I asked him how he was and he smiled a charming, wrinkled smile that reminded me of D. H. Lawrence.' See her *Tribute to Freud* (Manchester: Carcanet Press, 1985), p. 128; and cf. p. 141. H. D. also reports Freud's comment on reading one of Lawrence's works: 'Lawrence impressed him as "being unsatisfied but a man of real power"' (p. 144). Is it possible to read this attributed remark without seeing in it a self-reflexive dimension, in other words as being at the same time an evocation of Freud himself?

58   For Lawrence's arguments with Freud see especially his *Fantasia of the Unconscious* and *Psychoanalysis and the Unconscious* (1923; Harmondsworth: Penguin, 1971). For a thoughtful general account of Lawrence and Freud see Fiona Becket, *D. H. Lawrence: The Thinker as Poet* (Basingstoke: Macmillan, 1997), esp. Chapter 4, 'Language and the Unconscious: The Radical Metaphoricity of *Psychoanalysis and the Unconscious* and *Fantasia of the Unconscious* I', pp. 46–86.

59   See Leo Bersani's fine reading of Lawrence in a chapter entitled 'Lawrentian Stillness', in his *A Future for Astyanax: Character and Desire in Literature* (Boston: Little, Brown and Co., 1976), pp. 156–85: here, p. 180.

60 'The Reality of Peace', in *Phoenix: The Posthumous Papers of D. H. Lawrence*, pp. 669–98: here, p. 680. Further page references are given parenthetically in the main body of the text.

61 There was always something strange, I thought, about the blurb in the front of all the Penguin editions of Lawrence's work, claiming that 'Lawrence spent most of his short life living'. For an account of how 'Lawrence's pronouncements in his theoretical essays are not only frequently at odds with each other, but also with his writing practice, which especially in the great novels, *The Rainbow* and *Women in Love*, cultivates a differential rhetoric that undermines its own (often) strident assertions of meaning and truth', see Gerald Doherty, 'Lawrence and Jacques Derrida: A Dialog across the Abyss', in his *Theorizing Lawrence: Nine Meditations on Tropological Themes* (New York: Peter Lang, 1999), pp. 145–61: here, p. 145.

62 'The Rocking-horse Winner', in *The Collected Short Stories of D. H. Lawrence* (London: Heinemann, 1974), pp. 734–47. Further page references to 'The Rocking-horse Winner' will be given in the main body of the text. For an earlier reading of the uncanny and psychoanalysis in relation to this story, see W. S. Marks, 'The Psychology of the Uncanny in Lawrence's "The Rocking-horse Winner"', *Modern Fiction Studies* vol. 11, no. 4 (Winter 1965–66), 381–92.

6

Silence, solitude and ...

- Did you say something?

- I heard a voice.

- In your head?

- No, in yours.

7
Darkness

Full of ghostly omissions and emissions, Freud's 'The Uncanny' is an essay in the night, an investigation in the dark, into darkness. As he says near the outset: 'the uncanny would always, as it were, be something one does not know one's way about in' (U, p. 341). Throughout the essay Freud keeps coming back to the dark, or the dark keeps coming back to him. Repeatedly he evokes the uncanniness of moving about in the dark, without necessarily remarking that this is what he is doing. Darkness is a factor that stares us in the face, so to speak, when it comes to considering the various dictionary definitions of 'heimlich' and 'unheimlich'. The uncanny, he notes, is fundamentally concerned with what is '"Concealed, kept from sight"' (U, p. 344). A few moments later he cites a dictionary that cites the phrase '"The unheimlich, fearful hours of night"' (U, p. 345). And again, shortly after this, as a way of illustrating the uncanny logic whereby the meaning of a word can turn into its opposite ('"heimlich" comes to have the meaning usually ascribed to "unheimlich"' (U, p. 346)), he quotes Grimms' dictionary, quoting Klinger: 'At times I feel like a man who walks in the night and believes in ghosts; every corner is heimlich and full of terrors for him' (U, pp. 346–7). Darkness is at least implicitly involved in the crucial definition of the uncanny that Freud takes from Schelling: the unheimlich or uncanny is what 'ought to have remained secret and hidden but has come to light' (U, p. 345).

Already there is a certain paradox here: it is not so much darkness itself (whatever that might be), but the process of ceasing to be dark, the process of revelation or bringing to light, that is uncanny. As several writers have noted, the uncanny seems (at least for Freud) to involve a special emphasis on the visual, on what comes to light, on what is revealed to the eye. The uncanny is what comes out of the darkness. To recall a provoking formulation from Paul de Man: 'To make the invisible visible is uncanny.'[1] Such a proposition also neatly encapsulates the uncanny idea for which de Man himself will perhaps be best remembered, namely that every literary, critical or philosophical text is a work of blindness and insight, in which the moments of greatest authorial insight are characteristically moments of blindness, or vice versa. The two poles of an apparent opposition (blindness and insight) merge into one another: something becomes the negative, inversion or opposite of itself. In a trope familiar (from Sophocles' Tiresias to D. H. Lawrence's 'The Blind Man' or Raymond Carver's 'Cathedral') but still perhaps strange, blindness can be an especially powerful kind of seeing. The sense of a word changes into its opposite: blindness is seeing, the canny uncanny, the uncanny canny.² We have an inkling, perhaps, of what Milton calls 'darkness visible' (*Paradise Lost*, Book I, 63).

Darkness is repeatedly mentioned, implied, evoked in Freud's essay, often in terms of the darkness of night. But while references to darkness may recur, he never specifically tries to elucidate, as it were, the uncanny nature of darkness 'itself'. In the closing section of the essay he asks: 'And once more: what is the origin of the uncanny effect of silence, darkness and solitude?' (U, p. 369). The 'once more' is a little bizarre, for Freud has not, until now, asked this question as such. It is as if he has repeatedly been referring to darkness, losing his way in the darkness of the uncanny, and yet darkness remains as something constantly destined to return, 'once more'. Quite apart from the essay's numerous allusions to dictionary definitions concerned with darkness and night, and quite apart from the recurrent 'image' of losing one's way in the dark (the recurrent figure of 'the uncanny' as 'something one does not know one's way about in' (U, p. 341), the recurrent figure of recurrence whereby 'one may wander about in a dark, strange room, looking for the door or the electric switch, and collide time after time with the same piece of furniture' (U, p. 359), and so on), we might wonder what is going on in Freud's evocations of the fear of blindness or the fear of being buried alive. He proposes that, in the context of Hoffmann's Sandman, 'the feeling of something uncanny is directly attached … to the idea of being robbed of one's eyes' (U, p. 351), and later he asserts that 'To some people the idea of being buried alive … is the most uncanny thing of all' (U, p. 366). But in neither case does Freud make explicit the obvious (if also perhaps terrifying) connection with darkness as such.

'And once more: what is the origin of the uncanny effect of silence, darkness and solitude?' The form of the question suggests they all belong together: silence, darkness and solitude. And this is how the essay concludes – with a complex, shifting figuration of what remains enigmatic. Darkness remains uncanny, a 'site' of ghostly omissions and emissions. Freud declares:

> Concerning the factors of silence, solitude and darkness, we can only say that they are actually elements in the production of the infantile anxiety from which the majority of human beings have never become quite free. This problem has been discussed from a psychoanalytic point of view elsewhere. (U, p. 376)

These are the last words of Freud's great essay. The 'fear of the dark', as the English translator of 'The "Uncanny"' points out (U, p. 376, n. 1), has indeed 'been discussed from a psychoanalytic point of view elsewhere', namely in the *Three Essays on*

Sexuality (*PFL*, 7). The essay on the uncanny, then, ends with a supplement, a supplementary darkness. At the very end we are referred back – or forward – to something that comes before the beginning, to a passage in the *Three Essays* (1905). There Freud writes:

> Anxiety in children is originally nothing other than an expression of the fact that they are feeling the loss of the person they love. It is for this reason that they are frightened of every stranger. They are afraid in the dark because in the dark they cannot see the person they love; and their fear is soothed if they can take hold of that person's hand. (*PFL*, 7: 147)

In a footnote he records the indebtedness of his theory (theory in and of the dark) to the voice of a three-year-old boy:

> For this explanation of the origin of infantile anxiety I have to thank a three-year-old boy whom I once heard calling out of a dark room: 'Auntie, speak to me! I'm frightened because it's so dark.' His aunt answered him: 'What good would that do? You can't see me.' 'That doesn't matter,' replied the child, 'if anyone speaks, it gets light.' Thus what he was afraid of was not the dark, but the absence of someone he loved. (147, n. 1).

This footnote spectrally grafted on to the final paragraph of 'The Uncanny' might alert us, once again, to the importance for an understanding of the uncanny of the ear, of listening, of sound, voice and tone. Not that Freud is uninterested in the visible or invisible. Indeed, the ending of 'The Uncanny' could be taken to suggest that it is darkness (rather than silence or solitude) which finally haunts his project: it is specifically 'fear of the dark', rather than fear of silence or of solitude to which we are alerted, even if the discussion indicates that the three terms under consideration ('silence, solitude and darkness') are curiously entangled bed-fellows. Through its enigmatic, supplementary footnote-work (absent from the original German), 'The Uncanny' concludes not with any straightforward ocularcentrism (the uncanny as what comes to light, as what is to be seen, or as what represents a threat to vision), but with an eerily synaesthetic figure, a mixing of seeing and hearing, of a voice that lightens the dark ('if anyone speaks, it gets light'). The eeriness is doubtless accentuated by what is unspoken in Freud's account, namely that it is a curious night-scene of eavesdropping, a psychoanalyst overhearing or listening into a conversation between a small boy and his aunt. Where were the boy's parents? What was Freud doing there? Was he the father? How many rooms, how many beds and what occupants are we being asked to imagine here, in the darkness? There is something oddly resonant and moving about the fact that an essay that has been concerned to elaborate a critical detachment from the world of childhood (arguing that the uncanny is especially liable to occur, for example, 'when infantile complexes which have been repressed are once more revived' (U, p. 372)), sees fit to wrap up its case with textual support from a three-year-old. There is also something faintly, even perhaps 'irresistibly comic' (to recall a phrase from the penultimate paragraph of 'The Uncanny') about this allusive, elusive, illusive ending to Freud's essay. However obliquely, it refers to 'silence, solitude and darkness' as part of a problem which 'has been discussed from a psychoanalytic point of view elsewhere' – as if this disposes of the problem, indeed as if darkness (and its shady accomplices, silence and solitude) had always already been seen to, put to sleep, tucked up.

NOTES

1   Paul de Man, *The Resistance to Theory* (Minneapolis: University of Minnesota Press, 1986), p. 49.
2   On the uncanniness or *'disquieting strangeness'* of 'the eye of the blind man' and on the related notions that 'the blind man' can be 'the best witness' and that 'a witness, as such, is always blind', see Jacques Derrida, *Memoirs of the Blind: The Self-portrait and Other Ruins*, trans. Pascale-Anne Brault and Michael Naas (Chicago: Chicago University Press, 1993), pp. 104–6.

8

Night writing: deconstruction reading politics

> Those who think they see ghosts are those who do not want to see the night.
> (Maurice Blanchot)[1]

★ In such darkness. In my voice, in my language, which is not mine. 'Deconstruction reading politics': how to think about this in the so-called light of today?[2] What day? Night writing: a disordering of voice in the night. What follows is telegrammatic, fragmentary, a series of night letters, each marked with a star. The term 'night letter' is not (or, until a moment ago, was not) 'current English'. The *OED* explains that it was 'Said by the 1945 P.O. Guide "to be suspended"'. A night letter was 'a cheap-rate inland [or overseas] telegram delivered overnight' (*OED*). Hereby recalling and seeking to resuscitate the phrase, I wonder, isn't every letter, and in some sense every text, a night letter? An essay in the night, an investigation in the dark, an investigation into darkness: wouldn't Freud's essay on the uncanny be an exemplary case of such writing? Dispatched in such darkness: no letter, however fast, however cheap, however manual or electronic, without night, without the unforeseeable, the incalculable and death.

★ Start of second letter, introduced with a star, hence a so-called 'starred item', a phrase that will not signify in the same way for academics in Britain as for academics elsewhere. For those working in British universities, the phrase is associated with the RAE (the national Research Assessment Exercise). Everything in the present book, as the work of an academic employed by a British university, has been assembled in the shadow or night of the RAE. As in a cold war (an intellectual cold civil war), its eerie shadow is cast over everything. No analysis of the politics of the institution, of 'deconstruction reading politics', of the British University in deconstruction, without engaging with the insidious reality or reality-effects of the RAE. Analysis might start with the fact that, on a general level, national identity and all the related religious or mystical phantoms of nationalism ('British', but also 'Scottish', 'English' and so on) are determining the space of 'academic thought': in order to be counted 'academic thought' (and everything in the RAE has to do with counting, with disavowing the unaccountable and uncountable), the very 'freedom of thought' will already have been declared 'made in Britain'. At the same time, all British academic research is unblinkingly assigned to a particular discipline (philosophy, history, English, etc.). It is perfectly legitimate to talk about the interdisciplinary and multi-disciplinary, so long as it is realized that such talk has nothing to do with the real world of 'academic research' or with the running and financing of academic institutions. On a supposedly more 'individual' level (and the RAE takes as read all sorts of assumptions about the unitariness, as well as the mortgage-like porta-bility, of the individual and his or her 'work'), British academics are required to conceive their *raison d'être* in terms of the starred item. Each individual is expected to produce four starred items for each research assessment round. Each so-called research-active academic in Britain is monitored and evaluated accord-ingly. The item may be a book (the quasi-sacred 'monograph' if possible, but an edition or edited collection of essays also qualifies), or it may be an article published in a refereed journal. Other publications can be put forward as 'starred items', but they will not be ranked as highly and indeed *may not* 'count' for anything at all. It is necessary to say 'may not' because, while the RAE demands that academics think of what they do in terms of what can be counted and made accountable, the actual criteria and methods of counting and accounting pursued by those who sit in judgement on the RAE panel of assessors remain rigorously unaccountable. Fundamentally inscrutable, the panelists assess individual starred items above all in terms of whether or not they are examples of 'national excel-lence' and 'international excellence'. How can something be 'excellent' in a national context but no longer 'excellent' in some supposedly broader context? What is happening when a so-called English word ('excellent') is apparently sent abroad, smuggled out of its 'national' context, in order to appear not only to take account of views or assessments in an 'international' context but also, by this very appearance, to impose upon this 'international' context a language that is (one might reasonably suppose) foreign? Never really starting off from Britain in the first place, the word 'excellent' (or 'excellence') is in fact an exemplary instance of what is called Anglo-American, a language about which I will say more later. The term 'excellence' itself is, of course, not defined: it remains scrupulously empty, indeed nihilistically so.[3] No one is any longer to suppose that the small group of panelists can claim to read all the starred items submitted by every university department of X or Y discipline, but how do the panel-members decide which items (or 'forms of output') to assess? Do they, in fact, decide? What do they think about when they read? Do they think excellent thoughts? How do they distinguish between one monograph, one article (refereed or not), and another? If the length of a starred item is understood *not* to be a decisive criterion (otherwise there would indeed be no need for the assessment panel even to claim or to pretend that they read, to pretend or claim that they can or know how to read), in other words if it is granted that a certain twenty-page article can be assessed as more valuable, more 'excellent' than a particular book-length monograph, is it not possible that a starred item of only ten pages, or five, or less, might likewise be judged on a par with a book-length item? Suppose the starred item were unprecedentedly condensed, consisting of only a few words, for example

deconstruction reading politics
(non-RAE-compliant)

How would the assessors read that? What would they make of it? According to what models of reading and what criteriology? And with respect to what discipline or discourse? Perhaps a few years from now it will all seem merely fantastical. People will perhaps chuckle at the idea that the RAE really existed, that so-called free-thinking academic 'individuals' went along with it all, carried on their academic (and of course in some significant measure their non-academic) lives under its aegis, mostly without even a murmur against it, a society of academic somnambulists. For the moment let us simply note that, today, the RAE is the unbelievable night in which one is supposed to pretend to believe: non-transparent, invisibly dark machine that nevertheless monitors and infiltrates, overshadows and inflects all British university research. What would a research assessment exercise be like if it were to try to take account of deconstruction? Imagine an 'assessment exercise' that would seek to respond to a call, listen to a certain tone, that would seek to attune itself to the kind of thinking of identity and the 'we', of friendship and the New International, of originality and invention, of signature and expropriation, of citationality and grafting, of titles, borders and parerga, of all the *trans-* effects between and beyond disciplines and discourses, of mourning and the coming of the future, of spectrality, the incalculable, the undecidable and the uncountable, experiencing the impossible, multiple voices, deferred effects and deferred meaning, associated with deconstruction. End of second starred item.

★ But the RAE is only one aspect of a far more extensive kind of programming. Such, in effect, is the subject of Derrida's *The Other Heading*, in which he declares that one must not

> accept the capital of a centralizing authority that, by means of trans-European cultural mechanisms, by means of publishing, journalistic and academic concentrations ... would control and standardize, subjecting artistic discourses and practices to a grid of intelligibility, to philosophical or aesthetic norms, to channels of immediate and efficient communication, to the pursuit of ratings and commercial profitability.[4]

There is, he says, a new kind of '"cultural" discourse', one of whose 'master words' is 'transparency' (*OH*, pp. 54–5). It amounts to what he calls a '"new censorship"', a cultural discourse that massively 'de-politicizes' (100): 'Claiming to speak in the name of good sense, common sense, or the democratic ethic, this discourse tends, by means of these very things, and as if naturally, to discredit anything that complicates this model' (*OH*, p. 55). Work that does not comply, does not easily accommodate itself to the program of norms and standardization, to accredited models of intelligibility and so on, is 'relegated ... into the darkness of a *quasi-private* enclosure' (101). '"Difficult" research', Derrida notes, 'that which resists the stereotypes of the image or of narration, which does not submit to the norms of culture ... is excluded from the scene: occulted, deprived of the *light of day*. *As a result, such research is judged* to be more and more "obscure", "difficult", indeed "unreadable", and so it becomes what one says it is and wants it to be: inaccessible' (*OH*, p. 102). At issue here is the pursuit of research or writing that would be 'difficult' among other things in so far as it disturbs and interferes with distinctions between disciplines and discourses, above all perhaps in terms of an uncanny borderwork (for example, as neither and both philosophy and/or literature, literature and/or psychoanalysis). Work perhaps deprived of the light of day but impelled by the desire for a new enlightenment: night writing.

★ Night writing: of course there isn't any. In Maurice Blanchot's words: 'Whoever devotes himself [*sic*] to the work is drawn by it toward the point where it undergoes impossibility. This experience is purely nocturnal, it is the very experience of night.'[5] Night writing, in this sense, would be the very experience of the impossible. If night writing can be construed as another (non-synonymic) name for deconstruction, this would entail a thinking alien to any customary or conventional conception of night. In Blanchot's terms it is a question of 'the other night'. He observes: 'When we oppose night and day ... it is still to the night of day that we allude, to the night that is day's night, the night of which we can say that it is the true night, for it has day's truth just as it has day's laws, those which, precisely, assign it the duty of opposing itself to the day' (pp. 167–8).[6] The '*other* night', however, is 'always other'; it is neither 'comprehensible' not 'ascertainable' (p. 168). The example he gives is that of the beast, the *other* beast heard in Kafka's 'The Burrow':[7]

> What the beast senses in the distance – that monstrous thing which eternally approaches it and works eternally at coming closer – is itself ... The *other* night is always the other, and he who senses it becomes the other. He who approaches it departs from himself, is no longer he who approaches but he who turns away. (p. 169)

Strikingly, the form of this encounter with the 'other night' is sound. Night writing, in the context of Blanchot's thinking, would be an experience of hearing: 'There is always a moment when, in the night, the beast hears the other beast. This is the *other* night' (p. 168). So much for national research assessment exercises, so much for grids of intelligibility, norms and standardization.

★ Four starred items already. No point in going on: call it a day. What are you supposed to do when you have produced the required number of items? I may as well be dead. It is as if I were – as a so-called scholar (to use Marcellus's term in *Hamlet*) – already dead, or buried alive. In the burrow, lost for words. In this darkness, then, a few words about *Monolingualism of the Other*.[8] I know of no other text by Derrida that is so bristling and prickly, so dismayed yet powerful, around the deployment of particular words. In everything he writes, one may perhaps hear the reverberations of this engagement with the madness of writing. His sense of elementary incompetence and dismay is perhaps a key to beginning to feel towards any so-called politics of so-called deconstruction. As he has declared of the business of starting to write something:

> It is really as if I had never before written anything, or even known how to write (I mean, very sincerely, in the most elementary and almost grammatical fashion). Each time I begin a new text, however modest it may be, there is dismay in the face of the unknown or inaccessible, an overwhelming feeling of clumsiness, inexperience, powerlessness.[9]

Nowhere, it seems to me, is Derrida's dismay, and even revulsion, at 'his' language more pronounced (so to speak) than in *Monolingualism of the Other*. One could, and no doubt should, multiply the examples indefinitely. To recall just a few: he talks about 'All these problems of *identity*, as we so foolishly say nowadays' (*MO*, p. 10), referring to the meaning of this word ('identity') as what is 'always dogmatically presupposed by so many debates on monoculturalism or multiculturalism, nationality, citizenship, and, in general, belonging' (p. 14); he talks about 'what is, so hastily, named the body proper' (p. 27); he holds up the word 'interdiction' as 'too risky', the word 'transgression' as 'at once too facile and too loaded' (p. 32); he glosses the phrase 'educational system' with the words, 'as it has been called in France for some time now, without a smile, and without anxiety' (p. 37); he says he 'wouldn't like to make too easy use of the word "colonialism"' (p. 39); he refers to the expressions '"the relationship to the other"' and '"openness to the other"' as 'worn enough to give up the ghost' (p. 40), adding an aghast exclamation mark after each of them; he refers to '"the" Western metaphysics', then opens a parenthesis with the words 'which I have never identified, regardless of whatever has been repeated about it ad nauseam, as a single homogeneous thing' (p. 70); he speaks of 'All these words: *truth, alienation, habitation, one's home* [*chez-soi*], *ipseity, place of the subject, law,* and so on' as remaining 'problematic. Without exception' (p. 59); and so on; et cetera. In *Monolingualism of the Other*, more outspokenly perhaps – more harrowingly, more hatefully and lovingly – than in any other text by Derrida, one might hear him seeking to specify, at the instant of every syllable, a situation in which 'it is no longer possible to *use* seriously the words of the tradition'.[10] It is as if, as he puts it in the essay 'Some Statements and Truisms', 'the effects of a deconstructive process ... compelled us to add, more or less legibly, the mention "mention" to all the words' (pp. 74–5). In its singular way, then, *Monolingualism of the Other* might be described as one of those 'rare, strange, unbearable ... events of writing whose force nevertheless consists in "using" language again by submitting it to the effects of deconstruction', in other words 'destabiliz[ing] even the opposition between discourse *with* and discourse *without* quotation marks, [the opposition between] mention and use, and the entire system of associated values; that is, philosophy in its entirety, theory in its entirety' (*SST*, p. 75). Derrida emphasizes that what he is talking about in *Monolingualism of the Other* is what he calls '"my case"', but does so only in quotation marks. It is a matter, he says, of '"my case": the at once typical and uncommon situation of which I would like to speak' (*MO*, p. 15). Speaking as an 'exemplary Franco-Maghrebian' (p. 19), he expounds the force of the proposition that '*I only have one language, yet it is not mine*' (p. 2). *Monolingualism of the Other* is thus a political 'demonstration' (p. 72). 'All culture is originarily colonial', he argues: 'Every culture institutes itself through the unilateral imposition of some "politics" of language. Mastery begins ... through the power of naming, of imposing and legitimating appellations' (p. 39). But, as he stresses, 'contrary to what one is often tempted to believe, the master is nothing' (p. 23). For the so-called master 'does not have exclusive possession of anything', in particular he 'does not possess exclusively, and *naturally*, what he calls his language', 'he cannot maintain any relations of property or identity that are natural, national, congenital, or ontological, with it' (p. 23). This is most sharply demonstrated through Derrida's analysis of the word 'I'. Whatever the domain ('politics, religion, the arts, poetry [or] literature'), 'It is necessary to know already in what language *I* is expressed, and *I am* expressed' (p. 28). *Monolingualism of the Other* is not so much an autobiographical text, Derrida says, as an account of what makes 'auto-exposition' (p. 70) rigorously impossible. In whatever autobiographical context, he suggests, 'it is always *imagined* that the one who writes should know how to say *I*'. But 'an identity is never given, received, or attained; only the interminable and indefinitely phantasmatic process of identification endures' (p. 28).

★ Interruption and overlapping of another night letter. I note in passing why I started off with a quotation, with the three words 'in such darkness'. Is there not a sort of counter-example to this argument about 'always *imagin[ing]* that the one who writes should know how to say *I*', to wit in the work of Beckett, for instance from the very title and opening words of *The Unnamable* (*L'Innommable*)?

> Where now? Who now? When now? Unquestioning. I, say I. Unbelieving [*Où main-tenant? Quand maintenant? Qui maintenant? Sans me le demander. Dire je. Sans le penser*] … I shall not be alone, in the beginning. I am of course alone. Alone. That is soon said. Things have to be soon said. And how can one be sure, in such darkness?[11]

But to propose that 'it is always *imagined* that the one who writes should know how to say *I*' is already to be orienting us towards a sort of heterology of orientation, toward that 'thought that has no meaning' (*MO*, p. 6) of which Derrida speaks in *Monolingualism of the Other*. Example and counter-example do not constitute an opposition. In what language should we read Beckett's text and how construe its implications for the place and possibility of a mother tongue? 'The deconstruction of a pedagogical institution and all that it implies', we may recall, would turn above all on what one might call a deconstructive translation-ationality, interfering with the poles of 'nationalism and universalism': 'What this institution cannot bear, is for anyone to tamper with language, meaning *both* the *national* language *and*, paradoxically, an ideal of translatability that neutralizes this national language.'[12] *The Unnamable* and *Monolingualism of the Other* would uncannily harbour one another, sign and countersign one another, in such darkness. Allow me then, passing in the night, in the most telegrammatic fashion, simply to evoke here the thought of a reading of Beckett's work that would attend to its singular engagement with darkness and voice, its effectivity as a kind of night writing, and to suggest that *The Unnamable* / *L'Innommable* is one of the most formidable political texts of the twentieth century.

★ *Monolingualism of the Other* is a political 'demonstration', I was saying: it calls for another thinking of 'politics', starting with the '"politics" of language'. As always in Derrida, it is a matter of a night-voice, of hearing-oneself-speak as 'the most normal and the most impossible experience',[13] a trembling of tone. He declares:

I was the first to be afraid of my own voice, as if it were not mine, and to contest it, even to detest it.

If I have always trembled before what I could say, it was fundamentally [*au fond*] because of the tone, and not the substance [*non du fond*]. And what, obscurely, I seek to impart as if in spite of myself, to give or lend to others as well as to myself, to myself as well as to the other, is perhaps a tone. Everything is summoned from an intonation. (*MO*, p. 48)

If one wants to understand anything about 'deconstruction reading politics', it has to do with a certain tone, as of a certain 'come' of which Derrida has written:

The event of this 'Come' precedes and calls the event. It would be that starting from which there is any event, the coming, the to-come of the event that cannot be thought under the given category of event ... 'Come' no more lets itself be arraigned [*arraisonner*] by an onto-theo-eschatology than by a logic of the event, however new they may be and *whatever politics they announce* ... 'Come' cannot come from a voice or at least from a tone signifying 'I' or 'self', a so-and-so (male or female) ... 'Come' does not address itself to an identity determinable in advance.[14]

★ In such darkness. Bristling. Listen. There is a voice in you which says: Listen. What's in a name, a title, a word, even a hyphen? Out of the night Derrida writes:

therefore invent in *your* language if you can or want to hear mine; invent if you can or want to give my language to be understood, as well as yours, where the event of its prosody only takes place once at home, in the very place where its 'being home' [*son 'chez elle'*] disturbs the co-habitants, the fellow citizens, and the compatriots. Compatriots of every country, translator-poets, rebel against patriotism! Do you hear me! Each time I write a word, a word I love and want to write; in the time of this word, at the instant of a single syllable, the song of this new International awakens in me. I never resist it, I am in the street at its call, even if, apparently, I have been working silently since dawn at my table. (*MO*, p. 57)

Working silently, out of the night, at every word, at every instant recalling that (as Derrida has said elsewhere) 'silence is not exterior to language',[15] wanting to invent in my language, permit me to say a word about an instant that may not be a word, another invocation of silence that punctuates and haunts *Monolingualism of the Other*. Derrida's book is about being 'Franco-Maghrebian'. Everything, he says, is in a sense inscribed in the silence of its hyphen:

The silence of that hyphen does not pacify or appease anything, not a single torment, not a single torture. It will never silence their memory. It could even worsen the terror, the lesions, and the wounds. A hyphen is never enough to conceal protests, cries of anger or suffering, the noise of weapons, airplanes, and bombs. (p. 11)

I would like to consider another hyphen that punctuates *Monolingualism of the Other*, that occurs near the start of the book when Derrida refers to the excessive haste with which 'the reproach of "performative contradiction"' tends to be made nowadays. 'Certain German or Anglo-American theorists', says one of the voices that opens the essay, 'believe they have discovered an unanswerable strategy there. They make a specialty of this puerile weapon' (4). 'Performative contradiction' in this context, then, would be another of those phrases that Derrida finds glib and vacuous, calling to be fenced off with wrought ironic quotation marks. But what about 'Anglo-American'? What is going on with this word or phrase, one that Derrida and no doubt the rest of us use often enough but perhaps too hastily? What is going on in the silence of its hyphen?

★ Nearly twenty years ago, I began what is so inanely called an 'academic publishing career' with a short review of a book by Christopher Norris entitled *Deconstruction: Theory and Practice*. This review was taken up by Terry Eagleton and savaged by him in a further review, which was then taken up by Geoffrey Bennington who (in his characteristically gracious way) savaged Terry Eagleton's review of my review.[16] Such a chain, starting with Norris's book and my more or less insignificant review of it, might at least serve to recall that, how ever marginalized and minuscule, 'deconstruction reading politics' has a history in Britain – a sort of mental history, perhaps, a history that would have to do precisely with the madness of the day, with the nocturnal light of today, of a thinking of the day and of so many yesterdays that would break with any history of the sort that could suppose that deconstruction has done *isms* (in particular poststructuralism and postmodernism), done history, done ethics, and now it is time to do politics – as if Richard Beardsworth's book,[17] brilliant and indispensable as it is, were really completely new, as if 'reading politics' could be something for deconstruction to do, since it hasn't really before, and then it can move on to something else, such as animals ('man is not the only political animal', as Derrida has noted,[18] thereby recalling and affirming another massive dimension for the history and future of 'deconstruction', 'reading' and 'politics'). Rather it is a matter of trying to keep watch over other temporalities and other histories, such as Bennington evokes when he speaks, for example, of Derrida's reading of Rousseau: 'The event constituted by the reading of Rousseau in the *Grammatology*, for example, did not take place in 1967 only later to become absorbed into familiarity, but comprises an essential, persisting *Unheimlichkeit*.'[19] If deconstruction is 'uncanny philosophy' (to recall the terms of Sarah Kofman's reading of Derrida as 'uncanny philosopher'),[20] it is just as much also uncanny history. There is a history concerned with resistance to a certain kind of Marxist intimidation in Britain, a deconstructive history still to be written on the subject of what happened to deconstruction in Britain in the 1980s and 1990s and of what is still persisting. My review of Norris's book focused on deconstruction and institutions in relation to what Derrida, in *Positions*, had called 'The effective violence of disseminating writing'.[21] It spoke of a tampering with language that might begin with the word *déconstruction* itself (or with any other of the many terms singularly associated with Derrida's work): the translation of the word into English, but also the translations *within* 'English' itself. The review thus proposed questioning and tampering with the 'tacitly (institutionally) accepted unity of British and American English, the silent hyphen of "Anglo-American"'.[22] Has this been done? Or is it still to come?

★ It is, perhaps, a matter of voice – difference within hearing oneself speak. In English. We are already speaking English – as Derrida suggests, the living-dead language of Latin,[23] yes, in part, but more specifically what is called English. What is this English that I am speaking, or that I would most love to speak, this English that I dream of speaking, in this context of Derrida-in-English, in an English which is not mine but is also no one else's, above all not the master's, for the master is nothing? 'Anglo' is not the same as 'British'; 'England' is not 'Britain'; 'English' is not the same as 'British'; 'the United States' is not the same as 'America'. But all too frequently they go on being conflated. Derrida's own writings are not exempt in this respect. The aphoristic 'deconstruction is America', near the start of *Mémoires*, might have sounded rather less striking as 'deconstruction is the United States'.[24] In more than one context, both in interview and elsewhere, Derrida has spoken about Britain in terms that seem to suggest that 'Britain' is synonymous with 'England' and 'British' with 'English'.[25] One might say things come to a head, they capitalize themselves most problematically and strangely, in the term 'Anglo-American'. To recall Derrida's declaration in *The Other Heading*: 'the Anglo-American language is today the second universal language [after Latin] destined to overtake or dub all the idioms of the world; and this is one of the essential problems of our culture today, of European culture in particular, of which Anglo-American both is and is not a language' (*OH*, p. 23). Wanting to invent in my language, I have to say I do not imagine I, I do not say I in the 'being home' of something called 'Anglo-American', my I is not 'Anglo-American'. I subscribe entirely to what Derrida says here about 'the Anglo-American' or 'English' language; but I do so necessarily differently, in another language, from the angle of my language, which is not mine. Derrida is working from another angle. In an essay called 'Two Words for Joyce' he writes of 'a *war* through which English tries to erase the other language or languages, to colonize them, to domesticate them, to present them for reading from only one angle'. He goes on to say that 'one must ... write oneself against it'.[26] Me too: me already at least two. I must write myself against it: such would be the very condition of 'deconstruction reading politics'. To invent a language, out of English, against and through it. Night writing: I speak English, I am monolingual and speak a language that is not my own, but I do not have a mother tongue. There is no mother tongue, says Derrida, that is '"entirely" maternal' (*MO*, p. 36), no mother tongue that is not essentially susceptible to substitution, no mother tongue that is distinct from madness even if only as necessary possibility (see *MO*, pp. 87–9). Night writing: this would be a name perhaps for what I dream of, a dream (so powerfully evoked by Derrida in *Monolingualism of the Other*) of 'making something happen to this language' (*MO*, p. 51), to my English, this English.

★ In other words, for example, to Shakespeare's English. 'Political Shakespeare', I hear a voice say: hasn't that been done? One of the best-selling academic books of recent years, both in so-called Shakespeare and Renaissance Studies and more generally in the so-called field of so-called cultural materialism or new historicism (much work still required on the silent hyphen of Anglo-American inscribing itself in the untranslatability or untransatlanticatability of these isms), *Political Shakespeare* is a collection of essays edited by Jonathan Dollimore and Alan Sinfield, originally published in 1985, then reissued in a second edition (1994) with the following declaration on its back cover: '*Political Shakespeare* was a book which some academics tried to prevent being published and which others have been fulminating about ever since. For radical critics and students alike it quickly became a classic text.'[27] No time to dwell on the intricacies of that statement, except to say that I feel what Derrida would perhaps call a 'dual allegiance', and that, while I admire this book and admire the work of both its editors and support many of its proclaimed or implicit 'political aims', I also feel a distance and have to confess to a little uncertainty about its claims to radicalism ('for radical critics and students alike'). I feel this from the opening page of its Introduction. *Political Shakespeare* begins with the claim that 'One of the most important achievements of "theory" in English studies has been the making possible a truly interdisciplinary approach to ... the subject'; 'With the various structuralisms, Marxism, psychoanalysis, semiotics and post-structuralism, there occurred a significant dismantling of barriers (barriers of exclusion as well as of containment)'. This happened, we are told, because of the emergence of 'new conceptions of philosophy and history'.[28] I would like only to note that 'the subject' (i.e. so-called 'English studies') becomes the problematic, though tacit and apparently unquestioned, principle of unification here; that I cannot use or mention the phrase 'truly interdisciplinary' without smiling or pain; and that the 'new conceptions of philosophy and history' with which *Political Shakespeare* purports to be concerned have, apparently, nothing whatever to do with deconstruction. Some 'barriers of exclusion' or 'containment' may have undergone dismantling; but this particular exclusion is rigorously conformed to throughout the book. 'Political Shakespeare' has, apparently, nothing to do with the work of Derrida or deconstruction. Contrariwise, as Tweedledee might say, I would like to propose that there can be no 'political Shakespeare' today, in the madness of today, that does not go by way of deconstruction. A political reading of Shakespeare, in other words, at least in the sense in which Derrida's work might encourage us to think about it, has perhaps hardly begun, is still to come.

★ A question of voice, I was suggesting, of something that Derrida's work might lead us towards in relation to Shakespeare's English: another English, English otherwise, a monolingualism beside itself. Something to be thought starting out from a recognition of Shakespeare, the name and work, as linked to the very essence of so-called Englishness. 'The time is out of joint': Derrida's argument in *Spectres of Marx* is about a thinking of the political in terms of the *'non-contemporaneity with itself of the living present'*,[29] the darkness or blink of the madness of the day, of the eye on the clock-face. I quote:

> Time is off its hinges, time is off course, beside itself, disadjusted. Says Hamlet. Who thereby opened one of those breaches, often they are poetic and thinking peepholes [*meurtrières*, says the French, with a sense also then of something like 'death-trap' in English, as well as 'murderess'], through which Shakespeare will have kept watch over the English language and at the same time signed its body [*son corps*], with the same unprecedented stroke, of some arrow. (*SM*, p. 18/42, translation slightly modified)

If *Hamlet* is, for Derrida, an exemplary work for thinking together about the current state of the world as belonging to a time that is 'out of joint', for thinking about spectrality and for thinking about a future politics and new enlightenment, this exemplarity is indissociably bound up with what *Hamlet* might have to teach us about language. Shakespeare is viewed, then, as a sort of night watchman, *in arms*; 'Shakespeare' as the name of something, somebody, a ghost or gathering of ghostly effects, that keeps watch over the English language. Wouldn't Derrida be similar to Shakespeare, precisely in terms of this concern to keep watch over a language, knowing that there is no *one* language, that there is always more and other than *a* language? Isn't this his concern, in *Monolingualism of the Other*, when he talks of himself, or of someone in him, who is trying to 'listen' (in double quotation marks) to the 'last will of the language' as if he were the 'last heir, the last defender and illustrator of the French language' (*MO*, p. 47)? And isn't this how it is, whenever someone wants to invent? Isn't that the very desire of what is called 'love of the language'? How might we try to listen to Shakespeare's English in this context?

★ Derrida's published texts on Shakespeare are night letters of a sort, essays about *the night*. In particular his aphoristic essay on *Romeo and Juliet* and his account of *Hamlet* in *Spectres of Marx* are readings in the night: Shakespeare at night, on the night. Of *Romeo and Juliet* Derrida writes:

> This drama belongs to the night because it stages what cannot be seen, the name; it stages what one calls because one cannot see or because one is not certain of seeing what one calls. Theatre of the name, theatre of night. The name calls beyond presence, phenomenon, light, beyond the day, beyond the theatre. It keeps – whence the mourning and survival – what is no longer present, the invisible: what from now on will no longer see the light of day.[30]

Derrida's analysis of Juliet's analysis of the name ('O Romeo, Romeo, wherefore art thou Romeo?')[31] is doubtless not limited to the example of the name 'Romeo' but can be linked to his many other readings of the name, as uncanny bearer of death and principle of living on. One's name is familiarity itself, but it is also perhaps the strangest 'thing' in the world. It is one's own, the very home of who one is, of who it is who says 'I', even while it harbours, prescribes, programs the unthinkable: structured to outlive its bearer, it is an invisible tombstone one carries about every day.[32] It is the very night of the 'everyday'. Derrida's reading of *Romeo and Juliet* and especially of the so-called balcony scene might be traced out, in crepuscular fashion, as a reading of and in the name of 'night', the name as 'night' and 'night' as rigorously platitudinous name of the impossible. 'Bescreen'd in night' (2.2.52), Romeo declares: 'I have night's cloak to hide me' (2.2.75). Juliet remarks that she has 'the mask of night' (85) on her face. Romeo and Juliet personify night. Shakespeare's *Romeo and Juliet* is 'theatre of the name, theatre of night', it stages the night of the name, night in the name.

★ How might one hear the word 'night' in *Hamlet*, in Shakespeare's night watching death-trap English? Night is the name. 'A voice comes to one in the dark. Imagine.'[33] In such darkness. A solitary star. Unless another. Another still. Peeping through.

★ If Shakespeare through 'poetic and thinking peepholes ... will have kept watch over the English language', the rhythm or resonance of this might be felt in the operations and effects of a single word, if it is one: *night*. 'Night', in *Hamlet*, comports with the logic that Derrida analyses under the proposition that 'The time is out of joint'.[34] The play opens at night, with night, with a sense of fear around whether one can say, with assurance, with any sense of proper meaning, 'good night'.

> *Barnardo*: Have you had quiet guard?
> *Francisco*: Not a mouse stirring.
> *Barnardo*: Well, good night.
> (1.1.10–12)

When Horatio and Marcellus come to replace Barnardo, 'good night' returns, now in a form apparently more religious, more Christianizing, though the name of God is itself absent. It is as if 'good night' could be given, without a subject:

> *Francisco*:   Stand, ho! Who is there?
> *Horatio*: Friends to this ground.
> *Marcellus*:   And liegemen to the Dane.
> *Francisco*: Give you good night.
> *Marcellus*: O, farewell honest soldier, who hath reliev'd you?
> *Francisco*: Barnardo hath my place. Give you good night. [*Exit*]
> (1.1.15–19)

'Good night' is the time of exit, the time perhaps of Shakespeare's play as a whole. When is night? What is night? Or who? Can one ever say 'good night' or claim to understand what it could mean?

★ The time of night is the time of the Ghost. 'Fad[ing] on the crowing of the cock' (1.1.162), 'Doom'd for a certain term to walk the night' (1.5.10), the Ghost is identified with the night, but more particularly with an exact moment, 'jump at this dead hour' (1.1.68), 'the dead waste and middle of the night' (1.2.198). The scenes of *Hamlet* concerned with night watching are not only or not simply night-scenes: they also contain numerous evocations of an uncertain mixing of light and night, of 'night' as 'joint-labourer with the day' (1.1.81), of being 'sick almost to doomsday with eclipse' (1.1.123). As Horatio says, at the sound or thought of the ghost as the old mole, underground, in the dark: 'O day and night, but this is wondrous strange' (1.5.172). The Ghost is identified with the night, with the desert or what Horatio calls 'the dead waste' of the night. But the Ghost is *at the same time* that which 'usurp'st this time of night' (1.1.49). The 'jump' of the 'dead hour' of night is a jump, a usurping of time itself, absolute interruption and disordering of night. There is a need for new principles of intelligibility in reading, watching and listening to Shakespeare's plays, for example in terms of what might be called dramaturgic or theatrical telepathy, in other words in terms of the fact that in a play such as *Hamlet* characters seem to pick up on words, thoughts and feelings, resonances of words associated with other characters whose speech nevertheless they did not witness.[35] The logic of such telepathy bids good night to any conventional understanding of character, identity or subjectivity, plot or narrative. Polonius of course was not present (at least not in any conventional sense) and did not witness any of these discussions, these terrible uncertainties, these usurpations of time itself. Yet he seems, by this structure of theatrical telepathy, to pick up on it all when, in Act 2 scene 2, he expostulates on expostulating into what may be called the experience of tautology: 'to expostulate / What majesty should be, what duty is, / Why day is day, night night, and time is time, / Were nothing but to waste night, day, and time' (2.2.86–9). The 'waste' of 'night' returns, in this lucid interval of dramaturgic telepathy, in the madness of a juxtaposition in which 'night' both is and is not 'night': 'night' is beside itself, at the same time the same and another 'night' in 'night night'. Only with 'night' does Polonius elide the 'is'; the style, the syntax and, perhaps, the tone, the 'differential vibration' (as Derrida calls it)[36] would carry this singular telepathy of the waste of night.

★ One wants to be able to say 'good night'. But how? Can one ever truly say 'good night', in oneself, to oneself or to another, in the name of oneself or of another? Shakespeare's *Hamlet* hesitates here. Hamlet dies and Horatio says: 'Now cracks a noble heart. Good night, sweet prince' (5.2.364). Horatio's words, one may suppose, are spoken to the dead: 'Good night' would be prosopopoeia, delirious euphemism, impossible speech. Tracing out the strange lineaments of theatrical telepathy, Horatio's words 'Good night, sweet prince' uncannily pick up the mad Ophelia's 'good night. Sweet ladies, good night' (4.5.72–3). Similarly, Horatio cannot have known, cannot have heard the differently wild and whirling speech of Hamlet himself as he leaves his mother, lugging out the body of the man he has just killed, with the words, 'Good night, mother' (3.4.219). One is tempted to say that 'Good night' always sounds as if it is already a quotation, hence perhaps its peculiar ghostly effectivity in T. S. Eliot's *The Waste Land*);[37] but in 'quoting' Ophelia's words so closely and in 'quoting' (without knowing he is quoting) Hamlet's parting words to his mother, Horatio's final or post-final address, his posthumous spectralized and spectralizing 'Good night, sweet prince', is a madness. 'Good night' is, perhaps, the epitome of the colloquial: any and every-one can say it. The phrase is so conventional, so familiar, it doesn't require a second's reflection. And yet, it belongs to the liminal, belongs without belong-ing, at and as the very border: has 'night' ever quite begun when one says 'good night'? Strange 'object' of a performative, when will it have begun? In particular as a so-called euphemism for 'death' ('die well', 'happy death', 'have a good death now'), it names the unthinkable. But this unthinkable haunts every 'good night'. 'Good night' is mad. Impossible schibboleth. One might thus hear in it, at the very 'waste' of it, that 'differential vibration, without support, insupportable', as Derrida says of the 'come' in his essay on apocalyptic tone.[38] Madness of the 'good night' at the heart of Shakespeare, at the heart of 'his' English, at the heart of 'Englishness' perhaps (for let us not forget that 'good night' in *Hamlet* is not only specifically identified with ghosts, madness and death, but also with England: Hamlet's 'Good night, mother' are his parting words before going to England, to the country where, in the terms of this play, everyone is 'mad', 'strangely' mad (5.i.150–4)), telepathic 'good night' generated out of multiple voices, in a time belonging to no one, beyond any identity of writer, actor or character, spectator or listener, 'good night' to come, still to be understood, still to be heard.

★ Derrida's *Spectres of Marx* is night writing, on the subject of 'learning to live': this, he remarks, is 'ethics itself' (*SM*, xviii). 'What follows', he declares at the start of the book, 'advances like an essay in the night – into the unknown of that which must remain to come' (*SM*, xviii). A certain madness must keep watch over thinking, in other words a certain thinking of night, of nocturnal light, of a new enlightenment as heterophotological. But the movement into 'the unknown of that which must remain to come' is also linked to the sense that, as Derrida observes in 'Force and Signification', 'writing is inaugural'.[39] When one writes one does not know what one is going to find oneself saying or trying to say. To write is to advance into night, to engage with the unseen and unforeseeable, like some-one who is blind. Derrida is like a blind man. As he says in *Monolingualism of the Other*:

> Everything I do, especially when I am writing, resembles a game of blindman's buff: the one who is writing, always by hand, even when using machines, holds out his hand like a blind man seeking to touch the one whom he could thank for the gift of a language, for the very words in which he declares himself ready to give thanks. And to beg for mercy as well.
>
> While the other, more prudent, hand, another blindman's hand, tries to protect against the fall, against a headlong, premature fall, in a word, against haste. (*MO*, 64–5)

In this sense, writing is a kind of drawing. As Derrida remarks in *Memoirs of the Blind*, in the context of that '*trait*' which will have set drawing going: 'Even if drawing is, as they say, mimetic, that is, reproductive, figurative, representative, even if the model is presently facing the artist, the *trait* must proceed in the night.' This 'night', he goes on to say, can be interpreted either 'as a reserve of visibility (the draftsman does not presently see but he has seen and will see again)', or 'as radically and definitively foreign to the phenomenality of the day'.[40] *Spectres of Marx* is 'like an essay in the night', then, in at least these two senses. Derrida does not know, he cannot see, where he is going or being led: this is also the 'logic of spectrality', which, as he says, is 'inseparable from the very motif ... of deconstruction' (*SM*, 178, n. 3). Advancing into the night, where does he stop? *Spectres of Marx* concludes with a return to the night of *Hamlet*, to the responsibility of being a scholar, to the question of response and address in the night (*Thou art a scholar; speak to it, Horatio*: 176). In other words, it ends with a discussion of the uncanny.

★ Night spuks. Something, finally, 'blinks and sparkles' (*SM*, 174). Derrida concludes *Spectres of Marx* by suggesting that everything he has been saying is a matter of the uncanny, *das Unheimliche*. Marx, Freud, Heidegger – none of them, Derrida says, began 'where [they] ought to have "been able to begin" (*beginnen können*), namely with haunting, before life *as such*, before death *as such* ... Th[is] fault, in any case, by definition, is repeated, we inherit it, we must watch over it' (175). The uncanny is what will have come back, haunting Derrida's work from the beginning, or from 'where he ought to have "been able to begin"'. Of that essay or address in the night entitled *Spectres of Marx*, he observes in the closing pages: 'The subtitle of this address could thus have been: "Marx – *das Unheimliche*"' (174). Likewise in relation to the work of Freud and Heidegger. There is a 'recourse' to the uncanny, to a thinking of *das Unheimliche* and to 'the value of *Unheimlichkeit*' that might yet open on to a quite different thinking of ethics and politics. Derrida remarks:

> In both discourses, that of Freud and that of Heidegger, this recourse [to the uncanny] makes possible fundamental projects or trajectories. But it does so while destabilizing permanently, and in a more or less subterranean fashion, the order of conceptual distinctions that are put to work. It should disturb both the ethics and the politics that follow implicitly or explicitly from that order. (*SM*, 174)

★ Deconstruction would be uncanny politics. This is the point from which we ought to have been able to begin. A point that would be double, in accord with those figures of the double, double-consciousness, double gesture, double writing, 'dual allegiance' that pervade Derrida's work. As he remarks in an 1981 interview with Richard Kearney:

> the difficulty is to gesture in opposite directions at the same time: on the one hand to preserve a distance and suspicion with regard to the official political codes governing reality; on the other, to intervene here and now in a practical and *engagé* manner whenever the necessity arises. This position of dual allegiance ... is one of perpetual uneasiness.[41]

Deconstruction is not concerned with setting up an alternative politics that would take over and replace 'the official political codes governing reality'. As Derrida has elsewhere emphasised: 'the idea that a deconstructive discourse might come to command and replace other practices, discursive or not, is a kind of madness or comedy that doesn't interest me in the least'.[42] There is politics *and* politics: 'politics' beside itself, politics identifiable only through an uncanny 'and'.[43] It is a matter, then, of what he calls 'a different politics ... a different theory of politics, and a different delimitation of the *socius*, especially in relation to citizenship and State-nationhood in general, and more broadly to identity and subjectivity as well'.[44] The uncanny politics of deconstruction will have begun with the 'I', and first of all with the encounter between the 'I' and the uncanny, the 'I' and spectrality, the 'I' as a ghost. In *Monolingualism of the Other* Derrida remarks that the 'I' is 'not independent of language' but, as a prosthesis of origin, will only ever have '*formed* itself ... at the site of a *situation* that cannot be found, a site always referring elsewhere, to something other, to another language, to the other in general'. He adds: 'There was no thinkable or thinking *I* before this strangely familiar and properly improper (uncanny, *unheimlich*) situation of an uncountable language' (29).

NOTES

1   Maurice Blanchot, 'The Outside, the Night', in *The Space of Literature*, trans. Ann Smock (Lincoln: University of Nebraska Press, 1982), p. 163.

2   The present chapter is a modified version of a paper originally presented at a conference on 'Deconstruction Reading Politics', at the University of Staffordshire, July 1998.

3   I am here indebted to the work of the late Bill Readings, especially to his account of the 'university of excellence' in *The University in Ruins* (Cambridge, Mass.: Harvard University Press, 1996). I discuss this book in more detail in Chapter 3 above.

4   Jacques Derrida, *The Other Heading: Reflections on Today's Europe*, trans. Pascale-Anne Brault and Michael B. Naas (Bloomington: Indiana University Press, 1992), p. 39. Further page references will be given parenthetically in the text, abbreviated '*OH*' where appropriate.

5   Blanchot, 'The Outside, the Night', p. 163.

6   Cf. Derrida's remark in 'White Mythology': 'The very opposition of appearing and disappearing, the entire lexicon of the *phainesthai*, of *aletheia*, etc, of day and night, of the visible and the invisible, of the present and the absent – all this is possible only under the sun.' See Jacques Derrida, 'White Mythology: Metaphor in the Text of Philosophy', in *Margins of Philosophy*, trans. Alan Bass (London: University of Chicago Press, 1982), p. 251.

7   Franz Kafka, 'The Burrow', trans. Willa and Edwin Muir, in *The Complete Short Stories*, ed. Nahum N. Glatzer (London: Minerva, 1992), pp. 325–59.

8   Jacques Derrida, *Monolingualism of the Other; or, The Prosthesis of Origin*, trans. Patrick Mensah (Stanford: Stanford University Press, 1998). Further page references will be given parenthetically in the text, abbreviated '*MO*' where appropriate.

9   Jacques Derrida, *Points ... Interviews, 1974–1994*, ed. Elisabeth Weber, trans. Peggy Kamuf et al. (London: Routledge, 1995), p. 352. Further page references will be given parenthetically in the text, abbreviated '*P*' where appropriate.

10   Jacques Derrida, 'Some Statements and Truisms about Neo-logisms, Newisms, Postisms, Parasitisms, and other Small Seismisms', trans. Anne Tomiche, in *The States of 'Theory': History, Art and Critical Discourse*, ed. David Carroll (New York: Columbia University Press, 1990), pp. 63–95: here, p. 74. Further page references will be given parenthetically in the text, abbreviated '*SST*' where appropriate.

11   Samuel Beckett, *Molloy: Malone Dies: The Unnamable* (London: Calder and Boyars, 1966), pp. 294–5; *L'Innommable* (Paris: Minuit, 1959), pp. 7–8.

12   Jacques Derrida, 'Border Lines', trans. James Hulbert, in Harold Bloom et al., *Deconstruction and Criticism* (New York: Seabury Press, 1979), pp. 75–176: here, p. 94.

13   'Qual Quelle: Valéry's Sources', in *Margins of Philosophy*, trans. Alan Bass (Chicago: Chicago University Press, 1982), pp. 273–306: here, p. 297.

14   Jacques Derrida, 'Of an Apocalyptic Tone Recently Adopted in Philosophy', trans. John P. Leavey, Jr, *Oxford Literary Review*, vol. 6, no. 2 (1984), 3–37: here, pp. 33–4 (my emphasis).

15   Jacques Derrida, 'Force of Law: The "Mystical Foundation of Authority"', trans. Mary Quaintance, *Cardozo Law Review*, vol. 11, no. 5/6 (1990), 921–1045: here, p. 943.

16   See Christopher Norris, *Deconstruction: Theory and Practice* (London: Methuen, 1981); Nick Royle, 'Nor is Deconstruction', *Oxford Literary Review*, vol. 5, no. 1–2 (1982), pp. 170–7; Terry Eagleton, review of *OLR*, in *Literature and History*, vol. 10, no. 1 (1984), 134–6; Geoffrey Bennington, 'Deconstruction and the Philosophers (The Very Idea)' (1988), in his *Legislations: The Politics of Deconstruction* (London: Verso, 1994), p. 56, n. 45.

17   Richard Beardsworth, *Derrida and the Political* (London: Routledge, 1996).

18   Jacques Derrida, 'Afterword: Toward an Ethic of Discussion', trans. Samuel Weber, in *Limited Inc* (Evanston, Ill: Northwestern University Press, 1988), p. 136.

19   Geoffrey Bennington, 'Derridabase', in Bennington and Derrida, *Jacques Derrida*, trans. Bennington (Chicago: Chicago University Press, 1993), p. 252.

20   Sarah Kofman, 'Un philosophe "unheimlich"', in *Lectures de Derrida* (Paris: Galilée, 1984), pp. 11–114. Kofman gives particular emphasis to what Derrida does with 'the uncanny "disruptiveness of writing", "its aphoristic energy" (p. 15, quoting *Of Grammatology*), especially in relation to that other great modern uncanny discourse, psychoanalysis.

21   Jacques Derrida, *Positions*, trans. Alan Bass (Chicago: Chicago University Press, 1981), p. 85.

22   'Nor Is Deconstruction', p. 176.

23   See Jacques Derrida, 'Faith and Knowledge: The Two Sources of "Religion" at the Limits of Reason Alone', trans. Sam Weber, in *Religion*, ed. Jacques Derrida and Gianni Vattimo (Cambridge: Polity Press, 1998), p. 27.

24   See Jacques Derrida, *Mémoires: For Paul de Man*, trans. Cecile Lindsay, Jonathan Culler and Eduardo Cadava (New York: Columbia University Press, 1986), p. 18; and cf. 'The Time Is Out of Joint', trans. Peggy Kamuf, in *Deconstruction is/in America: A New Sense of the Political*, ed. Anselm Haverkamp (New York: New York University Press, 1995), pp. 16–17. It is significant, perhaps, that the word 'America' (in particular as an assumed synonym for 'the United States of America') is not subjected to questioning either in *Mémoires* itself or in the book *Deconstruction is/in America*. In the case of the latter, the closest thing to an exception comes, I believe, when Gayatri Spivak briefly refers to the tacit violence whereby 'The United States gives itself the right to the proper name "America"': see Spivak, 'At the *Planchette* of Deconstruction is/in America', p. 242.

25   See, for example, '*Honoris Causa*: "This is *also* extremely funny"', in *Points ...*, pp. 407, 413, and *Spectres of Marx: The State of the Debt, the Work of Mourning, and the New International*, trans. Peggy Kamuf (New York: Routledge, 1994), p. 178 n. 3.

26   Jacques Derrida, 'Two Words for Joyce', trans. Geoff Bennington, in *Post-structuralist Joyce: Essays from the French*, eds Derek Attridge and Daniel Ferrer (Cambridge: Cambridge University Press, 1984), 145–59: here p. 156.

27   Jonathan Dollimore and Alan Sinfield, eds, *Political Shakespeare*, 2nd edn (Manchester: Manchester University Press, 1994).

28   Dollimore and Sinfield, *Political Shakespeare*, p. 2.

29   Derrida, *Spectres of Marx*, p.xix. Further page references will be given parenthetically in the text, abbreviated '*SM*' where appropriate. These are followed by a slash and page reference to the original French text (*Spectres de Marx: L'État de la dette, le travail du deuil et la nouvelle Internationale* (Paris: Galilée, 1993)), where appropriate.

30   Jacques Derrida, 'Aphorism Countertime', trans. Nicholas Royle, in *Acts of Literature*, ed. Derek Attridge (London and New York: Routledge, 1992), 414–33: here, p. 425.

31   William Shakespeare, *Romeo and Juliet*, ed. Brian Gibbons (London: Methuen, 1980), 2.1.33. Further references are to this edition, given parenthetically in the text.

32   Cf. Derrida's poly-rhetorical question in 'Fors': 'To what does a name go back? But a *present* going back, a going back in the present, a bringing back to the present, to whatever kind of haunting return or *unheimlich* homecoming – isn't all that already the law of the name?' See Jacques Derrida, 'Fors: The Anglish Words of Nicolas Abraham and Maria Torok', trans. Barbara Johnson, in Abraham and Torok, *The Wolf Man's Magic Word: A Cryptonymy*, trans. Nicholas Rand (Minneapolis: University of Minnesota Press, 1986), p. xlviii.

33   Samuel Beckett, *Company* (London: John Calder, 1980), p. 7.

34   See 'The Time Is Out of Joint': Derrida takes this phrase from *Hamlet*, 1.5.196. Further references to *Hamlet* are to the Arden edition (London: Methuen, 1980), ed. Harold Jenkins, and will be given parenthetically in the text.

35   For further discussion of dramaturgic telepathy, see Nicholas Royle, *Telepathy and Literature: Essays on the Reading Mind* (Oxford: Basil Blackwell, 1991), esp. pp. 146–59.

36   See Jacques Derrida, 'Of an Apocalyptic Tone Recently Adopted in Philosophy', p. 24.

37   See *The Waste Land*, in T. S. Eliot, *Complete Poems* (London: Faber and Faber, 1962). For a fine account of uncanny citationality in Eliot's poem see Maud Ellmann, '*The Waste Land*: A Sphinx without a Secret', in her *The Poetics of Impersonality: T. S. Eliot and Ezra Pound* (Brighton: Harvester Press, 1987), pp. 91–113. For two further accounts of uncanniness in Eliot's poetry see James Longenbach, 'Uncanny Eliot', in *T. S. Eliot: Man and Poet*, ed. Laura Cowan, 1 (Orono, Maine: National Poetry Foundation, 1990), pp. 47–69; and Charles Ferrall, *Modernist Writing and Reactionary Politics* (Cambridge: Cambridge University Press, 2001), esp. Chapter 3,

'"Neither Living nor Dead": T. S. Eliot and the Uncanny', pp. 71–114.

38 Derrida, 'Of an Apocalyptic Tone Recently Adopted in Philosophy', p. 24.

39 Jacques Derrida, 'Force and Signification', in *Writing and Difference*, trans. Alan Bass (London: Routledge and Kegan Paul, 1978), pp. 3–30: here, p. 11.

40 Jacques Derrida, *Memoirs of the Blind: The Self-portrait and Other Ruins*, trans. Pascale-Anne Brault and Michael Naas (Chicago: Chicago University Press, 1993), p. 45.

41 Jacques Derrida, 'Deconstruction and the Other', Interview with Richard Kearney, in Kearney, *Dialogues with Contemporary Continental Thinkers* (Manchester: Manchester University Press, 1984), pp. 105–26: here, p. 120.

42 Jacques Derrida, 'Politics and Friendship: An Interview with Jacques Derrida', in *The Althusserian Legacy*, eds E. Ann Kaplan and Michael Sprinker (London: Verso, 1994), pp. 183–231: here, p. 229.

43 For an account of the supplementarity of the 'and' in this context see Jacques Derrida, 'Et Cetera', trans. Geoffrey Bennington, in *Deconstructions: A User's Guide*, ed. Nicholas Royle (Basingstoke and New York: Palgrave, 2000), esp. pp. 299–300.

44 Jacques Derrida, 'The Deconstruction of Actuality: An Interview with Jacques Derrida', trans. Jonathan Rée, *Radical Philosophy*, vol. 68 (1994), 28–41: here, p. 36.

9
Inexplicable

Darkness returns. Towards the end of Freud's essay on the uncanny there is a personal anecdote that has drawn comparatively little attention from readers and critics:

> In the middle of the isolation of war-time a number of the English *Strand Magazine* fell into my hands; and, among other somewhat redundant matter, I read a story about a young married couple who moved into a furnished house in which there is a curiously shaped table with carvings of crocodiles on it. Towards evening an intolerable and very specific smell begins to pervade the house; they stumble over something in the dark; they seem to see a vague form gliding over the stairs – in short, we are given to understand that the presence of the table causes ghostly crocodiles to haunt the place, or that the wooden monsters come to life in the dark, or something of the sort. It was a naïve enough story, but the uncanny feeling it produced was quite remarkable. (U, p. 367)

This is a key passage for exploring the idea that Freud's 'uncanny' turns upon the experience of reading. Recalling his experience of a short story about 'ghostly crocodiles', he highlights the uncanniness of reading as such, the capacity for reading to produce uncanny feelings. Just a moment earlier he has noted that 'an uncanny effect is often produced when the distinction between imagination and reality is effaced' (U, p. 367) – as if the terms 'reality' and 'imagination' were somehow written in stone, prehistoric in their meaning, impervious to any psychoanalytic thinking, as if psychoanalysis were ever concerned with *anything but* displacements, disturbances and refigurations of 'the distinction between imagination and reality'! The distinction between 'imagination and reality' (or, we might suppose, a short story and a psychoanalytic study) is now most dramatically effaced by the fact that Freud's story about the story about the ghostly crocodiles runs completely counter to his own claim to being someone who 'must plead guilty to a special obtuseness in the matter [of the uncanny]', someone for whom experiences of the uncanny are, at best, dim and distant memories. As he firmly declares near the beginning of the essay: 'It is long since he [i.e. this author, me, Freud] has experienced or heard of anything which has given him an uncanny impression' (U, p. 340). Here is the man who is not susceptible to having uncanny experiences, recalling a story that produced a powerful feeling of uncanniness in him: 'the uncanny feeling it produced was quite remarkable [*ihre unheimliche Wirkung verspürte man als ganz hervorragend*]' (U, p. 367/258). As the original German suggests, the uncanny effect of this story 'was felt very strongly', 'its uncanny effect was outstanding'. In recounting this story from the *Strand Magazine*, Freud makes himself double. In this way he repeats a gesture characteristic of his essay as a whole. As Robin Lydenberg has described it: 'In "The Uncanny" Freud defensively doubles himself in his personal anecdotes [such as his account of the story from the *Strand Magazine*], splitting into controlling narrator and helpless protagonist.'¹ As personal anecdote, Freud's account articulates an experience of reading that is cryptic, private, unverifiable. It generates a 'special obtuseness' of its own, disturbing any supposition of Freud as reliable narrator or as allegedly detached, objective, scientific observer. It accentuates the very effacement with which the uncanny is said to be associated: the uncanny undoes any certainty about what is real and what is not, about where literature ends and real life or science or psychoanalysis or philosophy or literary criticism begins.

There is something quite touching, even beautiful about Freud's account of reading 'a number of the English *Strand Magazine*'. We are drawn into the strange silence and solitude of reading, into a world where, we perhaps discover, we already were. Freud emphasizes the solitude of the scene: it is 'in the middle of the isolation of war-time'. As if from nowhere, by uncanny chance, 'a number of the English *Strand Magazine* fell into my hands' (or, more literally, 'came into my hand': *Mitten in der Absperrung des Weltkrieges kam eine Nummer des englischen Magazins 'Strand' in meine Hände* (258)). Freud is, literally, stranded.

He does not tell us what the story is called, or the name of its author, or where exactly it is to be found. He leaves us in the dark. What are we to make of this? Does he omit to provide a conventional 'scholarly' footnote reference to the title and location of this story because all readers can be assumed to have numbers of the *Strand Magazine* at their fingertips, potentially falling into their hands at any time? Or is it because Freud does not have the 'number' in question, it came into his hand and went away again, back into the dark, and he does not regard it as necessary or worthwhile or even practicable to track down the volume concerned and supply the reference? How should we read such omissions? It is always possible that Freud was concerned for us *not to know* more details about the story. Like Goethe, it might be said, Freud is at once 'a great self-revealer' and 'a careful concealer'.² If it suits Freud's purposes better, would this be a matter of suppression (he wants us to know only what he tells us, it is better that way) or repression (there are unconscious reasons for not recalling the text in greater detail)? We cannot know. Stranded in a reminiscence about a story that created a very strong uncanny feeling in him, Freud effectively strands us.

Entitled 'Inexplicable', written by L. G. Moberly, the story appeared in 1917. The text is embellished with illustrations, including a number of crocodiles, by Dudley Tennant.[3] Given the anonymity and obscurity in which Freud's essay leaves it, there is something curious about approaching the text. It is difficult not to feel, however flickeringly, the sense of an encounter with 'what ought to have remained … hidden but has come to light' (U, p. 345). There is the feeling of 'sharing Freud's reading', an impossible companionship, the strange 'isolation' of reading for the first time this 'secret story' of Freud. His summary of the text is misleading or incorrect in at least two ways. First, he says the couple move into 'a furnished house [*möblierte Wohnung*, "furnished apartment"], in which there is a curiously shaped table with carvings of crocodiles on it' (U, p. 367/258). In fact, it is a significant and emphatic point in the story that the house is very much a house (a property so substantial, indeed, that it transpires to have its own 'cottage at the end of the garden' (p. 579)), and that it is *not* furnished: the mystery is why the owner or owners, or previous tenant or tenants, have left the table behind. In other words, whether through misremembering or misrepresentation, it is more specifically a case of a 'haunted house' ('*ein Haus in dem es spukt*' (U, pp. 364/255)) than Freud's summary might seem to suggest. His describing the property as 'furnished' also suggests that there is something funny going on. It is as if he has felt a need to fill the house (or 'apartment') with his own furniture. Second, Freud's summary of the story condenses the action into one day ('Towards evening an intolerable and very specific smell begins to pervade the house'), and into a single shared experience ('they stumble over something in the dark'). In fact the action is spread over many days and entails (so to speak) various 'queer' (p. 573), 'funny' (p. 574) 'uncanny' (p. 578) slithering encounters with crocodiles, experienced not only by the couple (May and Hugh) themselves, but also by the servants and by an old friend of Hugh's, Jack Wilding.

In furnishing the house with his own imagination and telescoping the events into a single day, Freud's account presents another perspective for thinking about the initial supposition which appeared to get him started off on Moberly's story in the first place, namely that 'an uncanny effect is often and easily produced when the distinction between imagination and reality is effaced'. For there is a 'reality' of the story here which Freud, for whatever reasons, misses, misremembers, misrepresents, distorts. His account, in other words, presents us with an effacement of the distinction between imagination and reality before we even begin to consider how the story itself (rather than his fictionalizing recollection of it) is concerned with such an effacement.

L. G. Moberly's 'Inexplicable' begins:

The hinges were rusty, the gate swinging to behind me creaked dismally, and as the latch clicked into its socket with a sharp clang I started. That clanging sound drew from the depths of my subconscious self some old stories of prison doors and turn-keys. And I actually glanced nervously over my shoulder at the suburban road which trailed to right and left of the gate I had just entered, although anything less calculated to inspire nervous tremors than that stretch of ordinary road lined by ordinary houses could not be imagined! (p. 572)

This opening paragraph does at least three things that might be regarded as characteristic of 'the uncanny as it is depicted in literature' (U, p. 372). First, like so many other cases (from *Wuthering Heights* onwards), it is a story about a house, and more particularly a new 'home', and it begins at the threshold, with a complexity and uncertainty of crossing a threshold, with an experience of liminality (the word comes from the Latin 'limen', threshold). Second, it foregrounds a sense of the familiar or 'ordinary' (the house is in such an 'ordinary road lined by ordinary houses'): uncanniness is indissociably bound up with the ordinary or familiar. Finally, the opening paragraph of Moberly's story is self-reflexive in the sense that it remarks on its own participation in a certain tradition of supernatural, gothic or uncanny fiction ('old stories of prison doors and turn-keys'). In signalling its own status as a story, in implicitly evoking its own fictionality, 'Inexplicable' (like so many other uncanny literary narratives) does not reduce but rather complicates and even deepens the singularity of its claims to a certain eerie 'reality'.

Two other small but perhaps significant details might be mentioned in relation to the opening paragraph of 'Inexplicable'. First, there is a concern with the strangeness of sounds – a creaking, a click, a clang. This sense of eeriness in the ear, the 'eariness' of the uncanny, recurs throughout the story. There is, for example, the sound of the house-agent's clerk's repeated phrase about the crocodile-table ('in the dimness that had temporarily descended upon my brain I thought he went on repeating, like a parrot-cry, "It goes with the house. It goes with the house"': p. 572); the repeated 'prodigious crack', the 'funny sort of crack' p. (574) made by this piece of furniture; the sudden sound 'like a far-away bellowing – not precisely the bellowing of cattle, but a more sinister, more horrible sound, pregnant with evil' (p. 576); and last, but perhaps not least, the 'sliding and pattering' (p. 579) of crocodiles in the darkness overrunning the house. Once again, that is to say, this story provides striking examples of an auditory dimension that is crucial to a critical apprehension of 'the uncanny'.

The second detail is one Freud could hardly have failed to notice, namely the allusion to a 'subconscious self': 'That clanging sound drew from the depths of my subconscious self some old stories of prison doors and turn-keys.' However 'simple' or 'naïve' ('*einfältig*': p. 258) Freud may have considered Moberly's story to be, it shows certain slippery or slithery qualities from the start. Indeed, like any literary fiction, it starts before the start. This is evident in the way the text alludes to a tradition of narrative fiction ('old stories of prison doors and turn-keys'). But it is also evident in the play within the word 'start' itself – the verb that governs, as one says, the opening sentence: 'The hinges were rusty, the gate swinging to behind me creaked dismally, and as the latch clicked into its socket with a sharp clang I started.' The narrator's 'start', it turns out, may entail a sense of surprise, but it is also immediately subjected to a kind of involuntary auto-analysis, to a sense of 'old stories' stirring in the depths of her 'subconscious self'.

Freud's 'secret story' must remain unknowable, undisentanglable, in a word inexplicable; but one cannot help imagining his silent vexation at this talk of 'my subconscious self'. As he observes elsewhere, regarding the word 'conscious':

> We have no right to extend the meaning of this word so far as to make it include a consciousness of which the owner himself is not aware. If philosophers find difficulty in accepting the existence of unconscious ideas, the existence of an unconscious consciousness seems to me even more objectionable. (*PFL*, 11: 53)

Moberly's 'somewhat redundant' story is canny psychological fiction. It plays with and plays over the concepts and vocabulary of what was once familiarly (but still perhaps strangely) called 'popular psychology'. Jack Wilding comes to dinner and there is a recurrence of that 'most awfully queer smell' (p. 576), the 'strange and penetrating odour' (p. 573) that the narrator noticed when first looking around the house. Jack gives his hosts an 'oddly-bewildered glance':

> 'I must have had a nightmare – a waking nightmare,' he said, looking round him. 'I could have sworn that I smelt the alligator swamp in New Guinea – the place where –' He broke off short. 'I heard the loathsome brutes bellowing,' he began again; 'but, of course – of course, it was merely some association of ideas.' (p. 577)

The reference to 'association of ideas' is at once a 'realistic' appropriation of the language of psychology and psychoanalysis, and an eerie ironization. Apart from anything else it calls up the slithering, sliding sense of telepathy, since at this point in the text the reader already knows that the narrator has also heard this strange 'far-away bellowing' (p. 576). The 'association of ideas' is uncannily shared.

The foregoing examples may suggest at least some of the ingredients that nourish Freud's ambivalence about the world of literary fiction and the power of the 'imaginative writer'. As he puts it in 'The Uncanny': 'The imaginative writer

has this licence among many others, that he [*sic*] can select his world of representation so that it either coincides with the realities we are familiar with or departs
from them in what particulars he pleases. We accept his ruling in every case' (U,
p. 373). It seems that for Freud the imaginative writer is he, or rather perhaps *she*,
who must be obeyed.[4] What might he have made of the androgynous, furnished
or unfurnished authorial name, 'Moberly'? It would be conventional to infer that
'L. G. Moberly' is a woman from the fact that the narrator of the story, May, the
wife of the 'young married couple' to which Freud refers, is a woman.[5] But he
makes no mention of the fact that the narrator of 'Inexplicable' is a woman. In this
respect, Moberly's story presents us with another instance of the ghostly but
crucial figure of the woman in the workings of Freud's essay.[6]

Hugh finally burns the crocodile-encrusted table (a table for Freud, we
may recall, is a symbol of the feminine)[7] and he and May go to the house-agent's
to inform the clerk of this fact:

> 'I have burnt that infernal table,' Hugh went on, forgetting his manners for once;
> 'nobody will ever see it again. You can tell your late client so, with my compliments. To
> leave it in the house was an abominable and mean thing to do.' With that he marched
> out of the office, and we went back to our house, a house which, from that day to this,
> has shown no sign of abnormality.
>
> But it was many a long day before I could live down those weird experiences, and
> even now they are to me quite inexplicable.
>
> Does any explanation of it all occur to you? (p. 581)

Apart from the title, this is the only place in the text where the word 'inexplicable' occurs. It is perhaps not altogether inexplicable that Freud should have
suppressed any reference to this title-word. While not generally given to having
uncanny experiences, Freud nevertheless finds this particular story extremely
uncanny; but he is not one to find a work of fiction – let alone a piece of 'naïve' or
'somewhat redundant' fiction – 'inexplicable'. At the very least, mentioning the
title (or the androgynous author-name) would tend to corroborate his precursor
Ernst Jentsch's notion of the uncanny as bound up with 'intellectual uncertainty'
– a notion that, throughout 'The Uncanny', Freud is repeatedly concerned to
reject, but that repeatedly comes back to haunt. As Freud admits, in appro-
priately uncertain terms, towards the end of the essay: 'And are we after all justified in entirely ignoring intellectual uncertainty as a factor [in the understanding
of the uncanny]?' (U, p. 370).

L. G. Moberly's 'Inexplicable' is in some respects perhaps the most
enigmatically 'readerly' example of what Freud himself records as giving rise to
an experience of the uncanny. The readerly reminiscence from which his text

suffers (the strange irruption of this passage that begins 'In the middle of the isolation of war-time ...') is prefaced by the celebrated remark about an uncanny effect being 'often and easily produced when the distinction between imagination and reality is effaced'. He goes on to proffer two examples of such effacement: 'as when something that we have hitherto regarded as imaginary appears before us in reality, or when a symbol takes over the full function of the thing it symbolizes' (U, p. 367). He then mentions 'the uncanny effect attaching to magical practices' and 'the belief in the omnipotence of thoughts' (U, p. 367). It is not at all certain, however, if or in what ways these remarks are supposed to provide an indication of what, for Freud, makes Moberly's story so uncanny.

It is evident that the 'ghostly crocodiles' are a factor: the large reptiles apparently emerging from the carved table figure a powerful example of animism, of the inanimate becoming animate, of what is lifeless acquiring life. Again, this is the primary example that Freud's precursor had given of 'intellectual' or 'psychical' uncertainty, namely 'doubt as to whether an apparently living being is animate and, conversely, doubt as to whether a lifeless object may not in fact be animate'.[8] In his 1906 essay Jentsch offers this example: 'One can read now and then in old accounts of journeys that someone sat down in an ancient forest on a tree trunk and that, to the horror of the traveller, this trunk suddenly began to move and showed itself to be a giant snake' (p. 11).[9] The crocodiles in 'Inexplicable' body forth the truth of Jentsch's insight. Like the snake in 'old accounts of journeys', Moberly's crocodiles constitute an example of what is inanimate ('mere' wood – though wood is another feminine symbol, according to Freud) transpiring to be alive.[10] Jentsch says that the snake story is a 'good example' of when something 'that at first seemed completely lifeless suddenly reveals an inherent energy' (p. 11). But the snake, or the crocodile, is in a sense an even better example of the uncanny than Jentsch acknowledges. It is a sort of double-whammy uncanny. For what both creatures share is a capacity to produce *at the same time* 'doubt as to whether an apparently living being is animate *and*, conversely, doubt as to whether a lifeless object may not in fact be animate' (U, p. 347, my emphasis).

We could go on sniffing out the (un)canny nooks and crannies of Freud's 'secret story' indefinitely. Doubtless, for example, smell has a role. 'Towards evening an intolerable and very specific smell begins to pervade the house', recalls Freud: corresponding to the move of collapsing the narrative into a single day ('Towards evening'), his story of the story suggests a single, intensifying 'intolerable and very specific smell'. 'Inexplicable' is in fact concerned with the *recurrence* of smell, suggesting a clear link between smell, uncanny repetition and trauma: for Jack Wilding in particular there is the 'stench', the 'most awfully queer smell' (p. 576) which recalls him to the time in New Guinea when he 'crossed an alligator swamp ... with a friend ... It was dark, the place swarmed with those unspeakable devils, their stench was everywhere ... They dragged [his friend, Dawson] off the path of logs in the darkness' (p. 578).[11] In a more general way, Moberly's story invites us to savour how strange smell can be: it can be 'familiarity itself', and yet arise in the most unexpected context. Smell has an uncanny duplicity: it can in a split-second drop us out of the erstwhile familiarity of our present into the strange, painful and/or pleasurable, impossible country of the past; and yet a smell resists being recalled, in reality, even for a moment.[12]

'Inexplicable' strands the reader: Freud, me, 'you'. Such is the peculiar turn of address in its final sentence: 'it was many a long day before I could live down those weird experiences, and even now they are to me quite inexplicable. Does any explanation of it all occur to *you*?' (p. 581, emphasis added). Sharing Freud's sense that this story is indeed remarkably uncanny, I conclude with my own stranded attempt at summarizing in the teeth of the impossible. 'Inexplicable' generates uncanny feelings concerned with the liminal; with the strange solitude of being a reader; with the distinction between literary and psychological or psychoanalytical discourse; with what I have called 'eariness'; with the distinction between the homely and unhomely, or the 'ordinary' and the 'weird'; with the distinction between being awake and dreaming ('waking nightmare'); with telepathy or otherwise magical 'association of ideas'; with the figure of the woman; with androgyny and other senses of doubling or proliferation in sexual identity; with the hallucinatory perception of what is inanimate coming to life; with crocodiles and snakes; with symbols; with smell; with intellectual and other sorts of uncertainty, not least those formulated by Jentsch and disavowed or otherwise understated by Freud; and, finally, with darkness, with the sense of something 'lived down', going back into the dark, a 'secret story' sinking back down again, back (but it was never properly present) 'out of' Freud's essay, into the fictive, inexplicable darkness of its swamp.

NOTES

1   Robin Lydenberg, 'Freud's Uncanny Narratives', PMLA, vol. 112, no. 5 (1997), 1072–86: here, p. 1079. Lydenberg is one of the few critics who devotes any detailed attention to this passage in 'The Uncanny'.

2   See Freud's 'Address Delivered in the Goethe House at Frankfurt', PFL, 14: 472.

3   L. G. Moberly, 'Inexplicable', Strand Magazine, vol. 54 (1917), 572–81. Further page references are given in parentheses in the main body of the text. (Moberly's text is also reprinted in

Strange Tales from the Strand (Oxford: Oxford University Press, 1991), pp. 183–96. My thanks to Asko Kauppinen for locating a copy of the original 1917 publication.

4   Freud refers to Rider Haggard's *She* in *The Interpretation of Dreams*, describing it as 'A *strange* book, but full of hidden meaning … the eternal feminine, the immortality of our emotions' (*PFL*, 4: 586–7). To be in the presence of She herself, Haggard's novel suggests, was to be 'in the presence of something that was not canny': see H. Rider Haggard, *She* (1887; Harmonds-worth: Penguin Popular Classics, 1994), p. 140.

5   Lucy Gertrude Moberly was the author of many novels, published in the early decades of the twentieth century; largely forgotten now, they were regularly reviewed, for example, in the *Times Literary Supplement*.

6   Lydenberg, whose essay is especially interested in 'the relation between narration and the uncanny maternal' (p. 1078), also gives a fine account of some of the other narratologically significant details of 'Inexplicable' that Freud leaves out in his rendition. See 'Freud's Uncanny Narratives', esp. p. 1082.

7   See, for example, *PFL*, 1: 189, 191, 196; *PFL*, 4: 472, 496–7. As Freud puts it in the Introductory Lecture, 'Symbolism in Dreams': '*Tables* and *wood* [are] puzzling but certainly female symbols' (*PFL*, 1: 191).

8   Ernst Jentsch, 'On the Psychology of the Uncanny' (1906), trans. Roy Sellars, *Angelaki* vol. 2, no. 1 (1995), 11. Quoted by Freud in 'The Uncanny', p. 347. Further page references to Jentsch are given in parentheses in the main body of the text.

9   In this context we may recall that Freud elsewhere specifically refers to the uncanniness of snakes. In his lecture on 'Anxiety', in the context of a discussion of phobias, Freud writes: 'Some … dreaded objects and situations have something uncanny about them for normal people as well … Thus most of us have a sense of repulsion if we meet with a snake. Snake phobia, we might say, is a universal human characteristic' (*PFL*, 1: 447). Elsewhere, in *The Interpretation of Dreams*, Freud singles out snakes as the 'most important symbols of the male organ' (*PFL*, 4: 474). When is a snake a snake? What is happening, for example, when a table becomes a crocodile becomes snake-like? 'Inexplicable' makes a passing reference to snakes, when Hugh exclaims 'I shall be seeing rats and snakes next!' (p. 574). Snakes are certainly in the mind's eye as it were. In the suggestive words of the hurriedly-appointed and very temporary charwoman Mrs Jenkins, the crocodiles are 'Slithering in and out o' the scullery and kitchen … Runnin' on their underneaths, with paws as don't seem a bit o' use to 'em' (p. 579). In other words, we could readily construe Moberly's text as snake-infested, as well as crocodile-infested or, perhaps, table-infested. But what is happening here to Freudian symbolism? When is a symbol a symbol? If Moberly's story furnishes an example of 'when a symbol takes over the full function of the thing it symbolizes' (U, p. 367), any determinate 'symbolic' reading of the text simultaneously perhaps slithers out of view.

10 On 'wood' as 'feminine' see note 7 above. Cf. also Jentsch's later discussion of 'when one under-takes to reinterpret some kind of lifeless thing as a part of an organic creature', citing as an example: 'In the dark, a rafter covered with nails becomes the jaw of a fabulous animal' (p. 13).

11 As early as *Studies on Hysteria* (1893–95), Freud shows himself to be concerned with how 'the sensation of smell that was associated with [a] trauma persisted as its symbol': see *PFL*, 3: 179.

12 Cf. Gregory Ulmer: '*while smells may be recognized, they may not be recalled*. One may actively recall the image of a rose, but not its smell.' See Gregory L. Ulmer, *Applied Grammatology: Post(e)-pedagogy from Jacques Derrida to Joseph Beuys* (Baltimore: Johns Hopkins University Press, 1985), p. 95.

10
Buried alive

'What did you think?' one of them once asked impatiently; 'would we feel like enduring the estrangement, the cold and quiet of the grave around us – this whole subterranean, concealed, mute, undiscovered solitude that among us is called life but might just as well be called death – if we did not know what will *become* of us, and that it is only after death that we shall enter *our* life and become alive, oh, very much alive, we post-humous people!' (Friedrich Nietzsche)[1]

Seemingly out of the blue (for he has just been meditating, with admirable terseness, on the uncanniness of 'dismembered limbs, a severed head, a hand cut off at the wrist'), Freud declares:

> To some people the idea of being buried alive by mistake is the most uncanny thing of all. And yet psychoanalysis has taught us that this terrifying phantasy is only a trans-formation of another phantasy which had originally nothing terrifying about it at all, but was qualified by a certain lasciviousness – the phantasy, I mean, of intra-uterine existence. (U, pp. 366–7)[2]

Perhaps he should have started his essay with this 'most uncanny' example. Freud presents us here with a sort of micro-analysis of psychoanalysis in two sentences, the story of life from A to Z, or from Z to A, from death to birth, from the imminence of death to the timeless pleasure of womb-life, from terror to lasciviousness, from death to the mother (scrabbling to get out of the grave, 'when force is gone, there's always Mom', as Laurie Anderson's eerie, apocalyptic 'O Superman' has it).[3] What an incredible pair of sentences! What a fantasy coupling!

They trace a curious reversal of the truth, as Freud himself had formulated it in 'The Theme of the Three Caskets' (1913) (*PFL*, 14: 235–47). In 'The Uncanny' psychoanalysis teaches us how to get from death to Mummy: we move from smothering terror to mothering lechery, tranquillized by the assurance that this terrifying fantasy 'is only a transformation' of another, completely un-terrifying fantasy. In 'The Theme of the Three Caskets', the argument works in just the other direction: Mummy is not there. Man's fantasy of the end, as the point at which it is 'the Mother Earth who receives him once more', is blankly rejected in that earlier essay's concluding sentence: 'But it is in vain that an old man yearns for the love of woman as he had it first from his mother; the third of the Fates alone, the silent Goddess of Death, will take him into her arms' (*PFL*, 14: 247). Of course, Freud is still anthropomorphizing, feminizing and eroticizing 'death' –

the reversal comes back to the same, like 'the perpetual recurrence of the same thing'.[4] 'The Theme of the Three Caskets' works through a reading of Greek mythology, fairy tales and Shakespeare (*The Merchant of Venice* and *King Lear*), in order to arrive at a demystification that is also a sort of remystification (death as a silent Goddess, Atropos, who above or beneath all, after all, is supposed to castrate, cut a fellow down, sever the thread of life, not take him in her arms).[5]

'To some people the idea of being buried alive by mistake is the most uncanny thing of all.' There is a certain comedy in James Strachey's translation here. The English version might be taken as positing that being buried alive *per se* is not necessarily uncanny; what is really uncanny is when it happens *by mistake*. The German is more unequivocally sombre, indeed majestic: '*Manche Menschen würden die Krone der Unheimlichkeit der Vorstellung zuweisen, scheintot begraben zu werden*' (p. 257). More cloddenly than Strachey, we might say: 'Some people would regard as the crowning instance of uncanniness the idea of being buried because ostensibly dead.' This example of the uncanny is *die Krone*, literally, the crown. Finally one gets to be His or Her Majesty: a coronation fit for royalty. Freud's regal turn of phrase perhaps already suggests an air of fantasy missing from Strachey's translation: what tops the lot when it comes to measuring maximum uncanniness is being committed to the earth not because you are dead but because you *appear to be* dead. It is a matter of ostensibly or being seemingly dead [*scheintot*], as if in suspended animation.

In any case, this crowning achievement doesn't really mean anything, except as the 'transformation' of a different fantasy, namely 'intra-uterine existence'. This, Freud tells us, is what 'psychoanalysis has taught us'. (One of the most important things that psychoanalysis has perhaps taught us is to be especially critical and circumspect whenever we are being told what 'psychoanalysis has taught us'.) Again, the English phrase 'intra-uterine existence' is curious: it sounds very clinical and, dare one say, uninviting. The original German is *Leben im Mutterleib* (p. 257), 'life within the mother's body'. And in the original German text the statement is followed by three asterisks. It is very strange, as if one's supposed to see stars.

This is the only place in the text of Freud's 'Das Unheimliche' where this typographical intervention or embellishment appears. It is as if his account simply has to break off here: he can go no further.[6] But which way? Eyes shut, as tight as can be, seeing stars, are we pushing up daisies or back in Mummy's body?

Freud elsewhere writes of life in the womb in terms of uncanniness. In a footnote added to *The Interpretation of Dreams* in 1909, he talks about how long it was before psychoanalysis taught him, or he taught himself, on this topic:

> It was not for a long time that I learned to appreciate the importance of phantasies and unconscious thoughts about life in the womb. They contain an explanation of the remarkable dread that many people have of being buried alive; and they also afford the deepest unconscious basis for the belief in survival after death, which merely represents a projection into the future of this uncanny life before birth. (*PFL*, 4: 525–6, n. 2)

This is another extraordinary couple of sentences, proferring an explanation of the grounds of all religious belief in terms of the uncanny. 'Uncanny life before birth' provides the sole reason for all 'belief in survival after death'. But how exactly do 'unconscious thoughts about life in the womb ... contain an explanation of the ... dread ... of being buried alive'? Why should one be more original, 'prior' to the other at all?

The two sentences from 'The Uncanny' that we have been trying to read here seem to present a movement of tranquillization, of reassurance already assured. The fear of being buried alive is 'really' about something that had 'originally nothing terrifying about it at all'. It may appear as if the uncanny has been explicated, put to rest.[7] Yet the footnote from *The Interpretation of Dreams* specifically refers to life in the womb as 'uncanny' as well. We move, in fact, from one uncanny to another, remaining within a strange space of substitution, of one fantasy for another, womb for tomb and tomb for womb, a chiasmatic logic. Movement is limited, but seemingly interminable: we are left, as if in the uncanny time prior to what may be called the 'canny moment', in other words 'the moment of childbirth'.[8]

There is something left over, some remains or supplement: does Freud really think that the fantasy of 'intra-uterine existence' *explains* the uncanniness of 'the idea of being buried alive'? Does he really suppose that the latter ceases to be uncanny once we have had a lesson in psychoanalysis? For all their elegance and seeming self-assurance, there is a peculiar disjunction between the two sentences in question. Having advanced the singular proposition that the idea of being buried alive constitutes 'the most uncanny thing of all', he never says another word on the subject. Ostensibly. It is as if he walks away from this little textual diadem, this sparkling crown, lying on the ground, or half-buried there.

★ ★
★

Perhaps it is simply too much, a crowning example of the uncanny as what 'is too much intermixed with what is purely gruesome and is in part overlaid by it' (U, p. 364).[9] Certainly it seems to be too much, at first sight, for the narrator of Edgar Allan Poe's 'The Premature Burial' (1844), which begins:

> There are certain themes of which the interest is all-absorbing, but which are too entirely horrible for the purposes of legitimate fiction. These the mere romanticist must eschew, if he do not wish to offend, or to disgust. They are with propriety handled, only when the severity and majesty of truth sanctify and sustain them. We thrill, for example, with the most intense of 'pleasurable pain', over the accounts of the Passage of the Beresina, of the Earthquake at Lisbon, of the Plague at London, of the Massacre of St. Bartholomew, or of the stifling of the hundred and twenty-three prisoners in the Black Hole at Calcutta. But, in these accounts, it is the fact – it is the reality – it is the history which excites. As inventions, we should regard them with simple abhorrence.[10]

Of course, this is not how Poe's text begins. It begins with the title, a phrase – 'the premature burial' – that resounds, if in a strangely muffled way, through this opening paragraph. Or perhaps even more precisely, it begins with the author's name, Edgar Allan Poe, a name that doubtless already carries an overwhelming weight or freight of sense. Buried alive: isn't that what a proper name is?[11] A cadaverously 'rigid designator', it entombs its bearer from birth.[12]

What kind of text is 'The Premature Burial'? Is it 'legitimate fiction'? The opening sentence can hardly be held at a distance from our knowledge of the title: 'premature burial', we are invited to suppose, is precisely one of those 'themes' that the narrator has in mind. Its 'interest' may be 'all-absorbing' but it is 'too entirely horrible for the purposes of legitimate fiction'. The self-remarking or (as Todorov might say) 'meta-uncanny' allusion to 'legitimate fiction' generates a strange aporia concerning the very possibility of assigning the text to one or another 'genre' or discourse.[13] The narrator goes on to 'explain':

> To be buried while alive is, beyond question, the most terrific of these extremes which has ever fallen to the lot of mere mortality. That it has frequently, very frequently, so fallen will scarcely be denied by those who think. The boundaries which divide Life from Death, are at best shadowy and vague. (p. 955)

The seemingly superfluous 'while' in this first sentence is a fine, almost stately touch; 'fallen' comes with the gentlest, even imperceptible thud. The sentence that follows has a limbo quality all of its own. It may appear an aposiopoesis, an unfinished statement, a sudden breaking off in the midst of

'That it has frequently, very frequently, so fallen will scarcely be denied by those who think': by those who think what? 'Think' has no object. Thinking becomes its own 'stifling' object. To recall a phrase from Shakespeare (Sonnet 64): 'This thought is as a death.' Poe's text presents a kind of death sentence on a thought of overwhelming claustrophobia, a necessary but unthinkable stoppage of thinking.[14] There is also, perhaps, a sense of the 'irresistibly comic' to be excavated here, in this hyperbole of the qualifying 'very' ('frequently, very frequently'), in this seemingly gratuitous and perverse, yet continuing and indeed ever deepening disquisition on the enigmatically 'pleasurable pain' of what is at once of 'all-absorbing interest' and 'too entirely horrible'.

One feels for a way out: 'The boundaries which divide Life from Death, are at best shadowy and vague.' One might be excused for supposing that the sense, and sentence, will have carried on; that sense need not, after all, be walled up in 'those who think'; that the boundaries between sentences are at best shadowy and vague, indeed that the boundaries between *clauses* need not be claustrophobic (for surely that comma after 'Death' is a charming superfluity, flourishing symptom and symptomatic flourish of a literary claustrophilia). The text goes on:

> Who shall say where the one ends, and where the other begins? We know that there are diseases in which occur total cessations of all the apparent functions of vitality, and yet in which these cessations are merely suspensions, properly so called. They are only temporary pauses in the incomprehensible mechanism. A certain period elapses, and some unseen mysterious principle again sets in motion the magic pinions and the wizard wheels. (p. 955)

The 'cessations' or 'suspensions, properly so called', concern the eerie, as yet concealed 'other side' of Poe's text. As 'The Premature Burial' continues, so readerly curiosity gathers: who *is* this narrator? And *why* is he *telling* all this stuff? On the one hand, we may feel ourselves being drawn into the catacombs of a literary genealogy here, one that would link Poe's text with the figure of the apparently drowned Rogue Riderhood in Dickens's *Our Mutual Friend* (1864–65) or the undecidably dead-alive J. in Maurice Blanchot's *Death Sentence* (1948): Poe's story is likewise focused on an uncanny suspension, the sense of being, at the same 'incomprehensible' time, both dead and alive, neither dead nor alive.[15] On the other hand, 'The Premature Burial' seems to make something peculiar happen to our sense of Freud. But of course these two hands are linked, working together.

In keeping with the seemingly fantastical logic articulated by Harold Bloom, according to which an earlier writer can come to sound more like a later one (Milton, for example, more like Wordsworth than Milton himself, Shelley more like Yeats, Stevens more like Ashbery), we may begin to feel that 'The

Premature Burial' is in some respects more rigorously, even *rigidly* Freudian than Freud allows himself to be, for example, in 'The Uncanny'.[16] Bloom calls this seemingly fantastical logic 'the curious magic of the positive *apophrades*'.[17] *Apophrades* is the last and most explicitly uncanny of what he calls the six revisionary ratios or movements which make up a strong poem or other work of 'great writing'.[18] He defines it as follows:

> *Apophrades*, or the return of the dead; I take the word from the Athenian dismal or unlucky days upon which the dead returned to reinhabit the houses in which they had lived. The later poet, in his [*sic*] own final phase, already burdened by an imaginative solitude that is almost a solipsism, holds his own poem so open again to the precursor's work that at first we might believe the wheel has come full circle, and that we are back in the later poet's flooded apprenticeship, before his strength began to assert itself in the revisionary ratios. But the poem is now *held* open to the precursor, where once it *was* open, and the uncanny effect is that the new poem's achievement makes it seem to us, not as though the precursor were writing it, but as though the later poet himself had written the precursor's characteristic work.[19]

Bloom's celebrated 'theory of poetry' is altogether a sort of theory of *apophrades* writ large, since it is fundamentally concerned with poetry (or 'great writing') as an encounter with the dead, with the ghostliness of ancestral voices and intertextual hauntings. In this context it is especially intriguing and significant, I think, that he seems to have very little time for Poe. He scarcely merits a mention in Bloom's *The Western Canon: The Books and School of the Ages*: the most we are given is a passing reference to Poe's writing as 'almost invariably atrocious'.[20] My reading of 'The Premature Burial' here is in part concerned to suggest how badly Bloom evidently needs to misread Poe; how poetic, strange and compelling the 'atrocious' becomes in the context of reading Poe's work; and, above all, how the figure of being 'buried alive' might be in some respects as productive as 'apophrades' as a way of construing the uncanniness of 'great writing'. In other words, what is perhaps at issue in Bloom's misprision of Poe is the figure of live burial as a way of thinking 'the Western canon'. Poe's writing shows up a questionable vitalism in Bloom's and testifies to the possibilities of a displaced conception of the canon in terms of what might be called a posthumism.[21]

It is a question, then, of an uncanny intertextuality, a catacomb-effect of voices. This would have nothing to do with Poe's 'influence' on Freud, or Freud's being unconsciously 'indebted' to Poe. Rather, it would be to engage critically with a well-known Freudian psychoanalytic tradition of reading Poe as a means of elucidating what is meant by 'Freud'. It is not only that the tone and quasi-scientific, clinical precision and 'propriety' of 'The Premature Burial' can seem strangely to prefigure that of Freud's Bloomsbury English (Strachey's clinical 'intra-uterine existence', for example). Certain unsuspected resemblances may begin to show up between the opening sentences of the two texts in question:

> There are certain themes of which the interest is all-absorbing, but which are too entirely horrible for the purposes of legitimate fiction. These the mere romanticist must eschew, if he do not wish to offend, or to disgust.

> It is only rarely that a psychoanalyst feels impelled to investigate the subject of aesthetics, even when aesthetics is understood to mean not merely the theory of beauty but the theory of the qualities of feeling. (U, p. 339)

Both openings involve the remarking and the making of a foreign genre or foreign body of writing that is strangely mixed up, already grafted on to what is implied as being distinct (in other words, what is not 'legitimate fiction' in Poe, the discourse of 'aesthetics' in Freud). Both involve, also, a rendering foreign of the speaker or writer: he becomes detached, other to himself, estranged in the third person singular ('he' in Poe's text, 'a psychoanalyst' in Freud's). But more strikingly, perhaps, we become conscious of the fact that *Poe's text begins as Freud's could or should have begun*, with a focus on that 'gruesome' (U, p. 364) crowning instance of the uncanny, 'premature interment' (p. 956). The adjective 'clinical' – seemingly so decisively different in literary and psychoanalytic usage – acquires a broader and altogether stranger resonance in the wake of reading Poe's text. The various senses of 'clinical' as 'hospital-like', 'concerned with or based on observation', 'strictly objective', 'analytical', 'plain, functional in appearance' derive from the Greek *klinikos*, from *kline* 'a bed' (*Chambers*). The clinical becomes a place of trance, at once a bed of repose and suspension, and a death-bed. Words get tangled up, buried in their bed-sheets.[22]

It is also the case that 'The Premature Burial' makes Freudian connections, on the subject of being buried alive, that 'The Uncanny' itself does not quite make. The allusions that Poe's anonymous narrator makes to 'these cessations', 'suspensions', 'temporary pauses in the incomprehensible mechanism' in a sense become 'properly' meaningful only when – after devoting several pages to what might be called clinical accounts of 'living inhumation' (p. 957) and 'seeming decease' (p. 959) – the narrator finally tells us 'of [his] own actual knowledge – of [his] own positive and personal experience' (p. 962). For the narrator, it transpires, is himself 'subject to attacks of the singular disorder which physicians have agreed to term catalepsy, in default of a more definite title' (p. 962). 'Catalepsy' is defined in *Chambers Dictionary* as 'a state where one is more or less completely incapacitated, with bodily rigidity, as in hypnotic trances and sometimes in schizophrenia; cataplexy in animals'. And 'cataplexy' (this word thus presuming a distinction between humans and animals that Poe's text might be said to keep uncertain, in suspension) is given as 'a condition of immobility induced by extreme emotion, eg shock (*med*); a physical state resembling death, adopted by some animals to discourage predators'.

Poe's text, in other words, is not only a gruesome 'clinical' account of various 'premature interments' in Europe and America, but also an uncertainly fictional, autobiothanatoheterographical account of the narrator's own experience of what had, at the outset, perhaps seemed a smilingly implausible fate.[23] Of the trance-like condition of catalepsy, he explains that 'the closest scrutiny, and the most rigorous medical tests, fail to establish any material distinction between the state of the sufferer and what we conceive of absolute death' (p. 962). Premature burial being so very frequent an event (as the preceding pages of Poe's text have made hammeringly clear), someone suffering from catalepsy is all too likely to get 'buried alive by mistake'. At once reassuring and crazy, Poe's narrator informs us that: 'Very usually he is saved from premature interment solely by the knowledge of his friends that he has been previously subject to catalepsy, by the consequent suspicion excited, and, above all, by the non-appearance of decay' (p. 962). What 'The Premature Burial' digs up and analyses, in effect, is the peculiar connection that is made and not made in Freud's text, the peculiar gap or cover-up, the elision rendered even less visible in Strachey's English translation by the mistaken 'by mistake' ('buried alive *by mistake*'). For what Freud is referring to, in particular, is the singularly 'uncanny' idea of being buried because *seemingly dead*. Suspended animation, in other words, is crucially part of what is uncanny here, though Freud says nothing more about it: his 'seemingly' ('*schein*') haunts his own text like a phantom (*Scheindasein*).

Freud does not say it quite, but what is happening at this moment in his essay is an acknowledgement of the eerie power of hypnotic or trance-states and more particularly of what Poe calls 'catalepsy'. Elsewhere, in *Group Psychology and the Analysis of the Ego* (1921) (*PFL*, 12: 95–178), Freud notes that 'hypnosis has something positively uncanny about it' (p. 157), though oddly this example of the uncanny does not explicitly appear in the essay of that title. It is also the case that the figure of the 'seemingly dead' recalls or revivifies the 'waxwork figures, ingeniously constructed dolls and automata' (U, p. 347), which Freud is at pains earlier in the 1919 essay to keep at a distance, identifying them as he does with the theory of the uncanny elaborated by his so-called 'conscious' precursor, Ernst Jentsch.[24] In other words, there is further corroboration here perhaps of the sense that Jentsch is subjected to a premature burial in Freud's essay.

But there is another subterranean shift or movement to be detected here. It has to do with the notion of the fit, the uncanny seizure or attack. For something else that Freud acknowledges Jentsch also to have discussed is epilepsy or *morbus sacer* (literally, the sacred disease): no doubt it is in part because the latter devotes some time to this topic that Freud seems to give it such short shrift. He says that Jentsch refers to 'the uncanny effect of epileptic fits, and of manifestations of insanity, because these excite in the spectator the impression of automatic, mechanical processes at work behind the normal appearance of mental activity'. He then adds, without further explanation: 'Without entirely accepting this author's view, we will take it as a starting-point for our own investigation' (U, p. 347). If Jentsch provides Freud with his 'starting-point', however, the topics of 'epileptic fits' and 'manifestations of insanity' themselves disappear, only briefly to resurface, named as such, some twenty pages later (U, p. 366), just before the cryptic, star-crossed sentences about being buried alive. In his 1906 essay on the psychology of the uncanny, Jentsch discusses the 'demonic effect' of epileptic fits, observing that:

> It is not unjustly that epilepsy is therefore spoken of as the *morbus sacer*, as an illness deriving not from the human world but from foreign and enigmatic spheres, for the epileptic attack of spasms reveals the human body to the viewer – the body that under normal conditions is so meaningful, expedient, and unitary, functioning according to the directions of his [*sic*] consciousness – as an immensely complicated and delicate mechanism. (p. 14)[25]

Now epilepsy (Jentsch) and catalepsy (Poe) are not necessarily the same thing, but they do come together in Freud. This happens not in the text of 'The Uncanny' itself, but in a deferred fashion, as if after a mole-like progression, in the essay 'Dostoevsky and Parricide' (1928) (*PFL*, 14: 437–60). This '"occasional" piece' (p. 439), as the Penguin editor Albert Dickson calls it (thereby evoking, perhaps, the rhetoric of a certain 'fitfulness' in Freud's writing in general), can be read in part as a sort of uncanny outgrowth of the 1919 essay. It presents a return to Jentsch (and to the ghost of Poe) that is not registered or apparently recognized as such. 'Dostoevsky and Parricide' has a fit, a sort of absent-minded Jentschian seizure.[26] The 1928 essay also follows on from 'The Uncanny' in that it is a further or repeated attempt to struggle with the impossible, namely the interminable resistance of the literary to psychoanalytical accountability.

Freud starts 'Dostoevsky and Parricide' with what appears to be a literally disarming humility: 'Before the problem of the creative artist analysis must, alas, lay down its arms' (p. 441). But this of course does not stop Freud: he was already up in arms, it is what compelled him to begin. He feels he has to try to deal with the question of Dostoevsky's 'epilepsy'. He admits that there are a couple of rather basic problems in this regard: first, that this 'epilepsy' is only 'alleged', the data is 'defective and untrustworthy' (p. 444); and, second, that it is in fact impossible to define 'epilepsy' at all! It is just so 'clinically' ambiguous or ambiguously 'clinical': 'it has been found impossible', he declares, 'to maintain that "epilepsy" is a single clinical entity' (p. 445).

On the one hand, then, Freud seems to be 'remembering' what Jentsch says, and what he himself has elliptically repeated in 'The Uncanny'. Thus, he says, there is that 'uncanny disease', 'the old *morbus sacer* ... still in evidence as an ostensible clinical entity' (p. 444). *Morbus sacer* is 'the uncanny disease with its incalculable, apparently unprovoked convulsive attacks, its changing of the character into irritability and aggressiveness, and its progressive lowering of all the mental faculties' (p. 444). But on the other hand, as Freud goes on to make clear, 'the outlines of this picture are quite lacking in precision' (p. 444). And here, we might say, his writing takes on a more Poe-like character. 'Epilepsy' can, Freud says, take the form of 'brief periods of *absence*, or rapidly passing fits of vertigo or ... short spaces of time during which the patient does something out of character, as though he were under the control of his unconscious' (p. 444). Indeed, the sense of 'epilepsy' – like the uncanny itself – spreads out, spreads back, diffusing and grafting itself everywhere. For example, in sex: as Freud notes, 'the earliest physicians described coition as a minor epilepsy, and thus recognized in the sexual act a mitigation and adaptation of the epileptic method of discharging stimuli' (p. 445). Sex: the epileptic uncanny.

Freud has to give up on this speculative line of approach in what is already an avowedly failed attempt to write about the 'creative artist' Dostoevsky. He has to go back to what came 'long before the incidence of the "epilepsy"' (p. 447). Long before this, and constituting a much better 'starting-point' in Freud's view, there are the 'attacks' that Dostoevsky had in his boyhood, attacks that were 'heralded by a fear of death and consisted of lethargic, somnolent states' (p. 447). Freud writes:

> The illness first came over him while he was still a boy, in the form of a sudden, groundless melancholy, a feeling, as he later told his friend Soloviev, as though he were going to die on the spot. And there in fact followed a state exactly similar to real death. His brother Andrey tells us that even when he was quite young Fyodor used to leave little notes about before he went to sleep, saying that he was afraid he might fall into

> this death-like sleep during the night and therefore begged that his burial should be
> postponed for five days. (p. 447)

'Epilepsy' seems to have been translated out of another, earlier language, more
akin to what Poe's text calls 'catalepsy'. Freud traces everything back to this 'one
certain starting-point' (p. 447), this allegedly true story about the young Fyodor's
cataleptic writing, 'little notes' written on the verge of sleep, texts fitfully
produced on the subject of 'death-like sleep' and premature burial.

Do we believe this story?[27] Everything seems to fit – and not – at the same
time. From this passage concerning Dostoevsky's 'little notes … saying that he
was afraid he might fall into this death-like sleep during the night and therefore
begged that his burial should be postponed for five days', we might reasonably
suppose that what is at issue is a fear of being buried alive. But we would be
wrong, seemingly: for Freud confidently turns, as it were, to begin a new
paragraph with the following declaration:

> We know the meaning and intention of such death-like attacks. They signify an
> identification with a dead person, either with someone who is really dead or with
> someone who is still alive and whom the subject wishes dead. The latter case is the
> more significant. The attack then has the value of a punishment. One has wished
> another person dead, and now one *is* this other person and is dead oneself. (p. 447)

Like incest, killing one's father (or the guilt to which it might be expected to give
rise) is an uncanny idea. Freud's '"occasional" piece' is concerned to explain it: he
concludes that 'for a boy this other person is usually his father and … the attack
… is thus a self-punishment for a death-wish against a hated father' (p. 447).
Freud is in such a rush to get there. It doesn't matter that these 'death-like
attacks' can equally well signify an identification with 'someone who is really
dead'. The 'more significant' meaning is that of an identification with 'someone
who is still alive and whom the subject wishes dead'. It is 'more significant'
because it is, how should we say, more significant – in other words for no reason
other than it fits, apparently snug as a bug, with the story Freud wishes to tell.
'Now one *is* this other person and is dead oneself': here is Freud's version of M.
Valdemar's 'I *have been* sleeping – and now – now – I *am dead.*'[28]

But why should *either* of Freud's interpretations in 'Dostoevsky and Parricide' be 'more significant' than the interpretation he gives, so unhesitatingly, in
'The Uncanny'? It seems as if he needs to suppress or repress the fact that what he
is dealing with, in the essay on Dostoevsky, is an example of someone with a fear
(a recurrent fear) of being buried while seemingly dead, a classic case of what
Poe's text calls 'catalepsy'.[29] Freud has patricide on his mind; his 'explanation' of

Dostoevsky's cataleptic writings is pushed through accordingly. His account thus surreptitiously covers up the earlier, equally 'legitimate' explanation of 'intra-uterine' fantasy. Is this because Freud thinks that a boy (as Dostoevsky allegedly then was) is not yet old enough to have a fantasy or idea of being in the womb? The Oedipal desire to kill the father appears – absurdly, impossibly, in every sense of the word *inconceivably* – to come *before* 'life in the maternal body'. The mother is the substitute, the site of a matricidal hermeneutics. Our Poe-impelled inter-ruption of Freud's reading of Dostoevsky's 'little notes' suggests that it is not necessarily a matter of supposing that one interpretation simply invalidates the other. Rather, it may appear, the uncanniness of the fantasy or idea of being buried alive has to do with impossible, tell-tale-less substitution: one fantasy or idea as the unarrestable 'transformation' of another, substituting for another substitute.

Darkness returns. Finally revealing his 'positive and personal experience' regarding this topic of such 'interest profound' (p. 961), Poe's narrator describes how 'the idea of premature burial held continual possession of my brain' (p. 963). Like Dostoevsky, he is afraid of going to sleep:

> it was with a struggle that I consented to sleep – for I shuddered to reflect that, upon awaking, I might find myself the tenant of a grave. And when, finally, I sank into slumber, it was only to rush at once into a world of phantasms, above which, with vast, sable, overshadowing wings, hovered, predominant, the one sepulchral Idea. (p. 963)

This terror of what he had earlier referred to as being 'consigned alive to the tomb' (p. 962) breathes new life into the word 'tenant' – not only through the sense of 'temporary possession or occupant' but also, in a way at once more gruesome and more touching, through its haptic derivation from the Latin *tenere*, 'to hold'.

Perhaps the most energetic or allergenic, eerily activated word in this passage, however, is 'slumber'.[30] The narrator (in that always at least faintly disturbing anonymity with which Poe signs and seals his first-person fictions) goes on to recount 'a solitary vision' (p. 964). In a 'cataleptic trance of more than usual duration and profundity', he is visited by a cold-handed figure with chattering teeth. 'The darkness was total', we are told. But the 'unseen figure' leads him into 'the outer Night', into an apocalypse of what ought to have remained secret and hidden:

> [he] caused to be thrown open the graves of all mankind; and from each issued the faint phosphoric radiance of decay; so that I could see into the innermost recesses, and there view the shrouded bodies in their sad and solemn slumbers with the worm. But, alas! the real sleepers were fewer, by many millions, than those who slumbered not at all. (p. 964)

It is as if words themselves are being opened up, and sealed again, in their 'innermost recesses'. 'With the worm', 'slumber' means death. The so-called figurative sense of death as a sleep or slumber turns over, restlessly. The 'real' (as in 'real sleepers') is buried alive.

The narrator concludes: 'Phantasies such as these, presenting themselves at night, extended their terrific influence far into my waking hours' (p. 965). A pseudo-iterative 'phantasy' then: there is always more than one. His 'mortal terrors' induce him to take the most meticulous preventive action:

> I had the family vault so remodelled as to admit of being readily opened from within. The slightest pressure upon a long lever that extended far into the tomb would cause the iron portals to fly back. There were arrangements also for the free admission of air and light, and convenient receptacles for food and water, within immediate reach of the coffin intended for my reception. (p. 965)

And of course what happens? A time comes when he wakes up, incapable of moving, in darkness, in 'the intense and utter raylessness of the Night that endureth for evermore', inside a structure of 'solid wooden substance' (p. 967), in what transpires *not* to be the family vault. In fact, he is in a berth on board a sloop, immersed in the cataleptic (un)familiarity of not being capable of 'collecting [his] senses' until 'a long time after awaking from slumber' (p. 968). This, seemingly, is his 'premature burial'.

The very 'excess' of this experience transforms him. As he puts it:

> I breathed the free air of Heaven. I thought upon other subjects than Death. I discarded my medical books. 'Buchan' I burned. I read no 'Night Thoughts' – no fustian about church-yards – no bugaboo tales – *such as this*. In short I became a new man, and lived a man's life. (p. 969)

The tale ends with a turning away from its own subject, a self-reflexive or meta-uncanny claim to having dismissed 'bugaboo tales – *such as this*'. Not yet finished, it makes out that it has been, finished with, finished off. It wants to bury the past, as if burying the past were not always and necessarily to bury alive. But if the past does indeed seem to be done and dusted, the last sentence of the text signifies a cryptically suspended resuscitation: 'Alas! the grim legion of sepulchral terrors cannot be regarded as altogether fanciful – but, like the Demons in whose company Afrasiab made his voyage down the Oxus, they must sleep, or they will devour us –

they must be suffered to slumber, or we perish' (p. 969). The text closes with a figuration not so much of apophrades (the Bloomian 'return of the dead') as of *sense itself* buried alive. Suffering to slumber or perishing: take your hypnopoetic pick.

By way of moving towards a conclusion, I would like to suggest that a literary preoccupation with being buried alive is more general and pervasive than has perhaps been realized. By way of illustration, let us wander down into the catacombs, in a long and twisting passage down the so-called English literary canon, passing in this sepulchral half-light:

Geoffrey Chaucer, whose Pardoner is that inaugural 'character' in English literature, as Harold Bloom describes him, the first example of what Nietzsche calls 'the uncanniest guest', the figure of nihilism from whom all the 'great villains' in Shakespeare descend,[31] the Pardoner who declares that 'dronkenesse is verray sepulture / Of mannes wit and his discrecioun',[32] hypocritically embodying as he does so the archetypal version of this 'verray sepulture'

William Shakespeare, who deserves perhaps a double-casket: we might think first of his *Romeo and Juliet* (the 'star-crossed lovers' who both end up alive in the tomb, Juliet 'newly dead / Who here hath lain this two days burièd' (5.3.174–5)); or *Hamlet* (from the figure of the King who has 'burst [his] cerements', 'cast … up again' from 'the sepulchre' in which he had been 'quietly inurned' (1.5.48ff.), to the climactic confrontation between Hamlet and Laertes in Ophelia's grave,

the 'mere madness' of that 'fit' in which Hamlet exclaims: 'Be buried quick with her, and so will I' (5.1.274)); or *King Lear* (with its eerily posthumous dimension figured in Lear's 'You do me wrong to take me out o' the grave' (4.7.45)); or *The Winter's Tale* (with Hermione its 'royal piece' (5.3.38), 'the life as lively mocked as ever / Still sleep mocked death' (5.3.19–20)); or so many other characters from other Shakespeare plays long assumed dead, lost, drowned at sea, effectively 'buried quick', but coming back

John Milton: how else *think* that 'deep world / Of darkness', that 'palpable obscure' which Satan and other fallen angels inhabit? Or that place where Sin and Death 'shall dwell at ease, and up and down unseen / Wing silently the buxom air, embalmed / With odors'?[33] Or the dark speculation on Lycidas, 'wash[ed] far away... / ... beyond the stormy Hebrides, / Where thou perhaps under the whelming tide / Visit'st the bottom of the monstrous world'?[34] Or the blindness of Samson, who experiences 'a living death, / And buried; but, O yet more miserable! / Myself my sepulchre, a moving grave, / Buried, yet not exempt / By privilege of death and burial / From worst of other evils'?[35]

William Wordsworth, whose sister Dorothy documented the poet's fondness for lying down in a trench and thinking 'that it would be as sweet thus to lie so in the grave, to hear the *peaceful* sounds of the earth & just to know that ones dear friends were near', Wordsworth whose *Prelude* is impelled by 'reverence for the glorious dead, the sight / Of those long vistos, catacombs in which / Perennial minds lie visibly entombed', and whose perennial fascination lies in accounts of the child as 'embalmed / By nature', of childhood as the place of 'those truths ... / Which we are toiling all our lives to find, / In darkness lost, the darkness of the grave'[36]

John Keats: everything that could be said to take place within the darkness of the Chamber of Maiden Thought and along all the 'dark passages' leading from it, from the 'swallow'd up / And buried' voicings of 'The Fall of Hyperion: A Dream' (in which the speaker 'breathe[s] death' with inferior poets but claims 'it will be life to see them sprawl before me into graves'), to that ode to a nightingale whose 'high requiem' causes the poet to 'become a sod', and whose song is finally, still alive but 'buried deep / In the next valley-glades', to the uncanny strangeness of that so-called posthumous poem in which 'This living hand, now warm and capable', reaches out towards us within 'the icy silence of the tomb')[37]

Emily Brontë: her poetry with its multiple tracings of the thought that 'All my life's bliss is in the grave with thee',[38] but most of all, *Wuthering Heights* with all its strange figurations of stifling claustrophobia, not only in such details as Lockwood's being locked up in the coffin-like wood of the 'large oak case' in which he spends his first night at Wuthering Heights or Catherine's insistence to Heathcliff that 'should a word of mine distress you hereafter, think I shall feel the same distress underground', but more generally in the experience of the eponymous house-as-text-as-buried-alive[39]

Emily Dickinson, with her numerous poems that are explicitly composed as posthumous exclamations ('I heard a fly buzz – when I died', 'I died for Beauty – but was scarce / Adjusted in the Tomb / When One who died for Truth, was lain / In an adjoining Room', and so on), but whose entire oeuvre of secreted 'packets' seems to comport a kind of live burial and perhaps thus to suggest that what has come to be known as 'women's writing', especially in the nineteenth century, might just as accurately be associated with being 'buried alive' as with the well-known 'madwoman in the attic'[40]

and so many other no-longer-if-ever-upright cases of 'men's writing', no less mad, from Matthew Arnold ('Lines Written in Kensington Gardens', 'The Buried Life' and so on)[41] to T. S. Eliot (perhaps most of all, *The Waste Land* with its relentless 'burial of the [living] dead', with all its claustrophobia of being 'neither / Living nor dead', of sprouting corpses, of being 'in rats' alley', and 'walk[ing] among the lowest of the dead');[42]

from the poetry of Thomas Hardy ('Ah, Are You Digging on My Grave', 'I Rose Up as My Custom Is', 'Lying Awake' and so on)[43] to the fiction of D. H. Lawrence (not only an explicit case such as 'The Man who Died', which itself prompts a radical rethinking of the question of the victim of the first Christian live burial, in other words a quite different conception of Christianity,[44] but everything in his novels and short stories that encouraged H. D. to distil her thinking on Lawrence, and doubtless also herself and Freud, within the proposition: 'We are all buried alive');[45]

from James Joyce (the snowy burial of 'all the living and the dead' at the end of 'The Dead',[46] *Ulysses* with Stephen haunted by thoughts of the 'allwombing tomb' and Leopold Bloom funereally '[w]onder[ing] does the news go about whenever a fresh one is let down. Underground communication',[47] not forgetting the uncertain wake of a certain Finnegan) to Samuel Beckett (not only Winnie up to her neck in sand in *Happy Days* or the buried alive world of *Endgame*, but all over – from *The Unnamable* to *How It Is* to *Not I* to *Company* to 'Stirrings Still').

From such a twisting passage we may gather some dusty sense that if (as Harold Bloom contends) the canonical is always uncanny, this uncanniness is in turn bound up with a thinking about literature itself in terms of being buried alive.

Let us return to Poe. If the figure, the image, the fear and desire of being buried alive is, as I have just tried to suggest, more insidiously and profoundly characteristic of 'literature' than has been supposed, there is doubtless also something historically specific, singular and cryptic about Poe's 'case'. In an essay on *Antigone* (and Antigone is of course, along with Jesus Christ, among the most haunting examples of the classical lineage of our topic),[48] George Steiner remarks:

> There is … a very curious motif prevalent from about the 1780s on – in the Gothic novel at a low level [how 'low'? six feet below?], but also in elevated speculation. It is the strange theme of live burial. It haunts the literary and philosophical imagination. Personages are buried alive. The symbolic meanings of live burial are explored. It is difficult to know why, just at this period, this motif should begin to concentrate great emotional malaise and philosophic speculation. But the fact is undeniable.[49]

In fact, this 'haunting' is a good deal less mysterious or incomprehensible than Steiner seems to think. As Jan Bondeson makes clear in his recent study, *Buried Alive: The Terrifying History of Our Most Primal Fear*, this new 'haunted' concern with live burial emerged through a range of practices and discourses, in particular medicine and religion, as well as literature and philosophy.[50] Bondeson follows the work of Philippe Ariès and other commentators, in emphasizing the combined effects of eighteenth-century medical and more popular concerns about the uncertain boundaries between life and death, in other words anxieties about 'apparent death' and the 'living dead'.[51] Elaborating on the effects in particular of the highly influential book by Jean-Jacques Bruhier, *Dissertation sur l'incertitude des signes de la mort*, first published in two volumes (1746–49) but quickly translated and published in numerous other languages (an initial English translation, *The Uncertainty of the Signs of Death*, appeared in 1746, another in 1751), Bondeson remarks:

> In a way, the 1740s were exactly the right time for fears of being buried alive to develop: there was still a good deal of superstition about abnormal fasts, hibernating swallows, and submarine humans, but the rationalist eighteeenth-century medical scientists no longer considered these matters to be supernatural.[52]

Perhaps most of all, to adopt Bondeson's rather bureaucratic phrasing: 'the fear of being buried alive was a by-product of the ongoing process of dechristian-ization'.[53] Without the comfort, hope or presumed assurance of a heavenly afterlife, the business of dying became, in new and different ways, exercisingly grave. In Philippe Ariès's terms, 'the great modern fear of death' thus began.[54] As Bondeson summarizes it: 'By the early nineteenth century, the danger of pre-mature burial had become one of the most-feared perils of everyday life, and a torrent of pamphlets and academic theses were dedicated to this subject by writers all over Europe.'[55]

George Steiner's observation can perhaps be formulated slightly differ-ently: around the end of the eighteenth and beginning of the nineteenth centuries, literature and live burial became curiously entwined bed-fellows. In particular, I would like to suggest, what emerges in the nineteenth century – and in an exemplary fashion in the writings of Poe – is a peculiar exposition of 'literature' itself *as* live burial. 'The Premature Burial' may seem to present a somewhat gruesome and exceptional example of what Freud calls the 'crown' of the uncanny. But in fact premature burial is everywhere in Poe's work.[56] His tales are pervaded by images and figurations of being buried alive, not only in an explicit way in texts such as 'Loss of Breath', 'Berenicë', 'Morella', 'Ligeia', 'King Pest', 'The Colloquy of Monos and Una', 'The Fall of the House of Usher', 'The Black Cat' and 'The Cask of Amontillado', but also, everywhere, in the experience of narrative suspension or catalepsy, in the sort of narratorial 'live burial' that we encounter in 'The Facts in the Case of M. Valdemar' (on the subject of being 'mesmerized *in articulo mortis*') or 'The Imp of the Perverse' ('But why shall I say more? To-day I wear these chains, and am *here*! To-morrow I shall be fetterless! – *but where*?').[57]

How conclude an account – whether first-person or (telepathic) third-person – of being buried alive? 'The Premature Burial' conveys a strong sense of the interminable. It is interminable in at least two, conjoined senses: first, as we have seen, in leaving us with an aporetic decision *between* death and 'slumber'; and second, in what we may describe as its prematurity. For the title of this text is, after all, curiously misleading, a sort of anamorphic misnomer. The 'the' of 'The Premature Burial', like the 'the' of 'The Uncanny', is always premature. Why is Poe's text called 'The Premature Burial'? If there is *a* specific premature burial which the text seems above all to want to tell us about, it would be the innocuous night on the sloop, an occasion that precisely is *not* a case of premature burial. The title of Poe's story is, 'very properly and very peculiarly' (p. 961), self-referential. If there is *a* premature burial, a single, singular one, *the* premature burial, it would be the text. 'The Premature Burial' will have been the premature burial. Above all, Poe's text makes clear an intimate cohabiting between being buried alive and *writing*.[58] Such would be the strangeness of his illegitimately 'legitimate fiction'.

Magical realist supplement. Permit me, if you will, a few terminal words concerning Gabriel García Márquez's story 'The Third Resignation', a (telepathic) third-person account.[59] Like 'The Premature Burial', 'The Third Resignation' conveys a strong sense of the interminable. García Márquez is of course most commonly associated with the literary genre known as magical realism. There are doubtless innumerable ways in which we might seek to explore the relations between magical realism and the uncanny. In an essay entitled 'Derek Walcott and Alejo Carpentier: Nature, History, and the Caribbean Writer', David Mikics notes:

> Magical realism, like the uncanny, a mode with which it has strong affinities, projects a mesmerizing uncertainty suggesting that ordinary life may also be the scene of the extraordinary. Such dreamlike suspension on the border between the fantastic and the mundane offers a utopian, if evanescent, promise of transfigured perception, the hypnotic renewing of everyday existence. Both the uncanny and magical realism narrate fantastic events not merely alongside real ones, but as if they were real.[60]

He goes on to argue that 'magical realism is a mode or subset of the uncanny in which the uncanny exposes itself as a historical and cultural phenomenon'.[61]

We might take issue with various aspects of Mikics's account: the assumption that 'the uncanny' is a 'mode'; the presentism implicit in his characterization of the 'promise' as something that passes by, in 'evanescent' fashion, rather than as something that haunts and is perhaps still to come; the governing opposition of 'fantastic' and 'real events', apparently left intact and unaffected by the 'modes' of writing in question; and, finally, the apparent incongruity whereby 'the uncanny' can operate as at once a 'mode' *like* magical realism *and* as a 'set' for which magical realism would be a 'subset'. This last point, in particular, serves to foreground a notion of the uncanny as 'essentially' bound up with supplementarity, reversibility and substitutability, with a destabilizing of inside and outside, part and whole, set and subset, with an overflowing of genre or mode. We would thus have to call into question the claim that 'magical realism is a mode or subset of the uncanny in which the uncanny exposes itself as a historical and cultural phenomenon'. Magical realism has no privileged role here: one could just as well substitute 'gothic fiction' or 'surrealism' or indeed any other 'ism' in so far as this might be conceived as a genre or mode. The uncanny can (and indeed perhaps must) always be exposed as 'a historical and cultural phenomenon'; but it can (and indeed perhaps must) also, *at the same time*, be what questions, unsettles and defamiliarizes any 'ordinary' sense or understanding of the 'historical', the 'cultural' and the 'phenomenon'.

Lois Parkinson Zamora and Wendy B. Faris note that, in works of magical realism,

> the supernatural is not a simple or obvious matter, but it *is* an ordinary matter, an everyday occurrence – admitted, accepted, and integrated into the rationality and materiality of literary realism. Magic is no longer quixotic madness, but normative and normalizing.[62]

If magical realism can be an 'uncanny' discourse on account of its defamiliarizing of the ordinary, it is also quite capable of 'normalizing' and neutralizing itself.[63] This danger of neutralization seems to me evident not only in the work of García Márquez but also, for example, of Salman Rushdie, Angela Carter and Jeanette Winterson. It has to do with the paradoxical constraints of freedom: works of magical realism can be fictions in which anything can happen or un-happen. Such narratives are not governed, in the way that realist narratives are, by the 'sense of an ending' (in Frank Kermode's phrase).[64] They need not conform to notions of 'ordinary' or 'familiar' plot development or characterization. By the very tension and irresolution of the compound (both 'magical' and 'realist'), this discourse is condemned to an enclosure within the interminable.

'The Third Resignation' is suggestive in this context. From the outset, we are told that the protagonist is subjected to a terrible noise: it is said to be 'interminable, like a child beating his head against a concrete wall' (p. 2). A little later we are informed that the protagonist has been 'carefully placed inside a coffin of hard but transparent cement' (p. 2). He has, seemingly, been buried alive: 'He was in his coffin, ready to be buried, and yet he knew that he wasn't dead. That if he tried to get up he could do it so easily' (p. 3). We are given to understand that he died when he was a child of seven and again when he was twenty-five. The story goes on to recount his day-to-day 'death', year upon year 'in the solitary company of his own corpse' (p. 7). But then 'suddenly fear struck him in the back like a dagger … The phantom of fear opened the window of reality to him: They were going to bury him alive!' (p. 8). The story ends with an allusion to its title (the protagonist evidently having already 'resigned' himself to death twice): 'But most likely he is so resigned to dying now that he might well die of resignation' (p. 10). What kind of 'sense of an ending' is at stake here?

'The Third Resignation' might, in fact, have been 'The Fourth Resigna-tion', or 'The Fifth Resignation', or 'The Sixth Resignation', and so on: having died or been buried alive once, there is no reason why it should not happen again and again. Freed from the constraints of an 'ordinary' figuration of death as 'final', seduced again and again by the 'immortal' possibilities of being buried alive, the narrative need never end, indeed in some sense can never end. Like 'The Premature Burial', García Márquez's story thus exemplifies a relationship between live burial and writing. 'To write': a vivisepultural verb. The relationship is compounded by the use of a third-person narrative perspective, in which we are granted access to the thoughts and feelings of the unnamed protagonist thanks to an unnamed narrator, in other words we are kept constantly aware of the writing and writerliness of the text, the fabricated and fictive, fantastical or 'magical' nature of the narrative. Not all, indeed perhaps very few, works of magical realism are explicitly focused on live burial in the way that 'The Third Resignation' is; but García Márquez's story suggests that being buried alive is an apt figure for the interminable, enclosed world of fantasy that is known as magical realism.

'The uncanny as it is depicted in *literature*, in stories and imaginative productions, merits in truth a separate discussion' (U, p. 372). Of course, as Freud's essay itself shows in so many ways, 'a separate discussion' is impossible.

> To some people the idea of being buried alive by mistake is the most uncanny thing of all. And yet psychoanalysis has taught us that this terrifying phantasy is only a transformation of another phantasy which had originally nothing terrifying about it at all, but was qualified by a certain lasciviousness – the phantasy, I mean, of intra-uterine existence. (U, pp. 366–7)

These fantastical, chiasmatically self-enclosed sentences about the idea or fantasy of being buried alive that seem to come out of the blue, in 'The Uncanny', seem 'in truth' to have no bearing on literature. Nor, for that matter, do they seemingly have any bearing on the 'real' – if by that term we are thinking for example of the dreadful instances such as the earthquakes that happen every year in different parts of the world, all too terribly burying people alive.[65] We might say that these sentences about the 'crown of uncanniness' are, in a strange way, concerned with neither 'literature' nor 'the real'. At the same time, however, they throw new and unfamiliar light on both. As if suspended in a stellifying world of their own, they are like a miniature work of magical realism.

★ ★
★

UNDER-NOTES

1   Friedrich Nietzsche, *The Gay Science*, trans. Walter Kaufmann (New York: Vintage, 1974), section 365.

2   Only 'seemingly' out of the blue, because there is also a certain rationale here, in turn suggestive of an uncanny mechanical repetitiveness. In the preceding paragraph Freud had pointed out how psychoanalysis 'has itself become uncanny to many people': the next paragraph then gives these two instances (dismembered limbs, live burial) of how psychoanalysis can uncannily lay bare the hidden the hidden forces *behind* or *beneath* them. Regarding the 'peculiarly uncanny' impression that can be generated by 'dismembered limbs, a severed head, a hand cut off at the wrist' and 'feet which dance by themselves', Freud 'reminds' us that he has already severed this from any possibility of further discussion: 'As we already know, this kind of uncanniness springs from its proximity to the castration complex' (U, p. 366).

3   Laurie Anderson, 'O Superman', *Big Science* (Warner Bros Records, 1982).

4   Such an animistic rhetorical flourish (death as the 'silent Goddess' who 'take[s man] into her arms') redoubles itself, acting out the logic according to which (as Freud puts it in a footnote, a curiously 'double' footnote in that it appears both in 'The Uncanny' itself and in *Totem and Taboo*) 'We appear to attribute an "uncanny" quality to impressions that seek to confirm … the animistic mode of thinking, after we have reached a stage at which, in our *judgement*, we have abandoned such beliefs' (U, 363, n. 1; *PFL*, 13: 144, n. 1).

5   In 'The Theme of the Three Caskets', Freud explores the idea that, in the myth of the Moerae and in a variety of other mythical and literary material, 'the Goddess of Death was replaced by the Goddess of Love and by what was equivalent to her in human shape' (p. 244). He goes on to suggest that 'The fairest and best of women, who has taken the place of the Death-Goddess, has kept certain characteristics that border on the uncanny' (p. 245). For further discussion of beauty and femininity in this context see Elisabeth Bronfen, *Over Her Dead Body: Death, Femininity and the Aesthetic* (Manchester: Manchester University Press, 1992), pp. 59–75. Bronfen contends that 'Pleasure at the beauty of Woman resides in the uncanny *simultaneity* of recognising and misrecognising it as a veil for death' (p. 63). I discuss Bronfen's work at greater length in Chapter 5 above.

6   In the *Standard Edition* and in the *Pelican Freud Library* edition, there is simply a blank line.

7   There is a similar, perhaps rather too neat and cosy reversal and reassurance concerning the dissolution of the 'dreaded event' of being buried alive when Freud discusses the capacity of the dream-work for bringing about wish-fulfilments in *The Future of an Illusion*: 'The sleeper may be seized with a presentiment of death, which threatens to place him in the grave. But the dream-work knows how to select a condition that will turn even that dreaded event into a wish-fulfilment: the dreamer sees himself in an ancient Egyptian grave which he has climbed down into, happy to find his archaeological interests satisfied' (*PFL*, 12: 196–7). As the editor Albert Dickson notes (p. 197, n. 1), Freud is here recalling the analysis of one of his own dreams: see *The Interpretation of Dreams* (*PFL*, 4), pp. 587–8. There is a good discussion of this by Anthony Vidler, in a chapter called 'Buried Alive', in his *The Architectural Uncanny: Essays in the Modern Unhomely* (Cambridge, Mass.: MIT Press, 1992), pp. 45–55.

8   According to the *OED*, the 'canny moment' is a Scottish archaism for 'the moment of child-birth' (see *OED* entry for 'canny', sense 3).

9   For a fuller discussion of Freud's not starting his investigation of the uncanny where he perhaps ought to have done, see Chapter 8 above.

10   Edgar Allan Poe, 'The Premature Burial', in the *Collected Works of Edgar Allan Poe*, 3, ed. Thomas Ollive Mabbott (Cambridge, Mass.: Belknap Press, 1978), pp. 954–69: here, pp. 954–5. Further page references are given in parentheses in the main body of the text.

11   In this respect it seems especially appropriate that the strangely muted, chilling Dutch/ French film *The Vanishing* (dir. George Sluizer, 1988) ends with the male protagonist, buried alive, repeatedly calling out his name: 'Rex Hoffman'.

12   See the discussion of the living-dead name in the context of Nietzsche and Derrida in Chapter 3 above, and the discussion of the name in relation to death and the double in Chapter 12 below. 'Rigid designator' is Saul Kripke's term for the proper name: see his *Naming and Necessity* (Oxford: Basil Blackwell, 1980). On the notions of proper name and crypt, in which words themselves have been 'buried alive', see Jacques Derrida's 'Fors: The Anglish Words of Nicolas Abraham and Maria Torok', trans. Barbara Johnson, in Abraham and Torok, *The Wolf Man's Magic Word: A Cryptonymy*, trans. Nicholas Rand (Minneapolis: University of Minnesota Press, 1986), p. xxxv and passim. In their essay 'The Topography of Reality: Sketching a Metapsychology of Secrets', Abraham and Torok write of 'the depths of the crypt' in which 'unspeakable words buried alive are held fast, like owls in ceaseless vigil': see Nicolas Abraham and Maria Torok, *The Shell and the Kernel*, 1, ed. and trans. Nicholas Rand (Chicago: Chicago University Press, 1994), pp. 159–60.

13   Tzvetan Todorov, *The Fantastic: A Structural Approach to a Literary Genre* (1970), trans. Richard Howard (Ithaca: Cornell University Press, 1975), p. 48. I discuss the notion of the meta-uncanny in Chapter 1, above.

14   Poe's sentence suggests at the same time a weird foreshadowing of the sense of thinking one encounters in what is perhaps Samuel Beckett's greatest work about being 'buried alive', *The Unnamable*: 'I only think, if that is the name for this vertiginous panic as of hornets smoked out of their nest, once a certain degree of terror has been exceeded.' See *Molloy, Malone Dies, The Unnamable* (London: Calder and Boyars, 1959), p. 353.

15   See Charles Dickens, *Our Mutual Friend* (Harmondsworth: Penguin, 1971), pp. 503–9, and Maurice Blanchot, *Death Sentence*, trans. Lydia Davis, in *The Station Hill Blanchot Reader: Fiction and Literary Essays*, ed. George Quasha (Barrytown, NY: Station Hill, 1999), esp. pp. 131–51.

16   See, for example, Harold Bloom, *The Anxiety of Influence: A Theory of Poetry*, 2nd edn (Oxford: Oxford University Press, 1997), pp. 152–4.

17   Bloom, *The Anxiety of Influence*, p. 152.

18   In the Preface to the 1997 edition of *The Anxiety of Influence* he asserts: 'Like criticism, which is either part of literature or nothing at all, great writing is always at work strongly (or weakly) misreading previous writing' (p. xix).

19   Bloom, *The Anxiety of Influence*, pp. 15–16.

20   Harold Bloom, *The Western Canon: The Books and School of the Ages* (London: Macmillan, 1995), p. 288. He does at one point suggestively remark on Poe's uncanny 'ghostly presence' in the work of Dickens (p. 319).

21   Bloom is closer to such a posthumism than he perhaps recognizes or would wish to admit. While he maintains a fundamentally vitalist vocabulary, contending for example that '[t]he Canon is the very gauge of vitality' (*The Western Canon*, p. 39), his work is also acutely attuned to the power of the dead, the dead as the living dead, the dead as more alive than the living. Thus in the same passage of *The Western Canon* he writes contemptuously of the critical cliché about the western literary canon as comprising 'dead, white European males'. Naming Homer, Virgil, Dante, Chaucer, Shakespeare, Cervantes, Montaigne, Milton, Goethe, Tolstoy, Ibsen, Kafka and Proust, he goes on to declare: 'Livelier than you are, whoever you are,

these authors were indubitably male, and I suppose "white". But they are not dead, compared to any living author whomsoever. Among us now are García Márquez, Pynchon, Ashbery, and others who are likely to become as canonical as Borges and Beckett among the recently deceased, but Cervantes and Shakespeare are of another order of vitality' (p. 39). Instead of 'vitality' here, we could just as well, or still more appositely, speak of the 'posthumous power' of the buried alive.

22   Regarding the etymology of 'bed' itself, *Chambers* suggests that it is 'probably related to Latin *fodere* to dig (as *orig* a hole)'. Jacques Derrida makes a related comment in an essay on chance, coincidence and the uncanny possibilities of reading or writing in relation to 'juggling': 'The clinic, let it be said in passing, names the integral space of the retiring or bedridden position, which is the position of illness par excellence, and thus, one invariably "falls" ill.' See 'My Chances/*Mes Chances*: A Rendezvous with Some Epicurean Stereophonies', trans. Irene Harvey and Avital Ronell, in *Taking Chances: Derrida, Psychoanalysis, and Literature*, eds Joseph H. Smith and William Kerrigan (Baltimore and London: Johns Hopkins University Press, 1984), p. 7. The allusion to the uncanny and going 'beyond juggling' appears on p. 14. Commenting on Baudelaire's commentary on Poe, Derrida suggests that the uncanniness of Poe's writing comes from a combination of 'the art of the juggler' and a persistent openness to random effects of chance. Derrida writes: 'In itself juggling would imply too great a mastery in the art of coincidence, which must remain *unheimlich, uncanny*' (p. 14, translation slightly modified).

23   Thomas Ollive Mabbott notes that 'The impulse to write "The Premature Burial" presumably came from the publicity attendant on the "life preserving coffin" exhibited at the annual fair of the American Institute, New York City, 1843': see *Collected Works of Edgar Allan Poe*, 3: 954. Mabbott also provides valuable information about some of the original newspaper stories on which Poe drew for his account of the various recent cases of premature burial in Europe and America: see pp. 969 ff. On the autobiothanatoheterographical, see Jacques Derrida, 'Circumfession', in *Jacques Derrida*, trans. Geoffrey Bennington (Chicago: Chicago University Press, 1993), p. 213 and passim.

24   Ernst Jentsch, 'On the Psychology of the Uncanny', trans. Roy Sellars, *Angelaki*, vol. 2, no. 1 (1995), ed. Sarah Wood, pp. 7–16. Further page references are given in parentheses in the main body of the text.

25   Despite its exemplarity as an uncanny, 'foreign and enigmatic' disease, epilepsy can nevertheless be compared with numerous other mental and physical states, including 'alcoholic intoxication'. Jentsch remarks that, especially if it is not a 'familiar' occurrence, the sight of 'an alcoholic intoxication' can produce in the spectator an uncanny sense that 'mechanical processes are taking place in that which [the observer] was previously used to regarding as a unified psyche' (p. 14).

26   I explore the notion of textual fits in more detail in Chapter 22, below.

27   In the immediately preceding footnote Freud had bluntly declared his scepticism as regards the credibility of Fyodor Dostoevsky's own autobiographical accounts: 'Unfortunately there is reason to distrust the autobiographical statements of neurotics. Experience shows that their memories introduce falsifications which are designed to interrupt disagreeable causal connections' (p. 446, n. 2). We may take as reliable the evidence furnished by Fyodor's friend Soloviev and by his brother Andrey; but why should we assume the truth-status of these 'little notes' any more than the truth-status of what Poe's narrator tells us in 'The Premature Burial'? In any case, one is tempted to feel that some 'disagreeable causal connection' is here interrupted.

28   Edgar Allan Poe, 'The Facts in the Case of M. Valdemar', in the *Complete Works*, 3: 1240. We
      may here usefully recall Derrida's comment on this moment in the Valdemar text: far from
      seeing 'I am dead' as an impossible statement, Derrida contends that 'the condition for a true
      act of language is my being able to say "I am dead"... [T]he power of meaning of language is,
      to a point, independent of the possibility of its object. "I am dead" has a meaning [even] if it
      is obviously false. "I am dead" is an intelligible sentence. Therefore, "I am dead" is not only a
      possible proposition for one who is known to be living, but the very condition for the living
      person to speak is for him [sic] to be able to say, significantly, "I am dead".' See *The Structuralist
      Controversy: The Languages of Criticism and the Sciences of Man*, eds Richard Macksey and
      Eugenio Donato (1970; Baltimore: Johns Hopkins University Press, 1972), p. 156. Derrida is
      countering Roland Barthes's supposition, in 'To Write: An Intransitive Verb?', that '[one]
      can't say "I am dead"' (*The Structuralist Controversy*, p. 143). 'The Premature Burial' offers
      another enacting of the same spectral logic, this time in the seemingly opposing form of 'I am
      alive' (p. 961). Poe's narrator thus recounts the facts in the case of Mr Stapleton: 'dully and
      confusedly he was aware of every thing which happened to him, from the moment in which
      he was pronounced *dead* by his physicians, to that in which he fell swooning to the floor of
      the hospital. "I am alive," were the uncomprehended words which, upon recognising the
      locality of the dissecting-room, he had endeavored, in his extremity, to utter' (p. 961). As is
      suggested by a slightly earlier recounting of a case in which a man is dug up from a 'shame-
      fully shallow' grave, 'conveyed to the nearest hospital, and there pronounced to be still
      living' (p. 959), Poe's text brings to the surface, so to speak, the crucial yet spectral force of
      the performative utterance, in other words to pronounce dead *or* alive.

29   In *The Double: A Psychoanalytic Study*, trans. and ed. Harry Tucker, Jr (1914; Chapel Hill, NC:
      University of North Carolina Press, 1971), Otto Rank specifically draws attention to the
      similarity: 'As a youth in engineering school, according to his own statement, [Dostoevsky]
      is said to have had mild seizures (of an epileptic nature) – like those of Poe, with whom he
      also shared the fear of being buried alive' (p. 46). Freud of course read, or claimed to have
      read, Rank's study. It is indeed on account of that work that Freud restricts the amount of
      attention he gives, in his essay on 'The Uncanny', to the question of doubles. As he puts it:
      'The theme of the "double" has been very thoroughly treated by Otto Rank' (U, p. 356).
      Freud, in other words, could certainly be expected to have read Rank's parallel between Poe
      and Dostoevsky. But how familiar was Freud with the work of Poe? It is odd – given the
      formidable tradition of reading Poe with or through psychoanalysis, and vice versa – that
      Freud himself does not discuss Poe, either in 'The Uncanny' or indeed in any of his other
      essays or more major writings. The only text (as far as I have been able to discover) in which
      he writes about Poe is the short preface (comprising just four sentences) to Marie Bonaparte's
      Edgar Poe: Étude psychanalytique (Paris, 1933). Here, in a quite cursory fashion, Freud simply
      refers to Poe as 'a great writer of a pathological type'. See 'Preface to Marie Bonaparte's *The
      Life and Works of Edgar Allan Poe: A Psycho-analytic Interpretation*' (1933), SE, 22: 254.

30   In this respect, Poe's text seems to make contact with one of Wordsworth's most cryptic
      poems about being buried alive, 'A slumber did my spirit seal' (1800):

> A slumber did my spirit seal;
>   I had no human fears:
> She seemed a thing that could not feel
>   The touch of earthly years.

> No motion has she now, no force;
>   She neither hears nor sees;
>   Rolled round in earth's diurnal course,
>   With rocks and stones and trees.

(See *William Wordworth*, ed. Stephen Gill (Oxford: Oxford University Press, 1984), p. 147.) The sense and syntax of the opening line resists any reading that would finally put it to rest: the grammatical subject can be the 'slumber' or the 'spirit'. Wordsworth's astonishingly compacted elegy is concerned with a 'she' (usually identified by critics as 'Lucy') who is now in the grave, seemingly without 'motion'. Yet she is 'Rolled round in earth's diurnal course, / With rocks and stones and trees'. When alive she 'seemed a thing that could not feel / The touch of earthly years': does she feel this 'touch' now that she is a tenant of the grave? The 'slumber' – doubtless, as in Poe, in a tension of both sleep and inattentiveness – seems to suggest that the speaker was himself in a state of some kind of suspended animation (sealed up in spirit and/or slumber), beyond the 'touch of earthly years'. Everything is, in some sense perhaps, packed into the little word 'did' (palindromic, like the seizure of the 'sees' in the second stanza): with its evocations of doing and dying, 'died' and 'die', we are left to wonder: Who is dead, or buried alive? Has the slumber ended? Or is the very act of reading this hypnopoetic text not a slumber, its cryptic sealing?

31 See Bloom, *The Western Canon*, p. 120.

32 Geoffrey Chaucer, 'The Pardoner's Tale', ll. 558–9, *The Works of Geoffrey Chaucer*, 2nd edn, ed. F. N. Robinson (London: Oxford University Press, 1957).

33 John Milton, *Paradise Lost*, ed. Alastair Fowler (London: Longman, 1971), Book 2, ll. 262–3, 406, 841–3.

34 John Milton, 'Lycidas', ll. 155–8, in *Complete Shorter Poems* (London: Longman, 1971), p. 251.

35 'Samson Agonistes', ll. 100–5, in *Complete Shorter Poems*, p. 348.

36 See Dorothy Wordsworth, Journal entry for Thursday 29 April 1802, in *The Grasmere Journals*, ed. Pamela Woof (Oxford: Clarendon, 1991), p. 92; William Wordsworth, *The Prelude 1799, 1805, 1850*, ed. Jonathan Wordsworth, M. H. Abrams and Stephen Gill (New York: Norton, 1979), 1805 version, Book 3, ll. 344–6; Book 7, ll. 400–1; and the *Intimations* Ode, stanza 8, in *William Wordworth*, ed. Stephen Gill (Oxford: Oxford University Press, 1984), p. 300. For a discussion of 'the relationship between Romanticism and playing dead', focusing in particular on Byron, see Andrew Bennett, *Romantic Poets and the Culture of Posterity* (Cambridge: Cambridge University Press, 1999), pp. 179 ff. My thanks to Andrew Bennett for bringing the Dorothy Wordsworth journal entry (quoted in Bennett, p. 180) to my attention.

37 John Keats, Letter to J. H. Reynolds, 3 May 1818, in *Letters of John Keats*, ed. Robert Gittings (London: Oxford University Press, 1970), p. 95; 'The Fall of Hyperion: A Dream', Canto I, ll. 412–13, 208–9, 'Ode to a Nightingale', and 'This living hand' in *The Poems of John Keats*, ed. Jack Stillinger (London: Heinemann, 1978). The phrase 'swallow'd up / And buried' is Saturn's self-description, but 'The Fall of Hyperion: A Dream' is in more general respects preoccupied with such dark and subterranean feelings, not least in terms of the voice and voices – from the poet's amazement that death has not come 'To choak my utterance' (l. 140), having been granted (in Moneta's words) the opportunity to '[feel] / What 'tis to die and live again' (l. 142), to a more diffuse sense that this unfinished poem is too much 'swallow'd up / And buried' (ll. 412–13) in the voice and tonalities of Milton. On 'This living hand' and the uncanny see also Brooke Hopkins, 'Keats and the Uncanny: "This living hand"', *The Kenyon Review*, vol. 11, no. 4 (1989), 28–40.

38 Emily Brontë, 'Remembrance', in *The Complete Poems*, ed. Janet Gezari (Harmondsworth: Penguin, 1992), pp. 8–9.

39 Emily Brontë, *Wuthering Heights*, ed. William M. Sale Jr and Richard J. Dunn, 3rd edn (New York: W. W. Norton, 1990), pp. 15, 123.

40 Emily Dickinson, poems tagged and numbered (449, 465) as if in a textual mortuary, in *Complete Poems of Emily Dickinson*, ed. Thomas H. Johnson (London: Faber and Faber, 1975).

41 *The Poems of Matthew Arnold*, 2nd edn, ed. Miriam Allott (London: Longman, 1979), pp. 269–73, 286–91.

42 T. S. Eliot, *The Waste Land*, in *The Complete Poems and Plays of T. S. Eliot* (London: Faber and Faber, 1962), pp. 59–75.

43 See Thomas Hardy, *The Complete Poems* (London: Macmillan, 1976), pp. 330–1, 378–9, 863. Live burial would have a crucial role in the critical understanding of prosopopoeia in Hardy's poetry, of Hardy's poetry *as* prosopopoeia. In the elegy-sequence, 'Poems of 1912–13' (pp. 338–58), for example, we might consider in particular 'I Found Her Out There' (pp. 342–3), 'His Visitor' (p. 347) and 'The Spell of the Rose' (pp. 355–6).

44 D. H. Lawrence, 'The Man who Died' (1929) in *Love Among the Haystacks and Other Stories* (Harmondsworth: Penguin, 1960), pp. 125–73. Lawrence's powerful vision of Jesus Christ buried alive and coming back from the grave might lead us to wonder if Poe's narrator's vision of 'the shrouded bodies' of the 'many millions ... who slumbered not at all' ('The Premature Burial', p. 964) cannot perhaps be read as, among other things, the expression of a radical uncertainty as to whether a truly Christian burial will ever have taken place.

45 In her *Tribute to Freud*, rev. edn (Manchester: Carcanet, 1985), H. D. (Hilda Doolittle) repeatedly recalls the fact that Freud had a 'Buried Alive' print hanging on the wall of his waiting room: see for example pp. 61, 96, 131. She writes:

> I don't want to think of Lawrence.
> 'I hope never to see you again,' he wrote in that last letter.
> Then after the death of Lawrence, Stephen Guest brought me [a copy of 'The Man who Died'] and said, 'Lawrence wrote this for you.'
> Lawrence was imprisoned in his tomb; like the print hanging in the waiting room, he was 'Buried Alive'.
> We are all buried alive. (p. 134)

46 James Joyce, 'The Dead', in *Dubliners* (Harmondsworth: Penguin, 1956), p. 220.

47 James Joyce, *Ulysses*, ed. Jeri Johnson (Oxford: Oxford University Press, 1993), pp. 47, 110.

48 We might think, for example, of such lines as these:

> I go to my rockbound prison, strange new tomb –
>   always a stranger, O dear god,
>   I have no home on earth and none below,
>   not with the living, not with the breathless dead.

See Sophocles, *Antigone*, ll. 939–42, in *The Three Theban Plays*, trans. Robert Fagles (Harmondsworth: Penguin Classics, 1984). Let me here merely indicate a passageway, to be explored further, concerning the relationship between what I have been talking about as 'buried alive' and the death drive. For Lacan in particular, Antigone is the very incarnation of the death drive: see *The Ethics of Psychoanalysis 1959–1960*, *The Seminar of Jacques Lacan*, Book VII, ed. Jacques-Alain Miller, trans. Dennis Porter (London: Routledge, 1992), pp. 205–17, 243–87: here, p. 282. For some illuminating recent commentaries on Lacan's account in this context, see Caroline Rooney, 'Clandestine Antigones', in her *African Literature, Animism and Politics* (London: Routledge, 2000), p. 36–57; Judith Butler, *Antigone's Claim: Kinship Between Life and*

Death (New York: Columbia University Press, 2000), esp. pp. 27–55; and Jean-Michel Rabaté, '*Antigone*: Between the Beautiful and the Sublime', in his *Jacques Lacan: Psychoanalysis and the Subject of Literature* (Basingstoke: Palgrave, 2001), pp. 69–84.

49   George Steiner, 'Antigones', the 12th Jackson Knight Memorial Lecture (Exeter: Exeter University Press, 1979), p. 4. My thanks to Jennifer Cooke for bringing this text to my attention.

50   Jan Bondeson, *Buried Alive: The Terrifying History of Our Most Primal Fear* (New York: Norton, 2001).

51   See Philippe Ariès, *The Hour of Our Death*, trans. Helen Weaver (New York: Alfred A. Knopf, 1981), esp. Chapter 9 ('The Living Dead'), pp. 396–406; and 'The Eighteenth-century Debate', in Bondeson, *Buried Alive*, pp. 72–87.

52   Bondeson, *Buried Alive*, p. 80.

53   Bondeson, *Buried Alive*, p. 77.

54   Ariès writes: 'An early manifestation of the great modern fear of death now [in the eighteenth century] appears for the first time: the fear of being buried alive, which implies the conviction that there is an impure and reversible state that partakes of both life and death' (*The Hour of Our Death*, p. 609).

55   Bondeson, *Buried Alive*, p. 156.

56   As Bondeson puts it, with number-crunching good humour: 'The writer with the most premature burials per page must be Edgar Allan Poe' (p. 208). The author of 'The Terrifying History of Our Most Primal Fear' has an ability to say things wittily and knowingly as well as, perhaps, inadvertently. On the one hand, he appears to have a rather conventional, apparently no-nonsense mind in terms of literary criticism. He begins by wondering 'whether [Poe] himself lived in fear of being buried alive or merely wanted to use a well-known and horrific subject to curdle the blood of his readers' (p. 208) – as if one could know, or as if it really mattered, or as if the two possibilities were readily distinguishable. He then devotes a page or so to 'The Premature Burial', concluding his critical evaluation as follows: '"The Premature Burial" is not one of Poe's better stories; it is marred by the contrast between the rising tension of the story and the tongue-in-cheek quality of the ludicrous ending' (p. 211). On the other hand, he has a notable sensitivity to uncanniness, and especially to uncanny inadvertency. After talking about Poe, he moves on to the case of a 'learned German lady' called Frederike Kempner, who 'at an early age … had chanced to read a horrid pamphlet about premature burial, and this experience marked her for life' (p. 214). She becomes, it seems, obsessed with live burial. Bondeson cites a poem that he describes as (this word again) 'ludicrous' (p. 216). Addressed to King Wilhelm of Prussia, it is concerned with German soldiers Kempner felt were in danger of being premature fatalities of the Franco-Prussian War:

> In the German race's
> Fight for land to live in
> These pale, heroic faces
> Of the dead – may still be living!

> Great Emperor, with France enslaved
> Remember that it's surely
> A dismal end to soldiers brave
> To be buried prematurely!

He then goes on to remark of Kempner's poetry: 'She had little sense of either grammar or meter, and an almost uncanny ability to just miss the mark in a poem, or to break the tone at the last moment' (pp. 216–17). No doubt 'inadvertency', supplementarity and 'just missing the mark' are characteristic features of the uncanny. The present study would be condemned to confirm or repeat this. But what these two literary critical evaluations from Bondeson might be said inadvertently to suggest is a sense of uncanniness about the ending, not of Kempner's poems, but of Poe's story. Bondeson is doubtless right to note something like a contrast between the way 'The Premature Burial' opens and the so-called bathetic quality of its so-called denouement. The concern of the present reading is, among other things, to suggest that this bathetic effect is in a sense programmed or prescribed, starting from the very title of Poe's text. It is perhaps not so much a question of a narrative that is 'marred' (to recall Bondeson's term), as it is a question of writing and the experience of the impossible. With regard to the latter, all conclusions (including a dependence on terms such as 'bathos' and 'denouement') will have been premature. Perhaps inadvertently, Bondeson at the same time draws attention to a rather different contrast or tension, namely between the 'tongue-in-cheek' and the 'ludicrous'. 'Ludicrous' may indicate something merely absurd, ridiculous, laughable; 'tongue-in-cheek', however, bears a sense of calculating (but not necessarily calculable or determinable) irony, insincerity, mischievous humour. There is, perhaps, something curiously intimate about the relationship between being buried alive and the figure of the 'tongue-in-cheek': to speak tongue-in-cheek, or to have spoken tongue-in-cheek, is to bury one's tongue in one's cheek, literally, vitally, cryptically. It is, if one may venture such an expression, a kind of auto-oscular vivisepulture. Like the celebrated 'hoax', hocus-pocus or *hic est corpus* of 'The Facts in the Case of M. Valdemar', all of Poe's writing in this respect is perhaps tongue-in-cheek.

57   The Facts in the Case of M. Valdemar', *Collected Works*, 3: 1227; 'The Imp of the Perverse', p. 1233. A Poetic series of 'P'-words begins to rouse itself: *purloined, perverse, premature …*

58   In this respect it may be worth emphasizing that it is indeed a question of writing here, rather than of 'authorial consciousness', artistic 'self-consciousness' and so on. In a thoughtful and provoking essay on live burial in James Hogg's *Confessions of a Justified Sinner*, Magdalene Redekop writes: 'Like Poe, Hogg uses the image of being buried alive as a metaphor for intensified self-consciousness, and the result is that as readers we become vividly aware of the free mind – our own participating intelligence – buried in the body of the text, engaged in a constant struggle to escape through understanding'. See Magdalene Redekop, 'Beyond Closure: Buried Alive with Hogg's *Justified Sinner*', *English Literary History* (Spring 1985), 159–84: here, p. 162. Poe's story may indeed evoke an uncanny feeling of claustrophobia and unease in the reader, but the figure of live burial is no more a matter of 'self-consciousness' than it is of 'metaphor'. It is a writing-effect. The 'premature burial' *is* the text. What we are left with is the strangeness of a text that never arrives at the referent of its title, a narrative that in a sense never gets underway but at the same time will never not have been underway, is always still to be read.

59   Gabriel García Márquez, 'The Third Resignation', trans. Gregory Rabassa, in *Collected Stories* (Harmondsworth: Penguin, 1996), pp. 1–10. Further page references will be given in the main body of the text.

60   David Mikics, 'Derek Walcott and Alejo Carpentier: Nature, History, and the Caribbean Writer', in *Magical Realism: Theory, History, Community*, ed. Lois Parkinson Zamora and Wendy B. Faris (Durham, NC: Duke University Press, 1995), pp. 371–404: here, p. 372.

61   Mikics, p. 373.

62   Lois Parkinson Zamora and Wendy B. Faris, 'Introduction', *Magical Realism: Theory, History, Community*, p. 3.

63   It is for this reason absurd to claim, as Zamora and Faris do in their 'Introduction' to *Magical*

Realism: Theory, History, Community, that magical realist texts are categorically 'subversive' (p. 6). No text is inherently subversive, any more than it is inherently uncanny. Once again, it is a question of reading.

64 Frank Kermode, *The Sense of an Ending: Studies in the Theory of Fiction* (Oxford: Oxford University Press, 1967).

65 In this context, we should have to consider too a case such as that of Daphne Banks, discussed in Chapter 20, below. Every case is singular. No one, we might suppose, can be buried alive in the place of anyone else.

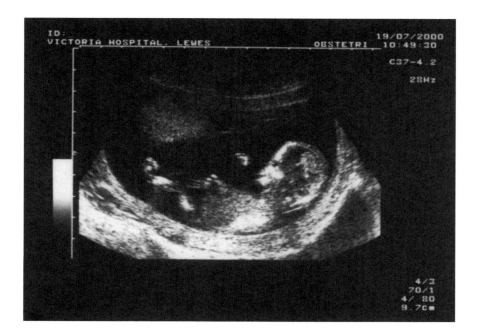

Antenatal photography

'That rather terrible thing which is there in every photograph: the return of the dead' (Roland Barthes)

11
Déjà vu

A belief like a guillotine, just as heavy, just as light. (Franz Kafka)[1]

If I had my life to live over again I should devote myself to psychical research rather than to psychoanalysis. (Sigmund Freud, attributed)[2]

What is *déjà vu*? If we consult a dictionary, as Freud does near the start of his essay on 'The Uncanny', we find that the term '*déjà vu*' is defined in two broadly distinct ways. Thus in the *OED*, for example, we discover:

  a. An illusory feeling of having previously experienced a present situation; a form of paramnesia ...
  b. occas. The correct impression that something has been previously experienced; tedious familiarity ...

The first recorded usage of the term in English in sense (a) is 1903; in sense (b) 1960. This historical detail is provoking: it suggests that we are living in the epoch of the double-sense of '*déjà vu*'.[3] '*Déjà vu*' seems to figure as a kind of primal word or phrase, one that carries an antithetical or contradictory sense within it, a kind of verbal double. What would it mean to suppose that a primal word is not only 'primal' but also '*déjà vu*'? '*Déjà vu*' signifies at once the illusion of 'having previously experienced a present situation' *and* 'the correct impression' of having really 'previously experienced' it. Given this semantic duplicity, a duplicity that menaces or haunts the very possibility of a dictionary (what could be called a *déjà vu* effect that necessarily makes every definition tremble, doubling and contradicting it, dividing it within), it is perhaps appropriate that dictionaries such as the *OED* and *Chambers* should emphasize the earlier or 'original' sense of '*déjà vu*' specifically and merely as 'illusion' or 'illusory'. *Chambers* thus gives its equivalent of *OED* sense (a): '*déjà vu*': 'an illusion of having experienced before something that is really being experienced for the first time'. This definition rests on an opposition of illusion and reality, presupposing the reality of what 'really' is 'being experienced' in a sense that is displaced and even proscribed by the *uncertainties* that could be said to characterize '*déjà vu*'. Both the *OED* and *Chambers* present '*déjà vu*' as a phrase whose meanings may be antithetical but can nevertheless be clearly distinguished and categorized as such. Yet what is perhaps most striking about '*déjà vu*' is the uncertainty, the deranging of definition that is, by definition, excluded by these various definitions of the term. Both the *OED* and *Chambers* see to it that '*déjà vu*' be defined as 'an illusion' or 'illusory' and both delegate the authority for such a definition to the discipline of psychology and in particular to the psychological concept of paramnesia. Thus in *Chambers* we read: '*déjà vu*': 'a form of the memory disorder paramnesia (*psychology*)'. If we then look in *Chambers* for a definition of 'paramnesia' we discover with seemingly unremarked irony: 'a memory disorder in which words are remembered but not their proper meaning'. (This is the first sense of 'paramnesia', according to *Chambers*, the second being: 'the condition of believing that one remembers events and circumstances which have not previously occurred'.) The dictionary itself seems subject to some sort of paramnesia.

What is the 'proper meaning' of '*déjà vu*'? If we go back to one of the earliest usages of the term '*déjà vu*', as specified in the *OED*, we find a reference to (who else but?) Freud, to Chapter 12 of *The Psychopathology of Everyday Life*.[4] Let us, then, return to Freud. Here, in the chapter on 'Determinism, Belief in Chance and Superstition – Some Points of View' (*PFL*, 5: 300–44), in a series of paragraphs dating from 1907, Freud writes:

> We must also include in the category of the miraculous and the 'uncanny' [*In die Kategorie des Wunderbaren und Unheimlichen* ...] [the English translator, Alan Tyson, puts the word 'uncanny' in quotation marks, as James Strachey does in translating the title of Freud's essay on this topic, i.e. 'The "Uncanny"': why? Might the implicit logic of quotation as duplication here signal something more intimate and essential about the rapport between the 'uncanny' and *déjà vu*? We shall return to this ...] the peculiar feeling we have, in certain moments and situations, of having had exactly the same experience once before or of having once before been in the same place, though *our efforts never succeed* in clearly remembering the previous occasion that announces itself in this way [*das sich so anzeigt*]. I am aware that I am merely following loose linguistic usage when I call what arises in a person at such moments a 'feeling' [*eine Empfindung*] [without any explanation 'feeling' too, then, joins the 'uncanny' as a word apparently always already 'in' 'quotes', at least in the English translation]. What is no doubt in question is a judgement [*es handelt sich wohl um ein Urteil*: 'it is probably a matter of a judgement'], and, more precisely, a perceptual judgement; but these cases have nevertheless *a character quite of their own*, and we must not leave out of account the fact that what is looked for is *never remembered*. (pp. 328–9/294, emphases added)

What must be remembered is that what is looked for is never remembered: so Freud, in effect, says. With that lucidity and fixity of purpose that is so grave and yet also sometimes so comical and affecting in his writing, Freud then goes on (at least on one level) to contradict his own thesis. For it turns out that, thanks to psychoanalysis, our efforts to remember at least in principle *can* succeed and what is looked for *can* be remembered: with the experience of *déjà vu*, he declares, something is really touched on which we have already experienced once before, only we cannot consciously remember it because it has never been conscious. To put it briefly, the feeling of '*déjà vu*' corresponds to the recollection of an unconscious phantasy. (*Die Empfindung des 'déjà vu' entspricht, kurz gesagt, der Erinnerung an eine unbewusste Phantasie.*) (p. 329/295)

(Freud then goes on to give an analysis of 'a single case', in which a woman's experience of *déjà vu* is explained as a sort of substitute for 'recalling', as if for the first time – *déjà vu* at the origin, we might say – a repressed or unconscious phantasy about wishing or expecting her brother's death.) It is in this context, then, that Freud is able to put forward a proposition that is also completely at odds with the dictionary definitions of '*déjà vu*', including the *OED* definition which refers to the Freud text for verification of the authoritative usage of the term! He states simply and categorically: 'It is in my view wrong to call the feeling of having experienced something before an illusion' (*Ich meine, man tut unrecht, die Empfindung des schon einmal Erlebthabens als eine Illusion zu bezeichnen*) (p. 329/295). But Freud makes a judgement here and in the very gesture of asserting that the feeling of *déjà vu* is not 'an illusion' and ascribing to it instead the seeming '"reality"' of 'the recollection of an unconscious phanstasy', he arrests, forecloses, shuts off consideration of the 'feeling' of *déjà vu* as 'a judgement' (a 'perceptual judgement') (*ein Urteil, und zwar ein Erkennungsurteil*: pp. 294–5) that is *in question*.

The author of *The Psychopathology of Everyday Life* says that he 'know[s] that the subject [of *déjà vu*] would merit the most exhaustive treatment (*der eingehendsten Behandlung würdig wäre*)' (p. 329/295), but he declines to give it. Or so it may appear. It may appear that *déjà vu* is a minor concern in the writings of Freud, in other words, but perhaps we should look again. In this way, like the question of telepathy, *déjà vu* may come to 'reappear' at the very heart of psychoanalysis, always already there *as a question*, and as the experience of a question. What would be going on in such an experience, as seen at once again and anew? What would it mean to suppose that the theoretical edifice of psychoanalysis lies here, trembling in the question of *déjà vu*, of actual and false recognition, of what is or is not really being experienced for the first time, of when experiencing is not dreaming, of arresting a judgement on or doing justice to an experience that has (in Freud's own words) 'a character quite of its own' (*ein ganz eigentümlicher Charakter*: p. 295)? This, to repeat Freud's words, 'would merit the most exhaustive treatment'.

References to *déjà vu* are scattered across the Freudian oeuvre.[5] I propose to concentrate here on two texts in which, it seems to me, the question of *déjà vu* is decisively at stake. First, a short piece which appears in volume XIII of the Standard Edition, immediately before 'The Moses of Michelangelo': it is an essay entitled '*Fausse Reconnaissance ("déjà raconté")* in Psycho-analytic Treatment', first published in 1914.[6] This essay focuses on the '*déjà raconté*', the already recounted or the '*But I've told you that already*' (*das habe ich Ihnen aber schon erzählt*) (p. 201/116). Freud observes that this situation 'not infrequently' (*nicht selten*: p. 116) arises in the course of an analytic treatment: the analysand believes, or claims to believe, that s/he has already told the analyst something or other. With the kind of amazing economy and precipitousness that is characteristic of certain passages of Freud's writing, this essay provides a sort of uncanny elliptical allegory or (we might say) *raconteurism* of psychoanalysis as a discourse about narrative and as a narrative about discourse. Thus the opening paragraph zooms in on the notion of bearing witness as the foundation of the analytic experience. What happens if the patient insists on the idea that s/he has already told the analyst this or that, whereas the analyst does not believe it? Freud writes:

> To try to decide the dispute by shouting the patient down or by outvying him [*sic*] in protestations would be a most unpsychological proceeding [*ganz unpsychologisch*]. It is familiar ground [*bekanntlich*] that a sense of conviction of the accuracy of one's memory has no objective value; and, since one of the two persons concerned must necessarily be in the wrong, it may just as well be the physician as the patient who has fallen a victim to a paramnesia. (p. 201/116)

'A most unpsychological proceeding': inadvertently perhaps, the comic scenario is evoked of analyst and analysand shouting at one another in a crazy agonistics. (But I've told you that already! No you haven't! I tell you I did! I swear this is the first I've heard anything about it! What's the point of analysis if you don't even listen to what I say? I *was* listening! *Und so weiter*, interminably.) 'It is familiar ground that a sense of conviction of the accuracy of one's memory has no objective value': thus Freud specifies the space of witnessing and self-witnessing. Although he does not say so, it is precisely this 'familiar ground' or sense of what is well-known (*bekanntlich*) that we might regard as susceptible to becoming unfamiliar, unheimlich.

Focusing on those cases where it is supposedly the patient who is in error, and in a peculiar conceptual sliding, Freud equates the *fausse reconnaissance* (or false recognition) of having already recounted a particular memory or particular story (the *déjà raconté*) with the experience of *déjà vu*:

> The phenomenon presented by the patient in cases like this deserves to be called a '*fausse reconnaissance*', and is completely analogous [*durchaus analog*] to what occurs in

certain other cases and has been described as a '*déjà vu*'. In these other cases the subject has a spontaneous feeling such as 'I've been in this situation before', or 'I've been through all this already'. (p. 202/117)

Freud is then apparently in a position to go on to explore the '*fausse reconnaissance*' of the *déjà raconté as déjà vu*. But why does he say that the '*But I've told you that already*' is 'completely analogous' to the 'feeling' or 'phenomenon' of *déjà vu*? What is the basis of this analogy? What *is* 'analogy' here? Is it perhaps because the '*But I've told you that already*' is in some sense bound to give rise to a feeling *in the analyst* of having had this experience before? The situation of being thus confronted, as he points out at the start of the essay, arises 'not infrequently' (*nicht selten*), after all. Is there not a suggestion here of a confusion of identities, the uncanny automatism of a kind of *déjà-vu*-finder, a certain transferential logic whereby the solitude of the patient's bearing witness is appropriated by the analyst and an effacement of the patient's experience is carried out through the very imposition of the 'analogy'?

It would at least seem possible to suggest that what is going on in this parallelism between the *déjà raconté* and *déjà vu* is a peculiar metaphorics, a seemingly compulsive metaphorization, a figurative transference or translation of the notion of *déjà vu*. Once *déjà vu* can be figured as a metaphor, transfer or translation (but was it ever anything else?), there is no limit to its applicability or replicability. It is as if Freud is led on by the ghostly myrmidons of *déjà vu*.[7] In any event, it seems that what he wants to tell us about in this little essay called '*Fausse Reconnaissance*' is not '*fausse reconnaissance*' so much as '*déjà vu*' itself – even though he has (by his own admission) *already told us* about it, some seven years earlier, in the *Psychopathology of Everyday Life*. Embedded within this *déjà* raconteurism is an intriguing example of what Harold Bloom has called the anxiety of influence.[8] Freud refers to an essay by J. Grasset, published in 1904, which argues that 'the phenomenon [of *déjà vu*] indicates that at some earlier time there has been an *unconscious* perception, which only now makes its way into consciousness' (p. 203). He then tells us about what he has supposedly already told us: 'In 1907, in the second edition of my *Psychopathology of Everyday Life* ... I proposed an exactly similar explanation for this form of apparent paramnesia without mentioning Grasset's paper or knowing of its existence' (*ohne die Arbeit von Grasset zu kennen oder zu erwähnen*: 'without knowing of the work of Grasset or mentioning it') (p. 203/119). The hesitation, the index of anxiety in the final part of that sentence again generates a certain comedy, this time of Freud mentioning Grasset's paper *without* knowing of its existence.

On the one hand, then, Freud's theory of *déjà vu* has no priority; it is *déjà raconté*, in Grasset. On the other hand, and in keeping with the notion of *déjà vu* that I am trying to trace in this chapter, Freud's theory is not a theory as such. This is clear, again, from the disquieting need for quotation marks around the question of what Freud (or his precursor Grasset) 'believes'. There are two 'class[es] of explanation' for the 'phenomenon' of *déjà vu*, says Freud: one 'looks upon the feeling that constitutes the phenomenon as deserving of credence'; the other, 'far larger class' 'maintain[s], on the contrary, that what we have to deal with is an illusory memory, and that the problem is to discover how this paramnesic error can have arisen' (p. 202). Freud then takes up a position against, for example, Pythagoras, for whom 'the phenomenon of *déjà vu* is evidence of the subject having had a former life' (pp. 202–3), and instead allies himself with Grasset as 'one of the group which "believes" in the phenomenon' (*Grasset hat im Jahre 1904 eine Erklärung des* déjà vu *gegeben, welche zu den 'gläubigen' gerechnet werden muß*) (p. 203 / 118). The word 'believes' ('*gläubigen*' ('believers')) is in quotation marks. In a way that is strikingly similar (we might say, indeed, 'completely analogous') to the case of telepathy, Freud presents himself as someone who '"believes"' in *déjà vu*.[9] I 'believe' in telepathy, I 'believe' in *déjà vu*, says Freud. The quotes around this word 'believes' point towards an experience of the undecidable. To 'believe' in *déjà vu* can no longer be construed as the opposite of *not* believing. *Déjà vu* can only ever be a question of belief but it is necessarily belief in quotation marks, in suspense, a suspension of the very subject of belief, a suspension which is moreover not a neutralization but rather a trembling of the 'I' in the very intimacy of its bearing witness.[10]

And if one wanted to *believe*, let us say, that there were some pure, non-metaphoric 'concept' or 'phenomenon' of *déjà vu*, and that this logic of an experience of the undecidable could or should be confined to a specific kind of context or situation, that its propensities for analogical application or replication could and should be carefully controlled and restricted, the conclusion to Freud's essay provides cold comfort. On the contrary, this conclusion makes an extra-ordinarily daring and violent gesture of appropriation in order to suggest that, indeed, *fausse reconnaissance*, *déjà raconté* or *déjà vu* is the very ground ('the familiar ground', we could say) on which psychoanalysis comes to rest. Freud's final paragraph runs as follows:

> There is another kind of *fausse reconnaissance* which not infrequently [*nicht selten*: the same phrase that Freud has already used, a revenant from the beginning of his essay] makes its appearance at the close of a treatment, much to the physician's satisfaction. After he has succeeded in forcing the repressed event (whether it was of a real or of a psychical nature) upon the patient's acceptance in the teeth of all resistances, and has

succeeded, as it were, in rehabilitating it – the patient may say: 'Now I feel as though I had known it all the time.' With this the work of the analysis has been completed. ('Jetzt habe ich die Empfindung, ich habe es immer gewußt.' Damit ist die analytische Aufgabe gelöst.) (p. 207/123)

Does Freud believe in this déjà vu? Or does he merely 'believe' in it? What is psychoanalysis if its most satisfying and complete achievement consists in the transference of an acredible déjà raconté déjà vu?

Déjà vu: the uncanny figure of that which is irreducible to the psychical or the real, an undecidable trembling that phantomizes the possibility of 'belief'.

What Freud's essay 'Fausse Reconnaissance' shows is finally, perhaps, the uncanny, protean power of déjà vu as an explanatory 'concept', 'analogy' or 'theory'. It is uncanny because it entails a logic that cannot be confined but rather operates as a kind of dangerous supplement. Not only does déjà vu work as a promiscuous term for 'analogy' with other feelings or experiences seemingly heterogeneous to it (for instance, the déjà raconté or the psychoanalytic experience itself), not only does this 'concept' serve as a means of describing both a symptom or affect and the experience of the cure ('Now I feel as though I had known it all the time'), not only does Freud use déjà vu as a 'theory' by which simultaneously to appropriate and to represent the patient's experience of psychoanalysis (the satisfaction provided at the close of a treatment, though also, it hardly needs be said, at the close of Freud's essay itself: the close of a narrative treatment, the apparent satisfaction of a narrative desire); but before and beyond anything else, déjà vu just is the experience of a supplement (and it is this, paradoxically, that gives cases of déjà vu 'a character quite of their own'): it is itself nothing other than supplementarity-as-experience, the experience of a supplement without origin, a disturbance of any sense of 'familiar ground'.

The second Freud text on which I wish to focus here is the essay entitled 'The Uncanny' (1919). This may appear to be a rather obvious choice of text. But here is a remarkable thing which, as far as I am aware, has not been drawn attention to before: in Freud's essay 'The Uncanny', there is not a single reference to déjà vu. Freud never explicitly mentions the 'feeling' or 'phenomenon' of déjà vu, even though years earlier in The Psychopathology of Everyday Life he had specifically referred to déjà vu as something that 'we must ... include in the category of the miraculous and the "uncanny"'. Why this omission? Why doesn't Freud discuss, or even make passing reference to what he himself elsewhere describes as something that must be included in the category of the uncanny and therefore in any theory of the uncanny? How might we construe this exclusion of what must be included, this strange theoretical supplement called 'déjà vu'?

Such questions may lead into strange fields of thought and feeling. If such spaces are in some sense speculative (theoretical, conjectural, risky, non-demonstrable, etc.), they also engage a certain conceptual twist, entailing the curious cohabitations of speculation with a logic of *déjà vu* 'itself'. Where could speculation be said to begin, for example, if it is only initiated on the basis of a singularly spectral *déjà vu*?

To repeat: How construe this exemplary 'Freudian slip', this uncanny exclusion of the feeling or phenomenon of *déjà vu* from 'The Uncanny'? It evokes, perhaps, a duplicitous sense, a double feeling: (1) for Freud to introduce the question of *déjà vu* in a categorical and systematic fashion into a theoretical account of the uncanny would be to introduce a sort of demonic logic capable of contaminating the entire project of the essay and of psychoanalytic theory in general; (2) *at the same time*, it will not have been possible for the question of *déjà vu* to be excluded in any case: it can be *already seen* to be in operation in Freud's essay. Like the supposedly normal 'abnormal' feeling called *déjà vu* (whereby one feels that one has experienced before something that is really being experienced for the first time), the 'place' of *déjà vu* in Freud's essay would be itself only thinkable in the light of the readerly experience of a sort of double-take. Excluded, *déjà vu* is more uncannily active in Freud's essay than if it were included. And it is because it is excluded that it is included. *Déjà vu* is present *and* absent in Freud's essay; and it is *neither* present *nor* absent.

Without ever being named as such, *déjà vu* haunts this great Freud text from start to finish. Indeed, from *before* the beginning and beyond its final words, *déjà vu* frames or supplements the text. We could multiply indefinitely the examples and possible re-readings of 'The Uncanny' as an essay about *déjà vu*. To conclude, I would like to consider three ghostly 'cases' of this uncanny supplement, this strange figure that haunts, that comes back without perhaps ever appearing.

First, *déjà vu* would be at once that which conditions and phantomizes the possibility of 'belief'. There is no believing without the ghost of *déjà vu*. This ghost haunts Freud's argument that beliefs which have been surmounted have not entirely been surmounted. The uncanny, he contends, has to do with the revival of surmounted beliefs (belief in 'the prompt fulfilment of wishes' and in 'secret injurious powers', the belief in the 'omnipotence of thoughts', the belief in 'the return of the dead': U, p. 370). He writes:

> We – or our primitive forefathers – once believed that these possibilities were realities, and were convinced that they actually happened. Nowadays we no longer believe in them, we have *surmounted* these modes of thought [*wir haben diese Denkweisen überwunden*]; but we do not feel quite sure of our new beliefs, and the old ones still exist

within us ready to seize upon any confirmation. As soon as something *actually happens* in our lives which seems to confirm the old, discarded beliefs we get a feeling of the uncanny; it is as though we were making a judgement something like this: 'So, after all, it *is* true that one can kill a person by the mere wish!' or, 'So the dead *do* live on and appear on the scene of their former activities!' and so on. (U, pp. 370–1/262)

Freud effectively presents himself here as a double, and imposes on his reader the same structure of being-two ('we' as Freud and the reader, but also the reader, you or me for example, as already a double): we non-religious, non-primitive, non-mystical people do *not* believe; and yet these 'surmounted' modes of thought 'still exist within us ready to seize upon any confirmation'. Not believing is still believing. These phantom 'modes of thought' will have seen us coming. A feeling of the uncanny comes when 'something *actually happens* in our lives which seems to confirm the old, discarded beliefs'. Like junk, beliefs are discarded but hang around; belief is cryptic, the experience of a foreign body within ourselves.[11] And this scenario of when something '*actually happens*' is one of *déjà vu*. It entails a fundamental unsettling of the 'first time' of an experience. The moment when something '*actually happens*' is a moment of '*Now I feel as if I had known it all the time*'.[12]

Second, *déjà vu* leads us back to *The Interpretation of Dreams* (PFL, 4) and indeed into an encounter with the question of the very definition of dreams and thus the very possibility of an interpretation of dreams. Without being named as such, *déjà vu* provides Freud with what he himself singles out as being 'the most beautiful confirmation' (*die schönste Bekräftigung*: U, p. 258) of his 'theory of the uncanny'. In 'The Uncanny', he writes:

> It often happens that neurotic men declare that they feel there is something uncanny about the female genital organs. This *unheimlich* place, however, is the entrance to the former *Heim* [home] of all human beings, to the place where each one of us lived once upon a time and in the beginning ... [W]henever a man dreams of a place or a country and says to himself, while he is still dreaming [*und wenn der Träumer von einer Örtlichkeit oder Landschaft noch im Traume denkt*]: 'this place is familiar to me, I've been here before', we may interpret the place as being his mother's genitals or body. (U, p. 368/259)

There is a moment of apparent *déjà lu* here for Freud-readers, since this 'same' example is also considered years earlier in *The Interpretation of Dreams* (first edition 1900). What is uncanny about this example, however, may be in the way it provokes a sort of retroactive 'new' reading of *The Interpretation* itself. Far from being merely familiar (*déjà lu*), *The Interpretation of Dreams* is rendered suddenly unfamiliar by this ghost of *déjà vu* that hovers over Freud's essay of 1919. In *The Interpretation* he had observed:

> In some dreams of landscapes or other localities emphasis is laid in the dream itself on a convinced feeling of having been there once before. (Occurrences of '*déjà vu*' in dreams have a special meaning.) These places are invariably the genitals of the dreamer's mother; there is indeed no other place about which one can assert with such conviction that one has been there before. (*PFL*, 4: 524: second sentence added in 1914; the remainder first published in 1909)

With his argument that *déjà vu* in dreams 'invariably' means that one (as a man or as a woman?) is dreaming of one's mother's genitals, it is perhaps impossible either to agree or disagree. If, as Freud maintains, 'there is indeed no other place about which one can assert with such conviction that one has been there before', it may be equally valid to maintain that there is no other place about which one can assert with such conviction that one cannot possibly know what one is talking about in supposing that 'one has been there before'.

But there is another question, another uncertainty that perhaps unsettles the ground of Freud's argument in advance, viz.: can we move so unfalteringly, as Freud implies we can, from talking about *déjà vu* in waking life to talking about *déjà vu* in a dream? Are they the same? Limiting ourselves to the sense of *déjà vu* as 'the peculiar feeling we have, in certain moments and situations, of having had exactly the same experience once before or of having once before been in the same place' (Freud, 1907), we may wonder whether it makes sense to speak of '*déjà vu* in a dream' at all. In a dream, we might suppose, there is not the feeling of anguish, excitement or surprise identifiable with the experience of *déjà vu* in waking life. There is no 'reality-testing'.[13] *Déjà vu* in a dream is much more concretely a determined experience of repetition (and in this respect perhaps not an 'experience' at all, at least to the extent that 'experience' belongs with the possibility of the unprogrammed or unprogrammable), than it is the *surprising* of a dreamer's 'perceptual judgement' (to recall Freud's phrase). According to Freud, *déjà vu* in a dream involves the dreamer thinking or 'say[ing] to himself, while he is still dreaming: "this place is familiar to me, I've been here before"'. In the case of *déjà vu* in waking life, however, it is a question of an experience which (to use Freud's phrase in *The Psychopathology of Everyday Life*) 'announces itself' (p. 329). In waking life, *déjà vu* comes from the other: it may appear, in some sense, the very announcement of the other.

These distinctions are perhaps not insignificant. By talking about *déjà vu* in dreams at all and more particularly by asserting that the 'special meaning' of *déjà vu* in dreams has to do with men dreaming of intra-uterine existence,[14] Freud is no doubt concerned to promote the authority of psychoanalysis and to extend its empire as a science. But this appropriation of *déjà vu* in the context of dreaming perhaps generates more questions than it puts to rest. In speaking of *déjà vu* in dreams Freud is, in effect, providing a further example of the necessary impurity, the dangerous supplementarity of the concept and proper meaning of '*déjà vu*'. His account might thus lead us to ask: When is a dream *not déjà vu*? How could we know? When or where would '*déjà vu* in dreams' begin or end? Here we might draw on a point made by Freud's precursor or 'double' in this field, Havelock Ellis, who remarks on the links between dreaming and suggestibility: 'some degree of suggestibility, some tendency to regard the things that come before us in dreams as familiar – in other words, as things that have happened to us before – is ... one of the very conditions of dreaming. It enables us to carry on our dreams.'[15] And conversely, how might the uncertainty of *déjà vu* impact on the nature of the assumed boundaries between dreaming and waking experience? Is the 'peculiar feeling' of *déjà vu* the invasion of a dream-state or of a different wakefulness? Or is it perhaps irreducible to either? Paradoxically, in seeking to export *déjà vu* directly from the context of waking life into that of dreams, Freud effectively disavows the singularity of *déjà vu* experiences as having 'a character quite of their own'. In not respecting this singularity he subordinates the notion of *déjà vu* to the theoretical indifference of dreaming or waking. *Déjà vu* cannot perhaps be so easily appropriated.

Third, it is difficult to imagine a theory of the ghost or double without a theory of *déjà vu*.[16] The examples of the double and the ghost are central to Freud's attempt to provide a full and systematic account of the uncanny under the rubric of the 'theory of the qualities of feeling' (339). Following Otto Rank, he explores the idea of the double as both 'an assurance of immortality' and 'the uncanny harbinger of death' (357) and concludes: 'When all is said and done, the quality of uncanniness can only come from the fact of the "double" being a creation dating back to a very early mental stage [*seelischen Urzeiten*: i.e. an early time in human history], long since surmounted – a stage, incidentally, at which it wore a more friendly aspect' (p. 358/248). Freud sees the desire to invent the double as one which springs 'from the soil of unbounded self-love, from the primary narcissism (*primären Narzißmus*) which dominates the mind of the child and of primitive man' (357/257).[17] Jacques Derrida has written at length, for example in 'To Speculate – On "Freud"', about the logic of the double in Freud's essay and in particular of its strange status as 'apparition', involving an experience of 'duplicity without an original'.[18] The double is always ghostly and cannot be dissociated from a sense of *déjà vu*. We might illustrate this, in a rather condensed fashion, with an observation about *déjà vu* made by Fouillée and discussed by Havelock Ellis: paramnesia or *déjà vu* is 'a kind of diplopia or seeing double in the mental field'; the feeling of *déjà vu* involves 'the impression that the present reality has a *double*'.[19] *Déjà vu* is the experience of the double *par excellence*: it is the experience of experience *as* double. There can be no uncanny, perhaps, without some experience of this duplicity.

In the closing pages of his book *Spectres of Marx* Derrida makes much of what Freud calls '*es spukt*' ('it ghosts', 'it comes back', 'it spooks') in 'The Uncanny'. In particular Derrida elaborates on this '*es spukt*' as being where (by Freud's own admission) he could and should have begun his attempt to write a theory of the uncanny.[20] How should we try to conceive the *es spukt*? It is, Derrida suggests, a matter of becoming ready to welcome the stranger,

> a stranger who is already found within (*das Heimliche-Unheimliche*), more intimate with one than one is oneself, the absolute proximity of a stranger whose power is singular *and* anonymous (*es spukt*), an unnameable and neutral power, that is, undecidable, neither active nor passive, an an-identity that, *without doing anything*, invisibly occupies places belonging finally neither to us nor to it.[21]

This leads perhaps to another sense of *déjà vu*: it is to be oneself *already seen*, watched (over). The ghost or double *is déjà vu*. This 'stranger within' has no name or finally assignable place, either in Freud or in Derrida or in ourselves. If (as Derrida stresses) Freud '*ought* to have begun' with 'the strongest example of *Unheimlichkeit*, the "es spukt", ghosts, and apparitions', we can equally well argue that Freud ought to have begun with *déjà vu* (*das Heimliche-Unheimliche*).[22] And in a sense of course he does: he advances it initially some twelve years earlier, in 1907, in *The Psychopathology of Everyday Life*, as what 'must be included' in any account of the uncanny. Without saying or indeed perhaps realizing that he is doing it, in 1914 he even writes an essay about it, a text that is at once a preface and a postscript to 'The Uncanny', entitled '*Fausse Reconnaissance ("déjà raconté")* in Psycho-analytic Treatment'.[23]

NOTES

1   Franz Kafka, *The Collected Aphorisms* (London: Syrens, 1994), p. 21.

2   See Ernest Jones, *Sigmund Freud: Life and Work*, vol. 3 (London: Hogarth Press, 1957), p. 419.

3   Cf. Jacques Derrida's discussion, near the beginning of *Spectres of Marx: The State of the Debt, the Work of Mourning, and the New International* (London: Routledge, 1994), of the 'troubling effect of "*déjà vu*"' (p. 14) whereby the question 'Whither Marxism?' can be posed in the 1990s, as if it had not been *the question* confronting so-called western intellectuals for 'at least forty years'. Derrida's specific inflection of the term is worth noting: it is a 'troubling' sense of *déjà vu*, even if '*déjà vu*' here is taken as *OED* sense (b).

4   Sigmund Freud, *The Psychopathology of Everyday Life*, trans. Alan Tyson, *PLF*, 5 (Harmondsworth: Penguin, 1976); *Gesammelte Werke*, 4 (London: Imago, 1941).

5   For Freud, it may appear, there is a point at which one has to stop: *déjà vu* may be a *question of a 'perceptual judgement'* but judgement on this predicament must be passed. Yet his relation to this subject is that of an uncanny double-bind: he never finishes with the question of *déjà vu*, or, perhaps we should say, it never finishes with him. In the late essay 'A Disturbance of Memory on the Acropolis' (1936), Freud returns (still, again) to the subject. (See 'A Disturbance of Memory on the Acropolis', trans. James Strachey, *PFL*, 11 (Harmondsworth: Penguin, 1984), pp. 447–56; *Gesammelte Werke*, 16 (London: Imago, 1950), 250–7.) Here he speaks of *déjà vu* as a 'positive counterpart' (*die positiven Gegenstücke*: 16: 255) of the phenomenon of derealization and depersonalization. It would be, in some sense, a 'positive' experience of the situation in which, he says, 'the subject feels either that a piece of reality or that a piece of his [*sic*] own self is strange to him' (*entweder erscheint uns ein Stück der Realität als fremd oder ein Stück des eigenen Ichs*) (11: 453/16: 254–5). He writes: 'derealizations and depersonalizations are intimately connected. There is another set of phenomena which may be regarded as their positive counterparts – what are known as *"fausse réconnaissance"*, *"déjà vu"*, *"déjà raconté"* etc., illusions [*sic*] in which we seek to accept something as belonging to our ego, just as in the derealizations we are anxious to keep something out of us. A naively mystical and unpsychological attempt at explaining the phenomena of *"déjà vu"* endeavours to find evidence in it of a former existence of our mental self. Depersonalization leads us on to the extraordinary notion of *"double conscience"* [in French in original: "double consciousness"], which is more correctly described as "split personality". But all of this is so obscure and has been so little mastered that I must refrain from talking about it any more to you. [*Das ist alles noch so dunkel, so wenig wissenschaftlich bezwungen, dass ich mir verbieten muß, es vor Ihnen weiter zu erörtern.*] (*PFL*, 11: 453–4/16: 255). This fascinating passage provokes numerous questions. Do we necessarily 'seek to accept something as belonging to our own ego' in the experience of *déjà vu*? How is 'double consciousness' distinct from the notion of 'a former existence of our mental self'? According to what criteria and authority should 'double consciousness' be '*more correctly* described as "split personality"' (my emphasis)? Freud stops himself, apparently, from saying any more: 'I must forbid myself to expound it any further in front of you (*ich mir verbieten muss, es vor Ihnen weiter zu erörtern*).' Who is forbidding whom here? In refraining from saying any more about this subject that is so resistant to scientific mastery, Freud paradoxically puts himself on the very stage of *déjà vu*, on to the scene, that is to say, in which the 'I' trembles *in secret*. As may become clearer as we go on, the sense of '*déjà vu*' as it emerges in Freud's work is in some ways strangely similar to deconstruction (*das Heimliche-Unheimliche*). Like deconstruction, *déjà vu* can be described as the experience of a trembling which is the trembling of experience itself. It is concerned with an absolute past, a past that was never present. It has to do with an experience of the undecidable that may be erotic and 'positive' as well as strange and frightening. It is not 'mystical' (cf. *PFL*, 11: 453). It is the experience of the being-promise of a promise in all its disruptive perversity *and* affirmation. It 'announces itself', it is the announcement of the other, it says 'come' to a future that cannot be anticipated. How long will it last? Is this an event? To whom is it happening?

6   Sigmund Freud, 'Fausse Reconnaissance ("*déjà raconté*") in Psycho-analytic Treatment', trans. James Strachey, *Standard Edition*, XIII (London: Hogarth Press and the Institute of Psycho-Analysis, 1955), pp. 201–7; *Gesammelte Werke*, 10 (London: Imago, 1946), pp. 116–23.

7   It is with the sense of these myrmidons that one might begin to consider the possible uncanny rapport between *déjà vu* and what Freud calls the repetition compulsion: how would

one distinguish between such conceptual ghosts? Would the repetition compulsion be a form of *déjà vu* or would the latter be merely an 'analogy' for the irruptive yet inaccessible character of the former?

8   Is the anxiety of influence not in some sense an anxiety of *déjà vu*? If one tracks off here to another of the precursor texts to which Freud specifically refers (see '*Fausse Reconnaissance*', p. 202, n. 1) in his own account of *déjà vu*, namely Havelock Ellis, *The World of Dreams* (London: Constable, 1911), and in particular Chapter IX, 'Memory in Dreams' (pp. 212–60), one finds the following Bloomian observation: 'We may read a new poem with a vague sense of familiarity, but such an experience never puts on a really paramnesic character, for we quickly realise that it is explainable by the fact that the writer of the poem has fallen under the influence of some greater master' (pp. 242–3). Alongside this conception of the anxiety of influence, however, one might also set the figuration of *déjà vu* implicit in a remark Geoffrey Bennington makes about the writings of Plato and Derrida: 'from a certain point of view the whole of Derrida is already "in" Plato (for those who read … like Derrida, and therefore do not believe that we really know what "in Plato" means), as his ghost or double'. See Bennington and Derrida, *Jacques Derrida*, trans. Bennington (London and Chicago: Chicago University Press, 1993), p. 273.

9   For a fuller account of Freud and telepathy, see, for example, Jacques Derrida, 'Telepathy', trans. Nicholas Royle, in *Deconstruction: A Reader*, ed. Martin McQuillan (Edinburgh: Edinburgh University Press, 2000), 496–526; and 'The Remains of Psychoanalysis (i): Telepathy' in my book *After Derrida* (Manchester and New York: Manchester University Press, 1995), pp. 61–84.

10   Cf. Jacques Derrida, *The Post Card: From Socrates to Freud and Beyond*, trans. Alan Bass (Chicago: Chicago University Press, 1987), where he describes a similar process or interruption of process at work in the logic of Freud's *Beyond the Pleasure Principle*: 'A certain *I*, the same but immediately an other, does not know to what extent *I* believes in them [i.e. in Freud's hypotheses]. It is not only belief, but the relation to belief which finds itself suspended, the relation of science or of consciousness' (p. 379).

11   'A piece of junk' is how he describes '*Fausse Reconnaissance* ("*déjà raconté*") in Psycho-analytic Treatment', in a letter to Ferenczi in February 1914. It is not a question of dismissing the essay for this reason. Rather the reverse: junk can be crucial. See *The Correspondence of Sigmund Freud and Sándor Ferenczi: Volume 1, 1908–1914*, eds Eva Brabant, Ernst Falzeder and Patrizia Giampieri-Deutsch, trans. Peter T. Hoffer (Cambridge, Mass.: Belknap Press, 1993), p. 540. Freud writes: 'The paper about déjà vu that you asked about is a piece of junk.' In another essay written around the same time, 'The Moses of Michelangelo' (*PFL*, 14: 249–82), Freud remarks that psychoanalysis 'is accustomed to divine secret and concealed things from despised or unnoticed features, from the rubbish-heap, as it were, of our observations' (p. 265).

12   Our primitive forefathers are ghosts within us, it may seem. Yet it is impossible to remember what our forefathers felt: come back as if from nowhere, it is belief itself that is ghostly. This temporal phantom-effect is perhaps evident in a slightly different way in an observation made by Havelock Ellis at the end of his essay on paramnesia and *déjà vu* ('the best known form of paramnesia': p. 230). These phenomena, he says, 'are of no little interest since, in earlier stages of culture, they may well have had a real influence on belief, suggesting to primitive man that he had somehow had wider experiences than he knew of, and that, as Wordsworth put it, he trailed clouds of glory behind him' (p. 260). Rather than, as Freud suggests, the beliefs of our primitive forefathers providing a rationalization for understanding why we have 'uncanny' experiences, might we not just as well suppose (following the

line of Ellis's proposal in what could nevertheless be called a Freudian spirit) that in some sense everything comes back to *déjà vu*, in other words that every belief (whether hypothetically 'primitive' or not), belief *in general*, passes by way of a *déjà vu* structure?

13   Cf. Freud, 'An Outline of Psychoanalysis' (*PFL*, 15: 371–443), where he suggests that '*reality-testing*' is an 'institution … which is allowed to fall into abeyance in dreams on account of the conditions prevailing in the state of sleep' (p. 435). From a different perspective, see Lacan's remarks about the 'ambiguous phenomenon of déjà vu' in *The Seminar of Jacques Lacan: Book I. Freud's Papers on Technique, 1953–1954*, ed. Jacques-Alain Miller, trans. with notes by John Forrester (Cambridge: Cambridge University Press, 1988), p. 59. Lacan claims that 'Freud is talking of nothing other than [*déjà vu*] when he tells us that any experiencing [*toute épreuve*: John Forrester suggests the connotation here of *épreuve de la réalité*, "reality-testing"] of the external world implicitly refers to something which has already been perceived in the past.'

14   See 'The Uncanny', p. 367, and cf. *The Interpretation of Dreams, PFL* 4: 525, n. 2.

15   Ellis, *The World of Dreams*, p. 232.

16   I borrow the style of this formulation from Jacques Derrida who makes an analogous claim with respect to telepathy and a theory of the unconscious: 'Difficult to imagine a theory of what they still call the unconscious without a theory of telepathy. They can be neither confused nor dissociated.' See 'Telepathy', p. 505.

17   But what would be the 'primary' of 'primary narcissism'? What self would indulge in a self-love that was not love of an other? Can one love one's self, oneself, without loving one's double? It would perhaps accord with the drift of the present chapter to supplement these questions with another: what might it mean to suppose that, following the logic of Freud's account, primary narcissism is a *déjà vu* concept? The sense of such a supposition may present itself in encountering the following passage, for example, from 'On Narcissism: An Introduction' (1914) (*PFL*, 11: 65–97): 'The primary narcissism of children *which we have assumed*, and which forms one of the postulates of our theories of the libido, is less easy to grasp by direct observation than to confirm *by inference from elsewhere*. If we look at the attitude of affectionate parents towards their children, we have to recognise that it is *a revival and reproduction* of their own narcissism, which they have long since abandoned' (p. 84, my emphases).

18   'To Speculate – on "Freud"', in *The Post Card*, pp. 257–409: see p. 270.

19   Quoted by Ellis, p. 252.

20   For more extended discussion of this spectrality of 'where one ought to have begun' see Chapter 8 above.

21   Jacques Derrida, *Spectres of Marx: The State of the Debt, the Work of Mourning, and the New International*, trans. Peggy Kamuf (London: Routledge, 1994), p. 172.

22   See Derrida, *Spectres of Marx*, p. 173.

23   The ascription of 'The Uncanny' to 1919 is, of course, contentious in various ways. As Neil Hertz puts it: 'Even the simple facts concerning the writing and publication of "The Uncanny" seem designed to raise questions about repetition. The essay came out in the fall of 1919, and a letter of Freud (12 May 1919) indicates that it was written in May of that year, or, rather, rewritten, for the letter speaks of his going back to an old manuscript that he had set aside, for how long is not clear – perhaps as long as a dozen years.' See Neil Hertz, 'Freud and the Sandman', in *The End of the Line: Essays on Psychoanalysis and the Sublime* (New York: Columbia University Press, 1985), pp. 97–121; here, p. 98.

12

The double

There is nothing more uncanny than seeing one's face accidentally in a mirror by moonlight. (Heinrich Heine)[1]

One cannot help having a slightly disagreeable feeling when one comes across one's own name in a stranger. Recently I was very sharply aware of it when a *Herr S. Freud* presented himself to me in my consulting hour. (Sigmund Freud)[2]

It was only a glass because he looked in it. It was nothing he could be told.
It was a language he spoke, because he must, yet did not know.
It was a page he had found in the handbook of heartbreak.

(Wallace Stevens)[3]

At first our correspondence was sparse. I think we were a little wary. We had both read Poe's 'William Wilson'. If … we doppelgängers met, might we not cancel each other out? (Nicholas Royle)[4]

This comes to you from the heart, on the heart – the heart and everything with which one might associate it: feeling, memory and desire, the innermost part of me, what Hamlet calls 'my heart of heart' (3.2.69), or Yeats, perhaps playing on a Latin etymology of the core, calls 'the deep heart's core'.[5] For Nicholas Royle, with him, I wish to write on the matter of the heart. To a perhaps unprecedented degree, this desire is today inscribed within questions concerning technology and the 'regime of telecommunications'.[6] The matter of the heart is a matter of desire, of a rhythm of singularity and generality, and of a logic of the foreign body, the automaton and spectre at the heart of the matter.

Let us have some sex to start off with – in this case, I am sorry to say, some 'bad sex'. In December 1997 Nicholas Royle was awarded the London *Literary Review*'s Grand Booby Prize for Bad Sex in Fiction, given for the most 'tasteless', 'charmless' and 'unskilled' description of sex in a work of fiction published that year.[7] Here is the prize-winning passage, from his 1997 novel *The Matter of the Heart*:

> But Ambrose banished the thought and reached for a condom. Yasmin grinned and writhed on the bed, arching her back, making a noise somewhere between a beached seal and a police siren. And then he was there. Slowly at first, dead slow – she liked that, he knew. Then speeding up gradually to gain a rhythm until he was punching smoothly in and out of her like a sewing machine. Her noises increased in volume until she was producing a throaty ululation. He sensed that unmistakeable stirring common to all men, that loosening, as he liked to think of it, of the bow ropes on the big white submarine.[8]

This passage is perhaps more comical and thought-provoking than the *Literary Review* gives it credit for. However deserving it is of the illustrious booby-prize, there are intriguing, unsteadily funny things going on in its mixing of the body and technology: the girl making 'a noise somewhere between a beached seal and a police siren'; the man 'punching smoothly in and out of her like a sewing machine' and experiencing his body in terms of a 'loosening ... of the bow ropes on [a] big white submarine'. *The Matter of the Heart* is a novel about the technologized nature of experience: 'the thought' that Ambrose 'banishe[s]' in the opening sentence, for instance, is the thought of a certain phantasmagoric technician, referred to as 'the Projectionist'. Ambrose, in other words, is inhabited, with penis-dwindling effectiveness, by a technological phantom, a kind of double who, even as Ambrose prepares for orgasm, is himself 'setting up. Plugging in his machine. Loading his magazine, checking its orientation' (p. 128). Royle's novel suggests that there is no natural body or art; thinking itself is indissociable from technology. If there are, in Judith Butler's phrase, bodies that matter, the matter in question is inseparable from the prosthetic, the mechanical and, above all perhaps, from writing itself. For as I hope to make clear, Royle's text, bad sex or otherwise, graphically demonstrates that there is no writing about the matter of the heart without a self-remarking, without the supplementary or prosthetic, mechanical and duplicitous re-marking of 'the matter of the heart' as a writing project, inscribed as at once the subject and object of the text entitled *The Matter of the Heart*. Writing is the double, writing is a double writing, from the beginning.

In the wake of the *Literary Review*'s publishing details of its award, and stimulated by discussion of the passage in question on national television (Chris Evans, *TFI*, in early December 1997), students and colleagues at my university began to confront me: 'Is it true that you write pornography?', 'Congratulations on the Bad Sex Prize!', and so on. It was like experiencing a kind of heartbreak, even a sort of open heart surgery, still conscious. To whom could I speak, whom could I get in touch with, in order to 'clear my name'? To quote another Nicholas Royle, on the subject of British Telecom:

> But I wanted my bloody telephone installed and wasn't going to miss this opportunity, not for the world ... I'd read about getting a pacemaker fitted, but that was nothing compared with this. The operation alone lasted forty-eight hours and I was conscious throughout. But I didn't let on about the fact that I was conscious and I'm quite sure I felt no pain, just the agony of looking with my screwed-up eyes at all those faces, and the pincers, and the screwdrivers and wirecutters, and listening to all the engineer's little requests like 'Can you connect ...?' and 'Could you give me a line on ...?', I thought it would never end. Even now maybe I'm wrong, and it's still being fitted, how are you supposed to know?

> The first person I called was Tel, but his line was engaged and then, much worse than that, I remembered that he was dead.

This is a passage from another apparently bad-sex text, a text about 'rape' and BT entitled 'Telephoning Home', which appeared as a footnote in a book called · *Telepathy and Literature: Essays on the Reading Mind.*[9] My book? Whose book? I, Nicholas Royle, am not Nicholas Royle. Nicholas Royle is not I. There is another Nicholas Royle, author of *The Matter of the Heart* and three other novels, *Counterparts* (1993), *Saxophone Dreams* (1996) and *The Director's Cut* (2000).

Nicholas Royle and I are connected, counterparts in a very familiar, all 'too familiar', scenario. His first novel, *Counterparts*, was a novel about doubles; my first novel, *Finnish Romance* (1988), was a novel about doubles, about a man called Tone and a man called Tel. I have just quoted Tone, trying to get through to Tel, only to find his double not simply engaged but dead, engaged *and* dead. I haven't published *Finnish Romance*: I believe it will not be published now until after my death, if it is published at all. It is a matter of the heart. And even after my death, and after the death of my double, Nicholas Royle and I will continue to be engaged to one another, engaged and dead. This really does sound like bad sex. Diabolical, even. Email (the usual means by which he and I communicate) facilitates and exacerbates the confusions. We receive messages and invitations, where 'we' means one or the other, or both of us, or a bit of one and a bit of the other. The author of *Counterparts* and *Telepathy and Literature*, for example, was invited in 1997 to speak at a conference at the University of Jyväskylä in Finland, on the subject of 'creative writing'. Which of us should have gone? Whichever was to go, we knew he would not simply be going alone.[10] The British Library Cataloguing system and Books in Print make no differentiation between us. Even our own publishers get us confused. According to the conventions of bio-bibliographical data, he was born in 1963, I was born in 1957. In a recent collection of essays entitled *Deconstructions: A User's Guide*, the editor requested that, in order to minimize such confusion, the publishers ensure that his year of birth be specified on the verso of the title-page. Sure enough, the name is there: 'Royle, Nicholas, 1963– '.[11] Doubtless it will not be long before we cease to exist, and the records become entirely uncertain which of us wrote what – for instance, this sentence. We are locked into a life-and-death struggle which is also a romance, the finish of all romance and struggle, heartbreak at the origin.

I admire and detest *The Matter of the Heart*; it impresses and appals me; it is entirely alien to me and yet I am mortgaged in an identification with it, in spite of myself. It's funny: it *matters* to me and yet of course doesn't matter to me in the slightest. Who 'me'? The scenario is strangely literary. For example, we may recall Edgar Allan Poe's great story, 'William Wilson', published in 1839.[12] 'William Wilson' is a fiction, a self-remarking fiction, a fiction in abyss. It is a text about a double with a title that is thus double, narrated moreover by one who describes his name as 'a fictitious title' (p. 431). William Wilson's words, thinking back to his first day at school, reverberate here:

> when, upon the day of my arrival, a second William Wilson came also to the academy, I felt angry with him for bearing the name, and doubly disgusted with the name because a stranger bore it, who would be the cause of its twofold repetition, who would be constantly in my presence, and whose concerns ... must inevitably, on account of the detestable coincidence, be often confounded with my own. (p. 434)

In his commentary on this story, Otto Rank remarks: 'Despite this uncanny imitation, the main character is incapable of hating his counterpart.'[13] Indeed, Poe's story suggests feelings at once of strange 'animosity' *and* 'affectionateness' (pp. 432–3) for one's double. Correspondingly, the figure of the double is also a figure of humour. This is a connection that Rank makes clear early on in his study *The Double*.[14] Such humour is inscribed in the very heart of Poe's work (just as it is, for example, in Shakespeare's doubles-based comedies), though this connection is intriguingly absent, or apparently absent, from Freud's account of the double in 'The Uncanny'. Freud suggests that the double, in the ancient past, 'wore a more friendly aspect' (U, p. 358), but his essay completely disregards, suppresses or represses the comic dimensions of this figure. The double is *funny*, in the most strongly antithetical or duplicitous sense of 'funny'.

What makes 'William Wilson' funny is partly its sense of absurdity, playfulness, hyperbole, perversity and hocus-pocus, but partly also its implacable earnestness, its peculiar, deadly seriousness. The story seems to be implicitly immersed, and explicitly to culminate, in a funny cross-talk involving death, the double and telepathy. The telepathic dimension becomes evident in the bizarre, murderous double-identity of the voice that concludes the text:

> It was Wilson; but he spoke no longer in a whisper, and I could have fancied that I myself was speaking while he said:
>   '*You have conquered, and I yield. Yet, henceforward art thou also dead – dead to the World, to Heaven and to Hope! In me didst thou exist – and, in my death, see by this image, which is thine own, how utterly thou hast murdered thyself.*' (p. 448)

To recall Freud's formulation, the double is 'the uncanny harbinger of death' (U, p. 357). One may want one's double dead; but the death of the double will always also be the death of oneself.

To the extent that writing is impelled by an authorial desire to be read and remembered after death, Nicholas Royle and I are mortgaged beyond the hilt. The literary desire to 'live on', buried alive in writing, is perhaps most clearly epitomized in a desire for the survival of the name. A logic of survival or live burial is of course already at work in the name. A name is capable of outliving its bearer: that is what a name 'is'. The name itself becomes an 'uncanny harbinger'. William Wilson has 'always felt aversion' (p. 434) to his name: he is 'doubly disgusted' when he discovers a stranger also bears it. Whether one loves or hates one's name, one is already in a double bind; for the name is always in some sense the name of a stranger. One's name is something at once crucial and superfluous, at once a part of, yet also apart from, oneself. Perhaps the best-known literary instance of this is in Shakespeare's *Romeo and Juliet*, in that illusory soliloquy in which Juliet exclaims, by moonlight, to or about her beloved Romeo: 'O be some other name' (2.2.42). Commenting on this passage, Jacques Derrida writes:

> A proper name does not name anything which is human, which belongs to a human body, a human spirit, an essence of man. And yet this relation to the inhuman only befalls man, for him, to him, in the name of man. He alone gives himself this inhuman name. And Romeo would not be what he is, a stranger to his name, without this name.[15]

The name is double, the double is already in the name: such is the logic elaborated in Jorge Luis Borges's brief masterpiece, 'Borges and I', with its uncanny final sentence concerning the figures invoked in its title: 'I do not know which of us has written this page.'[16]

The Matter of the Heart is a novel about coincidence, telepathy and doubles, starting off with a narrator called Chris who is in various respects wired and cross-wired to the figure of the author: they double for one another. Most resonantly perhaps, they double for one another in terms of sharing the experience of the death of the father. Nicholas Royle dedicates his novel to the memory of his father; the narrator Chris is mourning the death of his father: both in the novel and in so-called real life, the father was born in 1930 and died in 1994 (see pp. 75, 305). Nicholas Royle thus inscribes his name in this figure of mourning: it is one of the many ways in which he signs his book, inscribes the autobiographical within the fictional, signs their inextricable interlinking, registering death in the name. Chris is writing a book about the matter of the heart. As he tells us: 'For some time I'd been gathering material for a book. A book about the heart, although I didn't really know what *kind* of book it would be. Max, of course, had a pretty good idea' (p. 11). It is as if Max (the name of a fictional character though also, I must note in passing, the name of my own father) is telepathic. To recall here what Royle says, in *Telepathy and Literature*: any theory of the novel is also a theory of telepathy. Novels are telepathic structures, starting out from the fact of having a telepathic or misleadingly termed 'omniscient' narrator (the one in *The Matter of the Heart* who says, as we remarked earlier, 'Ambrose banished the thought' or 'She liked that, he knew'). More generally, telepathy haunts literature in the form of strange coincidences, doubles, uncanny communication or sharing of thoughts and feelings, above all in 'literature today' in relation to the disturbances of identity, time and place generated by so many kinds of automation and programming, simulation, virtuality and prosthesis, from mobile phones, email and the internet, to organ transplants and genetic engineering – in short the sorts of disturbances explored in Nicholas Royle's fiction.

In *The Matter of the Heart* the concern with telepathy is inscribed, above all, in the figure of the heart. Royle plays with the heart to the point, no doubt, of overkill: a journalist called Charlie has a heart attack in a hotel room that in the late nineteenth century had been a room in St George's Hospital, the site of the world's first (fictive) heart transplant; the flow of the novel is repeatedly arrested by references to characters' hearts, heart-shapes, having one's heart in the right place, being sick at heart, London as the heart, the hospital as the heart of London, and so on.[17] The novel is divided up into sections entitled 'Superior Vena Cava', 'Right Atrium', 'Tricuspid Valve', 'Right Ventricle', 'Pulmonary Valve', 'Left Atrium', 'Mitral Valve', 'Left Ventricle' and 'Aorta'. Heart-stopping stuff. *The Matter of the Heart* is a kind of limit-text which asks: What is the heart? In the time of the heart transplant, the pacemaker complete with its radioactive core, the non-human heart in the human, the human heart now separable from its 'home' (at least since October 1998 when television offered us images of a heart lying on a table, recovering from its 'own' body), how does the heart relate to writing, thinking and feeling? What is the matter of the heart?

Royle's novel belongs with certain other contemporary works that trace the rhythm of what could be called a cardiogrammatology. I am thinking here not only of the writings of Jacques Derrida but also of Jean-Luc Nancy. The great twentieth-century philosopher of the heart, Nancy is of course also (at least to my knowledge) the first great philosopher to have had a heart transplant. His book *The Inoperative Community* includes a remarkable essay called 'Shattered Love', a shattering text about the heart.[18] It is a love letter of sorts, about the strangeness of the heart but also about the heart as what dictates the love of thinking, the love of writing, the very possibility of literature or philosophy. Nancy proposes: 'The heart is not an organ, and neither is it a faculty. It is: [the fact] that *I* is broken and traversed by the other where its presence is most intimate and its life most open' (p. 99). To feel and think the heart today, in one's heart, from the heart, is to engage with the matter of the heart as other, as the workings and the passion of a foreign body, as what is not and cannot be reduced to a subject. Nancy writes:

> in its modes of affirmation and negation, the heart does not operate by reporting its own judgment to itself (if it is a judgment). It does not say 'I love', which is the reflection or the speculation of an *ego* (and which engages love neither more nor less than the *cogito*), but it says 'I love you', a declaration where 'I' is posed only by being exposed to 'you'. That is to say the heart is not a subject, even if it is the heart of a subject. (p. 89)

Alongside this, we might consider an extraordinary little text by Derrida entitled 'Che cos'è la poesia?', which responds to the question 'what thing is poetry?' by suggesting that this is in some sense the same as asking 'what is memory?' and 'what is love?' It is a matter of the heart. 'Che cos'è la poesia?' suggests that at the heart of the poetic, and of love and memory in general, is the desire to 'learn by heart', to take something within oneself and keep it. Derrida writes:

> I call a poem that very thing that teaches the heart, invents the heart, *that which*, finally, the word *heart* seems to mean and which, in my language, I cannot easily discern from the word itself. *Heart*, in the poem 'learn by heart' (to be learned by heart), no longer names only pure interiority, independent spontaneity, the freedom to affect oneself actively by reproducing the beloved trace.[19]

No art without the heart, but the heart names nothing human and is, as Derrida goes on to make clear, inseparable from 'a certain exteriority of the automaton' (p. 231). One's heart, even or especially when learning by heart, is never one's own. At the heart of desire, of the desire to write, of the desire to remember and of the desire to appropriate, to have as one's own, to have as one's own thing, is the otherness of a foreign body, a mechanical and deathly power of repetition.

Consider, for example, the case of a signature. At the start of the Genet column of *Glas*, Derrida characterizes the 'great stake of literary discourse' as the transformation of the writer's signature 'into things, into the name of things'.[20] This stake is traumatic, ecstatic, compulsive, a sort of writing drive. It is linked to what Derrida proposes elsewhere in that provocatively double-columned book when he says: 'The signature is a wound and there is no other origin of the work of art.'[21] Such a conception of the signature touches upon what is secret, secret within and to oneself, in one's heart. It has to do with the secret as described by Derrida when he says: 'I call secret not only that which is intimate but that which is like a style: inimitable.'[22] The desire to write, leave one's mark, be remembered in and for one's writing, is doubtless at some level inseparable from the desire to be inimitable, a desire for one's name to live on thanks to a unique style or signature. But it is also about an engagement with the fact that death, machine-like repetition and otherness are always inscribed in the workings of the name and signature.[23] This strangely divided, dividing desire or need has been brilliantly expounded by Derrida in his book *Signsponge*.[24] His account of the signature harbingers a theory of the double. It is closely linked to the fascination with 'the paradoxes of the double' that he finds in Freud's essay 'The Uncanny'.[25] The signature is double-hearted. The desire to sign is caught up in what Derrida calls a double-bind or 'double-band' (p. 56). Focusing on the work of Francis Ponge, he proposes that the writer's desire to sign involves a 'duel ... to the death' (p. 14). There cannot be a pure and proper signature: in order to be a signature, it must be repeatable, and this repeatability (or 'iterability' as Derrida also calls it) haunts and divides it from itself. This principle of repeatability that makes possible a signature also makes possible its forgery. Forgery, as he says elsewhere, 'is always possible'.[26] We could say that the signature functions according to the model of a 'duplicity without original', so long as this is understood to mean that there is no pure and proper double in the first place.[27] A signature is never finished: it always requires a countersignature; and that countersignature requires a countersignature, and so on.[28] Derrida argues that Ponge is driven by the impossible desire for his poetry to be both signature and countersignature, 'the absolute idiom' of 'one single countersigned signature, one single thing signing double' (p. 48). However obliquely, his poetry articulates a phallocentric longing to produce a signature that would be a 'stony double of the dead phallus' (p. 108) or what Derrida also calls a 'double of the dead man in erection' (p. 6). The proper itself is 'double' (p. 52), says Derrida.[29]

The other Nicholas Royle allows me to experience this strangeness in a striking way: I cannot recognize myself in his writing, perhaps especially when it comes closest to resembling my own. I cannot see its signature as being inscribable within 'my' name, 'Nicholas Royle'. His work has nothing to do with the signature which *I* recognize or desire to recognize as that of Nicholas Royle, my own heart's Nicholas Royle. 'My' double, or my 'double' – who is in many respects of course not a 'real' double at all – obliges me to recognize, more acutely than I might ever otherwise have done, the madness of the desire for the signature, the phallocentric laughableness of the 'duel'. And yet, as I have also indicated, there are strange 'resemblances' in or between the texts we have produced: are they coincidences? What are coincidences? What if one's name, in all its meagreness, insignificance and inessentialness ('Nicholas' – or 'Nick', as we are both also known – 'Royle'), were itself a sort of uncanny 'writing-machine', somehow itself capable of giving rise to the preoccupations and resemblances, especially of our so-called fictional writings? What if there really were effects bound up with the specificity of the name, effects which we Nicholas Royles ourselves neither intended nor even perhaps were aware of, effects as aleatory as the anagrammatic presence of a 'royle' in 'aleatory'? The 'coincidental' would here thus perhaps touch on a sense of the name as uncanny. We may recall Ernest Jones's story about Freud and Ferenczi's concerns with the question of telepathy in this connection:

Nicholas Royle and Nicholas Royle

on the occasion of a joint fiction-reading, Gantry Arts Centre, Southampton, October 1999

Ferenczi was now getting venturesome. Seeing a soldier in a tramcar he made a guess at his name and as they got out asked him, 'Are you Herr Kohn?' The astonished man answered in the affirmative. Freud found the story 'uncannily beautiful', but could not attribute it to telepathy because the man could hardly be expected to carry a visual picture of his name about with him. He said afterwards, however, that he was impressed by Ferenczi's argument that a man's name was a sensitive area and thus could more easily be communicated to a stranger.[30]

What is 'uncannily beautiful' here is specifically *not* to do with telepathy, it would seem, but rather with the strangeness of the name as a 'sensitive area' and with the strangeness of the 'coincidence' as such.

At the heart of Nicholas Royle's novel, announced on the opening page of Chapter One, is the idea of the heart in terms of 'emotional routes', in particular Max's idea that 'there are insubstantial but clearly defined thoroughfares all over [London]' (p. 7) and indeed all over the world, as becomes evident later when the narrative setting shifts to Australia. 'Emotional routes' is among other things a synonym for 'coincidences' (p. 33), and thus a way of describing the structure of the narrative: it is a novel about the fact that there are no novels without coincidences, without narratorial foreknowledge, clairvoyance and telepathy. 'Emotional route' is also a term used to describe the narrator's life, and his heart's trajectory. As he says early on in the novel: 'My emotional route was burning up' (p. 39). The 'emotional routes' of the heart are indissociable from the novel's quasi-obsessional concern with driving. It is in the various references to the signatures of drivers' tyre marks that one may feel the insistence of a kind of narratorial-authorial desire to affirm the singularity of the text. But this is also where one may feel particularly strongly the eerie presence of one of this novel's more powerful, overshadowing precursors, J. G. Ballard's *Crash* (1973).[31] Like *Crash*, *The Matter of the Heart* dramatizes the act of signing in the context of what, a few moments ago, I called the writing drive. In Royle's novel this link between the notion of the signature and the marks left by driving is perhaps most memorably evoked in the description of mad Danny, the scorch marks of whose tyres 'as good as signed his name on the macadam' (p. 280). As someone who has published fiction under the name Dan McAdam, I am particularly taken with that example of a scene of signature. It provokes, by one link-road or another, a quite different thinking of the autograph.

Above all, the term 'emotional routes' connects Royle's novel with the World Wide Web. In a crucial passage, set on a balcony at a party in New Orleans, Charlie tells the narrator about his heart attack and subsequent out-of-body experience at St George's Hospital. Charlie, we are given to understand, believes he has glimpsed the impossible: death, out-of-body experience. It has to do with what Charlie calls the 'subtle heart'. This ought to be read in a US accent:

> '... when you're up there, man –' he swept his arms high in the air '– you can see everything. The whole fuckin' lot, you know. It's all connected. Each one connected to the next in a giant fuckin' web. A net. Whatever you want to call it. It's the World Wide fuckin' Web of the heart, man, if that's what you wanna call it.' He knocked back another JD [that's a Jack Daniels, not Jacques Derrida], poured the next. 'And if you gotta subtle heart, man, you got other stuff too. 'Cause when you think about it, the heart is the cradle of time and space.' (p. 108)

This passage is concerned with an experience of the heart as an experience of the impossible, an experience that draws together writing itself (the very project of the writing of the novel) with a figural concatenation of the World Wide Web.

Royle's novel concludes with a parodic, gothic scene in which Max, Chris and his cardiologist lover Joanna dig up a lead box on Dartmoor and find inside it something like a heart, something that is presented (without being presented), a sort of figure for the novel, the heart and matter of *The Matter of the Heart*. As Chris recounts:

> Inside the lead box is something about the size of a large fist ... There are folds and crevices in the material. Lacking any distinct flux or whorl, the thing seems created by chaos. Looking at it cold, there's no way you'd guess what it was ...
>   It resembles the chamois heart. The unidentifiable object Danny found in the hospital all those years ago, which was neither an old window-cleaner's chamois leather scrunched up into a ball, nor an extracted heart inexplicably left lying around. (p. 289)

Unidentifiable yet textual, the heart is a crypt. Royle's novel, no doubt in some ways in spite of itself, beats to the rhythm of this cryptic heart: realistic, surrealistic, parodic, postmodern gothic. As an example of what the narrator at one point refers to as 'an experiment in psychogeography' (p. 287), Royle's novel makes my heart bleed. My heart is buried here, in Nicholas Royle's fiction, inseparable from my name which is not mine, my heart that is not mine, in this language which is not mine.

PS. In 1999 Nicholas Royle edited a collection of short stories which included a piece by the other Nicholas Royle, entitled 'Chance Encounter'.[32] It is a text about numbers and coincidences. Alluding to the Number of the Beast, it is also about the diabolical. In concluding with a recurring number ('10.09090909 ...'), 'Chance Encounter' affirms that 666 is not divisible by 66 and thus stages an encounter or coinciding that never takes place.[33] The text is written in the so-called omniscient or, more accurately perhaps, the telepathic third person: it thus testifies to that structure of doubling or 'being-two-to-speak' – and of being-two-to-think and being-two-to-feel – that Derrida has argued is a defining characteristic of literature.[34] With or without the other or any other Nicholas Royle, I, the writing I, am already a double, even or perhaps especially if the first person singular does not appear as such: the writing I is always inscribed in advance by its double. Joseph Conrad evokes something of this, perhaps, in his description of the experience of writing as the experience of having a secret sharer: it is a matter, he says, of 'wrestling as with a dumb devil for every line of my creation'.[35] What or where will this dumb devil have been? I hereby confess that, when writing this 'Chance Encounter', I had no 'conscious intention' of addressing the link between the double and the diabolical. Was it then simply writing 'by chance'? Analysing the figure of the devil 'in person' in the context of Freud's 'The Uncanny' and *Beyond the Pleasure Principle*, Derrida refers to the uncanny effect of 'duplicity without an original', before specifying that this is perhaps 'what the diabolical consists of'.[36]

PPS. More recently, I have died. I have been murdered or have at any rate been 'as good as murdered'. As Royle puts it: 'I as good as murder him [i.e. me] in my [i.e. his] new novel'.[37] He is referring to a passage in his latest novel, *The Director's Cut* (2000), in which a photographer called Fraser Munro stalks another man, also a photographer, also called Fraser Munro, and finally tracks him down to a cairn on the top of a munro, on the Scottish island of Mull. In this resolutely stony, deathly and monumental setting, complete with phalloid cameras and all the double-acting of photography, the duel, or at least the murder, or at least the attempted murder, can proceed:

> 'I make films.'
> 'Aye well, there's a coincidence, so do I.' ...
> 'What do you shoot with it?' the other man asked him, clearly wanting to redirect attention to Fraser's camera.
> 'Dead men,' Fraser replied, lifting the camera to his eye and squeezing off a few frames.
> Munro said nothing, but sat stiffly as the camera filmed him.
> 'How about yourself?' Fraser asked him. 'There's not much up here to film and the light's not great.'
> 'Mountains. Munros. That's my name, you see. Munro.' His voice wavered on the last word. He was definitely nervous now.

'There's another coincidence for you.' Fraser's delivery was deadpan.

'What's that?'

'Munro's my name, too.'

'Weird.'

'Definitely.'

'I don't usually believe in coincidence.'

'You're probably right not to.'

'Anyway, I have to be going.'

'Not so fast ... You're going nowhere.' ...

'Look, do you want my camera?'

'Aye. It's not all I want.'

'What do you want?'

'*I want to be me.*'

Munro had started to shake. With the cold? With fear?

'You want to be you?'

'I want to be me and you won't let me.'

Fraser stood up suddenly. Munro did likewise, taking a half-step back and falling against the wall of the cairn.

'What's your name?'

'I told you. Munro. Fraser Munro.'

'That was your last chance.'

'What do you mean? That's my name. Fraser Munro.'

'That's *my* name.'

Fraser raised his camera and Munro flinched, lifted an arm to ward off the blow that didn't come.

And then, along with a repetition of the phrase '*my* name', it did come. The camera struck him on the right temple, hard, hard enough to knock him down, and Fraser hit him again as he fell, twice, three times, repeating '*my* name'. He hit him on the ground, still inside the cairn, all the time with the camera and all the time with his fingers clutched around the handle, the soft whirr of the camera's motor the only sound apart from the repeated cracks to the victim's skull and the harsh rasp of Munro's breathing. After a while he stopped hitting him and for a short time he continued to film – then he stopped that as well.[38]

NOTES

1   Heinrich Heine, 'Die Harzreise', quoted in Otto Rank, *The Double: A Psychoanalytic Study* (1914), trans. Harry Tucker, Jr (Chapel Hill, NC: University of North Carolina Press, 1971), p. 43 n. 19.

2   Sigmund Freud, *The Psychopathology of Everyday Life* (1901), PFL, 5: 64. A few years later, in 1907, Freud added (in brackets) the following enigmatic attempt at differentiation from this person with his 'own' name: 'However, I must record the assurance of one of my critics that in this respect his feelings are the opposite of mine.'

3   'Madame la Fleurie', *The Collected Poems of Wallace Stevens* (New York: Knopf, 1954), p. 507.

4   Nicholas Royle, 'Royle We', *Dazed and Confused* (July 2000), p. 32.

5   See W. B. Yeats, 'The Lake-Isle of Innisfree', *The Collected Poems of W. B. Yeats* (London: Macmillan, 1977), p. 44.

6   In his 1954 lecture 'The Question Concerning Technology' (in *The Question Concerning Technology and Other Essays*, trans. William Lovitt (New York: Harper and Row, 1977), pp. 3–35), Heidegger elaborates on the uncanniness of what he calls the 'instrumental definition of technology', in other words the assumption that technology is 'a means and a human activity'. He notes: 'The instrumental definition of technology is indeed so uncannily correct that it even holds for modern technology, of which, in other respects, we maintain with some justification that it is, in contrast to the older handwork technology, something completely different and therefore new.' Stressing the paralysing movement whereby '[t]he will to mastery becomes all the more urgent the more technology threatens to slip from human control' (p. 5), he seeks to question and displace the deluded logic by which 'man ... exalts himself to the posture of lord of the earth' (p. 27). Heidegger's analysis of the 'instrumental' conception of technology remains uncannily apposite. Since 1954, the proliferation of so many sorts of 'new technology' has entailed only a continuing slippage from human control, indeed a decentring of the human. This is what Jacques Derrida, summing up the twentieth century, has called 'the techno-scientific ... decentring of ... the *anthropos* in its onto-theological identity or its genetic properties, of the *ego cogito* ... and of the very concept of narcissism': see *Spectres of Marx: The State of the Debt, the Work of Mourning, and the New International*, trans. Peggy Kamuf (New York: Routledge, 1994), p. 98. In the present chapter, I am especially concerned with trying to explore the question of literary writing, and its links with philosophy and psychoanalysis, in the light of Derrida's contention that 'an entire epoch of so-called literature, if not all of it, cannot survive a certain technological regime of telecommunications (in this respect the political regime is secondary). Neither can philosophy, or psychoanalysis.' See Jacques Derrida, *The Post Card: From Socrates to Freud and Beyond*, trans. Alan Bass (Chicago: Chicago University Press, 1987), p. 197.

7   See Auberon Waugh, 'A Sad Plop', *Literary Review*, December 1997, pp. 48–9, and 'Woe Be Unto Thee, O Moab!', January 1998.

8   Nicholas Royle, *The Matter of the Heart* (London: Abacus, 1997), p. 128. Further page references to this novel will be given in parentheses in the main body of the text.

9   Nicholas Royle, *Telepathy and Literature: Essays on the Reading Mind* (Oxford: Blackwell, 1990), p. 216.

10   Correspondingly, in 1996, in a review of an anthology entitled *Two, or the Book of Twins and Doubles*, ed. Penelope Farmer (London: Virago, 1996), the other Nicholas Royle begins: 'When I was offered this book for review, my first thought was to check I hadn't been mistaken for The Other Nicholas Royle – a literary theorist at a university in Scotland.' See Nicholas Royle, 'Secret Sharers', *New Statesman & Society* (7 June 1996), p. 38. For the record (as the saying goes), I should perhaps add a word of clarification here, namely that I do not think of myself as a 'literary theorist' and have never had any aspirations to being such. A 'writer', perhaps, but never a 'theorist'. I was teaching at the University of Stirling at this time: later Nicholas Royle and I were to give a joint seminar there (in February 1999) and he would base part of his novel *The Director's Cut* in the University's (fictive) medical school.

11   Nicholas Royle, ed., *Deconstructions: A User's Guide* (Basingstoke and New York: Palgrave, 2000).

12   'William Wilson', in *Collected Works of Edgar Allan Poe, vol. 2, Tales and Sketches 1831–1842*, ed. Thomas Ollive Mabbott (Cambridge, Mass.: Belknap Press, 1978), pp. 426–48. Further page references are given in the main body of the text.

13 Rank, *The Double: A Psychoanalytic Study*, p. 25.

14 Rank writes: 'It is noteworthy that some typical motifs of the double-phenomenon seem …
to be raised from their unconscious tragedy into the cognitive sphere of humour': see *The
Double*, p. 16.

15 Jacques Derrida, 'Aphorism Countertime', trans. Nicholas Royle, in *Acts of Literature*, ed.
Derek Attridge (London and New York: Routledge, 1992), p. 427.

16 Jorge Luis Borges, 'Borges and I', in *Labyrinths* (Harmondsworth: Penguin, 1970), pp. 282–3:
here, p. 283.

17 A concern with what might be called the palimpsestuous nature of the city is characteristic of
Royle's fiction. In this respect his work belongs with that group of 'uncanny' writers and
architects identified by Anthony Vidler in his book *The Architectural Uncanny: Essays in the
Modern Unhomely* (Cambridge, Mass.: MIT Press, 1992) where he talks about 'a posturbanist
sensibility that, from surrealism to situationism, has stood against the tendency of modern
urbanism to create so many *tabulae rasae* for the building of cities without memory'. Vidler
suggests that '[p]reoccupied with traces and residues – the material of the dreamwork –
rather than with the new, writers and architects have increasingly found ways to chart the
underground reverberations of the city' (p. xiii).

18 Jean-Luc Nancy, 'Shattered Love', trans. Lisa Garbus and Simona Sawhney, in *The Inoperative
Community*, ed. Peter Connor (Minneapolis: University of Minnesota Press, 1991), pp. 82–109.
Further page references are given parenthetically in the main body of the text.

19 Jacques Derrida, 'Che cos'è la poesia?', trans. Peggy Kamuf, in *A Derrida Reader: Between the
Blinds*, ed. Kamuf (London and New York: Harvester, 1991), p. 231.

20 Jacques Derrida, *Glas*, trans. John P. Leavey, Jr, and Richard Rand (London: University of
Nebraska Press, 1986), p. 5.

21 Derrida, *Glas*, p. 184.

22 See Jacques Derrida, 'The Deaths of Roland Barthes', trans. Pascale-Anne Brault and Michael
Naas, in *Continental Philosophy I: Philosophy and Non-Philosophy since Merleau-Ponty*, ed. Hugh
Silverman (London: Routledge, 1988), p. 263.

23 Cf. Jacques Derrida's remark in *The Post Card*: 'The desire for the idiom – nothing is less
idiomatic' (p. 360).

24 Jacques Derrida, *Signéponge/Signsponge*, trans. Richard Rand (New York: Columbia University Press, 1984). Further page references will be given in parentheses in the main body of the
text. For a more extensive account of *Signsponge*, in particular as inhabiting 'the uncanny and
perhaps finally undecidable space between science and belief', see Nicholas Royle, 'The Remains
of Psychoanalysis (ii): Shakespeare', in *After Derrida* (Manchester: Manchester University
Press, 1995), pp. 85–123: here, p. 91.

25 See Jacques Derrida, 'The Double Session', in *Dissemination*, trans. Barbara Johnson
(Chicago: Chicago University Press, 1981): here, p. 220, n. 32.

26 Jacques Derrida, 'Afterword: Toward an Ethic of Discussion', trans. Samuel Weber, in
Limited Inc (Evanston, Ill: Northwestern University Press, 1988), p. 133.

27 See Derrida, *The Post Card*, pp. 270, 342.

28 For a fine discussion of this uncanny supplementary logic in the context of being the
presumed author of a book, see Geoffrey Bennington, in Bennington and Derrida, *Jacques
Derrida*, trans. Geoffrey Bennington (Chicago: Chicago University Press, 1993), pp. 153–5.

29 The 'proper double or double proper' (*le double propre*), he suggests, involves 'propriety and
idiomatic property' (the desire for a proper signature, mine and no one else's) and also 'the
double *of* the proper *that is placed in abyss*' (the 'properness' of a signature is possible only on

condition of being repeatable, imitable, always already subject to 'death' or 'exappropriation', and on condition of there being a countersignature, another signature, the signature of another). See *Signsponge*, pp. 52/53, 132. It is in this context of the double that we might consider Paul de Man's suggestive characterization of how Derrida writes: 'Derrida's text is so brilliant, so incisive, so strong that whatever happens in Derrida, it happens between him and his own text. He doesn't need Rousseau, he doesn't need anybody else.' See Paul de Man, *The Resistance to Theory* (Manchester: Manchester University Press, 1986), p. 118.

30 Ernest Jones, *Sigmund Freud: Life and Work*, 3 (London: Hogarth Press, 1957), p. 415.

31 J. G. Ballard, *Crash* (London: Picador, 1973). Like Ballard's, Royle's text is repeatedly, compulsively concerned with driving and signing. For examples of where *The Matter of the Heart* speaks of tyre marks as signatures, see pp. 125, 212, 218, 271 and 280.

32 Nicholas Royle, 'Chance Encounter', in *Neon Lit 2*, ed. Nicholas Royle (London: Time Out Books, 1999), 47–9. This text reappears below: see Chapter 13.

33 The recurrence of the figure of 66 in the text inevitably resembles (or is it just 'chance'?) Freud's preoccupation with 62 (or is it 61 or 60 – or, why not, 66, since after all it seems to be the digit 6 that insists here?) in 'The Uncanny': see U, p. 360. In a letter to Jung on 16 April 1909, Freud writes: 'Some years ago I discovered within me the conviction that I should die between the ages of 61 and 62 [what is there, one wonders, *between* these ages?], which then struck me as a long time away. (Today it is only eight years off.) Then I went to Greece with my brother [Alexander] and it was really uncanny how often the number 61 or 60 in connection with 1 or 2 kept cropping up in all sorts of numbered objects, especially those connected with transportation.' See *The Freud/Jung Letters: The Correspondence between Sigmund Freud and C. G. Jung*, ed. William McGuire, trans. Ralph Manheim and R. F. C. Hull (London: Hogarth Press and Routledge and Kegan Paul, 1974), p. 219. Here, of course, is confirmation of another 'example' of the uncanny that is based on Freud's personal experience and that thus runs counter to the 'special obtuseness' (U, p. 340) to which he double-heartedly lays claim in his essay 'The Uncanny'.

34 Jacques Derrida, *Given Time: 1. Counterfeit Money*, trans. Peggy Kamuf (Chicago: Chicago University Press, 1992), p. 153. I consider this characterization of literature in greater detail in Chapter 19 ('The "telepathy effect"') below.

35 Joseph Conrad, letter to J. G. Huneker, 18 May 1909, in *The Collected Letters of Joseph Conrad*, 4, ed. Frederick R. Carl (Cambridge: Cambridge University Press, 1990), p. 235.

36 See Derrida, *The Post Card*, p. 270.

37 Royle, 'Royle We', p. 33.

38 Nicholas Royle, *The Director's Cut* (London: Abacus, 2000), pp. 142–4.

13

Chance encounter

For Asko Kauppinen

> Here is wisdom. Let him that hath understanding count the number of the beast; for it is the number of a man. (*Revelation* 13: 18)

> One can make the queerest play with numbers: so be careful. (Freud, in Jones 3: 111)

It was a sharp frosty morning and he was up early, before it was properly light, keen to get off to the library where he was working on an essay about numbers for a respectable academic journal whose editors had expressed cautious but positive interest. Drying himself from the shower, he noticed a distasteful black area developing on one of his toes. At first he supposed it fluff, which he made to brush away with the towel. The extuberance was odd, in the shape of two tiny comically squashed-up noses or opening quotation marks.

Reading can always have undesirable effects, including the worst. It was already mid-morning and he – for his name would never come to be of any significance – was very cosily ensconced in his regular seat in the main reading-room of the city library. Recent research had led him to Sigmund Freud, someone with a surprising amount to say on the subject of numbers. He had just come across a particularly intriguing paragraph in which Freud was reflecting on the idea of involuntary repetition. Involuntary repetition is something which can sometimes make us laugh, but which, in other circumstances,

> forces upon us the idea of something fateful and inescapable when otherwise we should have spoken only of "chance". For instance, we naturally attach no importance to the event when we hand in an overcoat and get a cloakroom ticket with the number, let us say, 62; or when we find that our cabin on a ship bears that number. But the impression is altered if two such events, each in itself indifferent, happen close together – if we come across the number 62 several times in a single day, or if we begin to notice that everything which has a number – addresses, hotel rooms, compartments in railway trains – invariably has the same one, or at all events one which contains the same figures. We do feel this to be uncanny.

He enjoyed Freud because his prose was so clear but contradictory, laughable but inescapable, rational and superstitious all in the same breath. A footnote at the bottom of the page (it was page 66 of the volume he was looking at) informed him that Freud himself had been 62 the year prior to the original publication of the paragraph in question. The twentieth-century master of post-Darwinian no-

nonsense was actually, if truth be told, superstitious as hell. Numerology fascinated this reader, more than he could realize. What Freud made especially clear was timing. Coincidences become significant only when close together in time. Snug in his seat, in the warmth of the library, looking out over the still icy street, he could not stop thinking about this paragraph of Freud's. His mind was frozen in the tantalizing possibilities it seemed to open up, like so many doors in an abandoned house. How many? Was it possible to count, if only in the back of his mind? And on to what did they open? How distant or near in time does a coincidence have to be to be a coincidence? What happens if we accept as genuine, like currency that is foreign but not counterfeit, that there are coincidences of which we are unaware?

He had arranged to meet someone for lunch at a restaurant on the High Street. He sat at a table by the window and waited, first consulting the menu, then pulling out from his shoulder-bag an old novel to pass the time. He had ordered a gin and tonic. The taste of the bubbles bursting on his tongue reminded him of the squashed-up noses. He became gradually more sceptical until finally convinced, the woman was not coming. And then a strange thing happened. The waiter returned to his table and graciously enquired: "Would Madam care to order now?" Taken aback, but saying nothing about it, he specified a dish from the copious main menu. As soon as the waiter had withdrawn he turned and checked himself in the reflections of the window. Obviously it was his hair, grown overlong and feminine. But what he saw in the reflections of the window was nothing of what he might have seen. Unbeknownst to him, an upper region of his mind even now was filling with blackness, light as the beginnings of cancer, dark and remote as a tarn. On the other side of the High Street, at Number 65, was the main branch of the city's largest bookshop: he did not consider what was to be inferred from this, regarding the number of the building where he was sitting. He had not noticed that from the restaurant menu he had ordered item sixty-six, or that the point at which he had given up reading his novel, never to return to it, was a sentence in which one character explains to another how to understand the currency of the foreign country in which they are just arriving: "Simply multiply by 10.09090909...."

14

Cannibalism: for starters

Cannibalism is not, perhaps, something to rush into. There is a real danger of – to inflect slightly differently the English version of one of Lacan's favoured idioms – getting ahead of ourselves. In what follows I wish only to sketch out a selection of very modest hors d'oeuvres, offered as a sort of textual thali. The subtitle suggests the colloquial phrase (as in 'What's for starters?') defined by *Chambers Dictionary* as: 'the first course of a meal; in the first place, for a start'. But the word 'starters' is ineschewably if not unchewably ironic in other ways: there is 'starter' also in the sense of 'a person who gives the signal for starting', 'an apparatus or device for starting a machine' or 'anything used to begin a process' (*Chambers*). The strange layers or skins of the term 'starters' might also include connotations of the 'start' as 'a startled feeling'; 'a queer occurrence'; 'a spurt, spasm, burst'.

If 'starters' has to do with what is 'in the first place', what is this 'first place' when it comes to cannibalism? I'm not trying simply to turn all of this into a joke. In fact I'm anxious not to do so – if only because I am apprehensive about the sense that laughter itself may be indistinguishable from cannibalistic desire. Any sense of comedy here has to be decidedly unsteady, even if an encounter with the question of the comic seems uncircumventable. Joseph Conrad's *Heart of Darkness* (1902) is not usually construed as a comic novel, though to try to conceive it as such seems to me a possible *starter*.

First starter then. I have to laugh, at least to myself (as one says), when I read the extraordinary passage in which the narrator Marlow is describing the steamer's journey up the river into the heart of darkness:

> I don't pretend to say that steamboat floated all the time. More than once she had to wade for a bit, with twenty cannibals splashing around and pushing. We had enlisted some of these chaps on the way for a crew [*for starters*, in other words]. Fine fellows – cannibals – in their place. They were men one could work with, and I am grateful to them. And, after all, they did not eat each other before my face: they had brought along a provision of hippo-meat which went rotten, and made the mystery of the wilderness stink in my nostrils. Phoo! I can sniff it now.[1]

The comic dimensions of Conrad's novel are doubtless linked to what Elaine Showalter would call male hysteria.[2] The hysteria is suggested, for example, in Marlow's final claim: 'Phoo! I can sniff it now' – for, as all non-hysterics are supposed to know, smells cannot be recalled: disturbances of smell are one of the primary symptoms of hysteria noted by Freud and Breuer.[3] More specifically of interest in the present context is the way cannibalism and language splash around together. It is as if cannibalism eats its way into the very words Marlow uses. There's the ambiguous playfulness of 'chaps' (both gentlemen and jaws), and even (in an intriguingly retrospective fashion) in the word 'bit' ('she had to wade for a bit, with twenty cannibals splashing around and pushing': 'bit' thus imprinted with the sense of 'bite' or 'morsel'). I can't help finding comical the oddity of 'before my face' ('And, after all, they did not eat each other before my face'): 'before' is intended in a spatial sense ('in front of my face') but also carries with it at least a soupçon of the temporal sense ('prior to my face'). The phrase 'before my face' leaves us to suppose that there certainly *was* cannibalistic activity going on (after all, the hippo-meat had gone rotten), only the cannibalism didn't happen in the narrator's presence. But what is perhaps most demanding of rumination in this enigmatic *bit* of Conrad is the 'Fine fellows – cannibals – in their place'. We could linger over this remarkable, six-word, verbless sentence for some time: why does the adjective 'fine' seem so provoking? Its aptness has echoed more recently in the name of a group of musicians called The Fine Young Cannibals. 'Fine' suggests 'excellent' and 'beautiful' but also 'sharp'. There is, in other words, a finely veiled if not finely filed evocation of sharp teeth in 'fine fellows'.

How are we (as it were) to get our heads round the claim that cannibals are 'fine fellows … *in their place*'? The comedy here touches on the very pulse of incongruity: *out of place* cannibals are not so fine; so long as they remain 'in their place' they are entirely acceptable. But what, in the first place, is the place of the cannibal? And what might it mean to suggest that the meaning of 'cannibalism' always already cannibalizes itself?

Second starter. For Freud, the place of the cannibal, of cannibalism and the cannibalistic, is at the origin. In the beginning was the cannibal. Psychoanalysis is first and foremost (foremost and hindmost, or perhaps hindforemost) a theory of cannibalism. Psychoanalysis gets started, in so far as it can or must get started, only on the basis of a theory of cannibalism. People may tend to associate psychoanalysis with a theory of sexuality but, as Freud makes clear in *The Future of an Illusion* (1927), cannibalism is what is most fundamental and decisive. More even than the 'instinctual wishes' connected with 'incest' and 'lust for killing' (*PFL*, 12: 189), cannibalism can be described as the taboo desire *par excellence*. As Freud puts it: 'Cannibalism alone [of the oldest instinctual wishes] seems to be universally proscribed and – to the non-psychoanalytic view – to have been completely surmounted' (p. 190). Psychoanalysis thus distinguishes itself as a discourse that caters for cannibals, indeed as a cannibalistic discourse. You can't subscribe to the psychoanalytic view without subscribing to cannibalism. In an uncanny sense that is perhaps untranslatable into the German *unheimlich*, the cannibalistic is uncannibalistic. Freud's text cannily divides, slices the addressee up. It is canny to believe that you are cannibalistic; but if you don't believe that you are cannibalistic, this is not surprising. After all, as he acknowledges in *The Future of an Illusion*, the practice of cannibalism is 'unacceptable' (*PFL*, 12: 190). In which case, you must be repressed. As with all the other examples of the uncanny that Freud deals with, in 'The Uncanny' and elsewhere, what may seem to have been sur- mounted can always come back; but to the psychoanalytic view cannibalism has in fact never been surmounted. If you think that cannibalistic desire has been 'completely surmounted', psychoanalytic thinking may itself seem uncanny, for here, as in so many other contexts, it is 'laying bare ... hidden forces' (U, p. 366). To work as a text that is addressed not merely to cannibalistic psychoanalytic 'believers', the rhetoric of *The Future of an Illusion* here conjures a sort of uncanny performativity, inviting those with a 'non-psychoanalytic view' to think or look again, and thus perhaps experience a sense of 'something which is secretly familiar [*heimlich – heimisch*], which has undergone repression and [has now] returned from it' (U, p. 368).

Third starter. In that great textual carnival *Totem and Taboo* (1913) Freud proposes that 'anything that is uncanny ... becomes subject to taboo' (*PFL* 13: 77) and goes on to inscribe cannibalism at the origin of human history: 'cannibal savages' 'killed' then 'devoured' their father, 'and in the act of devouring him they accom- plished their identification with him, and each one of them acquired a portion of his strength'. Freud concludes:

> The totem meal, which is perhaps mankind's earliest festival, would thus be a repetition and a commemoration of this memorable and criminal deed, which was the beginning of so many things – of social organisation, of moral restrictions and of religion. (*PFL*, 13: 203)

Does the accomplishment here come in finishing off or getting started? And what would be the difference between the wish and the act, 'knowing' (as psycho- analysis has shown us) that the unconscious recognizes no such distinction (as Freud put it, 'there are no indications of reality in the unconscious')?[4] Where does cannibalism start if wishing itself is cannibalistic? The aporetic nature of such questions perhaps characterizes the strange 'place' of cannibalism. To adopt a formulation from James Risser: 'An uncanny space is thus first of all a space of a place of displacement.'[5]

The decisive question of the place of cannibalism vis-à-vis psychoanalysis is not, however, limited to Freud's 'monstrous' hypothesis (*PFL*, 13: 203, n. 2) concerning the origins of human history. What is enigmatic in his work is his desire, his consuming desire to formulate a theory of the development of the individual psyche on the same cannibalistic model. His appetite for this 'theoretical cannibalism' is quite voracious. We thus have a theory of cannibalism, cannibalism as theory, theory as cannibalization and even, as the opening allusion to Lacan may have intimated, theory as autophagy. To recall a marvellous phrase from Shakespeare, Freud seems to be 'cannibally given'.[6] He's given and driven to it. As he declares in 'The Wolf Man' (1918 [1914]): 'I have been driven to regard as the earliest recognisable sexual organisation the so-called "cannibalistic" or "oral" phase' (*PFL*, 9: 347). The formulation here corresponds to what is first propounded in the *Three Essays on Sexuality* (in a passage added in 1915), where Freud asserts of the 'pregenital' organizations of sexual life: 'The first of these is the *oral* or, as it might be called, *cannibalistic* pregenital sexual organisation' (*PFL*, 7: 116). Another reference at around the same time comes in 'Mourning and Melancholia' (1917 [1915]) in the context of a definition of identification as 'a preliminary stage of object-choice'. Freud writes: 'The ego wants to incorporate this object into itself, and, in accordance with the oral or cannibalistic phase of libidinal development in which it is, it wants to do so by devouring it' (*PFL*, 11: 258).

What is this cannibalistic drive in Freud? He is himself clearly aware that the relationship between the 'oral' and the 'cannibalistic' is an *analogy* – at least at the start, in its first formulation, it is a sort of 'take or leave it': thus he speaks of 'the *oral* or, *as it might be called* [my emphasis], *cannibalistic*'. As anyone who has observed babies will be aware, there is at the start nothing at all ostensibly 'cannibalistic' about a baby's 'orality': 'I am the breast' might as well be 'I am the table'. It is a question, as Freud makes clear, of 'the earliest recognizable sexual organization', in other words of *when* an organization becomes recognizable, of the moment of recognition as indeed a repetition, a cannibalization, a performative act of naming: 'the *oral* or, as it might be called, *cannibalistic*'.

Fourth starter. Cannibalism is not something to 'baulk at', as Freud breezily declares, in *Moses and Monotheism* (*PFL*, 13: 325). There is, for him, no cannibalism without love, no love without cannibalism. We may recall here the unequivocally affirmative characterization of the cannibal in the 'Identification' section of *Group Psychology and the Analysis of the Ego* (1921): 'The cannibal … has a devouring affection for his enemies and only devours people of whom he is fond' (*PFL*, 12: 135). This corresponds, in turn, with the example Freud gives of one of the 'permanent marks'[7] left by the oral or cannibalistic phase 'upon the usages of language': 'People commonly speak for instance, of an "appetising" love-object, and describe persons they are fond of as "sweet" ' (*PFL*, 9: 348). One might thus imagine Freud beginning each of his Introductory Lectures, 'Ladies and gentlemen, you are a sweet audience and I have a fittingly sweet theory for you ...' Cannibalism is a crucial trope in his attempt to articulate an account of the history of humanity with the history of the individual: he cannibalizes the former for the latter. But at the same time this is cannibalism in one's mouth, cannibalism as performative, indissociable from an experience of the promise or threat, of naming and seduction. The metaphor of cannibalism in Freud is not 'just' metaphorical (whatever that might mean). Metaphor itself is cannibalized. The question of the performative and seductive power of a text or discourse becomes inseparable from a disturbance of any 'proper' relationship between the metaphorical and non-metaphorical, between orality and cannibalism.

Freud's work is not alone in foregrounding the power of a cannibalistic logic which is embodied in the very process of articulation. Again, Conrad provides one of the most dramatic examples of this, in his 1907 novel *The Secret Agent*, where the following is put into the mouth of the old terrorist Karl Yundt:

> 'Do you know how I would call the nature of the present economic conditions? I would call it cannibalistic. That's what it is! They are nourishing their greed on the quivering flesh and the warm blood of the people – nothing else!'
>
> Stevie swallowed the terrifying statement with an audible gulp, and at once, as though it had been swift poison, sank limply in a sitting posture on the steps of the kitchen door.[8]

It is not only that cannibalism is a powerful way of figuring political and economic inequality and exploitation (as it is, for example, in Jonathan Swift's 'A Modest Proposal' in 1729),[9] but rather its figuration is explicitly and inextricably linked to the performative effects of language itself. This is cannibalism not simply in-your-face but in-your-mouth. Stevie's response to Yundt's speech suggests that Conrad, like Freud, is doing something with words, doing something with the cannibalistic power of the language of cannibalism. The question of cannibalism becomes strangely but unavoidably bound up with the question of language.

In cannibalizing cannibalism, in making cannibalism a defining concept in the psychoanalytic account of identity and in highlighting the 'devouring affection' of the cannibal, Freud eroticizes both the concept and the discourse of cannibalism. We can nibble, so to speak, once again at that delicious sentence in *The Future of an Illusion*: 'Cannibalism alone [of the oldest instinctual wishes] seems to be universally proscribed and – to the non-psychoanalytic view – to have been completely surmounted' (*PFL*, 12: 190). Freud goes on to talk about murder, incest and various other 'cultural prohibitions' (p. 191); but intriguingly makes no further reference to cannibalism anywhere in the remaining fifty pages of the text. In so far as it lurks in the pages that follow, cannibalism has a sort of spectral, comical incongruity: it raises, perhaps, the ghost of a smile. Freud goes on to remark, for example, that '[t]here are countless civilized people who would shrink from murder or incest but who do not deny themselves the satisfaction of their avarice, their aggressive urges or their sexual lusts, and who do not hesitate to injure other people by lies, fraud and calumny, so long as they can remain unpunished for it' (p. 191): it is easy to see why Freud, the great headshrinker, might shrink here from an evocation of 'shrink[ing] from cannibalism'. It is as if he is keeping cannibalism in reserve, even when he does speak of it: he refers only to 'the non-psychoanalytic view', according to which cannibalism '[has] been completely surmounted'. He leaves the psychoanalytic view to be inferred, something to be chewed over in silence.

Fifth and final starter. As he has put it elsewhere, 'an author's words are deeds'.[10] But with Freud, the deeds can be just as much an effect of the leftovers, of what is not said or left unsaid. Given his candid and positive evaluation, his fundamentally loving embrace of cannibalism, we should hardly be surprised to find that the topic does not come up in his essay, 'The Uncanny'. Nowhere in 'The Uncanny' does Freud explicitly speak of the uncanniness of cannibalism. On the one hand, we might surmise that cannibalism, for Freud, would be uncanny because it is 'too much intermixed with what is purely gruesome' (U, p. 364); on the other, we may suspect that discussion of the subject too readily breaks into a sense of comedy. Such an alternation resembles what Freud describes in Oscar Wilde's 'The Canterville Ghost' which, he says, 'loses all power of at least arousing *gruesome* feelings in us as soon as the author begins to amuse himself by being ironical about it' (U, p. 376).[11]

But is it, in fact, so clear that 'The Uncanny' does not engage with the issue of cannibalism? Perhaps we could productively reconsider the central 'image' of Freud's text, in other words 'the figure of the Sandman [in Hoffmann's story], that is … the idea of being robbed of one's eyes' (U, p. 351). This is the focal point of Freud's account of the uncanny: Jentsch's 'theory of intellectual uncertainty' must be dismissed here; 'fears about the eye' must be understood in terms of 'the castration complex' (U, pp. 352–3). But what does Hoffmann's text actually say in this context? Who or what is the sandman? The old woman who looks after Nathaniel's youngest sister explains:

It is a wicked man who comes after children when they won't go to bed and throws handfuls of sand in their eyes, so that they jump out of their heads all bloody, and then he throws them into his sack and carries them to the crescent moon as food for his little children.[12]

The sandman is a 'dreadful spectre' (p. 87), monstrous and protean, yet still some sort of man. His progeny may have 'crooked beaks like owls' (p. 87) but they are still 'children'. Transformed into the loathsome Coppelius, the sandman seizes the young protagonist:

'Little beast! Little beast!' he bleated, showing his teeth. Then he pulled me up and threw me on to the hearth, so that the flames began to singe my hair.
    'Now we have eyes – eyes – a lovely pair of children's eyes!' Coppelius whispered. (p. 91)

Is it not possible that the 'fear of blindness' – of which Freud makes so much of a meal in his essay on 'The Uncanny' – has something to do with a cannibalistic terror *and* desire? Doesn't the sandman evoke an uncanny trace or tang of cannibalism right from the start?

NOTES

1   Joseph Conrad, *Heart of Darkness* (Harmondsworth: Penguin, 1973), pp. 49–50.
2   See Elaine Showalter, *Hystories: Hysterical Epidemics and Modern Culture* (London: Picador, 1997), esp. the chapters on 'Hysterical Men' (pp. 62–77) and 'Hysterical Narratives' (pp. 81–99). Conrad is discussed briefly in both chapters: in the former, Showalter specifically compares *Heart of Darkness* with Charcot's 'case studies of male hysterics' (p. 69).
3   See, for example, *PFL*, 3: 169–70, 178–80, 182–6.
4   Sigmund Freud, *The Complete Letters of Sigmund Freud to Wilhelm Fliess, 1881–1904*, trans. and ed. Jeffrey Mason (Cambridge, Mass.: Harvard University Press, 1985), p. 264. Jacques Derrida also cites this formulation, in his reading of *Totem and Taboo* in an essay entitled 'Before the Law', in *Acts of Literature*, ed. Derek Attridge (London: Routledge, 1992), pp. 183–220: here, p. 192. In both Freud's work and in the little masterpiece by Kafka from which he borrows his essay-title ('Before the Law'), Derrida focuses on the peculiarites of the origin of morality, on the nasal, on narrativity and on the nature of decision and law itself as 'uncanny, *unheimlich*' (pp. 195, 199).
5   James Risser, 'Siting Order at the Limits of Construction: Deconstructing Architectural Space', *Research in Phenomenology*, vol. 22 (1992), 62–72: here, p. 70. Risser's remark arises in a discussion of Heidegger concerned with the fact that the ancient Greeks had no word for 'space'.
6   See *Coriolanus*, 4.5.188.
7   'Teeth marks?' as Diana Fuss asks, regarding this phrase 'permanent marks', in an endearing and helpful account of psychoanalysis, cannibalism and male homosexuality: see 'Oral Incorporations: *The Silence of the Lambs*' in her *Identification Papers* (London: Routledge, 1995), pp. 83–105: here, p. 97.

8   Joseph Conrad, *The Secret Agent* (Harmondsworth: Penguin, 1992), p. 80.

9   Jonathan Swift, 'A Modest Proposal', in *The Writings of Jonathan Swift*, ed. Robert A. Greenberg and William Bowman Piper (New York: Norton, 1973). Swift, it should perhaps be stressed, does not use the term 'cannibalism' itself: according to the *OED*, the earliest recorded instance of this '-ism' is 1796.

10 Sigmund Freud, letter to Thomas Mann, *SE*, XXII: 255. We might here recall also the splendidly ironic, Goethean verbal flourish at the end of *Totem and Taboo*: 'in the beginning was the Deed' (*PFL*, 13: 224); or the affirmation of the magical power of the word, in 'The Question of Lay Analysis': 'Words can do unspeakable good and cause terrible wounds. No doubt 'in the beginning was the deed' and the word came later ... But originally the word was magic – a magical act [*sic*]; and it has retained much of its ancient power' (*PFL*, 15: 287–8).

11 For an account of Freud's 'The Uncanny' and Wilde's story see Phillip McCaffrey's 'Freud's Uncanny Woman', in *Reading Freud's Reading*, eds Sander L. Gilman, Jutta Birmele, Jay Geller and Valerie D. Greenberg (New York: New York University Press, 1994), pp. 91–108. McCaffrey argues that 'the story's humorous tone veils some satisfactorily gruesome material which might easily have been turned to uncanny effect' (p. 92).

12 E. T. A. Hoffmann, 'The Sandman', in *Tales of Hoffmann*, trans. R. J. Hollingdale (Harmondsworth: Penguin, 1982), p. 87. Further page references to this story will appear in the main body of the text.

15

Manifestations of insanity: *Hunger* and contemporary fiction

Breathless, my hunger, I can't write, can't speak, can't hold my breath, must, must stop, breathing, breathless, 'out of breath', breathless, 'with the breath held or taken away, from excitement, interest, etc', breathless, 'breezeless, airless; dead' (*Chambers Dictionary*), can't write or speak of Knut Hamsun's *Hunger*[1] and contemporary fiction, I have to look at my shoes, 'When I looked at my shoes, it was as though I had met a good friend or got back a torn-off part of me' (*H*, p. 18), 'manifestations of insanity', my title must be a joke, a madness, who made it up, it wasn't me, I remember I was breathless, aphasic, aphonic, at best or worst I must merely have been having a 'silent chat with myself' (p. 73), in other words with my hunger, a silent chat, that's it, with my hunger, not mine, impossible appropriation, it's only that that speaks, breathless, to say '*Hunger* and contemporary fiction', what a madness, 'manifestations of insanity', that's Freud's phrase, he talks of how they 'excite in the spectator the impression of automatic, mechanical processes at work behind the ordinary appearance of mental activity' (U, p. 347), in doing so he is doing little other than repeat, mechanically, as if a little madly, Ernst Jentsch's observations in 'On the Psychology of the Uncanny', 'most mental and many nervous illnesses', says Jentsch, 'make a quite decidedly uncanny impression on most people',[2] out of breath, madly breathless, as in *Alice in Wonderland* and *Through the Looking-glass*, texts of such relentless breathlessness, I must sober up, Good afternoon, ladies and gentlemen, I begin, my intention in this brief expiration is to consider Hamsun's *Hunger* (1890) as a way of trying to say something about what is called 'contemporary fiction', a phrase that is itself a manifestation of insanity, manifestations of insanity most of all perhaps in the formula 'contemporary American fiction', or 'English', or 'Scottish', all such terms binding so-called 'contemporary fiction' together with the mystico-religiousness of nationalism, since that is ultimately what every nationalism amounts to, phew, 'Suddenly one or two good sentences occur to me, suitable for a sketch or story, nice linguistic flukes the likes of which I had never experienced before … It was as though a vein had burst inside me – one word follows another … I write as if possessed, filling one page after another without a moment's pause. My thoughts strike me so suddenly and continue to pour out so abundantly that I lose a lot of minor details I'm not able to write down fast enough, though I am working at full blast. They continue to crowd in on me, I am full of my subject, and every word I write is put in my mouth' (pp. 27–8), breathless without a moment's pause, it's words that aren't mine that fill me up, my mouth is crammed with them, impossible after this text of 1890 to speak of hunger without speaking of speaking, of what has to be and cannot be spoken, impossible to appropriate, assimilate or digest the time of *Hunger*, but also impossible to throw up, make a clean breast of it, disengage from the time of *Hunger*, that's the first reason why 'contemporary fiction' is a joke, or madness, if *Hunger* is the first modern novel, it is because it breaks with the conventions of the novel as a genre ('My book is not to be looked upon as a novel', as Hamsun observed),[3] and because it breaks with time, it's a phantom Kit-Kat, it interrupts, it is impossible to get it down you, in time, a phantom-break, I must be off my head, as John Vernon put it, in *Hunger* 'a pure narrative present, a sense of time continuously billowing and literally getting nowhere, for the first time fully occupies fiction',[4] in a sense neither modern nor a novel, *Hunger* won't stay on a plate with so-called 'contemporary fiction' or indeed with any concept of the contemporary, now or then, then as now, the shortest word in my subtitle (the 'and' in '*Hunger* and contemporary fiction') is also perhaps the most unreadable, 'Something new is happening here, some new thought about the nature of art is being proposed in *Hunger*' as Paul Auster wrote in his essay 'The Art of Hunger' (1970), but this 'newness' is not (as Auster claimed) to do with 'the art of hunger ... as an existential art',[5] this 'newness' is not inscribed in any present, it has to do with an experience of the breathless, breathless writing, we can consider historical precursors and parallels for Hamsun's book, such as Poe for perversity, Strindberg and Nietzsche for fragmented self and multiple identity, Mark Twain for humour, Dostoevsky for narrative delirium, Baudelaire for the twisting and twisted *flâneur*,[6] Dickens or Hardy or Gissing or George Douglas Brown for the maddening misery of a character going from bad to worse, but the something new that is happening in *Hunger*, if it happens, breaks with linearity, dislocates every historicism, fits quite otherwise, a singular breathlessness, just as necessary but impossible we can sketch a sort of direct or inadvertent legacy for Hamsun's text, such as Bataille for violence to the sacred, Blanchot for the madness of the day, Kafka for the madness of the night, Beckett for failure, contemporary fiction for, for what, what for, 'I was drunk with starvation, my hunger had made me intoxicated' (p. 52), 'I laughed, laughed and slapped my knees, laughed like a madman. And not a sound emerged from my throat; my laughter was feverish and silent, with the intensity of tears' (p. 53), I'm just having a silent chat with myself, I'm feeling provoked, something is provoking my 'emaciated brain' (p. 123), apart from the lack of oxygen, it's the provoking similarities between Hamsun's *Hunger* and an example, I'll limit myself to just one, of what is called 'contemporary fiction', or even more insidiously and insanely 'contemporary Scottish fiction', I'm thinking of Janice Galloway's 1989 novel *The Trick Is to Keep Breathing*,[7] both of these texts are first-person narratives concerned with hunger and madness, with someone who does not or will not eat and whose disturbed state of mind is disturbing to others, not least the reader, for instance in the eerie epiphany of Galloway's narrator pouring away the vegetable soup that was to have been a meal, 'There, my cupped hands over the sink, I split my fingers and let the puree slither, spattering unevenly onto the white porcelain. I was learning something as I stared at what I was doing; the most obvious thing yet it had never dawned on me till I stood here, bug-eyed at the sink, congealing soup up to my wrists. I didn't need to eat. *I didn't need to eat*' (p. 38), but within these similarities there are equally provoking differences, first, hunger or the experience of eating disorder is not, in Galloway's novel, explicitly elaborated with the question of writing as such, and, second, mental disturbance in Galloway's text is a controlled or pro-grammed representation, complying with medical conventions concerning anorexia and mental breakdown and treatment in a state mental hospital, whereas in *Hunger* the madness is at once *in* the writing and *in* the streets, perhaps the narrator of *Hunger should* 'go and ask to be locked up', but he doesn't, and these crucial distinctions operate, above all, in terms of time, for both *Hunger* and *The Trick Is to Keep Breathing* mess with time, Galloway's narrator, the wittily named Joy Stone (yet the very imposition of a name is, among other things, what radically distinguishes this text from Hamsun's, with its uncanny anonymity prefiguring E. M. Forster's proposition, in an essay of 1925, that 'all literature tends towards a condition of anonymity'),[8] Joy Stone complains about her 'terrible timing' (p. 83) and the fact that she has 'problems with tenses' (p. 133), and in its insistent switches from present tense to flashback Galloway's novel might seem to corres-pond with the kind of phantom Kit-Kat effect, the temporal phantom effects generated by *Hunger*, 'I began … running my head against the lampposts on purpose … and biting my tongue in frenzy when it didn't speak clearly, and I laughed madly whenever it fairly hurt. "Yes, but what shall I do?" I asked myself at last. I stamp my feet on the pavement several times and repeat, "What shall I do?" A gentleman just walking by remarks with a smile, "You should go and ask to be locked up"' (p. 81), but other things are going on in *Hunger*, at the level of the breathless sentence, something 'strangely ruined' (p. 119) and irreducibly estranging in the phanstasmagoric shifts from past to present that characterize the grammatical structures of Hamsun's book ('"Yes, but what shall I do?" I asked myself' … 'I stamp my feet on the pavement several times and repeat, "What shall I do?"'), *The Trick Is to Keep Breathing* shifts about, it's unsettling, funny, and ironic, but it is quite different from the uncanny irony of the breathless writing of *Hunger*, a ghostly irony that is a power of interruption, discontinuity, non-presence, as evoked by Donald C. Riechel, when he observes that 'Hamsun's style ... has a vehemence and haste about it, a paratactical, often hyperbolic abruptness, and an insistent hypnotic rhythm that suggest the opposite of ironic utterance',[9] Galloway's novel *plays with* breathlessness, it is a study in breathing and the desire for breathlessness, for desire *as* breathless, as a narrative it holds its breath and asks readers to hold theirs for a long time, not only in its oscillations between present and flashback and its withholding of the fresh air of new information (in the sense of the reader's desire to know what has happened to Joy Stone, what's so to speak eating her, what's going to happen to her), but also because it is only at the very end of the novel that we come to the title-phrase ('Shadows in the corner of the room give me away. I'm gawky, not a natural swimmer. But I can read up a little, take advice. I read somewhere the trick is to keep breathing, make out it's not unnatural at all. They say it comes with practice': p. 235), the ending of Galloway's novel is recuperative in a double sense, it suggests recovery and conservation, both in terms of the narrator's mental health and in terms of the society and culture in which this 'mental health' is defined, the ending of Galloway's novel is redemptive, it signs up for what Leo Bersani has called the culture of redemption,[10] 'The voice is still there. I forgive you' (p. 235), we are told, this moment of forgiveness affirming the model of the American guide to *Courage and Bereavement*, quoted earlier on, from which the narrator learns that 'I should shout all the anger out of my system. Then I should say I Forgive You' (p. 172), the ending of the novel lets its title-phrase finally sound as a pathetic wisdom, a closing down of the strangeness of the 'trick' and of the suggestion, evident elsewhere in the text, that the trick is in fact to stop breathing, that there is breathlessness, breathless at the very opening of the future, *The Trick Is to Keep Breathing* suggests this, for example, in its figuration of the telephone, 'The phone is an instrument of intrusion into order. It is a threat to control. Just when you think you are alone and safe, the call could come that changes your life. Or someone else's. It makes the same flat, mechanical noise for everyone and gives no clues what's waiting there on the other end of the line' (p. 57), this breathless call, I have to stop, I'm going to stop any minute now, 'I can read up a little, take advice. I read somewhere the trick is to keep breathing, make out it's not unnatural at all. They say it comes with practice', *I read somewhere, they say*, the interest and the irony of Galloway's novel lies in the fact that is about the asphyxiating effects of a power/knowledge program (call it 'contemporary culture' if you like) according to which everything the narrator ever does or thinks appears to be articulated by or subject to the power/ knowledge of what 'they' say, of the media, of television and magazines, of the family, of the Scottish education system, of state psychiatry and institutions of mental health, but the program accommodates this ironic mode, it fairly gobbles it up, it's part of the culture of redemption, doubtless *Hunger* is also about the program, '"If you could just be a little more level-headed! There's always too much fever"' (p. 74) the narrator of *Hunger* is told, not insignificantly by a literary critic of sorts, a newspaper editor, but *Hunger* is concerned with the ironic undoing, interruption, impossibilization of every program, in the Foreword to Sverre Lyngstad's 1996 translation of *Hunger* Duncan McLean declares that 'This exciting new translation should introduce Knut Hamsun to a whole new readership – one which has been nourished on the equally startling and lyrical collisions of such writers as Alan Warner, A. L. Kennedy and Irvine Welsh' (p. v), 'nourished' is unfortunate, it suggests Duncan McLean hasn't really thought about the subject of his Foreword, unfortunate but suggestive, because perhaps it's the case that what is called 'contemporary fiction' has precisely the function of nourishing, nourishing the culture of redemption, nourishing more generally everything that so insidiously binds the madness of today, the assumption that we know what 'contemporary' means, and binds it at the same time with all the commercial, cultural, educational, legal apparatuses that fix and programme the production of what is called 'fiction', above all in the naming of a fictional but self-authorizing narrator (Joy Stone) and in the designation of the category 'novel' (Galloway's *The Trick Is to Keep Breathing* is specified as such on the inside front page of her book, alongside the observation that Galloway 'likes cities and lives in Glasgow'), so much for contemporary fiction, so much for all 'consumer fiction', edible and inedible, so much for the novel as redemptive, farewell to all that since at least 1890, 'I found myself before a special kind of darkness, a desperate element which no one had previously been aware of' (p. 60), it's the darkness of the 'I', I 'in a state of utter absence from myself' (p. 53), a breathless anonymous written I that, in an utter absence of self, can always be anyone, always in transit, indissociable from the I that reads or speaks of it, breathless, it's words that aren't mine that fill me up, every word is put in my mouth, impossible hunger that is mine, 'I break my pencil between my teeth, jump up, tear my manuscript to bits, every single sheet, toss my hat in the gutter and trample it. "I'm lost!" I whisper to myself. "Ladies and gentlemen, I'm lost!" I say nothing except these words as I stand there trampling my hat' (p. 176).

NOTES

1   Knut Hamsun, *Hunger*, trans. Sverre Lyngstad (1890; Edinburgh: Cannongate, 1996). Further page references are to this edition, abbreviated '*H*' where appropriate.

2   Ernst Jentsch, 'On the Psychology of the Uncanny' (1906), trans. Roy Sellars, *Angelaki*, vol. 2, no. 1 (1995), p. 14.

3   See Harald Naess, *Knut Hamsun* (Boston: Twayne, 1984), p. 33.

4   John Vernon, *Money and Fiction: Literary Realism in the Nineteenth and Early Twentieth Centuries* (Ithaca: Cornell University Press, 1984), p. 117; cited in Donald C. Riechel, 'Knut Hamsun's "Imp of the Perverse": Calculation and Contradiction in *Sult* and *Mysterier*', *Scandinavica: International Journal of Scandinavian Studies*, vol. 28, no. 1 (1989), p. 32.

5   Paul Auster, 'The Art of Hunger' (1970), in *Ground Work: Selected Poems and Essays 1970–1979* (London: Faber and Faber, 1991), pp. 105–15: here, pp. 113, 114.

6   It is in this context, too, that we might consider the importance of what Walter Benjamin calls 'the uncanny elements … of the physiognomy of the big city': see 'On Some Motifs in Baudelaire', in *Illuminations: Essays and Reflections*, ed. Hannah Arendt (New York: Schocken Books, 1969), p. 174. There are clearly parallels in the evocations of the incipient madness of city-life, in the nature of 'the crowd', in the experience of isolation, alienation and dislocation, between *Hunger* and the writings of Poe, Baudelaire and others. It is not insignificant that the very opening sentence of *Hunger* seeks to locate itself in terms of the 'strange city': 'It was in those days when I wandered about hungry in Kristiania, that strange city which no one leaves before it has set its mark upon him' (p. 3). For more on the city and the uncanny, see Anthony Vidler, *The Architectural Uncanny: Essays in the Modern Unhomely* (Cambridge, Mass.: MIT Press, 1991).

7   Janice Galloway *The Trick Is to Keep Breathing* (1989; London: Minerva, 1991). Further page references are given in parentheses in the main body of the text.

8   E. M. Forster, 'Anonymity: An Enquiry' (1925), in *Two Cheers for Democracy* (London: Edward Arnold, 1951), p. 92.

9   Riechel, 'Knut Hamsun's "Imp of the Perverse"', p. 30.

10 See Leo Bersani, *The Culture of Redemption* (Cambridge, Mass.: Harvard University Press, 1990).

16

A crowded after-life*

He seemed to have forgotten how to breathe, all these years, or never knew. In the dark, how to breathe, let alone speak, all these years, without a sound, and still going on. He had been asked to speak on the subject of 'Beckett Against the Grain', he said yes, his first word for many years. Without thinking properly, if thinking properly was something he or anyone else had ever done, he said yes. On further reflection he asked himself: 'Beckett Against the Grain'? Was that against the grain of Beckett, or Beckett against the grain of himself, or not Beckett at all, after all wasn't Beckett dead? Or was by 'Beckett' meant 'Beckett Studies', in other words, to quote his prospective hosts, 'new approaches in the field of Beckett Studies', in short new approaches in the field of Beckett Studies against the grain, and if so, he had to wonder, was it new approaches against the grain of the field of Beckett Studies, or new approaches in the field of Beckett Studies against the grain of the field of Beckett Studies, for there could surely be field without grain, even if, as seemed to be taken for granted, there could be no new approaches that were not already *in* the field, no chance seemingly of new approaches to the field or, better perhaps, away from it, new approaches away, as far and perhaps as fast away from the field as one's feet, hands or knees could carry one? And what of 'the grain'? Against the fibre of the wood, as for instance of a coffin, bog-standard, against the natural temper or inclination? Grain as in seed, as in something very small, as in truth, as in *Watt*, 'in the warm moonless night, when no one is looking, no one listening, in tiny packets of two or three millions the grains slip, all together'? *Glissement* without listening, no one listening, all together. Enough, more than enough of that. Like knocking his head against a door. The conference was like a door, he observed to himself in the silence of his head, 'open to any new approaches'. It aimed 'to encourage research … into aspects of Beckett's work that have hitherto received minimal critical attention'. How minimal, he asked himself in the silence, is minimal? To encourage research into something so minimal it would never previously have been thought to exist, indeed something that to all intents and purposes does not exist? No one listening, no one there, like knocking his head against a door. Buried alive. But what

* This text was originally written for a conference entitled Beckett Against the Grain, at the University of York, 8 May 1999. The author wishes to thank Ulrika Maude and Steven Connor for their invitation to speak. Unattributed quotations in the text ('someone said') are from the writings of Leo Bersani, Maurice Blanchot, Steven Connor, Simon Critchley, Jacques Derrida, Leslie Hill, James Joyce, Laura Mulvey and Lawrence Rainey.

was the door? More precisely, what was the door doing in a field? A mythological gateway, as someone said, a doorway against the grain, standing, no, lying in a field, no, not in a field, anything but that, if it was to be the door for him, the door he was dreaming of, or the door that was dreaming him, not a door in or to the field of 'Beckett Studies', but rather a door before, a door out, right out, completely out of doors, but where? And whose? He seemed to have forgotten how to breathe, all these years, or never knew, in the dark, let alone speak.

Asked to, he said yes I will, yes, I will speak of a crowded after-life, having like his progenitors an at best uneasy familiarity with 'educated' or academic discourse, thinking that 'against the grain' would enable him to express the milk of his strangeness, mother himself quite otherwise. He said yes, recalling that, as someone said, years ago, Beckett's writing marks a break with cultural discourse itself, intertextuality becomes the occasion for a kind of psychotic raving, what does it matter who's speaking. It pleased but also unnerved him to dream of the effacement of the proper names of critics and academics, eliminating them from the enquiry, and thus picture altogether differently the institutions called literary criticism, literary theory, philosophy, what you will, the entire edifice, the whole shebang.

He duly turned up, paper in hand, ready to speak. He had come to a decision, in fact he was already boxed in by more than one. Already it was evident that he would have to speak of 'Beckett'. Catastrophe from the start. What gives Beckett criticism such importance and cultural centrality, someone said, is the continued reassertion in that discourse of the myth of the author as creator, source and absolute origin. Continued reassertion, he asked himself, what is a continued reassertion? Sunk before beginning. The name of Beckett, at least, would be forced to make an appearance. And perhaps also one or two others, to keep him company. But out of his grave affection he was determined to follow his master's voice, at least when opportunity beckoned, and speak of him as a mole. That would be well said, he thought. 'A mole in a molehill', that's me, said Beckett, well said, old mole, thought he. Buoyed up by this, without the least reason, he had also decided to venture a neologism: disinterjecta. Ugly and almost unpronounceable expansion upon the old mole's disjecta, this was doomed to failure, he knew, just as he knew that Beckett against the grain must mean failure, a reimagining of academic discourse as charred remains, dust, at best, of shards, flints and pebbles, or ashes, at best, fantastically abandoned, aposiopoesis of the only and impure kind. Similarly lacking membra, it would be the cryptic business of disinterjecta to countersign the mole's scattering without limit, literary and otherwise, of monumental cremations: disinterring jetties, in the silence you don't know.

These were probably more than enough decisions to be going on with, but he felt himself pressed, to a nose-squashing degree, with at least one more. For he knew in his bones that he could not proceed without telling a story, one or more, knowing even as he did so that this was perceived to be against the grain, stories apart from anything else being, as someone said, what one doesn't relate in a university. He wanted to tell the story of a crowded after-life. Such a crowd, impossible to move, all these years, in the dark, in the ground, buried alive.

He and Beckett never met but corresponded on a couple of occasions, moles at a distance, unsettling solitude. Once, in August 1984, he wrote asking if he would be willing to contribute something to a literary magazine he was hoping to start up, against the grain. The mole's response was uncannily fast, almost as if he had received the letter before it could have arrived. I have literally nothing to offer you, he said, not the least presentable *inédit* to my name, and nothing new in sight. I am sorry to disappoint you. With best wishes for the success of your project. Yours sincerely, Samuel Beckett. Under ground, nothing new in sight. With best wishes for the success of the project. How was he ever to fathom these words, from this mole that was here popping its head out of prosopopoeia and evoking – how ever fleetingly, comically or terrifyingly – success? Projects belong to the future. As *The Unnamable* says, 'the mistake they make of course is to speak of him as if he really existed, in a specific place, whereas the whole thing is no more than a project for the moment'.

The project about which he had written to the mole never got off the ground, or out from under it. Disinterjecta, he reflected. And all the more so if, out of the silence of all these years, he were now to speak, if he were now to recite what the mole had said, thereby bearing testimony to the doublebind of every anecdotalism, of even the least presentable *inédit*, the words on that little card from Beckett themselves constituting this *inédit*, every anecdote being (as its etymology intimates) what is not given out, what is secret, private or hitherto unpublished, in other words what is revealed only by ceasing to be itself, anecdotal.

And then a few months later, he sent a story he had written, an abandoned work called 'A crowded after-life'. The mole replied, again with amazing alacrity, thanking him for the story, which he had 'read with interest'. Once more the precious little card from beyond, afar, away over wherever he was care of his publishers, expressing gratitude and, what was to become a new, implacably spectral word for him: interest. In what tone should one read someone's expression of interest in an account of their own cremation? Word of welcome and valediction, scene of writing and inheritance. Dig out a dictionary and rummage for the gospel on interest, it's what is between, being between; *inter est*, at once perhaps interred and disinterred. 'A crowded after-life' is written in what is comically known as the first person singular. It tells the story of how the narrator is cremated and, though perhaps at first, like the ashes of Murphy, 'well on four pounds', reduced to a single wafer of ash (first flake singular), and blown away, across a wilderness of meadow, until landing on a cowpat and meeting up with Samuel Beckett, likewise cremated and likewise reduced. A relationship gets under way. In fact things are going wonderfully. Phrases not yet coined, such as momentary coitus of signatures and telepathic hymen, suggest themselves, after the event. But there are complications. He thought to pick among the ashes, reiterate and interrupt the story, in disinterjected form, as follows:

It is not as you would imagine. Certainly not a voice. But let that rest a moment. I am striving to give an account of my crowded after-life. As a child I had foretastes, but I do not want red herrings. I am not even talking to you in fact. I thought we had cleared that up at the outset. As it happens, I was cremated. In a place near here. On the hot side, I can tell you. I was dispersed. You think perhaps I am pulling someone's leg, in the absence of having one of my own, but no, with a wave and a whoosh and the box disappeared, the brass fittings reclaimed, open country, plain sailing. Countless flakes of ash, launched across blank meadow. Each flake wafting a different story. There was not a cloud in the sky, and I was lying down. I had landed on a cowpat, if sight and smell were to be trusted. And then gradually I became aware that there was a person next to me, hardly a person, hardly me, no person at all, I regret having used the word, but Samuel Beckett. Likewise, a flake of ash. Well! This was indeed a tender moment. Shaking hands was, of course, out of the question. What was possible, to my extreme surprise and perhaps also to his, was conversation. Not articulate vibrations in the ether. Ashflakes are not charged with the capacity to speak, obviously. Yet there was dialogue so rapid and extreme that it became unclear whether we were in fact separate, two individual little ashflakes. We were bantering about stories, as if till the cows came home.

But at just this moment there is an interruption. It is the early summer of 1984 and their cowclap transpires not to have been the ideal resting place, set splat, as it was, in Ireland at the time of an official visit by the President of the United States. This is how it was described in the *Guardian* on 4 June:

> Estimates put the crowd who packed into Ballyporeen's two streets at about 3,000, only slightly outnumbering the droves of police, the troops in position on the surrounding hillsides manning missile launchers, and the wall of nervous, lightweight mac-clad secret servicemen who stood four deep around President Reagan and his wife.
>
> From early on in the day it was the security operation that caught the eye. Soldiers

could be seen up trees, shaking branches. Every drain was checked, every manhole cover lifted.

Not only did the American agents leave no stone unturned, they actually checked under cow pats in the surrounding fields. Police were installed in the front and rear of every house, along with marksmen.

President Reagan arrived by helicopter to visit the parish church and see for himself the register which marks the baptism in 1829 of his great-grandfather.

The ashflakes were a sitting target. What could they do? Shovelled up and carried off to an awaiting military vehicle, this was to be the beginning of a crowded after-life.

He and Beckett never communicated again. What does it mean to be buried? Isn't being buried always the thought of being buried alive? Apparently against cremation, feeling it to be against the grain, after Murphy and all the rest, what made the mole decide to be buried, if he was, if anyone ever can be, at Montparnasse on 26 December 1989? What kind of decision was this? Clov: Haven't I enough to do without burying people? Hamm: But you'll bury me. Clov: No I shan't bury you. Wonder, someone said, does the news go about whenever a fresh one is let down. Underground communication. Communication over. He buried a crowded after-life within himself. Or a crowded after-life buried him.

He knew that he, too, had to work in solitude, far away, in the darkness, silent as the grave. He knew that he, too, could only seek the congener he could not have, and that what ensnared him, too, in his own way, was the impression, as someone said, of impenetrable mystery but cryptic significance, of verbal concepts being overpowered by non-verbal affects and narrative clarity by intangible complications. It was enough to make him laugh, all these fine and perspicacious remarks made by someone, always someone or other. And even as he was about to laugh, he recalled what someone said about laughter in Beckett: it is a site of uncolonizable resistance to the alleged total adminstration of society, a node of non-identity. So laughable, if true. And node or unnode, past and present, he knew too that he must follow his master's voice in part by failing to hear it, as in the burrow, always the other, demonically elsewhere. The old mole working so fast, backwards and forwards, working at the door, past and present, buried alive, or not yet alive, the life to come, claw by claw, without escape, trying to find the door, he knew that if Beckett's work indeed breaks with cultural discourse, this must include breaking down, breaking through so-called clinical categories such as psychotic language, that it was a question of elaborating a discourse on the fact that the strategies for continuing talk survive the absence of psychological subjects, as someone said, that the heterophonic strangeness of the mole's work called for another thinking of mourning and spectrality, in short the impossible experience of posthumous culture. Clov: Do you believe in the life to come? Hamm: Mine was always that. Got him that time. A crowded after-life: such was Beckett's legacy.

'Birth was the death of him': so 'A Piece of Monologue' begins. For more than anything it was an issue, so to mince it, of never having been born, caput to cultural studies, certainly, from now on only posthumous cultural studies, but posthumous cultural studies aborted. The unnamable asks: 'Do they believe I believe it is I who am speaking? That's theirs too. To make me believe I have an ego all my own, and can speak of it, as they of theirs. Another trap to snap me up among the living. It's how to fall into it they can't have explained to me sufficiently.' To go on, to survive, not yet born, to be between, dead in-between, interred and disinterred, heshetheother, not gendered, but polysexual, cryptic beings. 'As thin as foil', thinner than a grain, with or against it, withered as ash, neither above nor below, 'I'm neither one side nor the other, I'm in the middle, I'm the partition … I don't belong to either, it's not to me they're talking, it's not of me they're talking, no … try something else, herd of shites … I can't get born.' A crowded after-life: a new elaboration of ghosts and crypts, posthumous culture not as something back in the past, a life over, dead and gone, but rather as an inter, an interring and disinterring of birth and death. A project for the future, then, as when the mole once said: 'I have always felt that there was within me a murdered being. Murdered before my birth. I had to find this murdered being again. To try to bring him back to life.'

Strange chiasmus of veritable reality and fiction. Stretch your mind back, if you have one. Meet President Ronald Reagan, the so-called person who, perhaps more than any other so-called public figure at that time, as someone said, was an image of the uncanny: made-up, artificial, and amnesiac. Neither doll nor auto-maton. Not one himself to stretch his mind back or, perhaps, to stretch one's mind back to. But there he was, or rather there was the stretch, stretch limo, death-black, motorcading down Ballyporean high street, beautiful June morning, 1984, what a crowd, spectral Sunday-best, the only sight of the made-up, artificial and amnesiac president in so-called propria persona being a hand, faintly waving, obtruding from the top inch or so by which the smoked-glass bullet-proof window had audaciously been lowered, pudgy fingers without evidence of a body, faintly moving, like an unshelled crab, greeting the crowd of thousands, as the vehicle swept on, back from the parish church where the so-called most powerful person in the world had been to see for himself the register which marked the baptism in 1829 of his great-grandfather. To have been born, to see for oneself that one has been born, or that someone has been born, not oneself obviously, can't stretch to that, but someone has been born, born in one's name, before oneself obviously, and again afterwards, in the wake of one's name: see the register, no birth without that, see oneself, see one's history in a word, against the grain, gather in one's mouth, in a world of writing, no birth without that. Once more, from 'A Piece of Monologue', always the same: 'Waits for first word always the same. It gathers in his mouth. Parts lips and thrusts tongue forward. Birth.'

Is Beckett dead? As someone said: in dying, did Beckett reach the end ... or ... by a cunning twist that would hardly be surprising, is he still keeping watch in order to find out what we intend doing with his silence, that silence that still speaks? He seemed to have forgotten, or never knew, how to breathe, let alone speak, all these years, without a sound, completely boxed in, nose pressed against the wood, heart against the grain. And then he thought he had found the door, or the door him. He duly turned up, paper in hand, ready to speak. It was time to begin, all but begin.

17

To be announced

Every uncanny figure or event is inevitably a substitute: the inexact double or surrogate of what we cannot know and cannot represent directly. Thus, in the system of the uncanny, a corpse cannot represent death (as it might in allegorical texts) but only our inability to know what death is. (David B. Morris)[1]

Who wants to substitute him- or herself for Freud's phantom? How can one not want to, as well? (Jacques Derrida)[2]

To be announced, that's my title and point of departure, the announcement of a departure and the departure of an announcement, what is departure, when will it have begun, to depart from everything or if nothing else to dream of a departing from everything.

> departure: act of departing; a going away from a place; deviation (from a normal course of action, etc); the distance in nautical miles travelled by a ship due east or west; a death (*euphem* [the dictionary uses this abbreviation for 'euphemism', in an act of euphemasia]) ... **the departed:** (*euphem*) a person (or people) who has (or have) died. (*Chambers*)

To be announced, to lie down, as if on your deathbed, with someone listening. Psychoanalysis, in a word, I'm with you, Sigmund, I'm in your dream, I'm holding your hand, or holding your head, I'm trying to hold you in my head, on the subject of what elicits 'the feeling [of uncanniness] in the highest degree' (U, p. 364), 'death' is the word, you feel it's death, as I feel you trying to hold me, your ear in my head, my ear in your voice, my voice in your ear, both of us out to the world. I'm trying to listen to all your death-sentences, attentive to the thought that the uncanniness of death to which you refer envelops everything you have to say, rendering 'the uncanny' more embracing, as well as a finer and more private place, than the discourse of psychoanalysis which might initially have appeared to subsume it, first of all in this short but amazing paragraph on 'Symbolism in Dreams' (1916) in the *Introductory Lectures*:

> Departure in dreams means dying. So, too, if a child asks where someone is who has died and whom he [*sic*] misses, it is common nursery usage to reply that he has gone on a journey. Once more I should like to contradict the belief that the dream-symbol [i.e. departure] is derived from this evasion. The dramatist is using the same symbolic connection when he speaks of the after-life as 'the undiscovered country from whose bourn no *traveller* returns'. Even in ordinary life [that's always been one of my favourite

Freud quips, 'even in ordinary life', as distinguished here, one might be expected to think, from literature and therefore from something like 'the psychopathology of literary texts'! – even in ordinary life, you were saying], it is common to speak of 'the last journey'. Everyone acquainted with ancient rituals [are we still talking about 'ordinary life'? I'm sorry, I'm interrupting you: to repeat: Everyone acquainted with ancient rituals] is aware of how seriously (in the religion of Ancient Egypt, for instance) the idea is taken of a journey to the land of the dead. Many copies have survived of *The Book of the Dead* [how to listen to you and interrupt, how to speak to you and how not to speak, on the subject of death, dead bodies, the return of the dead, spirits and ghosts, that is my question, it's the question of an auto-hetero-didactics, once more. I'm sorry, I'm interrupting again], which was supplied to the mummy like a Baedeker [or Blue Guide (Norwegian blue: it's not dead, it's resting)][3] to take with him [*sic*] on the journey. Ever since burial-places have been separated from dwelling-places, the dead person's last journey has indeed become a reality.[4]

'Departure in dreams means dying': what does this mean? Is the statement intelligible or is it such stuff as dreams are made on? Do you mean 'dying' or 'death'? And whose departure and from where? Is there departure? Does departure ever take place as such? Or conversely, when is one not departing in a dream, or when is a dream not a departure? No departures today, I'm sorry, there's a dream-strike. Earlier on in the same lecture you assert: 'Dying is replaced in dreams by departure, [for example] by a train journey, being dead by various obscure and, as it were, timid hints' (pp. 186–7). No doubt your comments in the 1916 lecture in some sense go back to the thinking of *The Interpretation of Dreams* (1900; *PFL*, 4) where you speak of '[d]reams of missing a train' as 'dreams of consolation for another kind of anxiety felt in sleep – the fear of dying. "Departing" on a journey is one of the commonest and best authenticated symbols of death. These dreams say in a consoling way: "Don't worry, you won't die (depart)"' (*PFL*, 4: 507). I like this last death-sentence especially, where your argument depends on an anthropomorphizing of the dream, where you listen, as it were in a telepathic rapport, to what the dream in its consoling way says to you; but I confess I can't be consoled by this account, in fact I confess to not being at all clear that there is an 'I' to be consoled, an I to whom dreams speak in a consoling or any other way, in particular I can't help wondering about this notion of symbols and the claim that there is such a thing as an 'authenticated symbol of death': who's authenticating here?

Not children, it may seem, at least from the way in which you carry on, in the little paragraph in the *Introductory Lectures*. To children, you say, we say a person who has died has gone on a journey. We do not dream of dying as departure because, for example, of the prevalence of this 'evasion' in so-called 'ordinary life'. Let us just repeat together: 'Once more I should like to contradict the belief that the dream-symbol is derived from this evasion.' In the previous paragraph, concerned with the argument that 'Birth is regularly expressed in dreams by some connection with water', you maintain that learning in childhood that storks bring babies (even if the child does not consider the fact that the stork fetches the baby from a pond or stream) 'contribute[s] nothing to the construction of the symbol' (*PFL*, 1: 194). The evasion as a departure from the truth, departure as euphem., a seeming departure for euphemland: this evasion (which can only be 'to be announced', since it is not an evasion of anything imaginable in short) is subordinated to a greater truth, to that great labyrinthine discourse of euphemism called psychoanalysis. *Chambers* defines 'euphemism' as '[1] a figure of rhetoric by which an unpleasant or offensive thing is described or referred to by a milder term; [2] such a term': this split definition ('euphemism' is at once the term itself and the process by which it works) points towards what 'euph' perhaps forgot, that euphemism is always itself euphemistic. No word can escape the law of euphemism, least of all perhaps 'death'. In speaking of death one has to speak well of it. As our telepathic friend Jacques Derrida has said: 'Let us not speak ill of death, not speak badly or unjustly of death. Let us not calumniate it; let us learn not to do so. We would run the risk of wounding, in our memory, those whom it bears.'[5] The context of his remark, the death of Paul de Man, bears on the notion of the limits of death: it is mistaken to speak of the limits of death in so far as such a phrase inevitably tends to imply a logic of surfaces or depths. From everything that one might want to say about death, Derrida suggests, from any and every possible word or sentence, 'nothing collects on the plane of a single surface or in the unity of some depth'.[6] One has to speak well of death and one can only do so thanks to writing, thanks to a logic of repetition that derails every departure while making it possible.

All of this is perhaps to be heard in the concluding sentences of your paragraph:

> Even in ordinary life, it is common to speak of 'the last journey'. Everyone acquainted with ancient rituals is aware of how seriously (in the religion of Ancient Egypt, for instance) the idea is taken of a journey to the land of the dead. Many copies have survived of *The Book of the Dead*, which was supplied to the mummy like a Baedeker to take with him on the journey. Ever since burial-places have been separated from dwelling-places, the dead person's last journey has indeed become a reality.

The labour of authentication is inseparable from the question of writing; the capacity for writing to survive, to endure, to 'travel well', is a crucial reference in an ostensibly historical micro-narrative that moves from 'ordinary life' in the second decade of the twentieth century back to ancient Egyptian times back to a time which one might say never existed or exists perhaps only as a fictive point of departure for this history of death in four easy sentences. 'Ever since burial-places have been separated from dwelling-places, the dead person's last journey has indeed become a reality.' What is this supposedly historical time when burial-places became separated from dwelling-places? Did it happen? Can it ever happen? The elegance of this paragraph-ending really makes me want to smile: 'Ever since burial-places have been separated from dwelling-places, the dead person's last journey has indeed become a reality.' It's so dead neat, this apparently straightforward literalization (what 'has indeed become a reality'). What is 'indeed' this 'reality' of a 'dead person' and of his or her 'last journey'? Where and when? Everything depends on the 'to be announced', the performative pronouncement of being dead when nothing, perhaps, is less certain. As Derrida puts it, in *Spectres of Marx*, to 'pronounce dead' is 'a performative that seeks to reassure but first of all to reassure itself by assuring itself, for nothing is less sure, that what one would like to see dead is indeed dead. It speaks in the name of life, it claims to know what that is.'[7]

'To be announced': this aphoristic phrase would be concerned (like every aphorism: Greek *aphorizein* to define, from *apo* from, and *horos* a limit) with limits. How ever elliptical or cryptic, the phrase perhaps conveys something of the trembling and hesitation, in particular regarding the time of death (when is it?) and place (where is it?) – especially as this is decisively affected by language, by a pronouncement or announcement in language. I think of a character of perhaps insufficiently recognized importance in Ibsen's *A Doll's House*, Dr Rank, Medical Practitioner, the one who has the legal authority to pronounce dead, sending a visiting card to the lawyer Torvald Helmer and his wife Nora.

> *Torvald*: There's a black cross above his name. Look. What an uncanny idea. It's just as if he were announcing his own death.
> *Nora*: He is.[8]

The announcement here is undecidably present-futural (to be announced), and additionally haunted by the dramaturgic context: it is writing (a play), writing about writing (a visiting card, 'a black cross above [the] name'), a writing characterized by the 'uncanny idea' of an absent character and an annunciative repeatability that is the condition of theatrical speech. I'll come back to this theatricality, I promise.

In suggesting that psychoanalysis is a great discourse of euphemism, I realize that I am contradicting what you say (in this same lecture, 'Symbolism in

Dreams') about its relentlessly non-euphemistic nature. You declare that only here, in the tenth of your introductory lectures, are you finally dealing with the subject-matter of sexual life. You claim not to beat about the bush then, despite having taken nine lectures to get here. I quote:

> Since this is the first time I have spoken of the subject-matter of sexual life in one of these lectures, I owe you some account of the way in which I propose to treat the topic. [This remark, by the way, makes little apparent sense: even if it were true, which one might find hard to credit (in the immediately preceding lecture, on 'The Censorship of Dreams', for example, one can find you getting diverted in a passage about 'love-services' and the satisfaction of 'erotic needs' (pp. 170–71)), but even if one were credulous enough to accept the claim that the first nine lectures of the *Introductory Lectures on Psychoanalysis* say nothing about the subject-matter of sexual life, why should you owe an account or explanation simply because you haven't spoken of it before? Concealing something? A calculated evasion? I'm sorry: you go on:] Psychoanalysis finds no occasion for concealments and hints, it does not think it necessary to be ashamed of dealing with this important material, it believes it is right and proper to call everything by its correct name, and it hopes that this will be the best way of keeping irrelevant thoughts of a disturbing kind at a distance. (*PFL*, 1: 187)

What is the founder of psychoanalysis doing when he evokes 'irrelevant thoughts of a disturbing kind' and the desire to keep them at a distance? What are 'irrelevant thoughts' when it comes to psychoanalysis? I can't help it, I get tangled up in this disturbing thought of disturbing thoughts at a distance. You know what I am talking about: telepathy. Let's not lose touch –

'Departure in dreams means dying ...': what a paragraph! So beautiful and lucid, so cannily open but strange. (And, in parenthesis – but everything here is that, parenthetical speech on the limits of parenthesis, digression, diversion, departure, the dash – let me just add that what makes the paragraph stand out is that it has nothing ostensibly to do with the so-called subject matter of sexual life: having promised that your lecture will focus on this topic and devoting the rest of the lecture to it, suddenly you seem to forget, your mind goes blank, as if something interposes, you are diverted, as if in a trance, you depart, as if into apparently irrelevant thoughts, into a parenthetical meditation on death, or into a sort of euphemistic meditation on departure itself (if there is such a thing). What is going on? What is passing or being passed by?) For you of course the psychoanalysis of dreams, here as it pertains to the dream-symbol of departure and death (or departure and dying, or departure as death – insuperable difficulties will have marked and complicated all these distinctions in advance, by a sort of uncanny advance booking), has conceptual and theoretical priority over everything else. This is, as you know, and as you know I know you know, the psychoanalytical gesture *par excellence*: to delimit the boundaries of dreams, and to institute a theory of dreams that works with this delimitation in order to colonize everything, including life, death and literature. But where does a dream begin? For example yours, Sigmund, in this paragraph about departure from which I seem to be having such difficulty departing or not so much departing, perhaps never departing, for in truth there is a part of me, departed or undeparted in me, that never wants to depart from the marvellous serenity of this paragraph. We'll be here for ever at this rate, I can hear you saying.

In order to corroborate your claim about the priority of psychoanalysis, here as the study of dream-symbols, in order to maintain psychoanalysis as a sort of a Baedeker of life and death, what do you do? You call on literature, and more specifically Shakespeare, or rather you call on 'the dramatist', a term which, in avoiding the name of Shakespeare, might be described as name-dropping with a difference, a contradiction (however apparently trivial) of the earlier commitment to the belief that 'it is right and proper to call everything by its correct name', in short as a euphemism and concealment. You think I am exaggerating, I know, you want to say Hey, come on, give me a break, I'm simply saying 'the dramatist' rather than 'Shakespeare' because I know that everyone knows what I am referring to, everyone knows the provenance of the phrase 'the undiscovered country from whose bourn no traveller returns': we all know it, the impossible package holiday, you've said so yourself, it's a euphemism. But hold on: what if we were to adhere as rigorously as possible to the methodological terms of the *Introductory Lectures* themselves, for example of the first of the three essays on 'Parapraxes' (Lecture 2)? What is at stake there is specifically the business of replying to 'someone who knows nothing of psychoanalysis' and who, in the face of the attempted psychoanalytical explanations of 'such apparent trivialities as the parapraxes of healthy people', comments: '"Oh! that's not worth explaining: they're just small chance events"' (p. 53). All of this will have been enough to give someone a headache. As you go on to remark: 'Slips of the tongue do really occur with particular frequency when one is tired, has a headache or is threatened with migraine … Some people are accustomed to recognise the approach of an attack of migraine when proper names escape them in this way.' To which the editor of the English translation adds, in a footnote in square brackets: 'This was a personal experience of Freud's' (p. 53, n. 1). I'm trying to share your headache now, in my mind. My mind? What mind? Do you mind? Doubtless one's not supposed to mind, or to pay it any mind, and yet I cannot help myself, I cannot help being seduced by the perhaps irrelevant thought of a kind of textual headache, a certain telepathy or suffering-at-a-distance perhaps, namely regarding the fact that you don't name Shakespeare: I just want to suggest that this omission of the name, this evasion, circumlocution, suppression, euphemism, theoretical parapraxis, this textual absentmindedness or chance remark if you want ('the dramatist'), signposts an uncanny area of Freudian land-slippage. My concern here is not simply with the argument that the empire of psychoanalysis is more literary than you are willing to allow,[9] but above all with the dream of another writing, a mutual contamination and reinscription of the relations between literature and psychoanalysis, dreaming of a jetty, the jetty of a departure from psychoanalysis *and* literature.

'Bourn' again: does your extraordinary paragraph about departure and death come out of an association-cum-dissociation of ideas whereby the two paragraphs preceding it, concerned with birth, give birth to this otherwise apparently digressive meditation on death as the impossible referent of dream-symbolism

Dancing on the Jetty

Hugo Simberg, *Dancing on the Jetty*, 1899
Ateneum Museum, Helsinki

(for let's recall, in case anyone was thinking of getting carried away, that psycho-analysis, for all its apparent pretensions to authenticity and to authority over the empire of dreams, cannot by its own admission tell us anything about death except on the euphemistic basis, at best, of 'various obscure and, as it were, timid hints')? Or is the paragraph set off by a translingual or interlingual pun, borne into existence by the words 'the undiscovered country from whose *bourn* no traveller returns'? I have no answer to these questions, Sigmund, I simply want to elucidate the amazing dream-thanatography of your writing, to think through the textual headache, to inhabit otherwise the edges or limits of Freudian *langue*-slippage, to highlight the literary or dramatic *intrigue* of this paragraph as a passage in which, as happens all the time in fact, your voice divides, the logic of your discursive 'place' disseminates. What is 'bourn'? The *New Shorter Oxford English Dictionary* specifies:

> 1. A boundary (between fields, etc.); a frontier. 2. A bound, a limit. 3. Destination; a goal. 4. Realm, domain … Senses 3 and 4 both arise from interpretations of Shakespeare.

And 'interpretations' here (as the fuller text of the *OED* makes clear) means 'mis-interpretations': a '*misunderstanding* (emphasis added) of the passage in *Hamlet*'. It's funny: it's as if readers or hearers of Hamlet's words, at least from the eighteenth century, couldn't accept that 'bourn' meant only 'boundary', 'frontier' or 'limit'. 'Bourn' cannot, as such, be 'bourn': it can't be borne. In a sense this may not be surprising: the boundary is always already departed: it is never present; it is the departure 'in' departure as such. In its syntax, Hamlet's 'undiscovered country from whose bourn' would parallel the peculiar possessive in 'the limits of death': the bourn would belong to the undiscovered country as much *and* as little as limits might be thought to belong to death. What is being, perhaps, announced here?

A small detail to begin with: you say that 'the dramatist is using the same symbolic connection [as yourself] when he speaks of the after-life', but it is not Shakespeare who is speaking here, it is Hamlet. Or, simultaneously, it is Shakespeare *and* Hamlet or rather, to employ your own loony terms, Edward de Vere and Hamlet.[10] For the moment, however, let me speak of the phrase simply as Hamlet's, in order to evoke a certain tele-scenario, in which one might be able to start to think at once the theatricality of Hamlet's voice as a voice that haunts and dislocates your discourse (Hamlet as a fictional being irreducible to any psychoanalysis) and the strange radicality of the 'To be or not to be' speech itself:

> To be, or not to be, that is the question:
> Whether 'tis nobler in the mind to suffer

> The slings and arrows of outrageous fortune,
> Or to take arms against a sea of troubles
> And by opposing end them. To die – to sleep,
> No more; and by a sleep to say we end
> The heart-ache and the thousand natural shocks
> That flesh is heir to: 'tis a consummation
> Devoutly to be wish'd. To die, to sleep;
> To sleep, perchance to dream – ay, there's the rub:
> For in that sleep of death what dreams may come,
> When we have shuffled off this mortal coil,
> Must give us pause …
> For who would bear the whips and scorns of time …?
>   … Who would fardels bear,
> To grunt and sweat under a weary life,
> But that the dread of something after death,
> The undiscover'd country, from whose bourn
> No traveller returns, puzzles the will,
> And makes us rather bear those ills we have
> Than fly to others that we know not of? (3.1.56–82)

Not to be is not to be borne, but what we bear cannot be 'bourn', can never be the 'bourn', not even with a 'bare bodkin' (3.1.76). Harold Bloom has called such speeches examples of 'self-overhearing'. Of Shakespeare's characters he observes: 'Overhearing their own speeches and pondering those expressions, they change and go on to contemplate an otherness in the self, or the possibility of such otherness.'[11] It is this sort of self-bugging, this responsiveness within the unfolding of the speech-act towards an otherness or foreign body within oneself (an otherness never simply separable from the unimaginable 'reality' of 'the undiscover'd country'), that illustrates what Bloom attributes to Shakespeare as 'the invention of the human'.[12] A danger here, as often with Bloom's work, is that this insight be recuperated within the logic of a sort of self-expansiveness or self-aggrandizement. Bloom, you may be pleased to hear, is something of a true Freudian in this respect. Less pleasing, I suspect, is his basic thesis on you and 'the dramatist', namely 'Shakespeare is the inventor of psychoanalysis; Freud, its codifier' or, again, 'Freud is essentially prosified Shakespeare'.[13] But if you don't mind my saying so, I don't think Bloom goes far enough in acknowledging and exploring the nature and implications of the invention. The speech from *Hamlet* is one that effectively breaks with all soliloquy (with every sense of an act of talking to oneself), not only because it's being overheard by others (by Claudius and Polonius) or by 'Hamlet himself', but more radically because it's speaking as a being perhaps as much dead as alive, it's a thanato-hypnagogics, 'to be announced'; it is the speech of a dramatic script, waiting to be announced, read, enacted by anyone, the dead, the living and the ghosts of those still to be.

The paragraph from your *Introductory Lectures* in turn belongs to this strange space of the 'to be announced'. On the one hand, there is the more or less acknowledged debt to literature, in particular the works of Shakespeare: you use *Hamlet* to support your claim about the symbolic significance of dreaming of going on a journey and thus to reinforce the proclaimed borders, to bolster the empire of the dream of psychoanalysis as a theory of dreams. On the other hand (and as the very obliqueness of the reference to *Hamlet* may already intimate), the passage from Shakespeare's play at issue here is perhaps less appropriate or appropriable than you are making out. It entails a living-dead recognition of a singular pause, the necessity of trying to respect the aporia or rub of dreams of death, of trying to disentangle the coil of infinitives that moves from 'To die, to sleep; / To sleep, perchance to dream' (3.1.64–5), while inhabiting the uncertainty of whether one's speech or thoughts are those of the living or the dead, the wakeful or the dreaming. Who speaks here, the subject of this experience of the 'perchance', is *to be announced* – irreducible to Hamlet or to Shakespeare, you or me, to any single speaker alive or dead, awake or dreaming.

Elsewhere too, if not in Elsinor, your thinking of departure, dying and dreams is spectralized by this passage of *Hamlet*: in a section of *The Interpretation of Dreams* entitled 'Dreams of the Death of Persons of Whom the Dreamer is Fond' (*PFL*, 4: 347–74), you talk again about the idea that 'To children ... being "dead" means approximately the same as being "gone"' (p. 355) and then discuss the example of a mother who 'does actually make the journey to that "undiscover'd country, from whose bourn no traveller returns"' (p. 356). In effect, it seems to me that you are subscribing to the children's view and to the notion of death as a journey but you do it without really saying so, and specifically by way of this reference (in quotation marks though unattributed) to *Hamlet*. (It is in a footnote to this passage, added in 1909, that you recall the observation of a 'highly intel- ligent' ten-year-old boy 'after the sudden death of his father: "I know father's dead, but what I can't understand is why he doesn't come home to supper"' (p. 355, n. 1). I am sorry, I have to ask myself, I have to ask you, is it possible to read this without recalling in turn Hamlet's apparent euphemism on the subject of the dead father in answer to the question 'where's Polonius?': 'At supper'; 'At supper? Where?'; 'Not where he eats, but where he is eaten' (4.3.16–19).) That Hamlet is the presiding madman of *The Interpretation of Dreams* perhaps goes without saying: he is the point of reference for what you no doubt regard ambivalently as the pitifully yet thankfully small number of thinkers who take an approach to dream interpretation similar to your own. Apparently inadvertently confusing dreams and waking life, you announce: 'It seems, however, to have dawned on *some* other writers that the madness of dreams may not be without method and may even be simulated, like that of the Danish prince on whom this shrewd judgment was passed' (p. 126, emphasis added). Goes without saying: such is the manner in which Shakespeare's *Hamlet* is passed off here. You go on to talk about some of your precursors but you don't mention again, at least by name, the text that has provided you with the very framework for your account. And yet the ghost of *Hamlet* returns, almost immediately. For you find yourself citing the 'sagacious Delbœuf' who writes (in 1885):

> In sleep, all the mental faculties (except for perception) – intelligence, imagination, memory, will and morality – remain essentially intact; they are merely applied to imaginary and unstable objects. A dreamer is an actor who at his own will plays the parts of madmen and philosophers, of executioners and their victims, of dwarfs and giants, of demons and angels. (cited in *PFL*, 4: 127, n.1)

The dreamer is an actor, I would say, but not one who plays multiple parts 'at his [or her] own will': this dream-acting, this deathlife, as Hamlet puts it, 'puzzles the will'.

To be or not to be announced: psychoanalysis as a dream of departure from literature, departing from it but by the same token irrevocably altering the bourn of literature and now, here and now, connecting up with the thought of a quite different departure. Jacques Lacan, another telepathic pretender of yours, demonstrates a similar furtiveness and embarrassment around naming Hamlet in his remarks on 'Desire, life and death' when he says:

> All that life is concerned with is seeking repose as much as possible while awaiting death ... [D]ozing off is the most natural of all vital states. Life is concerned solely with dying – *To die, to sleep, perchance to dream*, as a certain gentleman put it, just when what was at issue was exactly that – to be or not to be.[14]

(In parenthesis, let me briefly note the attempt – it does not matter if it is conscious or unconscious, it is the very lucidity of those distinctions that will have been dropping off here – to appropriate Shakespeare's play by speaking of it in the past tense ('as a certain gentleman put it'), even though, as Lacan immediately proceeds to make clear, it is all about a performativity of language right now, in the strange singularity of a speech act.) The Shakespearean séance continues:

> This *to be or not to be* [says Lacan] is an entirely verbal story. A very funny comedian tried showing how Shakespeare came upon it, scratching his head – *to be or not ...*, and he

would start again – *to be or not ... to be*. If that's funny [Lacan no longer seems to be sure, it was a 'very funny comedian' just a moment ago: I'm sorry, there I go, interposing again: If that's funny, says Lacan], that's because this moment is when the entire dimension of language comes into focus. The dream and the joke emerge on the same level. (p. 233)

Dream, what dream? The dream of 'a certain gentleman', and, if so, the dream of Shakespeare or the dream of Hamlet? No: it is the dream rather of psycho-analysis, again. An uncertain psychoanalyst follows you in the violence of his appropriation of Shakespeare's play, most notoriously in the seminar on 'Desire and the Interpretation of Desire in *Hamlet*', where the play's the thing above all in so far as it provides an allegory of the truth of psychoanalysis.[15] Lacan is right, I think, to identify the 'to be or not to be' as a 'verbal story' (even if the 'entirely' begs questions): as I've been trying to suggest, Hamlet's question is at least on one level the equivalent of 'Am I, as a speaking person, alive or dead?'[16] To be or not to be 'announced': for example, starting from the question of what we are doing here, of what is happening, what is going on when one does to, say, Freud and Lacan, what they do to Hamlet, in other words ventriloquize them, letting them speak for themselves while setting them off as slippery but thought-pro-voking characters in a new kind of writing, theatrical or filmic, that keeps the memory of psychoanalysis and literature without perhaps returning to either. Something else will always have been interposing: buzz, buzz.

> I heard a fly buzz – when I died –
> The Stillness in the Room
> Was like the Stillness in the Air –
> Between the Heaves of storm –
>
> The Eyes around – had wrung them dry –
> And Breaths were gathering firm
> For that last Onset – when the King
> Be witnessed – in the Room –
>
> I willed my Keepsakes – Signed away
> What portion of me be
> Assignable – and then it was
> There interposed a Fly –
>
> With Blue – uncertain stumbling Buzz –
> Between the light – and me –
> And then the Windows failed – and then
> I could not see to see –

The blue guide.[17] What interposes through Emily Dickinson's poem: the blue guide in the form of an interposing in interposing itself (the word 'interposed' occurs nowhere else in her poetry: an interposing that occurs, if it occurs, only once), an interring between the light and me, between the remains of the day and the remains of 'me' (having subtracted 'what portion of me be / Assignable'), between one stumbling sibilant and its seemingly stony recitation (you see to see, to see to see to see, you see?). In short, a question of sound and more specifically an experience of voice. It is easy enough, no doubt, to be distracted by the fly and miss the place of the other 'interposing' that is itself the condition of possibility of this fly, in other words the voice, or a trace in the voice, in a narrative lyrical voice that, initially sounding in around 1862, in a text published posthumously in 1896, interposes as what could be called an irrevocable tear or interring in the history of literature and its others (including literary criticism, philosophy and psychoanalysis). It is an example of prosopopoeia, a fiction of the voice from beyond the grave. It calls up what Paul de Man said about Wordsworth: 'Wordsworth', he declared in 'The Rhetoric of Temporality', 'is one of the few poets who can write proleptically about their own death and speak, as it were, from beyond their own graves'.[18] But something else is going on in the Dickinson poem: it sounds a small but dramatic shift, the interposing of a perhaps newly audible kind of foreign body. The voice in Dickinson's poem is, like any epitaph, an example of prosopopoeia, but it also narrates and listens to its own disappearance thanks to a logic that can be described as telepathic.[19] This cryptic text in which the 'I' narrates its own death exemplifies what might be called the telepathic structure *par excellence*: to be able to make contact with yourself as a dead person.

This then would be the final buzz here, the one you knew deep down inside was to be announced: no death without telepathy; no telepathy without death. You felt it all along: telepathy as a bourn of the undiscovered country. I've heard myself and others saying it before but I am hearing a certain difference in it now: telepathy is a foreign body within the theory of psychoanalysis, you cannot and cannot *not* admit this foreign body, Sigmund, it interposes everywhere and not least where it seems most distant. In the various short texts and other moments when you try to 'treat' telepathy (but there's no 'talking cure' for telepathy), it's invariably in the context of death.[20] Maria Torok goes so far as to assert that, as foreign body, telepathy, for you, is indissociable from the death drive: 'Freud's fable of Thanatos becomes justifiable only in relation to an internal and unknown area in Freud himself. In other words, the introduction of a "death instinct" into psychoanalytic theory makes sense only as a "foreign body".'[21]

Your secret, Sigmund, but still unimaginable for you: your very own unimaginable, unpossessable secret.[22] Permit me to recall what our mutual friend says, in his *Aporias*:

> *death* is always the name of a secret, since it signs the irreplaceable singularity. It puts forth the public name, the common name of a secret, the common name of the proper name without name. It is therefore always a schibboleth, for the manifest name of a secret is from the beginning a private name, so that language about death is nothing but the long history of a secret society, neither public nor private, semi-private, semi-public, on the border between the two.[23]

The name of death is always on the border between public and private – the limits of death are here, then, for our telepathic friend – and what 'death' means for you, Sigmund, or for him, or for me, might be figured as an encounter or experience of mind-reading, neither conscious nor unconscious, alive nor dead, awake nor dreaming, in telepathic writing. That's it, that's us. Curtains.

NOTES

1   David B. Morris, 'Gothic Sublimity', *New Literary History*, vol. 16 (1985), 311.

2   Jacques Derrida, *Archive Fever: A Freudian Impression*, trans. Eric Prenowitz (Chicago: Chicago University Press, 1996), p. 84.

3   The reference here is to the 'dead parrot' sketch: see *Monty Python's Flying Circus: Just the Words*, 1 (London: Methuen, 1989), p. 104.

4   Sigmund Freud, 'Symbolism in Dreams' (1916), in *Introductory Lectures on Psychoanalysis* (*PFL*, 1), trans. James Strachey, ed. James Strachey and Angela Richards (Harmondsworth: Penguin, 1973), pp. 182–203: here, p. 195. Further page references are given in brackets in the main body of the text.

5   Jacques Derrida, *Mémoires: For Paul de Man*, trans. Cecile Lindsay, Jonathan Culler and Eduardo Cadava (New York: Columbia University Press, 1986), p. 87.

6   *Mémoires*, p. 87. Derrida is commenting on a letter, the last letter de Man ever wrote to him, in which de Man quotes from the final line of Mallarmé's 'Tombeau [de Verlaine]', 'Un peu profond ruisseau calomnié la mort'. Jonathan Culler's translation, 'this shallow calumniated stream called death', misleadingly makes the 'this' part of the translated phrase (the original has 'Un peu profond …') and adds what is perhaps not insignificantly elided in the French: Weinfield's translation, 'A shallow stream calumniated death' (Stéphane Mallarmé, *Collected Poems*, trans. and with a commentary by Henry Weinfield (Berkeley: University of California Press, 1994, p. 73) avoids the 'called' and thus perhaps better evokes the trembling force of what is going on here: Mallarmé's poem suggests that any and every calling or naming of 'death' (though in particular in the context of the poet and poetry of Verlaine) is a calumniation. Derrida, on the other hand, evidently wants to avoid the language of calumniation altogether.

7   Jacques Derrida, *Spectres of Marx: The State of the Debt, the Work of Mourning, and the New International*, trans. Peggy Kamuf (London: Routledge, 1994), p. 48.

8   *A Doll's House*, in *Henrik Ibsen: Four Major Plays* (Oxford: World's Classics, 1981), p. 74.

9   As Paul de Man once observed, it's part of your literariness, it's part of the literarity of psychoanalysis, to 'know language's uncanny power to refuse the truth that nonetheless it never stops demanding'. The context of this remark is the occasion of introducing a lecture by Jacques Lacan, in New Haven in 1975. De Man prefaces the observation with a more critical assertion: 'I would say that we have not yet begun to suspect the extent to which this teaching [the teaching of psychoanalysis, what psychoanalysis has to teach] partakes of literature.' Paul de Man, cited by Shoshana Felman, in *The Lesson of Paul de Man*, *Yale French Studies*, vol. 69 (1985), 51. For further discussion of this question of teaching and the uncanny, see Chapter 3 above.

10   On the so-called 'Bacon–Shakespeare controversy', permit me to refer to my essay, 'The Distraction of "Freud": Literature, Psychoanalysis and the Bacon–Shakespeare Controversy', *Oxford Literary Review*, vol. 12 (1990), 101–38.

11   Harold Bloom, *The Western Canon: The Books and School of the Ages* (London: Macmillan, 1995), p. 70.

12   Harold Bloom, *Shakespeare: The Invention of the Human* (New York: Riverhead Books, 1998).

13   Bloom, *The Western Canon*, pp. 375, 371.

14   Jacques Lacan, 'Desire, Life and Death' in *The Seminar of Jacques Lacan, Book II: The Ego in Freud's Theory and in the Technique of Psychoanalysis, 1954–1955*, ed. Jacques-Alain Miller, trans. Sylvana Tomaselli, with Notes by John Forrester (Cambridge: Cambridge University Press, 1988), pp. 221–34: here, p. 233. Further references are given in brackets in the main body of the text.

15   'Desire and the Interpretation of Desire in *Hamlet*', trans. James Hulbert, *Yale French Studies*, no. 55/56 (special issue entitled *Literature and Psychoanalysis. The Question of Reading: Otherwise*), ed. Shoshana Felman, 11–52.

16   Cf. Julia Reinhard Lupton and Kenneth Reinhard, *After Oedipus: Shakespeare in Psychoanalysis* (Ithaca: Cornell University Press, 1993), p. 77.

17   The blue cover of my *Complete Poems of Emily Dickinson*, ed. Thomas H. Johnson (London: Faber and Faber, 1975) (for the poem in question, see pp. 223–4), has long been missing. It is the only one of my books that has come to resemble an unpackaged assemblage of packets in this way.

18   Paul de Man 'The Rhetoric of Temporality', *Blindness and Insight: Essays in the Rhetoric of Contemporary Criticism*, 2nd edn (London: Methuen, 1983), p. 225.

19   In this respect it can be distinguished from, for example, Poe's Monsieur Valdemar (1845), whose speech-from-beyond-the-grave appears as part of a third-person narrative.

20   Cf. Derrida, 'Telepathy', trans. Nicholas Royle, in *Deconstruction: A Reader*, ed. Martin McQuillan (Edinburgh: Edinburgh University Press, 2000), pp. 496–526, esp. pp. 514–18.

21   Maria Torok, 'Afterword: What Is Occult in Occultism? Between Sigmund Freud and Sergei Pankeiev Wolf Man', in Nicolas Abraham and Maria Torok, *The Wolf Man's Magic Word*, trans. Nicholas Rand (Minneapolis: University of Minnesota Press, 1986), pp. 84–106: here, p. 91.

22   Sigmund Freud, 'Thoughts for the Times on War and Death' (1915): 'It is indeed impossible to imagine our own death; and whenever we attempt to do so we can perceive that we are in fact still present as spectators.' See *Civilization, Society and Religion, Group Psychology, Civilization and Its Discontents and Other Works*, PFL, 12: 77.

23   Jacques Derrida, *Aporias: Dying – Awaiting (One Another at) the 'Limits of Truth'*, trans. Thomas Dutoit (Stanford: Stanford University Press, 1993), p. 74.

18

Mole[1]

He will return, that is certain: do not ask him what he is looking for down there, he will tell you himself of his own accord, this seeming Trophonius and subterranean, as soon as he has 'become a man' again. Being silent is something one completely unlearns if, like him, one has been for so long a solitary mole. (Friedrich Nietzsche)[2]

'Kafkaesque' has taken on an uncanny meaning for many among us; perhaps it has become a universal term for what Freud called 'the uncanny', something at once absolutely familiar to us yet also estranged from us. (Harold Bloom)[3]

Then all the stories would have to be told differently, the future would be incalculable, the historical forces would, will, change hands, bodies; another thinking as yet not thinkable will transform the functioning of all society. Well, we are living through this very period when the conceptual foundation of a millennial culture is in process of being undermined by millions of a species of mole as yet not recognized. (Hélène Cixous)[4]

('after a mole-like progression': how am I [N.W.O.R.] going to read this, eat or keep it, keep it by eating it? I have gathered the words together, like so many worms, I've bitten their heads, to immobilize them if only for a while, and I have placed them here, in my first tunnel. I'm worn out. The question of delay, detour, digression, deferred action, marked here in the first place by the lunar crescents of a tunnel '( )', known in English as parentheses, brackets or, perhaps most crepuscular, lunulae.[5] Worms of words squirming in the dark, and me worn to shreds. 'After a mole-like progression [après un cheminement de taupe]': this is a quotation from Derrida's 'Freud and the Scene of Writing'. It comes in the course of his meditation on pathbreaking, in particular regarding Freud's supposition of the logic of the memory-trace (Erinnerungsspur) as not yet 'conscious memory' and a notion of the 'itinerant work of the trace, producing rather than following its route, the trace which traces, the trace which breaks open its own path'.[6] He goes on: 'The metaphor of pathbreaking, so frequently used in Freud's descriptions, is always in communication with the theme of the supplementary delay and with the reconstitution of meaning through deferral, after a mole-like progression, after the subterranean toil of an impression. This impression has left behind a laborious trace which has never been perceived, whose meaning has never been lived in the present, i.e. has never been lived consciously' (p. 214). The mole might appear to be a promising figure for the trace. The mole, then, as the impossible figure, figure of the trace in Derrida's impression of the Freudian impression, the mole as the ghost of archive fever. Why a mole? What is the pertinence or impertinence of a mole here? As I said, I'm worn out, I'm going to sleep for a little now ...)

(What do animals dream of? We all know what Freud says about that – 'I do not know what animals dream of', he says in *The Interpretation of Dreams*, with that apparent naivety that is so lovable and yet in this case perhaps also so problematic. 'I do not know what animals dream of', he says. 'But a proverb, to which my attention was drawn by one of my students, does claim to know. "What", asks the proverb, "do geese dream of?" And it replies: "Of maize." The whole theory that dreams are wish-fulfilments is contained in these two phrases' (*PFL*, 4: 211–12). Then there are two footnotes (one added in 1911, the other in 1914) in which Freud remarks: 'A Hungarian proverb quoted by Ferenczi [1910] goes further and declares that "pigs dream of acorns and geese dream of maize." ... A Jewish proverb runs: "What do hens dream of? – Of millet"' (p. 212, n. 1). Doesn't the whole of *The Interpretation of Dreams* tremble here, in this question of animals' dreams, in this edgy configuration of ignorance ('I do not know what animals dream of') and desire (Freud's theory, 'the whole theory that dreams are wish-fulfilments')? Is Freud not an animal? And if geese and pigs and hens dream and in their dreams confirm the Freudian hypothesis, what or who is the subject of the wish: can there be wish, a desire for wish-fulfilment without an 'I'? I'm tunnelling, I'm dreaming of worms, I'm dreaming of a completely new tunnel ... ( )

('Those, and I am one of them, who find even a small ordinary-sized mole disgusting, would probably have died of disgust if they had seen the giant mole that a few years back was observed in the neighbourhood of one of our villages, which achieved a certain transitory celebrity on account of the incident.' Thus opens what is usually referred to in English as 'The Village Schoolmaster' but also known by the title 'The Giant Mole' (1914–15), a text described by its English language translator, Edwin Muir, as being among Kafka's most 'gravely incomplete'.[7] The gravely incomplete: such, perhaps, would be the condition of a discourse on the mole. 'The Giant Mole' is less about the creature evoked in its title than about the mad agonistics of writing about it: the narrator and the village schoolmaster both write pamphlets concerned to prove 'the existence of the mole' (p. 171), and despite the narrator's avowed desire to support the schoolmaster they fall into a dispute that is apparently interminable. The mole, it seems, exists only in the writings of this strange discoupled couple; and the pamphlets they write are themselves examples of the text in which they appear: the mole is textual, a writing-mole. And it is always already in retreat, burrowing away in a curious sort of textual-cum-'bestial oblivion': the most one hears or sees of it is in that opening sentence I quoted a moment ago.)

(In *The Natural History of Moles* (1990), Martyn L. Gorman and R. David Stone write: 'Once a suitable volume of soil has been accumulated the mole turns within the tight confines of the tunnel, either sideways or by somersaulting, and begins to push it back down the tunnel away from the working face. To do so, it places one of its forepaws diagonally to the body, rather like the offset blade of a bulldozer [elsewhere the authors talk of the Old World moles whose forelimbs 'have evolved into powerful digging tools and are turned permanently outwards from the body, like a pair of oars protruding from a rowing boat' (p. 10): no time to engage here with the whiffs of anthropocentrism coming downstream from *The Wind in the Willows*, with the prosthetico-catechresis whereby one's limb would be a supplementary tool or machine, or more broadly with the supposition, implicit here as well as elsewhere in Gorman's and Stone's book, that 'metaphor … is what is proper to man'],[8] and with two or three powerful thrusts of the body it moves the soil along the tunnel. It then changes over forepaws and continues its Herculean task until it reaches a *previously dug side tunnel* leading to the surface [I underscore the narratological *Nachträglichkeit* here: the necessary but out-of-place irruption of the reference to the 'previously dug side tunnel']. The soil is pushed up this sloping lateral shaft and out onto the surface to form a molehill. The mole then returns to the tunnel face and continues to dig … The result of all this unseen labour is a line of molehills marking the route of the subterranean passage.'[9] After a mole-like progression, after the subterranean toil of an impression: this, for Derrida, is Freud's great discovery. As he says in 'Freud and the Scene of Writing': 'The irreducibility of the "effect of deferral" – such, no doubt, is Freud's discovery' (p. 203). And in *Archive Fever*, in the context of an account of 'deferred obedience' which does not fail to make reference to Shakespeare's *Hamlet* (a reference to which I will try to somersault or come back in a moment or three), Derrida writes: 'the logic of the after-the-fact (*Nachträglichkeit*)' is 'at the heart of psychoanalysis', above all because it 'disrupt[s], disturb[s], entangle[s] forever the reassuring distinction between … the past and the future, that is to say, between the three actual presents, which would be the past present, the present present, and the future present'.[10] 'After a mole-like progression, after the subterranean toil of an impression': is this to be read from the point of view of being above ground or chthonically, from the point of view of man (say) or from the point of view of the mole? This very question is disturbed, embroiled, undermined by the law of supplementary delay. Each 'after' is 'at the same time', but one 'after' can never not be after the other ... No autobiography without a name or mole. The me is in the mole, the mole in me. '250 million years ago ... dinosaurs were not totally alone ... for scampering about in the leaf litter, amongst their great feet, were small furry animals whose descendants would, in the fullness of time, inherit the earth'.[11] I quote Gorman and Stone, *The Natural History of Moles*: what could 'fullness of time' mean, after a mole-like progression? And what of inheriting, without theology? Yes, the 'mole' in 'me', in what is called 'my' language, 'my' lifedeath caught up in 'mole'-effects. Which will entail, among other things, the task of reading 'mole', of thinking 'mole' as the secret that Derrida calls 'the functional possibility of homonymy',[12] of finding myself inscribed in the 'mole', not only as the so-called name of an animal, but also as identifying mark or stain, a fault or blemish, as foreign body or enemy within, and even as monstrosity (the 'mole' as 'false conception', a usage dating back to 1611, according to the *OED*, and synonymous with 'mooncalf').[13] **)**

(Derrida's 'Freud and the Scene of Writing' is concerned with thinking otherwise what he calls 'Hallucination as speech and hallucination as writing' (p. 197): Latin, *hallucinari*, to wander in the mind. It is a matter of what would be (in Derrida's words) 'before the distinction between man and animal, and even before the distinction between the living and the nonliving' (p. 197). A few of the many piquant formulations from the concluding paragraphs of his wanderings: 'We must be several in order to write, and even to "perceive"' (p. 226); 'The *sociality* of writing as *drama* requires an entirely different discipline' (p. 227); 'we must think of this scene [of writing] in other terms than those of individual or collective psychology, or even of anthropology' (p. 229). The scene or stage of the world would be that of 'the trace that is not yet language or speech or writing or sign or even something "proper to mankind" '.[14] Stop privileging a certain model of writing: that's what one's nose tells one, and Derrida is always led by the nose, close to or under the ground, on the scent of the trace.[15] 'There is no society without writing (without genealogical mark, accounting, archivalization), not even any so-called animal society without territorial mark. To be convinced of this, one need merely give up privileging a certain model of writing.'[16] **)**

(*On* or, better perhaps, *under* the stage: a question of the chthonic. What truth can I make of *Hamlet* in relation to the autobiographical animal? In *Spectres of Marx* Derrida does not, apparently, devote much attention to the figure of the mole in Shakespeare's play.[17] He seems to recognize the terrible, earthy darkness identifiable with this figure; but his only reference is in the form of a peculiar ellipsis, a contorted paralipsis, an admission of the apparent need to leave the mole out of account. He situates it in passing as something not even calling to be singled out for being passed over in silence. The allusion to the mole is subsumed or encrypted, as it were, within an observation about that 'fretful porpentine' (1.5.20) to which the Ghost of Hamlet's father refers.[18] Derrida writes: 'Every *revenant* seems to come from and return to *the earth*, to come from it as from a buried clandestinity (humus and mold, tomb and subterranean prison), to return to it as to the lowest, toward the humble, humid, humiliated. We must pass by here, we too, we must pass over in silence, as low as possible to the earth, the return of an animal: not the figure of the old mole ("Well said, old Mole"), nor of a certain hedgehog, but more precisely of a "fretfull Porpentine" that the spirit of the Father is then getting ready to conjure away by removing an "eternal blazon" from "ears of flesh and blood"' (p. 93). I would like to propose that this is what could be called a taupological ellipsis (for the suggestion of the word 'taupology' I am indebted to Ian Maclachlan who, with Michael Syrotinski, will have mined in advance everything I am saying here, if anything is being said: to them I would like, finally, humbly to dedicate this text – but where and in what language?). This ellipsis seems to me to be in communication with another, more general 'gap' in *Spectres of Marx*, namely the 'massively unavoidable' question of animals. I am thinking here of a singular tunnel that opens up immediately following Derrida's remark that 'no degree of progress allows one to ignore that never before, in absolute figures, have so many men, women, and children been subjugated, starved, or exterminated on the earth' (p. 85). In lunulae he adds: '(And provisionally, but with regret, we must leave aside here the nevertheless indissociable question of what is becoming of so-called "animal" life, the life and existence of "animals" in this history. This question has always been a serious one, but it will become massively unavoidable)' (p. 85). What is the time of the 'massively unavoidable'? Has it come? Derrida defers, he leaves aside the question of the animal and animals, even while acknowledging that it is 'indissociable' from everything he is saying. The massively unavoidable question is a ghost that haunts *Spectres of Marx*. I want to explore it by way of a smaller-scale question: what happens to the mole in *Spectres of Marx* and how does it relate to the more broadly political 'vision' of this book? The autobiographical here has to do with feeling: one's feeling (as Derrida puts it) 'projects itself necessarily into the scene I am interpreting … it is never possible to avoid this precipitation, since everyone reads, acts, writes with *his or her* ghosts, even when one goes after the ghosts of the other' (p. 139). 'Mole' appears twice in Shakespeare's play. On the first occasion, in Act 1 scene 2, Hamlet is with others on the watch, in a state of anticipation regarding the possibility of seeing his father's Ghost, and he is criticizing the Danish propensity for drunkenness: 'So, oft it chances in particular men / That for some vicious mole of nature in them, / As in their birth, wherein they are not guilty / (Since nature cannot choose his origin), / By their o'ergrowth of some complexion, / ... / ... / Shall in the general censure take corruption / From that particular fault' (1.4.23–36). 'Mole' here is taken to mean 'fault', 'defect', 'stain' or 'blemish'. It's there at the origin: a mole in one's birth. The second occasion, shortly after this, is when the Ghost has come and gone, but announces chthonically, from 'under the stage' (1.5.157), 'Swear by his sword', and Hamlet exclaims: 'Well said, old mole. Canst work i' th' earth so fast? / A worthy pioner!' (1.5.169–71). Already, then, the 'mole' is internally divided, divided on its 'first' appearance. As M. M. Mahood suggested in 1957, in her discussion of the 'vicious mole of nature': 'Since the *mole* as a burrowing animal is in Shakespeare's mind before this episode of the play ends ('Well sayd olde Mole'), it is perhaps not too far-fetched to indicate, in the word's use here, a nuance of "something that undermines from within" as well as the obvious meaning of a surface blemish.'[19] The second 'mole' comes before the first. The mole begins by coming back. 'Mole' is moled, mined from within: it mines the 'mine', even before Hamlet's characterization of the mole as 'worthy pioner' or 'miner', and before his later agonistic assertion of the 'I' against Rosencrantz and Guildenstern ('But I will delve one yard below their mines / And blow them at the moon' (3.4.210–11)). It ghosts the Ghost's words when describing the effects of the poison as it 'courses through / The natural gates and alleys of the body' (1.5.66–7). 'So did it mine', the Ghost says, 'And a most instant tetter bark'd about, / Most lazar-like, with vile and loathsome crust / All my smooth body' (1.5.70–3). There's a mole in me and mine. When Hamlet says 'Well said, old mole', the ghost becomes a mole but this mole is already spectralized. The out-of-joint tonality of this moment in the play, the irruption of what J. Dover Wilson called 'Hamlet's levity with his father's spirit',[20] constitutes what I would like to call, after Derrida or after Joyce, a peephole or portal. In *Spectres of Marx* Derrida speaks of Hamlet's expression 'The time is out of joint' as opening 'one of those breaches, often they are poetic and thinking peepholes [*meurtrières*], through which Shakespeare will have kept watch over the English language' (p. 18). This figure of the peephole bears an uncanny resemblance to that of the portal of which Stephen speaks in Joyce's *Ulysses*: 'A man of genius makes no mistakes. His errors are volitional and are the portals of discovery.'[21] This, it may be remembered, is the same passage in which Joyce recalls the apocryphal story (published in Nicholas Rowe's Preface of 1709) that Shakespeare himself played the mole ('Shakespeare who has studied *Hamlet* all the years of his life which were not vanity in order to play the part of the spectre': p. 188), and in which Joyce works with the molecular particles of 'mole' in 'molecules': 'Wait. Five months. Molecules all change. I am other I now … ' (p. 189). Portal: the opening of a tunnel. An air hole or breach. The word 'portal' comes in, or out of, *Hamlet*. As the Ghost disappears for apparently the last time, disappears as if for ever, Hamlet exclaims to his mother: 'Why, look you there, look how it steals away. / My father, in his habit as he liv'd! / Look where he goes even now out at the portal' (3.4.136–8). Even now: does this ghost-mole go out or go in? The mole is at the portal. The chiasmus of ghost becoming mole and mole becoming ghost is suspended here.)

(Derrida speaks, in *Spectres of Marx* and elsewhere, of the 'visor effect'. He defines this in terms of the formulation that 'we do not see who looks at us' and asserts that 'it will be presupposed by everything we advance on the subject of the spectre in general, in Marx and elsewhere' (p. 7). In 'The Time Is Out of Joint', the visor is integral to what Derrida offers, in passing, as a definition of deconstruction: 'Deconstruction is just visiting – and from the visitation one passes quickly to the visor, to the visor and haunting effect in *Hamlet* – return to Hamlet's father.'[22] In *Archive Fever* the visor effect is attached to Derrida's definition of the archive: the archive, he says, 'is spectral *a priori*: neither present nor absent "in the flesh", neither visible nor invisible, a trace always referring to another whose eyes can never be met, no more than those of Hamlet's father, thanks to the possibility of a visor' (p. 84). And in the context of his account of deferred action, and more specifically deferred obedience in Freud and Yerushalmi, he observes: 'The phantom thus makes the law – even, and more than ever, when one contests him. Like the father of Hamlet behind his visor, and by virtue of a *visor effect*, the spectre sees without being seen' (p. 61). All of this is slightly curious. If I contest a certain aspect of what Derrida is saying here I will of course be testifying to its truth. The word 'visor' does not occur in *Hamlet* and the suggestion of Hamlet's father concealing himself 'behind his visor' would appear to be a misreading.[23] As is evident from the following exchange between Hamlet and Horatio: *Ham.* Then saw you not his face? / *Hor.* O yes, my lord, he wore his beaver up. / *Ham.* What look'd he, frowningly? / *Hor.* A countenance more in sorrow than in anger. / *Ham.* Pale, or red? / *Hor.* Nay, very pale. / *Ham.* And fix'd his eyes upon you? / *Hor.* Most constantly. (1.2.228–34). Of course Derrida knows all this: he refers to this passage in *Spectres of Marx* in order to push through his point, which has to do with the *possibility* of the visor (or beaver): 'Even when it is raised, *in fact*, its possibility continues to signify that someone, beneath the armour, can safely see without being seen or without being identified' (*SM*, p. 8). Derrida toils at the visor-effect, as if preferring not to countenance this 'countenance more in sorrow than in anger'. Why does he put so much emphasis on something that runs counter to the words that actually appear in Shakespeare's text? Is it possible (such would be the feeling I have, and one of the possibilities I am interested in excavating here) that his concern with the visor-effect is traced, spectralized, 'supervised' by a certain mole? Isn't that above all what the figure of the mole evokes, at least in the West, namely an uncanniness around the question of seeing, an uncertainty about whether the mole sees or not, or, if it sees, how it does? Might this in turn throw another light or another sense on the logic according to which Hamlet addresses the figure with the visor-effect as a mole? Shakespeare will present the mole as blind, for instance in *The Tempest*, when that other mole, the 'moon-calf' (2.2.107) Caliban warns Stephano and Trinculo of their proximity to the mole called Prospero: 'Pray you, tread softly, that the blind mole may not / Hear a foot fall: we are now near his cell' (4.1.194). But the mole has eyes, it is just that they are largely hidden in fur. As Sir Thomas Browne remarked, in his *Pseudodoxia Epidemica* (1646): 'that [moles] have eyes in their head is manifest unto any, that wants them not in his own'.[24] I can feel it now, it's the visor-effect.)

(When Hamlet says 'Well said, old mole' he refers to the Ghost's saying 'Swear by his sword' (1.5.169), in other words to the only statement that the Ghost ever makes that is explicitly addressed to someone other than Hamlet: such is the significance of the word 'his'. The Ghost's repeated imperative 'Swear' (1.5.157, 163, 189) is not marked in this way. What is going on in this performative *en abyme* (cf. *SM*, p. 185, n. 10), this speaking well of speaking well of speech addressed to the other, the speech of a mole, at once interrupting and supplementing the performative? There is perhaps another haunting of the mole, by the mole, in *Spectres of Marx*, I mean in the speech or writing of another spokesperson for the mole, that is to say Marx himself. Marx's trope erupts in the Eighteenth Brumaire when he is describing the experience of being, as he sees it, in the middle or rather the purgatory or limbo of revolution: 'But the revolution is thoroughgoing. It is still journeying through purgatory. It does its work methodically. By 2 December 1851, it had completed one half of the preparatory work; it is now completing the other half ... And when it has done this second half of its preliminary work, Europe will leap from its seat and exultantly exclaim: Well grubbed, old mole! (*Brav gewühlt, alter Maulwurk!*)'[25] 'Old mole' here, as Bataille suggested, appears to be 'Marx's resounding expression for the complete satisfaction of the revolutionary outburst of the masses' and can be understood 'in relation to the notion of the geological uprising as expressed in the *Communist Manifesto*'.[26] Marx's exclamatory trope consists partly in the shift from saying to digging, searching, finding food ('grubbing'), and partly in the theriomorphic figuration of the completion of the revolution. In its programming of the future, catapulting the future into the past tense, and in its crucial elision of the notion of speech act, injunction and promise ('well said'), Marx's text perhaps speaks out against what has been called the opening of the future itself, that messianic that comes from 'the being-promise of a promise' (*SM*, p. 105) and that Derrida so patiently explores in *Spectres of Marx*. The mole, if there is one, comes from the future. I want to feel my way into a 'return of the animal' in *Spectres of Marx*, a return that would not, however, like Marx's rhetoric involve a metaphorical appropriation and effective objectification of the animal (mole as figure of the people or of the revolution) but would attempt to articulate slightly differently the taupological ellipsis in Derrida's book, concerning the 'massively unavoidable question' of the animal and animals. This ellipsis takes the form of a tunnel: it is placed in parentheses. The context of this seems to me significant. In a tunnel Derrida expresses his regret for not speaking of the animal, and this tunnel immediately precedes that moment in the text when he offers the most explicit 'working definition' of the New International: the New International, he says, 'is a link of affinity, suffering, and hope, a still discreet, almost secret link, as it was around 1848, but more and more visible, we have more than one sign of it. It is an untimely link, without status, without title, and without name, barely public even if it is not clandestine, without contract, "out of joint", without co-ordination, without party, without country, without national community (International before, across, and beyond any national determination), without citizenship, without common belonging to a class' (*SM*, p. 85). The New International, I would like to suggest, is not separable from the question of 'so-called "animal life"'. If there is a New International, it is not human, or at least not confined to the human.)

(Hamlet's praise for the Ghost's speech ('Well said, old mole') is, before anything else, a bearing witness to the thought that a mole can speak. The seeming madness of this testimony can be linked up with something else that is marked in the 'mole' and in the 'well said'. I have tried elsewhere to burrow away a little at what I call dramaturgic or theatrical telepathy, that is to say 'the provocative oddity, encountered elsewhere in Shakespeare's plays, of a sort of telepathic repetition of utterance, apparent displays of telepathy or thought-transmission which no amount of textual scholarship or editorial argumentation will efface'.[27] It breaks out all over the place in *Hamlet* and it is perhaps inseparable from the figure of the mole. At stake here would be the possibility of another way of thinking 'the *sociality* of writing as *drama*'. The phrase 'Well said', for example, is itself a sort of ghost, or mole, that comes back. It is put into the mouth of Polonius, in a quite different context, but just thirty-four lines after Hamlet uses it: 'You shall do marvellous wisely, good Reynaldo, / Before you visit him [i.e. Laertes], to make inquire / Of his behaviour.' Reynaldo: 'My lord, I did intend it.' Polonius: 'Marry, well said, very well said' (2.1.3–6). Dramaturgic telepathy would entail transposing or trans-lating otherwise the boundaries and marks of classification supposedly separating one character from another, one scene from another. It would mean trying to think differently what is happening when, for instance, Hamlet's 'private' vow to 'speak daggers to [his mother], but use none' (3.2.387) is picked up in the closet scene in his mother's exclamation, 'O speak to me no more. / These words like daggers enter in my ears' (3.4.94–5); or when, in the same scene, the Queen notes Hamlet's 'bedded hair, like life in excrements, / Start up and stand an end' (3.4.121–2) and thus eerily 'repeats' the Ghost's earlier evocation of Hamlet's 'each particular hair to stand an end / Like quills upon the fretful porpentine' (1.5.19–20); or when the Queen's dismissal of Hamlet's experience of the Ghost ('This is the very coinage of your brain': 3.4.139) refers back to Hamlet's numismatic phrase, to his verbal coinage at the moment the Ghost first cries under the stage: 'Ah ha, boy, say'st thou so? Art thou there, truepenny?' (1.5.158). To elaborate the notion of dramaturgic or theatrical telepathy in greater detail lies beyond the scope of the present text. I would say only this for now: rather than frame *Hamlet* accord-ing to the conventional boundaries of characterology, scenes and acts, and imagery (above all 'animal imagery'), wouldn't the logic of dramaturgic telepathy be a spectral logic, a logic indissociable from the mole? Wouldn't dramaturgic tele-pathy lead into a thought of spectral speech or writing within which the mole as much as the human 'speaks', that is, into a thinking of the trace impossibly figured in the mole, into a thinking of the secret as that which is 'no more in speech than foreign to speech'?[28] Nothing happens in *Hamlet* without a prior and radical putting into question of the opposition of the human and the animal, the living and the non-living, a questioning that begins with the (im)possible identification of a ghost ('Who's there?') and the ghostly negation of a mouse ('Have you had quiet guard?' 'Not a mouse stirring' (1.1.10–11)). I cannot get further into that labyrinth today. I'll stay here, in the outer labyrinth.)

(After a mole-like progression, after the subterranean toil of an impression, in the winter of 1923, who or what is the 'I' in the very great late text, also regarded as incomplete, 'The Burrow'? Everything is in this Kafka text, in the portal of its title and of its first sentence: 'I have completed the construction of my burrow and it seems to be successful' (p. 325). In the almost completely incredible, completely seductive voice of a burrowing animal (one whose mole-like characteristics lead me to want to call Kafka's story exemplary of a certain *animology*), in a trembling appearance of completion and of success that by the very terms of the description ('it seems') can be neither complete nor successful, the 'I' tells a fable about the anthropomorphism that permits this fabulous case of a speaking animal. It is an 'I' that reflects on itself and on the performativity of its speech, and that elaborates a deconstructive, animological discourse. 'Here is my main entrance, I said in those days, ironically addressing my invisible enemies and seeing them as already caught and stifled in the outer labyrinth' (p. 331): this 'I' knows that it is doing things with words, ironically, and that those it is addressing are not only invisible but already dead. And it proceeds to unfold a tale which suggests that, within the anthropomorphic projection, to speak or write as an anonymous, singular, autobiographical animal is to encounter the fabulous origins of the 'I' in a doubling or division. Such is the bizarre telephone-effect of the sound that the narrator comes to describe: 'I did not hear it at all when I first arrived, although it must certainly have been there; I must first feel quite at home before I could hear it; it is, so to speak, audible only to the ear of the householder' (p. 343). The 'I' is haunted by the ear, the whistling and the burrowing of the other. This other is variously figured as 'some animal unknown to me' (p. 347), a kind of double ('someone of my own kind, a connoisseur and prizer of burrows, a hermit, a lover of peace': p. 337), and as death: 'I know that my term is measured, that I do not have to hunt here forever, and that, whenever I am weary of this life and wish to leave it, Someone, whose invitation I shall not be able to withstand, will, so to speak, summon me to him' (p. 334). In its panic, anxiety and pleasure, 'The Burrow' presents the animological experience of the impossible. It recounts an allegory of the trace or difference within the ear of the householder who recounts: this trace is at the origin but will never have been lived in the present. It is the condition of having a burrow, of being in the burrow that is the text. Death, the one whose invitation cannot be withstood, is as unthinkable here as it is in *Aporias* when Derrida suggests that man has no more of a relation to death or to the 'name' of death than animals have.[29] One can call death a mole or call death through a mole, as Hamlet might appear to; or as Shakespeare's play might appear to, with all its labour of removing ground, delving and gravedigging (the fossorial and the fossor), relentlessly moving around the figure of death preparing its 'feast' in its 'eternal cell' (5.2.370); or as George Herbert might appear to in his poem 'Grace' ('Death is still working like a mole, / And digs my grave at each remove ...')³⁰ – but the itinerancy of the trace will always already have burrowed deeper or elsewhere.)

(Final tunnel or *afterw.rd.*³¹ When it comes to secrets, 'nonmanifestation is never assured'.³² I recall here Derrida's meditation on the question of whether animals can keep secrets. It is in 'How to Avoid Speaking', when he questions the 'somewhat naive philosophy' according to which 'animals are incapable of keeping or even having a secret' (p. 17). It is because 'the nonmanifestation is never assured' that it becomes necessary 'to reconsider all the boundaries between consciousness and the unconscious' and 'between man and animal' (p. 18). In an essay on *Hamlet* and *Mémoires: For Paul de Man*, published in *Diacritics* in 1990, I referred to the mole in the context of the promise and what Derrida calls 'a kind of irremediable disturbance or perversion' of 'the performative as promise': it is this that accounts for what he describes as 'the *unbelievable*, and comical, aspect of every promise'.³³ Isn't this also the experience of the non-assurance of the nonmanifestation of a secret? As that which haunts, as that which comes from the future, would the mole already have been 'in' *Spectres of Marx*? And would it be my mole or that of my telepathic friend Jacques Derrida or the mole of the other? When Derrida sent me a copy of *Spectres of Marx*, I wrote (2 March 1994) thanking him and, in a letter that included some remarks on molluscs (about which I was then writing) and a certain hedgehog, I also wondered about the possible communication between the *Diacritics* essay and *Spectres of Marx*. In his reply (6 March 1994) Derrida wrote: 'I am going to reread your text from *Diacritics* 1990 to see if it has made a mole-like progression in the unconscious of my memory' ('Je vais relire votre texte de *Diacritics* 1990 pour voir s'il a fait un chemin de taupe dans l'inconscient de ma mémoire'). The letter is typewritten or wordprocessed, but in pen he makes two alterations: originally he says 'mon mémoire' and changes the 'mon' to 'ma'; and around the word 'taupe' he adds, either side, the little claws or 'fossors' of quotation marks.)

SIDE TUNNELS

1   This text was originally presented at a conference on the autobiographical animal in relation to the work of Jacques Derrida ('L'animal autobiographique: Autour de Jacques Derrida') at Cerisy-la-Salle, in July 1997. It was first published in French (trans. Ian Maclachlan and

Michael Syrotinski), in *L'Animal autobiographique: Autour de Jacques Derrida*, ed. Marie-Louise Mallet (Paris: Galilée, 1999), 547–62. In the course of this chapter, I hope that the uncanniness of the mole might (as it were) speak for itself, in particular in terms of the relations between the human and the animal, of the animal *as* human, and in terms of deferred action or after-effect, writing, foreign body, secretiveness, solitude and death. Apparently 'by chance', immediately after writing 'Mole', in the summer of 1997, I began work on what I thought would be a very different project, a short account of the writings of E. M. Forster; but I quickly realized that it would be necessary to begin from the fact that, while still students at Cambridge, Lytton Strachey had nicknamed Forster 'the taupe' (or 'mole'). Focusing on the mole-like and the uncanny, *E. M. Forster* (Plymouth: Northcote House/British Council, 1999) thus became a sort of extended supplement to the present text.

2   Friedrich Nietzsche, *Daybreak: Thoughts on the Prejudices of Morality*, trans. R. J. Hollingdale (Cambridge: Cambridge University Press, 1982), p. 1.

3   Harold Bloom, *The Western Canon: The Books and School of the Ages* (London: Macmillan, 1995), p. 448.

4   Hélène Cixous, 'Sorties', in *Modern Literary Theory: A Reader*, 3rd edn, eds Philip Rice and Patricia Waugh (London: Edward Arnold, 1996), p. 140.

5   I borrow this word from John Lennard, who in turn takes it from Erasmus. See John Lennard, *But I Digress: The Exploitation of Parentheses in English Printed Verse* (Oxford: Clarendon, 1991), pp. 1, 249, n. 1.

6   Jacques Derrida, *Writing and Difference*, trans. Alan Bass (London: Routledge and Kegan Paul, 1978), p. 214, translation slightly modified. (See 'Freud et la scène de l'écriture', in *L'écriture et la différence* (Paris: Éditions du Seuil, 1967), pp. 293–340: here, p. 317.) Further page references to the English translation are given in brackets in the main body of the text.

7   See *The Complete Short Stories of Franz Kafka*, ed. Nahum N. Glatzer (London: Minerva, 1996), 470. Further page references are to this edition.

8   Jacques Derrida, 'White Mythology: Metaphor in the Text of Philosophy', in *Margins of Philosophy*, trans. Alan Bass (Chicago: Chicago University Press, 1982), p. 246.

9   Martyn L. Gorman and R. David Stone, *The Natural History of Moles* (London: Christopher Helm, 1990), p. 19.

10   Jacques Derrida, *Archive Fever: A Freudian Impression*, trans. Eric Prenowitz (Chicago: University of Chicago Press, 1996), p. 80. Further page references to this text are given in brackets in the main body of the text.

11   Gorman and Stone, *The Natural History of Moles*, p. 1.

12   Jacques Derrida, 'Passions: "An Oblique Offering" ', trans. David Wood, in *On the Name* (Stanford: Stanford University Press, 1995), p. 26.

13   As I hope will become clear from the reading of *Hamlet* advanced in the present chapter, I would contend that Shakespeare's text (1600–1) effectively offers an earlier construal of 'mole' as 'false conception'.

14   Jacques Derrida, 'The Almost Nothing of the Unpresentable', trans. Peggy Kamuf, in *Points ... Interviews, 1974–1994*, ed. Elisabeth Weber (Stanford: Stanford University Press, 1995), p. 79.

15   Cf. *Of Grammatology*, trans. Gayatri Chakravorty Spivak (Baltimore: Johns Hopkins University Press, 1976), p. 162, and *Points ...*, p. 48. Across the decades Derrida has followed the furrows of Freudian conceptuality and the contents of the Freudian archive about which he observes: 'These classical and extraordinary works move away from us at great speed, in a continually accelerated fashion. They burrow into the past' (*Archive Fever*, p. 18).

16   Derrida, 'The Almost Nothing of the Unpresentable', p. 84.

17 Jacques Derrida, *Spectres of Marx: The State of the Debt, the Work of Mourning, and the New International*, trans. Peggy Kamuf (New York: Routledge, 1994). Further references to this text are given in brackets in the main body of this essay, preceded by 'SM' where appropriate.

18 References to Shakespeare's play are to the Arden *Hamlet*, ed. Harold Jenkins (London: Methuen, 1982).

19 M. M. Mahood, *Shakespeare's Wordplay* (London: Methuen, 1957), p. 117.

20 J. Dover Wilson, *What Happens in Hamlet* (Cambridge: Cambridge University Press, 1935), p. 78.

21 James Joyce, *Ulysses* (Harmondsworth: Penguin, 1969), p. 190. Further references to this text are given in brackets in the main body of this essay.

22 Jacques Derrida, 'The Time Is Out of Joint', trans. Peggy Kamuf, in *Deconstruction is/in America*, ed. Anselm Haverkamp (New York: New York University Press, 1995), p. 29.

23 Derrida uses the Bonnefoy translation of 'beaver' as 'visière': see *Spectres of Marx*, p. 29. 'Beaver' is indeed the nearest word to 'visor' in Shakespeare's text. In a note to the Arden edition Harold Jenkins writes: 'Originally the beaver was drawn up from the chin and the vizor let down from the forehead. But in 16th-century helmets beaver and vizor had ceased to be distinct, and either word was applied to the whole face-guard, which "could be pushed up entirely over the top of the helmet" (Planché, *Cyclopaedia of Costume*, i.39), thus leaving the face free' (Arden *Hamlet*, p. 195).

24 Sir Thomas Browne, *Pseudodoxia Epidemica*, I, ed. Robin Robbins (Oxford: Clarendon Press, 1981), Chapter 18, 'Of Moles, or Molls', p. 233.

25 'The Eighteenth Brumaire of Louis Bonaparte', in Karl Marx and Frederick Engels, *Collected Works*, II (New York: International Publishers, 1979); *Marx–Engels Werke*, ed. Institut für Marxismus-Leninismus beim ZK der SED (Berlin: Dietz Verlag, 1969), 8, 196.

26 Georges Bataille, 'The "Old Mole" and the Prefix Sur', in *Visions of Excess: Selected Writings, 1927–1939*, ed. Allan Stoekl (Minneapolis: University of Minnesota Press, 1985), p. 35.

27 See my *Telepathy and Literature: Essays on the Reading Mind* (Oxford and Cambridge, Mass.: Basil Blackwell, 1991), p. 146. I explore further the notion of dramaturgic or theatrical telepathy, specifically in relation to *Hamlet*, in Chapter 8 ('Night writing'), above.

28 See Derrida, 'Passions', p. 27.

29 See Jacques Derrida, *Aporias*, trans. Thomas Dutoit (Stanford: Stanford University Press, 1993), p. 76.

30 *The Poems of George Herbert* (London: Oxford University Press, 1961), p. 52.

31 For the title of a short text concerned with the notion of the afterword and issues of after-effect, *après coup* and afterwards, specifically in relation to deconstruction, Derrida proposes 'Afterw.rd', noting of its dot that 'this furtive interruption mobiliz[es] two letters towards the improbable end of a word which hesitates between noun and non-noun'. 'Afterw.d', he stresses, 'does not belong to the dictionary of any known language'. See Jacques Derrida, 'Afterw.rds: or, at least, less than a letter about a letter less', trans. Geoffrey Bennington, in *Afterwords*, ed. Nicholas Royle (Tampere, Finland: Outside Books, 1992), pp. 197–203; here, pp. 198, 202.

32 Jacques Derrida, 'How to Avoid Speaking: Denials', trans. Ken Frieden, in *Languages of the Unsayable: The Play of Negativity in Literature and Literary Theory*, eds Sanford Budick and Wolfgang Iser (New York: Columbia University Press, 1989), p. 18. Further references to this text are given in brackets in the main body of the text.

33 'Nuclear Piece: *Mémoires* of *Hamlet* and the Time to Come', *Diacritics* vol. 20, no. 1 (Spring 1990), 39–55: here, p. 47. (Citing Derrida, *Mémoires: For Paul de Man* (New York: Columbia

University Press, 1986), p. 94.) In the *Diacritics* essay I also refer to the mole in a footnote (p. 41, n. 2), and in particular to Ned Lukacher's remarkable chapter entitled 'Shakespeare in the Ear of Hegel' (pp. 178–235) in his book *Primal Scenes: Literature, Philosophy, Psychoanalysis* (Ithaca: Cornell University Press, 1986), in which, I suggest, 'Lukacher plays Molecatcher, following the cryptic movements of this "figure of a figure" through [Shakespeare's play]'.

19

The 'telepathy effect': notes toward a reconsideration of narrative fiction

This chapter aims to explore what is perhaps the most intriguing feature of narrative fiction and to open up new ways of thinking about it. As Dorrit Cohn has described it: 'narrative fiction is the only literary genre, as well as the only kind of narrative, in which the unspoken thoughts, feelings, perceptions of a person other than the speaker can be portrayed'.[1] There is uncanny knowledge. Someone is telling us what someone else is thinking, feeling or perceiving. That someone else may not even be aware of experiencing these thoughts, feelings or perceptions. The history of criticism of the novel is the history of the attempt to deal, or avoid dealing, with this seemingly mad scenario. For this strange feature of literary fiction tends also to be the least questioned, most taken-for-granted. Passing without comment, it appears as a sort of somnambulism of critical common sense. Perhaps this is not surprising: after all, there can be no final assurance about an appropriate vocabulary for it. No doubt this lack of assurance helps to account for the labyrinthine intricacies of much writing in narratology and narrative theory. Might there be ways of construing narrative fiction that would be responsive to its complexity and strangeness but without 'losing the plot' in theoretical abstraction, in particular without collapsing into the sort of enervative taxonomizing to which narratological discourse seems prone?[2] Questioning a certain ethos and style of narrative theory, what follows is an attempt to sketch a rethinking of narrative fiction.

The task will consist principally in a re-examination of two of the most familiar and widely used critical terms of the past hundred years or so: 'omniscience' and 'point of view'. Recent narrative theory has tended to speak less of 'point of view' and more of 'focalization'; but, as will become evident, all three of these terms are linked, swimming or sinking together. First of all, then, the peculiar feature of narrative fiction at issue is closely identified with the concept of omniscience. An awareness of this is hardly recent. As Dorrit Cohn shows, it is explicitly formulated, for example, in Friedrich von Blanckenburg's *Essay on the Novel* in 1774, where he declares: 'A writer, lest he wish to dishonor himself, can not hold to the pretense that he is unacquainted with the inner world of his characters. He is their creator: they have received from him all their character traits, their entire being, they live in a world that he himself has fashioned.'[3] Lodged within this charming if deceptive candour – of not being able to pretend that one is unacquainted with such an 'inner world' – is an early Romantic formulation of what later came to be called authorial or narratorial omniscience. The writer is godlike, the creator who knows everything about the characters he (or she) has created. Blanckenburg's statement may now appear critically naive in its nondifferentiation between 'writer' and 'narrator': the twentieth century witnessed a slow but steadily sharpening sense that the 'I' of a narrative fiction cannot simply be talked about as if he or she were the author, and that this 'I' is just as much created *by* the narrative as s/he is the creator *of* it.[4]

But if the phrase 'authorial omniscience' now looks like a sort of redundant oxymoron (no author is omniscient, he or she can only ever have limited knowledge), 'omniscient narrator' and 'narrative omniscience' remain common critical parlance. Thus, for example, in his recent book on literary theory Jonathan Culler defines 'omniscient narration' as the situation in which

> the focalizer is a godlike figure who has access to the innermost thoughts and hidden motives of the characters ... Omniscient narration, where there seem in principle no limitations on what can be known and told, is common not only in traditional tales but in modern novels.[5]

Culler's characteristic clarity and serenity is somewhat troubling and ironic here. The trouble is indicated, first of all, in the hedging 'seem' and 'in principle'. Why 'seem' rather than 'are'? What does 'in principle' mean? What is this 'principle' of omniscience? The irony has to do with religion and can be brought out by quoting from another essay by Culler, from one of the least serene and most striking passages in all his writing. It comes in the essay 'Political Criticism: Confronting Religion', when he declares:

> The essential step is to take up the relation of our teaching and writing to religious discourse and to maintain a critical attitude when discussing religious themes – that is, not to assume that theistic beliefs deserve respect, any more than we would assume that sexist or racist beliefs deserve respect. This might involve us in comparing Christianity with other mythologies when we teach works imbued with religion, or making the sadism and sexism of religious discourse an explicit object of discussion, as we now tend to do when teaching works containing overtly racist language.[6]

We must, he suggests, be especially sensitive to – and critical of – anything that smacks of religion. Culler's advocacy of a heightened critical attentiveness to 'religious discourse', to all and any writing 'imbued with religion', becomes ironic because even a brief examination of the history of 'omniscience' indicates that it is a religious term, Judaeo-Christian or, rather, dominantly Christian, through and through.

For 'omniscience' the *OED* gives 'The quality of being omniscient. **a.** Strictly: Infinite knowledge; hence *transf.* the omniscient Being, the Deity': in the earliest sense of the term, it is the Christian God who, in His omniscience, 'searcheth the heart, discouereth the thoughts' (1612). The *OED* also records a 'hyperbolic' usage of the term (sense **b**), meaning 'Universal knowledge' (the first use in this sense being given as 1845). Correspondingly, the adjective 'omniscient' is defined as '1. Knowing all things, all-knowing, infinite in knowledge. **a.** Strictly: esp. Of God ... **b.** Hyperbolically: Having universal or very extensive knowledge.' 'Omniscience' is, strictly speaking then, a term for the Christian God; its deployment in any other sense is hyperbole.

What J. Hillis Miller once charted as 'the disappearance of God', looking back to Hölderlin and the late eighteenth century, might be rephrased here as the disappearance of omniscience; ghostly, like any thinking of disappearance, it would perhaps be legible in this hyperbolic appropriation of the 'omniscient'.[7] According to the *OED*, the earliest recorded use of 'omniscient' in this hyperbolic, i.e. ostensibly non-theistic context is in Boswell's *Life of Johnson* (1791), in the entry for 5 April 1776 where he refers to a man called Richard Jackson whom Johnson called 'the all-knowing'. In a footnote Boswell remarks of Jackson: 'A gentleman, who from his extraordinary stores of knowledge, has been stiled *omniscient*. Johnson, I think, very properly, altered it to all-knowing, as it is a *verbum solenne*, appropriated to the Supreme Being.'[8] The 'stiled' is a significant marker here. A curious thing seems to have happened to 'omniscience' since Boswell: in particular in the context of literary criticism and theory, the initially and explicitly 'hyperbolic' character of the word has tended to be repressed or disavowed.

A good example would be Robert Scholes's and Robert Kellogg's study *The Nature of Narrative* (1966). They have a number of critical reservations about 'the concept of omniscience' and are understandably cautious about its religious dimensions:

> 'omniscience' itself is not a descriptive term so much as a definition based on the presumed analogy between the novelist as creator and the Creator of the cosmos, an omniscient God. The analogy has a certain obvious relevance which has enabled it to maintain currency as a term in literary discussion. But it also, like most analogies, operates so as to prevent our seeing certain aspects of the thing analogized. In the case of omniscient narration in the novel, the analogy obscures an important duality in the fictional device. Omniscience includes the related god-like attribute of omnipresence. God *knows* everything because He *is* everywhere – simultaneously. But a narrator in fiction is imbedded in a time-bound artifact. He [*sic*] does not 'know' simultaneously but consecutively. He is not everywhere at once but now here, now there, now looking into this mind or that, now moving on to other vantage points. He is time-bound and space-bound as God is not.[9]

What Scholes and Kellogg seem to be describing here is a telepathic logic accord-ing to which a narrator – and thus a reader – is 'now looking into this mind', now into that. Their account motions toward a theory of narrative telepathy, not narrative omniscience. 'Omniscience', as they make clear, is a misleading and incoherent term: it 'obscures' the 'time-bound', 'space-bound' particularity of what is going on in literary fiction. Yet despite their reservations, Scholes and Kellogg continue to valorize and use the term, even when this entails depending on a nonsensical notion of 'full' (or non-full) omniscience.[10]

'Omniscience' has seemed useful in the context of literary studies as a means of gathering together the idea that a narrator or a narrative knows, or seems to know, not only what is going on in the minds and bodies of various characters, but also what is going to happen in the future. Just as a narrator inhabits the thoughts, feelings and perceptions of only one character at a time,[11] so the future that a narrator or narrative appears to know about is in fact highly circumscribed, limited and partial. The continuing use of the term 'omniscience' serves to promote and protect a thinking of the 'world' of narrative fiction as holistic, unified and closed. It colludes with a thinking of the experience of reading as asserting or presupposing a fixed and totalizing interpretation. It thus helps to ward off the transformative possibilities of reading, to limit and close down in advance what is incalculable and unprogrammable in the experience of a text.

A more precise way of talking about the fact that fictional narratives or narrators seem to have knowledge of the future might be in terms of clair-voyance. Again, as 'the alleged power of discerning things beyond the normal range of sense or perception' (*Chambers*), clairvoyance would be linked to a logic, not of omniscience, but of telepathy. God might be omniscient but one would not call her clairvoyant. To propose 'clairvoyance' as a more accurate term than 'omniscience' is not to advocate that narrative theory hurry up and become a branch of parapsychology. Rather it is to attempt to move away from uncritical, religious and other dogmatic assumptions about the nature of narrative fiction, while acknowledging and critically elaborating on what is uncanny, even 'magical' about such fiction. Concerned with seeing or feeling what is in the distance, clairvoyance is indissociably bound up with the telepathic. This might be succinctly illustrated by George Eliot's novella *The Lifted Veil* (1859, published 1878), a text which constitutes a meditation on the uncanny nature of story-telling, beginning: 'The time of my end approaches ... For I foresee when I shall die, and everything that will happen in my last moments.'[12] The narrator, Latimer, can read the minds of some but not all others (crucially, not his wife

Bertha's); he becomes appalled witness to 'all the suppressed egoism' (p. 19) of other people's speech and behaviour; he is subject of and to what in the mid nineteenth century was known as 'sympathetic clairvoyance' and what came in 1882 to be classified as telepathy.[13]

Omniscience is not simply a hyperbole, it is an incoherent and flawed plot-device in a story that critics and theorists have been telling for a hundred years and more. Why retain the concept of omniscience at all? The use of the words 'omniscient' and 'omniscience' in the context of narrative fiction remains inextricably entangled in Christian motifs, assumptions and beliefs. To assume the efficacy and appropriateness of discussing literary works in terms of 'omniscient narration' is, however faintly or discreetly, to subscribe to a religious (and above all, a Christian) discourse and thinking. But a continuing reliance on the term 'omniscience' in the context of literary studies could be said to testify to something else as well. This might be illuminated by taking up some observations made by Wallace Martin in his book *Recent Theories of Narrative* (1986).[14] Focusing on Ernest Hemingway's short story 'The Short Happy Life of Francis Macomber', Martin writes: 'One telltale sign of omniscience, beyond the third-person narrator's unnatural access to the minds of others, appears in the story: comments on what a character did *not* think' (p. 146). In his critical pursuit of what he calls 'an adequate account of omniscient narration' (p. 144), Martin speaks of 'omniscience in the usual sense (access to consciousness)' (p. 146): the force of what is strange or 'unnatural' here is at once registered and norm-ativized. The 'telltale' feature of omniscience, on the other hand, the feature that evidently helps to make omniscient narration so full of 'contrivance' and 'shortcomings' (p. 144), is that it enables the reader to discover what a character is *not* thinking. What would be an 'adequate account' of this 'unnatural' world of narrative fiction? Why should 'omniscience' be presumed an 'adequate' term for glossing 'comments on what a character did not think'?

What the continuing use of the term 'omniscience' masks is not only the religious and more specifically Christian ambience of literary criticism, even in some of its most sophisticated contemporary forms, but also any obligation to engage with the question of psychoanalysis. It is as if criticism were prepared to acknowledge the force and necessity of a logic of the unconscious, of presentations or representations of what a character does not realize he or she is thinking or feeling; but this acknowledgement is immediately, as if magically translated 'back' into a pre-nineteenth-century religious discourse. Reliance on the term 'omniscience' thus acts as a means by which criticism can avoid the obligation to reflect more rigorously on what psychoanalysis might have to say about unconscious knowledge and desire or, conversely, what literary fiction may have to say about psychoanalysis.

In historical terms, 'omniscience' became a widespread literary critical term just as psychoanalysis was establishing the structural and conditioning impossibility of complete knowledge of one's own thoughts and feelings, let alone complete knowledge of everyone else's. It is not a matter of arguing that literary criticism ought to adopt a more specifically psychoanalytic vocabulary, but rather of elaborating the space for a critical thinking that does not fall in with the scientistic elements of a psychoanalytically inflected critical approach to literary fiction either. The concept of telepathy is historically and epistemologically crucial in this context. Introduced in the late nineteenth century as a term to designate 'all cases of impression received at a distance without the normal operation of the recognised sense organs',[15] the emergence of 'telepathy' figures an important moment in what we have called the disappearance of omniscience, as well as in the origins of psychoanalysis. The significance of this emergence for a historical understanding of modern (and postmodern) fiction is considerable though remains insufficiently acknowledged. Telepathy is both thematically and structurally at work in modern fictional narratives, and calls for a quite different kind of critical storytelling than that promoted by the religious, panoptical delusion of omniscience. In particular, it calls for more rigorous critical reflection on the links between allegedly literary and non-literary discourses for, as the brief example from George Eliot may already have intimated, the emergence of 'telepathy' via 'clairvoyance' and 'sympathetic clairvoyance' is inextricably bound up with the language and forms of nineteenth-century literary fiction. In other words, 'telepathy' in its restricted, conventional, parapsychological sense (as 'communication between mind and mind otherwise than through the known channels of the senses' (*Chambers*)) is more literary than has generally been recognized.

'Telepathy' opens up possibilities of a humbler, more precise, less religiously freighted conceptuality than does 'omniscience', for thinking about the uncanniness of what is going on in narrative fiction. Such a conceptuality entails an unsettling and reworking of narratological and psychoanalytic vocabulary alike. The pertinence (and impertinence) of telepathy in the context of psychoanalysis lies in its status as a foreign body that, exemplarily in Freud's own writings, can be neither accepted nor rejected. The question of telepathy was one of the things that, by his own admission, drove Freud to distraction.[16] He just could not make up his mind about it. As Jacques Derrida has observed, it is 'difficult to imagine a theory of what they still call the unconscious without a theory of telepathy. They can be neither confused nor dissociated.'[17] Telepathy introduces a *literary scenario* into any account or thinking of the unconscious. In offering another way of describing what is happening to the thoughts and feelings of a given fictional character without the knowledge of that character, telepathy dislocates all notions of *applying* psychoanalysis to literary fiction, of psychoanalysing fictional characters or of deriving psychoanalytic 'truths' from narrative fiction.

The other critical term widely used over the last century for describing what is perhaps the most intriguing feature of narrative fiction is 'point of view', that is to say (in the words of Gerald Prince), 'The perceptual or conceptual position in terms of which the narrated situations and events are presented'.[18] In this way, an author or narrator inhabits the mind and/or body of a character and describes things from their point of view. The use of this term can be traced back, in particular, to the critical prefaces of Henry James (1907–09), and to influential critical studies by Joseph Warren Beach (1918) and Percy Lubbock (1921).[19] Point of view and omniscience seem to go hand-in-hand. Consider the following remarks on Flaubert and *Madame Bovary* (1857), in Lubbock's *The Craft of Fiction:*

> Flaubert, the author of the story, must intervene with his superior knowledge. Perhaps it is something in the past of the people who have been moving and talking on the scene; you cannot rightly understand this incident or this talk, the author implies, unless you know – what I now proceed to tell you. And so, for a new light on the drama, the author recalls certain circumstances that we should otherwise have missed. Or it may be that he – who naturally knows everything, even the inmost, unexpressed thought of his characters – wishes us to share the mind of Bovary or of Emma, not to wait only on their words or actions; and so he goes below the surface, enters their consciousness, and describes the train of sentiment that passes there.[20]

Here, as elsewhere in his book, Lubbock talks about the 'omniscient author'. Of Thackeray's *Vanity Fair* (1847–8), for example, he says that, when not narrated from Becky Sharp's point of view, 'It is the omniscient author, and the point of view is his'.[21] The concept of omniscience is natural, without need of question or definition: the author 'naturally knows everything'. Again, however, what is in operation here is a logic not of 'natural' omniscience but rather of something like narrative telepathy: the ability to present things from Bovary's or Emma's point of view involves the familiar-unfamiliar logic of a narrator 'enter[ing a character's] consciousness', becoming temporary amanuensis to their 'inmost, unexpressed thought'. To recall the phrasing of Scholes and Kellogg, it is a matter of a narrator 'not everywhere at once' but 'now here, now there, now looking into this mind or that'.

Throughout *The Craft of Fiction* Lubbock privileges the visual. In this respect it might be said that he is simply following the example set by James, in his New York Prefaces. This privileging is evident in the extract just quoted, in the theatrical allusions to 'moving and talking on the scene' and 'a new light on the drama'. Above all, however, it is evident in the term 'point of view' itself. 'Point of view' is a visual metaphor that, for a hundred years and more, has worked to elide or negate the importance of voice, of narrative fiction in the sounds of words. Moreover, if its more colloquial sense ('point of view' as 'opinion') has contributed toward a further critical effacement of the *how* rather than the *what* of what is being said, the term has also carried with it a powerful set of assumptions about the unity of the speaker or thinker whose 'point of view' is being 'expressed'. 'Point of view' would be homologous with 'omniscience', in fact, in terms of a sense of unity and the One ('God', for example, or Molly Bloom). Together with 'omniscience', 'point of view' has been a key critical term for the safekeeping of the unitariness of the figures of 'author', 'narrator' and 'character' alike. For all its apparent commonsensicality, 'point of view' is a critical fallacy. There is no single, unitary or unified point of view in a work of fiction. *Point of view does not exist, any more than does omniscience.*

In recent years 'point of view' has become an object of suspicion among many narrative theorists. There is a preference for talking about 'focalization': this term was introduced by Gérard Genette, in his *Narrative Discourse* (1972), on the apparently non-comical basis that it is 'more abstract'.[22] In fact, the concept of point of view continues to remain in widespread critical use and indeed underpins the logic of the new term. 'Focalization' is deemed to be valuable because it avoids the confusions between 'who sees?' and 'who speaks?'. Wallace Martin, for example, sees it as 'crucial' for that 'adequate account of omniscient narration' he wishes to provide, observing:

> In treating grammatical person and access to consciousness as the defining features of point of view, traditional accounts of the subject overlooked a crucial distinction. 'Access to consciousness' has two meanings: a third-person narrator can look *into* a character's mind or look *through* it. In the first case, the narrator is the perceiver and the character's mind is perceived. In the second, the character is the perceiver and the world is perceived; the narrator seems to have delegated the function of seeing to the character, as if a first-person story containing phrases such as 'I noticed ... then I realized' had been rewritten in the third person ('she noticed ... then she realized'). (pp. 143–4)

Like 'point of view', 'focalization' is still being defined in terms of the visual (of who can 'look into' or 'look through' a character's mind).[23] Like 'point of view', 'focalization' – together with the related term 'focalizer' – continues to leave unquestioned the unity of the one who sees and of the one who speaks: the 'function' of seeing can simply be 'delegated' by one identity to another, without this apparently having any implications or effects for thinking about the unity of either of these identities as such. For all its 'abstract' attractions (leading Genette to his celebrated spinning out of classifications and sub-classifications around 'internal', 'external', 'fixed', 'variable' and 'multiple focalization' and so on),[24] 'focalization' reinstates the basic problems already outlined in relation to 'point of view'.

Shifting back a hundred years and more, let us drood:

> An ancient English Cathedral town? How can an ancient English Cathedral town be here! The well-known massive grey square tower of its old Cathedral? How can that be here! There is no spike of rusty iron in the air, between the eye and it, from any point of the real prospect. What IS the spike that intervenes, and who has set it up? Maybe, it is set up by the Sultan's orders for the impaling of a horde of Turkish robbers, one by one. It is so, for cymbals clash, and the Sultan goes by to his palace in long procession. Ten thousand scimitars flash in the sunlight, and thrice ten thousand dancing-girls strew flowers. Then, follow white elephants caparisoned in countless gorgeous colors, and infinite in number and attendants. Still, the Cathedral tower rises in the background, where it cannot be, and still no writhing figure is on the grim spike. Stay! Is the spike so low a thing as the rusty spike on the top of a post of an old bedstead that has tumbled all awry? Some vague period of drowsy laughter must be devoted to the consideration of this possibility.
>
> Shaking from head to foot, the man whose scattered consciousness has thus fantastically pieced itself together, at length rises, supports his trembling frame upon his arms, and looks around.[25]

This is 'The Dawn', the beginning of Dickens's *The Mystery of Edwin Drood* (1870), the dawn of 'The Dawn' and of a narrative fiction. Dicken's unfinished, final work opens with a dramatic scatter of questions and exclamations concerned primarily with the visual. What is it that is being presented? Is it really here? From what or whose 'point of view'? Who narrates who perceives or perceives who narrates? By the logic of what Henry James named 'aftersense',[26] some attempt may be made at rationalizing, naturalizing or normativizing what will have been going on. Thus, it may be proposed, Dickens's novel is a work of omniscient narration in which the narrative perspective moves from one character to another, in which the narrator-figure is aware of 'the secret springs of this [or that] dialogue' (p. 97), drifting in and out of what characters are thinking and feeling, in the 'twilight depths' (p. 176) of their waking and sleeping.[27] In particular here, in the opening paragraph of the novel, it is John Jasper, waking up from an opium binge, unsure of where he is or what he is seeing. But to do this would be to disregard, or fail to listen to, what is perhaps most forceful about this passage, namely its strange uncertainties of identification and perception, seeing and hearing. Published forty years and more before the establishment of the conventions of 'point of view' and 'omniscience', the opening of Dickens's novel marks, in effect, a scattering of the logic of such conventional terms of literary criticism. Where is the omniscience in this writing? Is there a place for asking questions in the logic of putative omniscience? Is this a real or hallucinated dawn? If 'The Dawn', which is the dawn of a literary fiction, begins only after itself, in aftersense, when and what is it? And what is happening when, as here, a narrative appears to be referring the force of such questions to the figure of a spike: 'What IS the spike that intervenes, and who has set it up?'

The opening of Dickens's novel seems to remark upon its own origination, its own dawn, upon a spike that appears to have intervened as the very condition of seeing or reading. It prompts the thought that every novel or narrative fiction stages its own dawn: every literary work entails a singular and different kind of seeing, a new readerly eye. The dawn of Dickens's novel is unlike any other, even if it is recognizable as the dawn of another narrative fiction. And it is a mad dawn, a luculent cocktail of the real and hallucinatory. There is a madness of the day (to borrow Maurice Blanchot's phrase) from the very dawn of the dawn (from the very 'the' of 'The Dawn'). Despite the apparent emphasis on the visual, however, there is no sense here of a single, unified 'point of view': rather this mad dawn of writing seems to be explicitly remarking a phantasmagoric destabilization of 'any point of the real prospect'. Moreover, it is not simply a matter of light and vision run wild; it is a question of voice and thus of a new readerly ear. Above all, we are left to wonder of the opening passage of Dickens's novel: who is speaking, allowing all of this to seem 'fantastically pieced together', and in how many voices? To whom should we attribute the source of these numerous questions and exclamations, this 'drowsy laughter'? If, as the opening of The Mystery of Edwin Drood might have us suppose, narrative fiction presents a spiking of vision, there is also a spiking of narrative voice. In or on the verge of aftersense, we hear at least two voices, always at least two, spiked in advance. In order to describe what is going on here, neither 'omniscience' nor 'point of view' nor 'focalization' seems apt. They don't respond to the senses of hallucination, spiking and laughter, to the psychological, tonal and semantic scatteredness of this uncanny Dickensian dawn. They are not adequate to the psychic and textual peculiarity of what is sounding here.

In his book *Given Time: 1. Counterfeit Money*, Jacques Derrida discusses this sort of peculiarity of fictional narrative in terms of the secret, situating it as the very 'truth' of literature. In the context of a reading of Baudelaire's 'Counterfeit Money', a narrative poem which poses the question of whether the narrator's friend gave genuine or counterfeit money to a beggar, he writes:

> [T]here is no sense in wondering what actually happened, what was the true intention of the narrator's friend and the meaning hidden 'behind' his utterances. No more, incidentally, than behind the utterances of the narrator. As these fictional characters have no consistency, no depth beyond their literary phenomenon, the absolute inviolability of the secret they carry depends first of all on the essential superficiality of their phenomenality, on the *too-obvious* of that which they present to view. This inviolability depends on nothing other than the altogether bare device of being-two-to-speak [*l'être-deux-à-parler*] and it is the possibility of non-truth in which every possible truth is held or is made. It thus says the (non-)truth of literature, let us say the secret *of* literature: what literary fiction tells us about the secret, of the (non-) truth of the secret, but also a secret whose possibility assures the possibility of literature.[28]

The essential secret of literature has to do with 'the altogether bare device of being-two-to-speak'. As soon as there is the explicit figuration of someone speaking as someone else, of an author speaking as a narrator, or of a narrator speaking as (or for) a character, there is literature and there is something essentially secret going on. This essentiality of the literary secret is not something concealed, to be revealed or disinterred: it just is, and its being 'altogether bare' is what makes literature possible.

Derrida's work puts out of joint all normative thinking about the 'I' and/ or the identity of the narrator in a work of narrative fiction. Having written at length about narrator-figures and 'I'-focused narratives (especially in the work of Kafka and Blanchot),[29] however, he has shown little interest in the analysis of character in fictional narratives.[30] Is there perhaps a way of grafting his insights concerning secrecy and the 'being-two-to-speak' on to a more conventional critical discourse concerned with, for example, character and character-study?[31] The value of Derrida's account lies most of all, perhaps, in a certain humility: there is a humility before the narrative fiction (it is inexhaustibly cryptic and rigorously, demandingly, lucidly unreadable), but there is also a humbling of origins and horizons. One does not need to invoke omniscience (explicitly religious or not) in order to describe what is going on in an allegedly 'knowing' third-person fictional narrative. Moreover, all the implicit self-assurances of 'point of view' or 'focus of narration' or subject of 'focalization' ('who sees' or 'who speaks') become uncertain, unfamiliar, strange: there is, from start to finish, no purity or propriety of a single 'point of view', no single perspective or position or focus for 'focalization'. Instead there is a different logic of identity, voice and knowledge, encapsulated in the structure of 'being-two-to-speak'.

Wallace Martin has remarked:

> When focalization is not treated as an independent category in the definition of point of view, 'omniscient narration' becomes a kind of dumping-ground filled with a wide range of distinct narrative techniques. A narrator may 'see with' one or more characters, presenting what they see, as if looking over their shoulders. A shift from one position to another does not imply omniscience in the usual sense (access to consciousness), but we have no other word to name the technique. (p. 146)

In the obscure midst of his ocularcentric language ('focalization', 'point of view', '"see[ing] with"', 'presenting what they see', 'looking'), Martin nudges towards a truth: we are dealing with something elusive and resistant to naming, something touching on the very essence of secrecy and literature, something which, by definition, cannot indeed be simply a 'technique'. This 'shift' of perception, thinking and affect whereby a text can enable us to have sudden, but temporary and circumscribed 'access to [the] consciousness' of another – a shift that involves a strange communication (whether one-way or undecidably more-than-one-way) between narrator and character – belongs to a world of telepathy and clairvoyance. Derrida's 'being-two-to-speak' is a telepathic structure. It entails an uncanny logic, a strangeness at the heart of the identity of a narrator or character alike: being-two-to-feel and being-two-to-think, as well as being-two-to-speak.

From Drood to Dalloway:

> 'Who can – what can – ' asked Mrs Dalloway (thinking it was outrageous to be interrupted at eleven o'clock on the morning of the day she was giving a party), hearing a step on the stairs. She heard a hand upon the door. She made to hide her dress, like a virgin protecting chastity, respecting privacy. Now the brass handle slipped. Now the door opened, and in came – for a single second she could not remember what he was called! So surprised she was to see him, so glad, so shy, so utterly taken aback to have Peter Walsh come to her unexpectedly in the morning! (She had not read his letter.)
>
> 'And how are you?' said Peter Walsh, positively trembling; taking both her hands; kissing both her hands. She's grown older, he thought, sitting down. I shan't tell her anything about it, he thought, for she's grown older. She's looking at me, he thought, a sudden embarrassment coming over him, though he had kissed her hands.[32]

To consider this passage from Virginia Woolf's *Mrs Dalloway* (1925) after the Dickens passage may be helpful in various ways, not least in suggesting how 'modernist' the latter seems. As with the opening of *Edwin Drood*, the religious, totalizing notion of ominiscience is not apposite in the context of Woolf's text; 'point of view' is correspondingly reductive and misleading. Neither takes account of the force of what is not conscious, of what is not present, of what is felt without being said, of what is undecidably conscious and unconscious, undecidably the articulated or partially articulated thought or feeling of *more than one* identity or speaker: the narrator, Clarissa Dalloway, Peter Walsh.

Mrs Dalloway is pervasively concerned with 'telepathy' in its so-called conventional, restrictive sense: the relationship between Clarissa and Peter, in particular, is crucially preoccupied with what is described as their 'queer power of communicating without words' (p. 55). But it is not just a question of an apparently telepathic or hyperbolically sympathetic rapport between characters, even though this is a pervasive feature of Woolf's fictional writing in general. It is also a question of telepathic bonds and connections at the most decisive and elementary structural level, between narrator and character.[33] What Derrida calls the secret of literature is in play here – in the undecidability of the structure of being-two-to-speak or being-two-to-feel, in, for example, the exclamation 'Now the door opened, and in came – for a single second she could not remember what he was called!' (p. 37). In the 'single second' of this strange third-person narrative 'now', whose voice is to be heard, whose thought and feeling, whose ability or inability to 'remember'? We move from the mind and body of Clarissa to the mind and body of Peter ('She's grown older, he thought ... She's looking at me, he thought, a sudden embarrassment coming over him'), but in a way that sustains a 'queer power' of uncertainty, of mixed and mixing identities, mixed and mixing inside and outside, detachment and intimacy. The novel thus also engages with a more generalized, less restrictive sense of 'telepathy', opening it up along the lines of a sort of affective and conceptual dissemination: 'tele-' evoking everything that has to do with distance and absence (not least, death), and 'pathos' as mind, feeling and suffering.

We move from a restrictive and no doubt restricting notion of telepathy as something that presupposes the identity and unity of a subject (he or she who receives or transmits a telepathic communication) to a writing of distant minds, apprehensions of feeling and suffering in and of the distance, phantom communications, unconscious, absent or ghostly emotions, without any return to stabilized identities. This is why it becomes misleading, in the context of Woolf's work, even to talk about a narrator: it is not so much a matter of a telepathic narrator (the fiction of someone who has a fixed identity and consciousness, moving in and out of characters' minds and bodies, fundamentally unaffected in its identity by such moves), but rather any identity that one might assign to a narrator would be inseparable from the movements it enacts. It would be more accurate to speak of a fictional narrative like *Mrs Dalloway* in terms of its telepathic narration (as distinct from narrat*or*). The novel is a telepathic network or tunnel-work.[34] 'Tunnelling' – the term Woolf herself proposes as a means of describing the way *Mrs Dalloway* works[35] – is a telepathic principle. It operates at unseen, unforeseen and unforeseeable depths, in darkness, never appearing in its entirety, always lacking totalization or completion, at once conditioning and interrupting the 'now'. Mole-like, it is foreign to both 'omniscience' and 'point of view'.

In order to conclude this tentative historical sketch of the disappearance of omniscience and the case for a rethinking of the role and effects of telepathy in an understanding of modern narrative fiction, we could consider a more contemporary work, Salman Rushdie's *Midnight's Children* (1981).[36] The telepathic here accedes to a new level of explicitness.[37] The novel's canonical significance, indeed, might be judged in terms of how it situates telepathy as a determining figure within so-called 'postcolonial literatures in English', 'magical realism' and 'postmodern fiction'. The narrator, Saleem Sinai, is 'a radio-receiver' (p. 164), his head full of voices: he is telepathic. As Patricia Merivale has remarked, his telepathic powers constitute 'the primary self-reflexive image for the creative imagination in *Midnight's Children*'.[38]

Rushdie himself has pointed out that this novel was initially begun as a third-person omniscient narrative.[39] The very composition of *Midnight's Children* thus dramatizes the untenability of 'omniscient narration'. What the novel instead offers is the metadiscursive trope of 'omniscient third-person' reconfigured as 'telepathic first-person' – in other words, it demonstrates in a new, even unprecedented way the fundamentally telepathic (rather than omniscient) structure of fictional narration more generally. To begin with, Saleem regards his telepathic 'gift' as explicitly corresponding with authorial omniscience: 'I had entered into the illusion of the artist, and thought of the multitudinous realities of the land as the raw unshaped material of my gift. "I can find out any damn thing!" I triumphed, "There isn't a thing I cannot know!"' (p. 174). But this is pointedly an 'illusion', one that ignores or takes refuge from the other, more radical consequences of the telepathic, as the narrator also makes clear: 'If I had not believed myself in control of the flooding multitudes, their massed identities would have annihilated mine' (p. 175). Thus his telepathic gift enables him to realize that death exceeds, dislocates, fragments any thought of omniscience. As he goes on to confirm: 'death … still managed to take me by surprise' (p. 175).

Midnight's Children also offers a provoking account of telepathy in relation to history, historiography and historical narrative. As one of the midnight children born at the same time as 'India's arrival at independence' (15 August 1947), the narrator came into the world already 'heavily embroiled in Fate' (p. 9). Telepathy allows Saleem access to the thoughts and feelings of the other midnight children, but it is also the enabling fiction for an understanding of history itself. To the extent that *Midnight's Children* can be read as a so-called 'historical novel', its conception of history is inextricably bound up with telepathy. It explores the notion that any given moment, indeed the very possibility of time, depends on the fiction that everyone is experiencing the *same moment*, uncannily interconnected, sharing the same 'now'. Rushdie's novel analyses the ways in which history is inevitably conceived in narrative terms, but complicates this with the sense that what we might traditionally think of as history is in some respects itself grounded in telepathic fantasy.

Saleem describes his 'gift' as follows:

> Telepathy, then; the kind of thing you're reading about in the sensational magazines. But I ask for patience – wait. Only wait. It was telepathy; but also more than telepathy. Don't write me off too easily.
>
> Telepathy, then: the inner monologues of all the so-called teeming millions, of masses and classes alike, jostled for space within my head. In the beginning, when I was content to be an audience – before I began to *act* – there was a language problem. The voices babbled in everything from Malayalam to Naga dialects, from the purity of Lucknow Urdu to the Southern slurrings of Tamil. I understood only a fraction of the things being said within the walls of my skull. Only later, when I began to probe, did I learn that below the surface transmissions – the front-of-mind stuff which is what I'd originally been picking up – language faded away, and was replaced by universally intelligible thought-forms which far transcended words ... but that was after I heard, beneath the polyglot frenzy in my head, those other precious signals, utterly different from everything else, most of them faint and distant, like far-off drums whose insistent pulsing eventually broke through the fish-market cacophony of my voices ... those secret, nocturnal calls, like calling out to like ... the unconscious beacons of the children of midnight, signalling nothing more than their existence, transmitting simply: 'I.' From far to the north, 'I.' And to the South East West: 'I.' 'I.' 'And I.'
>
> But I mustn't get ahead of myself. In the beginning, before I broke through to more-than-telepathy, I contented myself with listening; and soon I was able to 'tune' my inner ear to those voices which I could understand; nor was it long before I picked out, from the throng, the voices of my own family; and of Mary Pereira; and of friends, classmates, teachers. In the street, I learned how to identify the mind-stream of passing strangers – the laws of Doppler shift continued to operate in these paranormal realms, and the voices grew and diminished as the strangers passed.
>
> All of which I somehow kept to myself. (pp. 168–9)

This passage foregrounds several issues already at stake in the emergence of 'telepathy' in the late nineteenth century. There is always 'a language problem'. Telepathy is always 'more than telepathy'. The attempted appropriations or transpositions of 'telepathy' into mystical, psychoanalytic or scientific understanding alike ('universally intelligible thought-forms which far transcended words', 'the unconscious beacons of the children of midnight', 'the laws of Doppler shift') remain caught up in 'a language problem' – even as the '-pathy' of 'telepathy' signals the possibilities and desires of an affectivity beyond the normal and thus perhaps 'beyond' any ordinary notion of language.[40] Despite the apparent straightforwardness of the metadiscursive gesture by which Saleem distinguishes his account from 'the kind of thing you're reading about in the sensational magazines', 'telepathy' remains a cryptic and uncanny term, always already other and 'more than itself', figuring a crisis in intelligibility and sensibility, an irreducibly interruptive moment in *reading*.

Hence, perhaps, the curious absurdity and intractable paradoxes of Saleem's account. What allegedly 'far transcended words' is nevertheless claimed to be 'universally intelligible': what is the fiction of the 'universally intelligible' if not some kind of a language? Telepathy, for Saleem, comes down to a sort of minimal (but therefore also maximal) egoism – 'the children of midnight … transmitting simply: "I" … "I." "I." "And I"' (p. 168). The 'And' is crucial here, the last of these 'unconscious beacons' signalling not only 'I', but the inevitable grafting of an 'and' that accompanies any and every 'I': identity is never absolutely pure or singular; it is always iterable, *anded about*. Despite having a mind constantly invaded by the voices and 'mind-stream' of others, Saleem claims that everything in his head is 'simply' his own ('All of which I somehow kept to myself'). In this respect, *Midnight's Children* is strikingly consonant with George Eliot's *The Lifted Veil*. Both are concerned with the revelation of a 'suppressed egoism' concealed beneath everything. Both could thus be said to subscribe to the conservative conception of telepathy as something that is figured on the basis of the assumed unity and identity of a subject. But, as we have seen, this conception is necessarily haunted by a more radical, indeed strictly incalculable notion of telepathy as (in the words of Claudette Sartiliot) what 'breaches the discreteness and unity of the subject, as well as the systems of thought derived from it'.[41]

Some sense of the ineluctable modality of the telepathic, as a characteristic of narrative fiction in general and of modern fiction in particular, provides a basis for thinking literary narrative differently. It is not a matter of asking, 'Are there any examples of telepathy in this narrative?', for there are no literary fictional works that do not involve a thinking of telepathy. The question is rather: 'How does this narrative engage with the telepathic, and how are we as readers already embroiled in it?'

The obligation, desire or anxiety to provide some sort of metadiscursive level, frame or register within which to talk about narrative fiction has no doubt been crucial in the production and institutionalization of such terms as 'omniscience', 'point of view' and 'focalization'. These terms are also self-remarking, plotting and defining the space of a certain discourse. In other words, they perhaps describe critical and theoretical writing rather better than they do literary works themselves. At the very least it may be suggested that they leave their traces as, for example, an implicit drive towards epistemological mastery over the literary work (omniscience) and an upholding of the rhetoric and culture of the authoritative, autonomous, individual subject-as-critic (point of view, focalization). All of these institutionalised terms ('omniscience', 'point of view', 'focalization') are in fact critical fallacies. We have attempted to sketch some of the possibilities for a new and different historical understanding of narrative fiction, from at least George Eliot to the present.

We have to reckon with telepathy as a concept and effect intimately bound up with writing and death, the spectral and unprogrammable. 'Telepathy' calls to be considered perhaps first of all as a *literary phenomenon*, rather than as a psychological problem.[42] There is a kind of madness or 'magical thinking' in literature, and in particular in the narrative scenario of being-two-to-speak. The uncanny nature of narrative fiction is indissociable from the strange telepathic reality of being-two-to-speak or being-two-to-feel: the question remains how to countersign this peculiar feature in a critical, faithful and productive way. New kinds of critical writing concerned with this 'telepathy effect' would seek to elucidate, to affirm and keep generatively open the strange uncertainties of identity, thought and feeling in the world of narrative fiction.[43]

NOTES

1   Dorrit Cohn, *Transparent Minds: Narrative Modes for Presenting Consciousness in Fiction* (Princeton: Princeton University Press, 1978), p. 7. See also Käte Hamburger, *The Logic of Literature*, trans. Marilyn J. Rose (Bloomington: Indiana University Press, 1973), p. 83.

2   In this respect it seems especially appropriate, if ironic, that Mieke Bal should make lamenting reference in her recent Preface to the Second Edition of *Narratology: Introduction to the Theory of Narrative* (Toronto: University of Toronto Press, 1997) to narratology's 'positivistic claims, formalist limitations, and inaccessible, idiosyncratic jargon' (p. xiv). The present account shares Bal's stated desire to focus more carefully on the strange nature of

narrative fiction as such. She rightly notes the irony that, in recent years, 'with the growth of the study of narrative, interest in what makes narratives "be" or "come across" has only declined' (ibid.).

3   Quoted in Cohn, *Transparent Minds*, p. 8.

4   Freud evidently subscribes to the Romantic conception of the author as godlike. There is no obvious attempt, either in the essay on 'The Uncanny' or elsewhere in his writings on literature, to think through questions and problems concerning distinctions between author and narrator in this context. Doubtless there *is* something potentially uncanny about the notion of author (or narrator) as godlike. This is perhaps most clearly suggested in 'The Uncanny' when Freud evokes a sense of the eerie machinations by which the reader becomes a sort of automaton, controlled and manipulated in whatever way the 'imaginative writer' may choose. He writes: 'The imaginative writer has this licence among many others, that he [*sic*] can select his world of representation so that it either coincides with the realities we are familiar with or departs from them in what particulars he pleases. *We accept his ruling in every case*' (U, p. 373, emphasis added). He goes on to refer to the '*peculiarly* directive power' (p. 375, Freud's emphasis) of the 'storyteller' (this last term characteristically by-passing any problems or questions concerning distinctions between 'author' and 'narrator'). This uncanny power is perhaps difficult to dissociate, in Freud's work, from the significance that he gives to the notion of the 'omnipotence of thoughts'. In *Totem and Taboo* (1913; *PFL*, 13: 43–224), we may recall, Freud talks of how he has borrowed this phrase, 'omnipotence of thoughts', from a patient (the 'Rat Man'). Freud remarks on the essentially 'uncanny' nature of this idea: the 'omnipotence of thoughts' constitutes, for Freud, the 'principle governing magic' (see *PFL*, 13: 143–4 and 144, n. 1). 'Omnipotence' and 'omniscience' are not identical, of course, but there is perhaps a crucial connection here for thinking about what may be called the 'magic of literature'. In the context of our own concerns, it is striking that Freud characterizes the 'world of magic' in terms of a specifically telepathic logic. Evidently playing upon the inscription of 'distance' in 'tele-', he writes: 'Since distance is of no importance in thinking – since what lies furthest apart both in time and space can without difficulty be comprehended in a single act of consciousness – so, too, the world of magic has a telepathic disregard for spatial distance and treats past situations as though they were present' (*Totem and Taboo*, *PFL*, 13: 143). Or as he remarks a little earlier in the same text, in a formulation that bears a special ironic resonance in the context of our concerns in the present chapter: 'telepathy is taken for granted' (p. 138).

5   See Jonathan Culler, *Literary Theory: A Very Short Introduction* (New York: Oxford University Press, 1997), p. 91.

6   Jonathan Culler, 'Political Criticism: Confronting Religion', in his *Framing the Sign: Criticism and Its Institutions* (Oxford: Basil Blackwell, 1988), p. 80.

7   J. Hillis Miller, *The Disappearance of God: Five Nineteenth-century Writers* (London and Cambridge, MA: Oxford University Press and Belknap Press, 1963).

8   James Boswell, *Life of Johnson* (London: Oxford University Press, 1953), p. 730.

9   See Robert Scholes and Robert Kellogg, *The Nature of Narrative* (New York: Oxford University Press, 1966), pp. 272–3.

10   Thus they propose, for example, that 'the authoritarian monism of the fully omniscient mode of narration has become less and less tenable in modern times, while the multifarious relativism of that same mode has seemed increasingly appropriate' (p. 276).

11   There is a principle of telepathic proliferation here. If a narrator inhabits (or is inhabited by) only one character at a time, the scenario is telepathic. If a narrative presents an inhabiting of

more than one character at a time, the telepathic dimension only becomes more accentuated: there is telepathy *between* characters. In neither case, however, is it a matter of omniscience.

12 George Eliot, *The Lifted Veil*, with an Afterword by Beryl Gray (London: Virago, 1985), p. 1. Further page references are given parenthetically in the text.

13 See Beryl Gray, Afterword to *The Lifted Veil*, p. 84; and also the chapter on George Eliot, entitled 'On Second Sight', in Nicholas Royle, *Telepathy and Literature: Essays on the Reading Mind* (Oxford and Cambridge, Mass.: Blackwell, 1991), pp. 84–110.

14 Wallace Martin, *Recent Theories of Narrative* (Ithaca: Cornell University Press, 1986), p. 146. Further page references will be incorporated in the main body of the text.

15 'First Report of the Literary Committee' (9 December 1882) by W. F. Barrett, C. C. Massey, Rev. W. Stainton Moses, Frank Podmore, Edmund Gurney and Frederic W. H. Myers, in *Proceedings of the Society for Psychical Research*, vol. 1, pt 2 (London: Trübner, 1883), 81.

16 See Ernest Jones, *Sigmund Freud: Life and Work*, vol. 3 (London: Hogarth Press, 1957), p. 462.

17 Jacques Derrida, 'Telepathy', trans. Nicholas Royle, in *Deconstruction: A Reader*, ed. Martin McQuillan (Edinburgh: Edinburgh University Press, 2000), pp. 496–526: here, p. 505.

18 Gerald Prince, *A Dictionary of Narratology* (Lincoln: University of Nebraska, 1987), p. 73.

19 See Henry James, *Literary Criticism: French Writers, Other European Writers, The Prefaces to the New York Edition* (New York: Library of America, 1984), pp. 1035–341; J. W. Beach, *The Method of Henry James* (New Haven: Yale University Press, 1918); Percy Lubbock, *The Craft of Fiction* (London: Jonathan Cape, 1921). A by now classic historical survey is Norman Friedman, 'Point of View in Fiction: The Development of a Critical Concept', *PMLA*, vol. 70 (1955), 1160–84. Wallace Martin's remarks on omniscience appear in a chapter entitled 'Points of View on Point of View': see *Recent Theories of Narrative*, pp. 130–51.

20 Lubbock, *The Craft of Fiction*, p. 65.

21 Lubbock, *The Craft of Fiction*, p. 115. See also p. 120.

22 See Gérard Genette, *Narrative Discourse*, trans. Jane E. Lewin (Oxford: Basil Blackwell, 1980), p. 189. Genette notes that his use of the term is in turn indebted to Cleanth Brooks's and Robert Penn Warren's phrase 'focus of narration' in their *Understanding Fiction* (1943).

23 Cf. Shlomith Rimmon-Kenan's argument that 'the term "focalization" is not free of optical-photographic connotations, and – like point of view – its purely visual sense has to be broadened to include cognitive, emotive and ideological orientation'. See her *Narrative Fiction: Contemporary Poetics* (London: Methuen, 1983), p. 71. It should perhaps be stressed that it is not our aim here simply to dismiss the importance of the visual in thinking about narrative fiction, but rather it is to argue for a more affectively and sensorily complex and differentiated conception.

24 See Genette, *Narrative Discourse*, pp. 189 ff.

25 Charles Dickens, *The Mystery of Edwin Drood* (Harmondsworth: Penguin, 1974), p. 37. Further page references are to this edition.

26 Henry James, Preface to *What Maisie Knew*, in *Literary Criticism: French Writers, Other European Writers, The Prefaces to the New York Edition* (New York: Library of America, 1984), p. 1165.

27 With respect to this last, one thinks especially perhaps of the extraordinary account of 'the unconscious Durdles', both prior to and during sleep: see *The Mystery of Edwin Drood*, pp. 155 ff.

28 Jacques Derrida, *Given Time: 1. Counterfeit Money*, trans. Peggy Kamuf (Chicago: Chicago University Press, 1992), p. 153.

29 On Kafka see for example 'Before the Law', trans. Avital Ronell and Christine Roulston, in Jacques Derrida, *Acts of Literature*, ed. Derek Attridge (New York: Routledge, 1992), pp. 181–220;

on Blanchot, see for example 'The Law of Genre', trans. Avital Ronell, in *Acts of Literature*, pp. 221–52, and 'Living On: Border Lines', trans. James Hulbert, in Harold Bloom et al., *Deconstruction and Criticism* (New York: Seabury, 1979), pp. 75–176.

30   His standoffishness in this context is suggested by the remark that he has 'never drawn great enjoyment from fiction, from reading novels, for example, beyond the pleasure taken in analyzing the play of writing, or else certain naive movements of identification'. See Derrida, *Acts of Literature*, ed. Derek Attridge (New York: Routledge, 1992), p. 39.

31   Conventional critical discourse here might be said to include the work of Mikhail Bakhtin. The concepts of polyphony, heteroglossia and dialogism have no doubt significantly altered English-language critical perceptions of narrative fiction and its workings over the past two decades in particular. Approaching literary narrative in terms of the telepathic offers a new and different, though in some respects complementary framework. The importance of Bakhtin's work lies in its foregrounding of the social nature of language-use in a literary context. The concern of the present chapter is with what might be called Bakhtin back to front, with the possibilities of a *socius* conceived *in the wake of* the telepathic.

32   Virginia Woolf, *Mrs Dalloway* (London: Granada, 1976), p. 37. Further page references are given parenthetically in the text.

33   For a reading of one of Woolf's works of short fiction in this context, see 'A Walk in "Kew Gardens"', in *Telepathy and Literature*, pp. 111–20.

34   A similar point could indeed be made about *The Mystery of Edwin Drood*, with its crypt-like narrative passages, constructions and excavations. To reiterate the broader historical argument here, critical terms such as 'omniscience' and 'point of view' (or 'focalization') were *already* anachronistic, inappropriate and reductive by the time of *Edwin Drood*, let alone by the time of modernist fiction.

35   In a diary entry for Monday, 15 October 1923, and in a spirit of explicit disagreement with Lubbock's assumptions about writing and conscious control, she writes of *Mrs Dalloway*: 'It took me a year's groping to discover my tunnelling process, by which I tell the past by instalments, as I have need of it. This is my prime discovery so far; and the fact that I've been so long finding it proves, I think, how false Percy Lubbock's doctrine is – that you can do this sort of thing consciously.' See Virginia Woolf, *A Writer's Diary* (London: Granta, 1976), pp. 66–7. In an earlier entry (30 August), she describes how she 'dig[s] out beautiful caves behind [her] characters … The idea is that the caves shall connect and each comes to daylight at the present moment' (p. 65).

36   Salman Rushdie, *Midnight's Children* (London: Pan Books, 1982). Further references are given parenthetically in the text.

37   'New', for example, in comparison with E. M. Forster's telepathically preoccupied *A Passage to India* (1924), a novel that is in this and various other ways an important intertext for *Midnight's Children*. For a reading of *A Passage to India* in terms of telepathy, see Nicholas Royle, *E. M. Forster* (Plymouth: Northcote House, 1999), pp. 72–84.

38   Patricia Merivale, 'Saleem Fathered by Oscar: *Midnight's Children*, Magic Realism, and *The Tin Drum*', in *Magical Realism: Theory, History, Community*, eds Lois Parkinson Zamora and Wendy B. Faris (Durham, NC: Duke University Press, 1995), p. 339.

39   See John Haffenden, *Novelists in Interview* (London: Methuen, 1985), pp. 237–8.

40   For a sense of Rushdie's own commitment to the mystical see his comments on 'trans-cendence' in the essay 'Is Nothing Sacred?': 'What I mean by transcendence is that flight of the human spirit outside the confines of its material, physical existence which all of us, secular or religious, experience on at least a few occasions … The soaring quality of

transcendence, the sense of being more than oneself, of being in some way joined to the whole of life, is by its nature short-lived. Not even the visionary or mystical experience ever lasts very long. It is for art to capture that experience, to offer it to, in the case of literature, its readers.' See Salman Rushdie, *Imaginary Homelands: Essays and Criticism 1981–1991* (London: Granta Books, 1991), p. 421.

41 See Claudette Sartiliot, 'Telepathy and Writing in Jacques Derrida's *Glas*', *Paragraph*, vol. 12, no. 3 (1989), 215.

42 The only reference that Freud makes to telepathy in 'The Uncanny' would seem, at least indirectly, to corroborate this view. Discussing E. T. A. Hoffmann's *Die Elixiere des Teufels* (*The Devil's Elixir*), he refers to the novel's emphasis on 'mental processes leaping from one [character] to another – by what we should call telepathy – so that one possesses knowledge, feelings and experience in common with the other' (U, p. 356). Freud is using the term 'telepathy' to describe the relation between characters; but his phrasing ('one possesses knowledge, feelings and experience in common with the other') would also be apt for what we have been saying about the relation between character and narrator. It strangely anticipates – or recalls – the definition of narrative fiction from Dorrit Cohn with which we began.

43 'Telepathy effect' is a phrase used by J. Hillis Miller in a statement published on the back cover of *Telepathy and Literature*: 'Royle argues that literature as a whole is a "discursive formation" penetrated through and through by what he calls a "telepathy effect".' The author of *Telepathy and Literature* encountered these words not long before receiving final proofs of the book. He looked through his typescript in vain for the presence of the phrase in question. Feeling that Miller had understood his work far better than he himself ever might, Royle inserted, at the end of a sentence in a chapter on *Wuthering Heights*, the 'missing' supplement: 'Thus the telepathic, foretelling, foretune-telling, mad network of narrators and narrating that constitutes the text, weaving and crisscrossing it: telepathy effect' (p. 53).

20
Phantom text

Nihilism stands at the door: whence comes this uncanniest of all guests? Point of departure: it is an error to consider 'social distress' or 'physiological degeneration' or, worse, corruption, as the *cause* of nihilism. Distress, whether of the soul, body, or intellect, cannot of itself give birth to nihilism (i.e., the radical repudiation of value, meaning, and desirability). Such distress always permits a variety of interpretations. Rather: it is in one particular interpretation, the Christian-moral one, that nihilism is rooted. (Friedrich Nietzsche)[1]

How can [one] claim to *prove* an absence of archive? How does one prove in general an absence of archive, if not in relying on classical norms (presence/absence of literal and explicit reference to this or to that, to a this or to a that which one supposes to be identical to themselves, and simply absent, *actually* absent, if they are not simply present, *actually* present; how can one not, and why not, take into account *unconscious*, and more generally *virtual* archives? (Jacques Derrida)[2]

As remarked at the beginning, this study is haunted by the many texts that have explicitly addressed the question of the uncanny, especially in relation to the ghostly. One of the most obvious of its inexorable revenants is Jacques Derrida's *Spectres of Marx*.[3] In the following few pages, I propose to consider not only what *Spectres of Marx* has to say about spectrality and phantoms, but also what it does *not* say, or says (perhaps) without saying. *Spectres of Marx* is concerned with another thinking of the spaces of academic research and scholarship. Scholars and phantoms make strange bedfellows. As Derrida remarks, near the beginning of the book:

There has never been a *scholar* who really, as such, deals with phantoms [*fantômes*]. A traditional *scholar* does not believe in phantoms – nor in all that one might call the virtual space of spectrality. There has never been a *scholar* who, as such, does not believe in the sharp distinction between the real and the unreal, the actual and the inactual, the living and the non-living, being and non-being ('to be or not to be', in the conventional reading), in the opposition between what is present and what is not, for example in the form of objectivity. Beyond this opposition, there is, for the *scholar*, only the hypothesis of a school of thought, theatrical fiction, literature, and speculation. (p. 11/33)[4]

This quotation provides, in a sense, the framework of Derrida's book. The context, as indicated by the parenthetical reference 'to be or not to be', is that of a reading of Shakespeare's *Hamlet*. Derrida is meditating on Marcellus's words in the face of the Ghost of Hamlet's father: 'Thou art a scholar, speak to it, Horatio.'

He describes this member of the King's Guard as suffering from the 'Marcellus complex', that is to say a blindness to, or ignorance of, that 'singularity of a place of speech, of a place of experience, and of a link of filiation, places and links from which alone one may address oneself to the phantom' (p. 12). Derrida is here focusing on something which has become particularly evident in his more recent writing, namely the uncanniness of solitude, the experience of the impossible, the aporias of what happens in 'my life' as 'what only happens to me'. ('It only happens to me' is an insistence made in the autobiothanatoheterographical text entitled 'Circumfession'.)[5] Or as he puts it elsewhere in *Spectres of Marx*: 'everyone reads, acts, writes with *his or her* ghosts' (p. 139).

'"Thou art a scholar, speak to it, Horatio" ... ' (p. 279): these are also the last words of *Spectres of Marx* and they mark, in effect, a turning back to the reader or listener, a return to or revenance of the Marcellus complex but now, perhaps, in a more critical, even deconstructive form. Marcellus's apostrophe, then, provides the curtain on Derrida's book. It is with the notion of the phantom that the book concludes. Derrida asks:

> Could one *address oneself in general* if already some phantom did not come back? If he [*sic*] loves justice at least, the 'scholar' [*le 'savant'*] of the future, the 'intellectual' of tomorrow should learn it and from the phantom. He should learn to live by learning not how to make conversation with the phantom but how to talk with him, with her, how to let it speak or how to give it back speech, even if it is in oneself, in the other, in the other in oneself: they are always *there*, spectres, even if they do not exist, even if they are no longer, even if they are not yet. They give us to rethink the 'there' as soon as we open our mouths ... (p. 176/279)

These passages from *Spectres of Marx* suggest why one might want to describe Derrida as both scholarly and unscholarly. On the one hand, like the traditional scholar, he upholds 'the sharp distinction between the real and the unreal, the actual and the inactual, the living and the non-living, being and non-being'. It is in this context that he says of phantoms: 'of course they do not exist' (174). On the other hand, unlike the traditional scholar, Derrida looks towards a new notion of scholarship, other spaces of intellectual thinking, spaces that can be called affirmatively spectral or phantomistic. It is in this context that he says of phantoms: 'of course they do not exist, *so what?*' (p. 174, my emphasis); and that he argues that 'the logic of spectrality' is 'inseparable from the very motif ... of deconstruction' (p. 178, n. 3). There *are* phantom effects, even if phantoms do not exist. The unscholarly or perhaps one should say the ascholarly dimensions of deconstruction are linked to this spectrality or phantomistics. If beyond 'the opposition between what is present and what is not ... there is, for the *scholar*, only the hypothesis of a school of thought, theatrical fiction, literature, and speculation', deconstruction would be concerned with what may be uncannily glimpsed there, with new ways of thinking about 'schools of thought', 'theatrical fiction', 'literature' and 'speculation'. What today are the chances of writing *as* phantom text?

Everything begins by coming back to the question of mourning. Of mourning Derrida writes:

> It consists always in attempting to ontologize remains, to make them present, in the first place by *identifying* the bodily remains and by *localizing* the dead (all ontologization, all semanticization – philosophical, hermeneutical, or psychoanalytical – finds itself caught up in this work of mourning but, as such, it does not yet think it; we are posing here the question of the spectre, to the spectre, whether it be Hamlet's or Marx's, on this near side of such thinking). One has to know ... *who* and *where*, to know whose body it really is and what place it occupies – for it must stay in its place. In a safe place ... Nothing could be worse, for the work of mourning, than confusion or doubt: one *has to know* who is buried where – and *it is necessary* (to know – to make certain) that, in what remains of him, *he remain there*. Let him stay there and move no more! (p. 9)

This passage signals towards a certain phantomistic topography in *Spectres of Marx*, concerning what Derrida does *not* say in this book, areas of silence, unspoken or unspeakable. In a sense what I want to do here is elucidate in another way what has been called symptomatic reading, to unfold in a perhaps new way Pierre Macherey's thesis that 'The speech of a book comes from a certain silence ... [T]he book is necessarily accompanied by a *certain absence*, without which it would not exist.'[6] Such a phantomistic topography perhaps calls for a new terminology: neither 'subtext' nor 'intertext', neither 'source' nor 'precursor' seem to me appropriate critical vocabulary for the identification of what would be, perhaps, encrypted in this topography. In a text called 'Living On/ Border Lines', dating from 1979, Derrida declared: 'One text reads another ... Each "text" is a machine with multiple reading heads for other texts'.[7] *Spectres of Marx* provokes an elaboration on this claim and in particular it leads us towards an exploration of the effects or effectivities of *texts which do not exist*. It is a question of a feeling, to begin with, a feeling I have about the passage on mourning just cited and about the strange 'place' (atopical topos) of the work of Nicolas Abraham and Maria Torok in relation to this. In particular my feeling has to do here with Abraham's notion of anasemia as what is on the 'near side' (to pick up Derrida's phrase) of meaning, as what in some sense precedes 'all semanticization', 'psychoanalytical' or otherwise.

Although Derrida has written a book about spectres, spirits, ghosts and phantoms, nowhere in *Spectres of Marx* does he discuss the writings of Nicolas

Abraham and Maria Torok.[8] Given the amount of attention he gives to their work in other writings, Derrida's apparent silence on Abraham and Torok in *Spectres of Marx*, and in particular his silence about Abraham's so-called theory of the phantom, and even more particularly Abraham's theory as expounded specifically in relation to *Hamlet*, seems rather remarkable. Let me stress that I am not interested here in making hypothetical pronouncements about Derrida's 'debt' to or swerve away from Abraham, or about Abraham's theory of the phantom as a precursor, or even as an intertext, for Derrida's book. Rather I am interested in the way in which Abraham's theory might itself be said to constitute a phantom which, in motioning us towards a spectral topography in *Spectres of Marx*, might serve as a sort of model for thinking about texts in general in terms of phantom effects. It is a question, then, of phantom texts – textual phantoms which do not necessarily have the solidity or objectivity of a quotation, an intertext or explicit, acknowledged presence and which do not in fact come to rest *anywhere*. Phantom texts are fleeting, continually moving on, leading us away, like Hamlet's Ghost, to some other scene or scenes which we, as readers, cannot anticipate.

In his essay 'Notes on the Phantom: A Complement to Freud's Metapsychology' (*SK*, pp. 171–6), Abraham begins with the idea that 'the theme of the dead – who, having suffered repression by their family or society, cannot enjoy, even in death, a state of authenticity – appears to be omnipresent (whether overtly expressed or disguised) on the fringes of religions and, failing that, in rational systems' (p. 171). His emphasis is on the fact that 'the "phantom", whatever its form, is nothing but an invention of the living'. His argument is that phantom effects can arise if (and, it would seem, only if) 'the dead were shamed during their lifetime or … took unspeakable secrets to the grave'. The phantom is an invention of the living in so far as it embodies 'the gap produced in us by the concealment of some part of a loved object's life … what haunts are not the dead, but the gaps left within us by the secrets of others' (p. 171).

Abraham puts strange flesh on, or perhaps takes strange flesh off this argument in 'The Phantom of Hamlet' (*SK*, pp. 191–205), his posthumously published fictional supplementary Sixth Act to Shakespeare's play. 'The Phantom of Hamlet' was written, Abraham tells us in his introductory statement ('The Intermission of "Truth"', pp. 187–90), in response to his sense that 'The final scene of the *Tragedy of Hamlet* does not close the dramatic action, it simply cuts it off' (p. 187). He proposes that the characters in Shakespeare's play are, in fact, the 'puppets of a phantom' (p. 188). 'The Phantom of Hamlet' is a short text, composed in decasyllabic verse, in which the ghost of Hamlet's father returns and this time is obliged to confirm that the secret he took to the grave was not his death at the hands of his brother Claudius but another secret, namely the fact that, in collusion with Polonius, he had thirty years earlier murdered the father of Fortinbras. With this fictional supplement Abraham seeks to expose and transform that 'state of mind' which in Shakespeare's play (he says) 'forces itself upon us like an inescapable necessity emanating from some unknown source' (pp. 187–8). 'The Phantom of Hamlet' is Abraham's attempt to 'reduce the phantom'; 'to "cure" the *public* of a covert neurosis [which] the *Tragedy of Hamlet* has, for centuries, inflicted upon it' (p. 190); to exorcize the crypto-phantomatic power imposed on our culture by the silences in Shakespeare's play.

Abraham's account of the phantom, especially in the form of this poetic supplement to Shakespeare's *Hamlet*, is very different from Derrida's. I would suggest that there are at least four ways in which it would be necessary to distinguish between Abraham and Derrida here:

(1) Derrida's conception of revenants, spirits, ghosts or phantoms is specifically bound up with an experience of language as an experience of the impossible. If, as he says in *Spectres of Marx*, 'one cannot speak of generations of skulls or spirits ... except on the condition of language' (p. 9), this speech is caught up in a ghostly prosopopoeia: we are ourselves spoken by skulls and spirits. Whereas for Abraham and Torok, in *The Wolf Man's Magic Word*, there is the supposition of a magic word ('tieret') at the heart of a psychoanalytic treatment or case-history, for Derrida there is rather what he calls 'the *cryptic* structure of the ultimate "referent"'.[9] If deconstruction is inseparable from a logic of spectrality, it is because the trace or différance is ghostly: all language, every manifestation of meaning, is the phantom effect of a trace which is neither present nor absent, but which is the condition of possibility of the opposition of presence and absence. The trace cannot become present, or absent, in its essence: it is the revenant at the origin.

(2) In his essay 'Notes on the Phantom', Abraham's emphasis is quite heavily on what passes down from generation to generation – he speaks for example of '"phantomogenic" words' that can 'rule an entire family's history and function as the tokens of its pitiable articulations'. He contends that 'the "phantom effect" progressively fades during its transmission from one generation to the next and that, finally, it disappears' (p. 176). Derrida's position appears less teleological and less fixed. As if in passing, he remarks at one point in *Spectres of Marx* that ghosts 'trick consciousness and skip generations' (p. 30). However tacitly, Derrida's account breaks up the family, interrupts the logic of the linear, skips successiveness. His focus in *Spectres of Marx* is rather on anachronism, contretemps, time out of joint.[10]

(3) Derrida's conception of the logic of exorcism is in many respects less benign than Abraham's. In 'The Phantom of Hamlet', for example, Abraham is concerned with an 'exorcism' that may lead (as he puts it) to 'a higher wisdom about oneself and the world of humans at large' (p. 189). Derrida's account of ghosts and phantoms in *Spectres of Marx* would call, in effect, for a subsuming of the Abrahamic conception within a broader, distinctly less humanist and more troubling perspective in which ghosts do not die and exorcism is in some sense impossible. For Derrida, 'to exorcize' is 'to attempt to destroy and to disavow' – 'exorcism consists in repeating in the mode of incantation that the dead man [or woman] is really dead ' (p. 48). We may here recall the case reported in January 1996 of a sixty-one-year-old woman in Cambridgeshire, Daphne Banks, pronounced dead by her GP, but discovered, in 'her' body bag, to be still breathing.[11] Uncanny: to be, or not to be, buried alive. To 'pronounce dead' is, like exorcism, a performative. As Derrida points out, in *Spectres of Marx*: it is 'a performative that seeks to reassure but first of all to reassure itself by assuring itself, for nothing is less sure, that what one would like to see dead is indeed dead. It speaks in the name of life, it claims to know what that is' (p. 48). At issue here, among other things, is a strange but compelling shift in the definition and concept of murder. It is a question of rethinking the teleological work of mourning, such as one encounters in the writings of Freud or in Hamlet's uncle Claudius (mourning must have an end, it is something that we should know how to 'throw to earth', as Claudius says [1.2.106]). As Derrida observes in a related essay on *Hamlet*, entitled 'The Time Is Out of Joint', such a notion of mourning 'presumes ... that mourning depends on us, in us, and not on the other in us. It presumes above all a knowledge, the knowledge of the date. One must indeed know *when*: *at what instant* mourning began. One must indeed know *at what moment* death took place, really took place, and this is always the moment of a murder.'[12] To pronounce dead is to collude in murder. To pronounce dead or to exorcize, for Derrida, is '*effectively* a performative. But here effectivity phantomalizes itself' (p. 48). To exorcize is not to escape from phantom-effects, rather the reverse.[13]

(4) There are at the same time various respects in which Derrida's account of ghosts and phantoms is perhaps *more* benign, more open than Abraham's. This distinction is perhaps most evident in relation to the temporality of the phantom or ghost. For Abraham the phantom comes from the past. For Derrida it comes at least as much from the future: 'It is a proper characteristic of the spectre, if there is any, that no one can be sure if by returning it testifies to a living past or to a living future ... [A] phantom never dies, it remains always to come and to come-back' (p. 99). 'The thinking of the spectre',

he proposes, 'contrary to what good sense leads us to believe, signals toward the future' (p. 196, n. 39).

With these four distinctions in mind, I want to ask: What happens if one lets Abraham's account of the phantom come back, filtering itself through the singularity of Derrida's account, into a space which does not exist but which might be said nevertheless to appear 'through' *Spectres of Marx*? Into what space of virtual spectrality might a reading of Abraham-through-Derrida lead us? In particular, what happens if one follows the sense that *Spectres of Marx* is to a large degree silently, but perhaps all the more powerfully on that account, a book as much about Christianity as about Marxism, and above all a book that fastens on the notion of Jesus Christ as the most spectral force in politics today, in the 'world war', as Derrida calls it, that is all around us, even if it has its most concentrated focus on the question of 'the appropriation of Jerusalem' (p. 58)?

If there is a publication which (alongside *The Interpretation of Dreams* or *Finnegans Wake* or *Of Grammatology*) has claims to being among the most devastating texts to have appeared in the twentieth century, it might be *The Nag Hammadi Library*.[14] It consists of twelve books, plus eight leaves taken from a thirteenth, altogether amounting to fifty-two tractates. The manuscripts themselves are now in the Coptic Museum in Cairo and some readers may already be familiar, for example through the work of Elaine Pagels, with the bizarre history of the discovery of these texts in December 1945 by a cannibalistic murderer called Muhammad Ali of the al-Samman clan in the Naj Hammadi region of Upper Egypt.[15] Among the more striking details of the process by which these fourth century papyrus books came to be disseminated across the world and finally brought back together in Cairo and eventually published in a single volume in English are the fact that most of Codex I was acquired in May 1952 by the Jung Institute in Zurich and initially published as the 'Jung Codex' (the history and legacies of psychoanalysis are thus already implicated here, in the most material fashion) and the fact that Muhammad's mother, Umm-Ahmad, later admitted that she'd used up a fair amount of the papyrus for (one hastens to add, non-cannibalistic) cooking purposes at home.

The Nag Hammadi library is in Coptic, though thought to have been originally written in Greek. There is evidence in the texts themselves that they were intended to have been preserved in a jar in a mountain until the end of time. They are, in Freudian terms perhaps, uncanny texts *par excellence* – texts which ought to have remained secret and hidden but have come to light. The texts in the Nag Hammadi library transform the history and conception of Gnosticism and early Christianity. Of particular interest in the present context is the evidence furnished by some of these tractates showing that certain features originally thought to be characteristic of Christian Gnosticism are in fact non-Christian in their provenance. James M. Robinson refers to two of the tractates, 'The Three Steles of Seth' and 'The Paraphrase of Shem', as being 'without Christian ingredients' (p. 7). Perhaps most dramatic, however, is the double-tractate published as 'Eugnostos the Blessed' and 'The Sophia of Jesus Christ' (pp. 220–43), in which the latter emerges in a particularly explicit fashion as a fictional reworking into a Christian discourse of the pre-Christian discourse of the former.

Theologians have not, to date, rushed into the breach or into the strange aporias hereby generated. Thus Elaine Pagels, for example, argues that the Nag Hammadi library enables us to 'begin to see that what we call Christianity – and what we identify as Christian tradition – actually represents only a small section of specific sources, chosen from among dozens of others' (p. xxxv). While acknowledging that the discovery of the Nag Hammadi texts makes it more difficult than ever to argue the case for which of the sayings of Jesus may or may not be 'genuinely authentic' (p. 148) – in other words, while implicitly recognizing that the Nag Hammadi library fundamentally disturbs and even phantomizes the basis on which the teachings of Jesus have been read and understood – Pagels's account in her book *The Gnostic Gospels* remains a curiously static and conservative one. In her Conclusion she asserts that 'the discoveries at Nag Hammadi reopen fundamental questions. They suggest that Christianity might have developed in very different directions – or that Christianity as we know it might not have survived at all' (p. 142). History, in the eyes of Elaine Pagels, is finished, achieved, already written. Rather than speculate on the 'very different directions' in which Christianity 'might [or might not] have developed', would it not be more critical and productive to consider how the discoveries at Nag Hammadi *change* history by transforming our conception of Christianity *to date* and *in the present*? The history of Christianity in this sense would lie in 'the opening of the future itself' (to borrow a phrase from Derrida).[16]

It can perhaps readily be acknowledged that the Nag Hammadi library constitutes a scandal in its own right: it phantomizes our reading of the New Testament and suspends the possibility of Christianity 'as we know it'. Let us conclude with the evocation (in the strong sense of that word: to evocalize or call up from the dead) of another, perhaps differently scandalous text, a phantom text generated out of Abraham, Derrida and the Nag Hammadi library. This text does not have a name. It might be said to belong to a virtual archive, a palimpsestuous phantom text, an effect of the anasemic, spectral topography I have been trying to describe in these few pages.

This text is fragmentary. Like 'The Sophia of Jesus Christ' (*NHL*, pp. 220–43), it presents us with a revelation discourse spoken by Christ to Mary Magdalen after coming back from the dead. And like 'The Gospel of the Egyptians' (*NHL*, pp. 208–19) and 'Allogenes' (*NHL*, pp. 490–500), it refers to the idea of the text itself being concealed in a mountain until the end of time or until the coming of the 'dreadful one'. It reads as follows:

> And Jesus came back and appeared unto Mary Magdalen and this woman was greatly afraid. Fear not, Mary, saith the Lord; I am come as a spirit to comfort you and tell – [text missing] – thunder – [text missing] – and [why] this stone was rolled away, with trembling of the earth three days and nights, and why I now appear in cloth as fresh and smelling sweet as when my body was anointed for the tomb. Let the word pass to [the chosen?]: I am a spirit come back to tell the secrets of my time on earth. – [text missing] – The heaven and the earth will be rolled up in your presence. Know now that I am not he who died on the cross, but I replaced and hid myself. The one who died in my place was unknown, a stranger. I ask for your forgiveness, as I have asked forgiveness of my father. – [text missing] – Write down the things that I tell you and place this book in the mountain. Then you shall adjure the Guardian, 'Come Dreadful One'.

This fragment would presuppose a rereading of Christianity in its biblical and related contexts as the story of a phantom or phantom effects at once inaugurated and revealed, legible in a new way. It would constitute a sort of futuristic ur-text for Abraham's account of the phantom, a strange figuring of what Derrida calls the *arrivant* ('a thinking of the past, a legacy that can come only from that which has not yet arrived': *SM*, p. 196, n. 39).

Two supplementary remarks by way of cutting things off:

(1) As Geza Vermes has argued, if there is a single thing about which there would appear to be consensus regarding the death of Jesus, it is 'the one disconcerting fact … that the women who set out to pay their last respects to Jesus found to their consternation, not a body, but an empty tomb'.[17] The various Gospel, Nag Hammadi and other accounts of seeing the dead Jesus alive again, together with the discovery of an empty tomb, constitute a testimony to what can be described, in Abraham's terms, as a vast phantom effect. Christian belief would be structured by the phantom effect of a figure whose reappearances beyond the grave, bolstered by the disappearance of his corpse, testify to unspoken or unspeakable secrets. In this context we might turn round Elaine Pagels's question: 'Why does faith in the passion and death of Christ become an essential element – some say, *the* essential element – of orthodox Christianity?' (p. 75). Rather than, like Pagels, wonder at it, wonder at our supposed wonder, might we not then reflect and elaborate in a critical, even deconstructive fashion on the

passion, death and resurrection scene as precisely cryptic and phantomatic? Jesus did not die on the cross but rather had himself substituted – an unknown man, an anonymous stranger, perhaps someone who looked similar to him, was taken away and crucified in his place. This shameful secret will have been at the heart of the ghost-story called Christianity. The crucifixion might then call to be re-thought as the passion of (to borrow Maurice Blanchot's fragmentary formulation) 'The unknown name, alien to naming'.[18]

(2) At the same time, we would be impelled to read this phantom text in terms of the way Derrida in *Spectres of Marx* seeks to situate the significance of Jesus Christ for Marxism and deconstruction. Following Marx and Max Stirner, Derrida declares: 'Christ is the most spectral of spectres. He tells us something about absolute spectrality' (p. 144). Marx, like Stirner, was concerned to dissolve 'the mirages of Christian onto-theology' (p. 191, n. 14). Derrida is willing to describe this as a work of deconstruction. But Marx's and Stirner's attempts to dispose of 'that arch-ghost in flesh and blood that is … Christ, God made Man in the incarnation' are themselves haunted, Derrida suggests:

> Their 'deconstruction' is limited at the point at which they *both* oppose this spectral onto-theology … to the hyper-phenomenological principle of the flesh-and-blood presence of the living person, of the being itself, of its effective and non-phantomatic presence, of presence in flesh and blood. (pp. 191–2, n. 14)

Spectres of Marx delineates a Marxist deconstruction of Christian onto-theology but suggests that the Marxist conception is itself still too much bound up in another kind of mirage, namely that of 'non-phantomatic presence, of presence in flesh and blood'. To be mere 'flesh and blood', to have 'ears of flesh and blood', is to be a ghost. The word 'Christ' is Greek for Messiah. *Spectres of Marx* calls for a de-Christification of experience, for 'a messianism without religion' (p. 59). This messianism or 'messianic' is desert-like and strange: Derrida remarks that one could consider it to be 'uncanny' (p. 168). This messianic is 'irreducible to any deconstruction', he suggests; it entails a 'suspension', 'trembling' or 'hesitation' that is 'essential to the messianic in general', a 'thinking of the other and of the event to come'. He writes: 'what remains irreducible to any deconstruction, what remains as undeconstructible as the possibility itself of deconstruction is, perhaps, a certain experience of the emancipatory promise' (p. 59). The 'perhaps', as elsewhere in Derrida's writing, testifies to the trembling that *is* the messianic. The messianic 'would no longer be messianic if it stopped hesitating' (p. 169). This hesitation is the destabilization of every identification and localization, and it is promised, if one can say this, by mourning.

The phantom text evoked here concerns the logic of what Derrida speaks of as the 'furtive passage' (p. 168): trembling in the unspoken of *Spectres of Marx* and the writings of Nicolas Abraham, it does not *belong*, it does not rest, perhaps, anywhere. The fragment would constitute a phantom effect of what Derrida elsewhere describes as the project of an 'internal critique' of Christianity and the 'putting on trial' of a 'fabricated mystery', the deconstruction of what is private, of privacy as such.[19]

NOTES

1   Friedrich Nietzsche, *The Will to Power*, trans. Walter Kaufmann and R. J. Hollingdale (New York: Vintage, 1968), p. 7.

2   Jacques Derrida, *Archive Fever: A Freudian Impression*, trans. Eric Prenowitz (Chicago: Chicago University Press, 1996), p. 64.

3   Jacques Derrida, *Spectres of Marx: The State of the Debt, the Work of Mourning, and the New International*, trans. Peggy Kamuf (New York: Routledge, 1994). Further page references are given in the text, preceded by the abbreviation '*SM*' where clarity dictates. Where appropriate, references to the French text, *Spectres de Marx: L'État de la dette, le travail du deuil et la nouvelle Internationale* (Paris: Galilée, 1993), are given in parentheses, following the English translation page number and a slash.

4   The translation/untranslatability of '*fantôme*' in Derrida's text is ultimately perhaps indissociable from that of the '*es spukt*' (it spooks, it apparitions, it phantoms) on which Derrida meditates in relation to Freud's 'The Uncanny': see *Spectres*, pp. 172–4. For reasons which I hope may become more apparent as I go on, I have preferred to translate '*fantôme*' as 'phantom' rather than as 'ghost' (Peggy Kamuf's translation). Otherwise I have generally followed Kamuf's fine translation throughout.

5   Jacques Derrida (with Geoffrey Bennington), *Jacques Derrida*, trans. Bennington (Chicago and London: Chicago University Press, 1993), p. 305.

6   Pierre Macherey, *A Theory of Literary Production*, trans. G. Wall (London: Routledge and Kegan Paul, 1978), p. 85.

7   'Living On', trans. James Hulbert, in Harold Bloom et al., *Deconstruction and Criticism* (New York: Seabury Press, 1979), p. 107.

8   There is a footnote reference on p. 178 but this is to Derrida's 'Fors: The Anglish Words of Nicolas Abraham and Maria Torok', rather than to the book to which that essay formed the foreword, viz. *The Wolf Man's Magic Word: A Cryptonymy*, trans. Nicholas Rand (Minneapolis: University of Minnesota Press, 1986). In what follows I also refer to Nicolas Abraham and Maria Torok, *The Shell and the Kernel*, 1, ed., trans. and with an Introduction by Nicholas T. Rand (Chicago and London: Chicago University Press, 1994): further page references are given in brackets in the text, abbreviated '*SK*' where appropriate.

9   'Fors: The Anglish Words of Nicolas Abraham and Maria Torok', p. xxvi.

10 If there is what he calls the 'tableau of an ageless world' (the subtitle of Chapter 3 of *Spectres of Marx*), the 'ageless' here is not a reference to some putatively ahistorical notion of the 'timeless' but rather to a punctual anachronism – a two-timing or split-time that comports the very old and the very new *at the same time*. For comparison one might think here of the

proposition, in *Memoirs of the Blind: The Self-portrait and Other Ruins*, trans. Pascale-Anne Brault and Michael Naas (Chicago: Chicago University Press, 1993), that love is 'an ageless ruin – at once originary, an infant even, and already old' (pp. 68–9).

11 See Edward Pilkington, 'Thwarting the Grim Reaper', *Guardian*, 6 January 1996, p. 1.

12 Jacques Derrida, 'The Time Is Out of Joint', trans. Peggy Kamuf, *Deconstruction is / in America: A New Sense of the Political*, ed. Anselm Haverkamp (New York: New York University Press, 1995), p. 20.

13 As with his observation (quoted earlier) about mourning's enigmatic commitment to 'identifying the bodily remains and … *localizing* the dead', Derrida's conception of the place and time of death – and therefore of the place and time of life, of presence, of experience itself – is perhaps best described as a trembling, a trembling conception and trembling of the concept. His thought is oriented by a sense of the injustice and even impossibility of 'localizing the dead' or of knowing 'at what instant mourning began'. This thought is not to be confused, however, with mere 'confusion' or 'doubt' ('Nothing could be worse, for the work of mourning, than confusion or doubt: one *has to know* who is buried where': p. 9): knowledge itself is spectralized. Similarly, it is not a matter of mourning as something to be thought 'merely' within us. As he suggests, in a related context, in *Mémoires*: 'thought is not bereaved interiorization; it thinks at boundaries, it thinks the boundary, the limit of interiority' (*Mémoires: For Paul de Man*, trans. Cecile Lindsay, Jonathan Culler and Eduardo Cadava (New York: Columbia University Press, 1986), p. 71).

14 *The Nag Hammadi Library in English*, trans. and introduced by members of the Coptic Gnostic Library Project of the Institute for Antiquity and Christianity at Claremont, California, ed. James M. Robinson, 3rd, completely revised edn (New York: HarperCollins, 1990). Further page references are given in the text, preceded by the abbreviation '*NHL*' where clarity dictates.

15 See Elaine Pagels, *The Gnostic Gospels* (New York: Vintage, 1979), pp. xiii–xvi. Further page references to Pagels's book are given parenthetically in the text.

16 Jacques Derrida, 'Afterw.rds: or, at least, less than a letter about a letter less', trans. Geoffrey Bennington, in *Afterwords*, ed. Nicholas Royle (Tampere, Finland: Outside Books, 1992), p. 200.

17 Geza Vermes, *Jesus the Jew: A Historian's Reading of the Gospels*, 2nd edn (London: Collins, 1983), p. 41.

18 Maurice Blanchot, *Writing the Disaster*, trans. Ann Smock (Lincoln: Nebraska University Press, 1986), p. 47.

19 See Jacques Derrida, *The Gift of Death*, trans. David Wills (London and Chicago: Chicago University Press, 1995), especially pp. 109–12. I consider this issue in more detail in Chapter 21.

21

The private parts of Jesus Christ

private: *adj.* independent, own, relating to personal affairs, not public, not open to the public, not made generally known, retired from observation, alone.

part: *noun* something less than the whole, a portion, a member or organ, share, region, participation, concern, interest, a role or duty, a side or party, a character taken by an actor in a play, the words or actions of a character in a play or in real life, a voice or instrument in concerted music, a section of a work in literature or in music. (*Chambers*)

) *The private parts of Jesus Christ*, how will you read that, subvocalizing in silence, that is my question, I have no interest in getting beyond it, only in trying to think what might be going on in it, how to hear this phrase, if it is a phrase, in other words at once a small group of words expressing a single idea or constituting a single element in a sentence and also an idiomatic expression, a pithy saying or catchword, in short a kind of shibboleth. (

)

Already plural, irreducibly, despite the appearances of the single and unitary, for example in the 'the' or in the phrase 'phrase'. (

)

At issue are the writings of Jacques Derrida in relation to Christianity and the question of how to think, after Derrida, about writing and messianicity, in one's own manner, with a view to the solitude of an unidentifiable church, to inventing one's own religion or rather (as Derrida says) doing or making a truth that perhaps does not come 'under any religion, for reason of literature, nor under any literature, for reason of religion'.[1] (

)

The private parts of Jesus Christ: does this phrase, if it is a phrase, sound blasphemous, idolatrous, perverse? If so, to whom will one have been listening, to what voice or tone within oneself that would not be one's own, perhaps, but the voice or tone of another within oneself, one who speaks ill (as the etymology of the word 'blasphemy' suggests), one to whom blame might be assigned? Is the voice or tone of blasphemy within oneself or outside oneself, and who can bear witness to this? It is a matter of trying to think the question of religion, and specifically here Christianity, in terms of performative utterance. As Hent de Vries puts it:

> Religion is to be conceived of as the problem of performative utterance 'as such', but of
> an utterance that does not – not yet or no longer – attain the determinability *qua* content
> and structure that remains presupposed (without further justification, metaphysically,
> and in the guise of some 'presentism') by the modern theories of the performative
> (Austin) and of the speech act (Searle).[2]

In other words, it is a question of acknowledging and elaborating on the fact that,
as de Vries goes on to say,

> the possible success of the religious performative – the very performativity of *religion*,
> the word no less than its effects, but also the religiosity of every performative – is never
> guaranteed by preestablished or simply given contextual requirements … Any religious
> utterance, act, or gesture, stands in the shadow of – more or less, but never totally
> avoidable – perversion, parody, and kitsch, of blasphemy and idolatry.[3] (

)

The private parts of Jesus Christ: can this phrase not also sound perfectly dignified,
solemn and respectful? In other words, might it not be heard as belonging to the
category of what may provisionally be called successful religious utterance? But
if it were successful, it would only be thanks to the necessary possibility of failure,
of perversion, parody, blasphemy. And more (and less) than that, its success
might be identified with what Derrida describes as 'a promise that cannot be *sure
of succeeding* except by succeeding in failing'.[4] Everything comes down or comes
back to tone, to how one would fail in succeeding to hear, a tone one cannot trace.
This is, at least on one occasion, how Derrida defines God. *Tone* (*Ton*), he writes
in *The Post Card*, 'is the name of God, my God, the one that I do not find'.[5] (

)

'A title is always a promise', Derrida says.[6] If this is true it should be possible to
demonstrate it in the case of 'the private parts of Jesus Christ'. The being-promise
of this title will entail a sense of excess. As Derrida remarks in *Mémoires*:

> A promise is always excessive. Without this essential excess, it would return to a
> description or knowledge of the future. Its act would have a constative structure and
> not a performative one. But this 'too much' of the promise does not belong to a
> (promised) content of a promise which I would be incapable of keeping. It is within the
> very *act* of promising that this excess comes to inscribe a kind of irremediable
> disturbance or perversion. This perversion, which is also a trap, no doubt unsettles the
> language of the promise, the performative as promise; but it also renders it possible –
> and indestructible. Whence the *unbelievable*, and comical, aspect of every promise, and
> this passionate attempt to come to terms with the law, the contract, the oath, the
> declared affirmation of fidelity.[7]

Let me emphasize two words, adjectives designating a certain privacy, in that final sentence. The first of these Derrida himself stresses: it is the 'unbelievable'. There is something unbelievable about every promise. Nothing happens without an experience of the unbelievable; as he has said elsewhere, the essence of belief or faith can only ever be a matter of 'believ[ing] in the unbelievable'.[8] The unbelievable is happening as soon as we open our mouths. What Derrida calls 'the declared affirmation of fidelity' entails a notion of faith as 'Not religion, to be sure, nor theology, but that which in faith acquiesces before or beyond all questioning, in the already common experience of a language and of a "we"'.[9] It is a matter of what he refers to as 'faith in language': 'even perjury, lying and infidelity would still presuppose *faith in language*; I cannot lie without believing and making believe in language, without giving credence to the idiom'.[10] The second word is 'comical': there is something comical about every promise. To say this is not to suggest that we start taking Derrida less seriously, but rather that what is in some ways perhaps most serious about his work is its insistence on the necessary possibility of comedy even in the most solemn of performative utterances. There is here, as elsewhere in his work, a resonance between the minimal yes of the promise and what he calls 'the question ... of a laughter which *remains*, as a fundamental, quasi-transcendental tonality'.[11] (

)

No private parts of Jesus Christ without deconstruction, no deconstruction without the private parts of Jesus Christ. (

)

It has become increasingly clear – and this is in part the burden and force of Hent de Vries's *Philosophy and the Turn to Religion* (1999) – that the question of religion is at stake in the treatment of philosophy, psychoanalysis, literature, phenomenology, science and knowledge in Derrida's work from the very start, and at the same time that this is a question that is inseparable from the most everyday reality of the world, in particular in the form of what Derrida has called 'mondialatinization' (translated by Samuel Weber as 'globalatinization'), taking the form of a 'strange alliance of Christianity ... and tele-technoscientific capitalism' (FK, p. 13), or, as de Vries glosses it, 'the becoming Christian of the modern world (or, for that matter, the becoming worldly and, in a sense, abstract, of Christianity)', a process that 'is linked to the faith (and fate) of a certain Europe'.[12] How does Derrida talk about religion, and Christianity in particular? He has said that he is not an enemy of religion (FK, p. 7). At the same time he has said that his thinking is guided by a desire 'for what, in politics, is called republican democracy as a universalizable model, binding philosophy to the public "cause"', and that this entails a preference for 'the enlightened virtue of public space, emancipating it from all external power (non-lay, non-secular), for example from religious dogmatism, orthodoxy or authority (that is, from a certain rule of *doxa* or of belief, which, however, does not mean from all faith)' (FK, p. 8). The logic of this 'at the same time' is quietly spoken, even subvocal, but still perhaps cataclysmic. (

)

It might help to juxtapose Derrida's work here with that of Nietzsche. The latter observes: 'From the start Christianity was, essentially and fundamentally, the embodiment of disgust and antipathy for life, merely disguised, concealed, got up as the belief in an "other" or a "better" life.' Christianity, for Nietzsche, is the embodiment of 'Hatred of the "world", the condemnation of the emotions, the fear of beauty and sensuality, a transcendental world invented the better to slander this one, basically a yearning for non-existence, for repose until the "sabbath of Sabbaths".'[13] Derrida is in some sense perhaps more explicit than Nietzsche in foregrounding that strangely *unheard-of* force of affirmation which is the basis of hatred and love alike. His focus is less on the 'hatred of the "world"' *per se* that Nietzsche here identifies with Christianity, than on the *yes* of affirmation that is the condition of every 'I hate you' and every 'I love you'. It is this allergic condition of affirmation that Derrida refers to with the deconstructive notion of a new enlightenment and with what he says in *Politics of Friendship* about 'a friendship prior to friendships, an ineffaceable friendship, fundamental and groundless, one that breathes in a shared language (past or to come) and in the being-together that all allocution supposes, up to and including the declaration of war'.[14] Derrida's way of proceeding is crucially different from Nietzsche's. He has never spoken out, and it is difficult to imagine him ever speaking out, in this Nietzschean fashion against Christianity or any other religion. His style is rather that of the subvocal survey, ghost-writing, eerie elucidation of what (as will be seen) he calls 'internal critique'. (

)

Spectres of Marx (1993) has rightly attracted considerable attention among Marxists and others concerned with the future of world politics. It has been less noticed as a book about Christianity, about the continuing importance of Christ as 'the most spectral of spectres' (p. 144). The book is concerned with what (in Chapter 20) I have called a de-Christification of experience, that is to say with a thinking of messianicity that would not involve any 'identifiable messiah' (p. 28), with 'a messianism without religion' (p. 59), a non-messianic messianicity. Derrida stresses the notion of 'the *messianic* rather than *messianism*, so as to designate a structure of experience rather than a religion' (pp. 167–8). His messianic is concerned with

a 'formal structure of promise' that at once 'exceeds' and 'precedes' both Marxism
and the religions it criticizes (p. 59). Marxism's error and Christianity's error
would entail what Derrida calls 'the animist incorporation of an emancipatory
eschatology which ought to have respected the promise, the being-promise of a
promise' (p. 105). This messianic is itself 'irreducible to any deconstruction' (p. 59),
he suggests. It involves a suspension (*epokhe*), trembling or hesitation that is
essential to the messianic in general, for the messianic, he holds, 'would no
longer be messianic if it stopped hesitating' (p. 169). It is indissociably bound up,
he suggests, with the 'strange, strangely familiar and [at the same time] inhospit-
able' (p. 168) experience of the uncanny. *Spectres of Marx* is war literature, engaged
with and in 'the world war' that is gathered around the figure of Jerusalem but is
'happening everywhere' (p. 58). It is a work of war literature, calling for another
thinking of war and literature alike. The question is how to think, how to be open,
how to welcome the future without 'killing [it] in the name of old frontiers':

> Like those of the blood, nationalisms of native soil not only sow hatred, not only
> commit crimes, they have no future, they promise nothing even if, like stupidity or the
> unconscious, they hold fast to life. [The] messianic hesitation does not paralyse any
> decision, any affirmation, any responsibility. On the contrary, it grants them their
> elementary condition. It is their very experience. (p. 169) (

)

Subvocal frontiers. (

)

What is Jesus thinking, I ask myself, has this question ever been asked, feeling it
provoked in a singular, even unprecedented fashion by a painting by Leonardo
da Vinci known as the *Madonna Litta* (see Frontispiece to this volume), a picture
that is an art historian's nightmare, they all seem to want to condemn it, damn it,
write it off as 'ruined' (Kenneth Clark)[15] or as what Robert Payne calls 'a
mockery'.[16] It's not the Madonna herself that's the problem: her face, says Payne,
'remains to remind us of Leonardo's extraordinary accomplishment',[17] even if
that face raises a host of questions in turn, starting from the uncanny, uncannily
characteristic 'touch of something sinister' that Walter Pater identifies with the
'unfathomable smile' of Leonardo's women.[18] No, it's the baby that is the problem,
as Cecil Gould notes, between dashes – 'a very big baby'[19] – an infant Jesus that is,
in the words of Martin Kemp, 'so awkward that it can hardly have been executed
by Leonardo himself – even allowing for the oddness of his early works'.[20] It's as
if art historians cannot quite bear to look at this picture, don't know how to
countenance it, it's so odd it cannot be authentic, even granting in the first place
that the picture has been (as Clark points out) 'totally repainted at least twice'.[21]

Payne sums it up when he writes:

> The overall effect is static, overdecorative, intellectual; the wonder and the tenderness
> are absent; there is no flow of feeling between the Virgin and Child. Many things have
> gone wrong since Leonardo painted it, and what has chiefly gone wrong is the Child's
> face, which is almost a caricature, with an enormous disembodied eye demanding
> attention, and there are two fingers like fungi pressing against a breast that looks like a
> loaf of bread. It is as though two separate paintings have somehow become fused
> together and they cry out to be separated.[22] (

)

It's a hybrid, a chimera, postmodern Leonardo, but everyone sees something
different, each time a different witnessing, Robert Payne sees two fungi and a
loaf of bread, I see no fungi or loaf of bread, what makes it so monstrous to these
art historians I find stunning, of all the pictorial figurations of all the bodies of
Christ I know, this is perhaps the strangest and most haunting. What is it that
doesn't get said in the condemnation of this painting of the Child Jesus? Where
does the sense of horror, if that is what it is, come from? Doesn't this picture
stage the hesitation of the unbelievable as such? What is it that makes it so
difficult for the art historians to attribute it to Leonardo? The figure of Jesus has
been added on, so the argument would go, a supplement that can be confidently
condemned as not Leonardo's, too 'awkward', too 'odd', it's a vicarious or
substitute Jesus, standing in for the irreplaceable, like every substitution. Isn't
there a strange leap, the art historians' leap of faith, in the decision of classifying
this Jesus as a mockery, as if it were simply not possible to suppose that the
repainting of this figure were in fact a mockery in another sense, in other words
a faithful mimicry, faithful to Leonardo's supposedly non-existent original? It's as
if they were fearful of a ghost, a certain kind of spectrality, as in Macbeth's
exclamation: 'Hence horrible shadow! / Unreal mockery, hence! [Exit ghost] (3.4.
105–6). Why not spell it out, the necessary failure of the performative of such an
exorcism, what is really happening if one looks, what truth to make of this
picture of the infant Jesus too large, a little old or at least precocious, 'too old' or
'precocious' being already perhaps a kind of impossible formulation, for how can
one speak of a precocious Jesus, irresolvable questions concerning private parts
of Christ's life, the aporias generated by considering Jesus as an 'early developer'
or becoming 'old before his time'. (

)

'Cry out to be separated.' (

)

Parts of life as private as dreaming. As Leo Steinberg has put it: 'Jesus dreaming is inconceivable.'[23] It goes along with the state of childhood as characterized by what St Augustine calls 'irrational affections'.[24] Both dreaming and that 'strange intoxication' which Augustine attributes to children are states of human experience which 'Jesus does not assume', says Steinberg, 'evidently because they involve deprivation or suspension of consciousness'.[25] What truth to make, I ask, of this picture of an infant Jesus with a look not quite directed at the viewer, neither at the Virgin Mary nor at the viewer of Leonardo's painting, in short an uncanny look, as of what perhaps 'ought to have remained secret and hidden but has come to light' (U, p. 345),[26] a look reserved and apparently knowing, undecidably of satisfaction ('I am the breast', as a Freudian baby would have it) and indifference, absorbed and absorbing endlessly. (

)

Is this infant Jesus dreaming? How could one know? How can a painting depict the state of dreaming, or rather give assurance of a distinction between dreaming and vigilance, especially if the subject in question is at the mother's breast, twist the interrogative, trance a da Vincian contrapposto, 'strange intoxication' to recall Augustine's phrase, a speaking look that says nothing, an infantilism of secrecy, one need look no further for the private parts of Jesus Christ. It recalls what Derrida says of the Matthew Paris picture of Socrates and Plato: 'A pictorial performative which never ends.'[27] (

)

Above all what all these art historians seem to miss, or seem unwilling to remark upon, is the fact that the eye of the child in this Leonardo painting calls us in, even as it screens or rebuffs, it provokes the question, what is Jesus thinking, it draws us into an interiority, a private part or parts of what can be named, as equivocally as possible, the thinking of Jesus. In the head: even the windows in this picture give the appearance of eyes, as if we are lodged within the head of another, looking out, inside out of someone else's mind. What is he thinking? Divine. (

)

Already cut. At the heart of Derrida's essay published in English as *The Gift of Death* (1995, originally given as a lecture in 1990) is a question about the nature of the self and trembling, trembling in private, a trembling of the private. He writes: 'The question of the self [*moi*]: "who am I?" no longer in the sense of "who am I" but "who is 'I'"? who can say "who"? what is the "I", and what does responsibility become when, *in secret*, the identity of the "I" trembles?'[28] Derrida presents a reading of Christ's teaching in the Gospel of Matthew and in particular focuses on the conception of God as 'thy father which seeth in secret' (Matt. 6: 4, 6, 18), noting that Jesus uses the phrase three times and that, repeated 'like some obsessive reminder to be learnt by heart' (*GD*, p. 97), it takes on the force of a kind of shibboleth. *The Gift of Death* traces what Derrida describes as 'a mutation ... in the history of secrecy' (p. 100). This mutation has to do with how Christ's saying 'Ye are the light of the world (*lux mundi* / *phos tou kosmou*)' (Matt 5: 14) is understood as the specification of a light 'in us, within the interiority of the spirit'. Derrida asserts: 'The interiorization of the photological source marks the end of secrecy but it is also the beginning of the paradox of the secret as irreducible in its interiority' (p. 100). This leads him to formulate a 'new' definition of God. He proposes that 'We should stop thinking about God as someone, over there, way up there, transcendent, and ... capable ... of seeing into the most secret of the most interior places' (p. 108). Instead, he suggests:

> God is the name of the possibility I have of keeping a secret that is visible from the interior but not from the exterior. Once such a structure of conscience [*conscience*, also 'consciousness'] exists, of being-with-oneself, of speaking, that is, of producing invisible sense, once I have within me, *thanks to the invisible word as such*, a witness that others cannot see, and who is therefore *at the same time other than me and more intimate with me than myself*, once I can have a secret relationship with myself and not tell everything, once there is secrecy and secret witnessing within me, then what I call God exists, (there is) what I call God in me, (it happens that) I call myself God [*je m'appelle Dieu*] – a phrase that is difficult to distinguish from 'God calls me' [*'Dieu m'appelle'*], for it is on that condition that I can call myself or that I am called in secret. God is in me, he is the absolute 'me' or 'self' [*moi*], he is that structure of invisible interiority that is called, in Kierkegaard's sense, *subjectivity*. (pp. 108–9/101–2)

This reformulation of how to think of God (thanks to the teaching of Christ) is said to be 'at the same time evangelical and heretical' and is part of an '*internal* critique of Christianity' (p. 109, emphasis added). It affirms, following Christ, the presence or testimony of an other (here named 'God') that is '*at the same time other than me and more intimate with me than myself*'. It brings into play a spectrality, a sort of ghost-writing within and across the experience of belief, a trembling which at once belongs and does not belong to Christianity. This double movement is implicit in the phrase 'internal critique of Christianity' – the adjective 'internal' being at once supplementary and essential to what is going on in Derrida's account. (

)

Elaborated through readings of Baudelaire ('The Pagan School') and Nietzsche (*The Genealogy of Morals*), *The Gift of Death* expounds another thinking of God and, in particular, another understanding of Jesus Christ's words, 'and thy father which seeth in secret ... shall reward thee'. This exposition follows 'the traditional Judeo-Christiano-Islamic injunction' (p. 108) but does so explicitly at the risk of turning this tradition against itself. Derrida writes:

> It is a matter of unfolding the mystagogical hypocrisy of a secret, putting on trial a fabricated mystery, a contract that has a secret clause, namely, that, seeing in secret, God will pay back infinitely more ['thy father ... shall reward thee']; a secret that we accept all the more easily since God remains the witness of every secret. He shares and *he knows*. We have to *believe* that he knows. This knowledge at the same time founds and destroys the Christian concepts of responsibility and justice and their 'object'. (p. 112)

The focus is thus on 'the reversal and infinitization that confers on God, on the Other or on the name of God, the responsibility for that which remains more secret than ever, the irreducible experience of belief' (p. 115, translation modified). Derrida has more recently articulated this irreducible experience in terms of the trembling of the undecidable: 'To say "I made a decision" is a necessary lie, a presumption. That is the meaning of God, as the only one who can know if someone has made a decision.'[29] In *The Gift of Death* he stages this trembling in the first person plural, a royal 'we': 'We have to believe that he knows.' Only 'faith in language' secures this 'we' with the minimal coherence of an identity; it is the royal 'we' of a ghost-writing. For Derrida is not speaking for himself here, he is not a Christian, it is and is not 'his' *we* that is being testified to here.[30] *Spectres of Marx* suggests a further intertextual turn to this ghost-writing. For Derrida's description of God in *The Gift of Death* as '*at the same time other than me and more intimate with me than myself [à la fois autre que moi et plus intime à moi que moi-même]*' will uncannily come back in *Spectres of Marx*, when he talks about that 'stranger who is already found within (*das Heimliche-Unheimliche*), more intimate with one than one is oneself [*plus intime à soi que soi-même*], the absolute proximity of a stranger whose power is singular *and* anonymous (*es spukt*), an unnameable and neutral power, that is, undecidable, neither active nor passive, an an-identity that, *without doing anything*, invisibly occupies places belonging finally neither to us nor to it' (p. 172/273). The uncanny: God, *for example*.[31] (

)

In *The Gift of Death*, Derrida may appear to take on the position of Christ – in other words the position of postman, representative of the postal principle, the PP, the private parts.[32] He notes that one doesn't see God looking, but one 'can, and must, only hear him', and this 'most often' happens 'through the voice of another, another other, a messenger, an angel, a prophet, a messiah or postman [*facteur*]' (p. 91). Derrida does not, however, elaborate on this specifically in terms of Jesus. The entire account of how Christ's words about 'thy father who seeth in secret' produce a mutation in the nature of secrecy and therefore of privacy, alter the very history and thinking of private parts, alter the nature of the self in private – this entire account is mediated through the private parts of Jesus Christ himself, in other words through the role of Christ as messenger, as the one who knows what in effect God has communicated to him in private, we have to believe that Christ knows, we have to believe this the most spectral of postmen, at the same time as or even *before* believing that God knows, and without questioning, it would seem, whether or how far Christ himself might be thought to 'see in secret'. (

)

'The private parts of Jesus Christ': difficult to think about without engaging with the question of what we might call, in the wake of a kind of deconstructive anachrony, the telepathic. There are numerous occasions in the Bible when Jesus appears telepathic, apparently seeing in secret, knowing the thoughts of others. For example, in Matthew, Chapter 9:

> And, behold, they brought to him a man sick of the palsy, lying on a bed: and Jesus seeing their faith said unto the sick of the palsy; Son, be of good cheer; thy sins be forgiven thee. And, behold, certain of the scribes said within themselves, This man blasphemeth. And Jesus *knowing their thoughts* said, Wherefore think ye evil in your hearts? (Matthew 9: 2–4, emphasis added).[33]

What Derrida has elsewhere talked about as the angelic structure of all discourse[34] means here of course that Christ's apparently telepathic powers are indissociably linked with the telepathic narration: Jesus may know the thoughts of the scribes, but the narrator already has to know not only this but also what the scribes 'said within themselves'. The stakes of such a telepathic performativity perhaps remain to be thought.[35] (

)

Uncanny vicar. Not I. (

)

When Derrida says that 'We should stop thinking about God as someone, over there, way up there, transcendent, and, what is more – into the bargain, precisely – capable, more than any satellite orbiting in space, of seeing into the most secret of the most interior places' (p. 108), he invokes a 'we' that is only made possible by that which exceeds it, by a solitude that can be identified with the secret: it is, as he describes it in *The Gift of Death*, a secrecy that is 'incommensurable with knowing', concerned with the innermost possibility of having private parts, that is to say with the notion of having a secret self. This secret self, 'which can be revealed only to the other, to the wholly other, to God if you wish, is a secret that I will never reflect on, that I will never know or experience or possess as my own' (p. 92). Consequently, asks Derrida,

> what sense is there in saying it is 'my' secret, or in saying more generally that a secret *belongs*, that it is proper to or belongs to some 'one', or to some *other* who remains some*one*? It is perhaps there that we find the secret of secrecy, namely, that it is not a matter of knowing and that it is there for no-one. A secret doesn't belong, it can never be said to be at home or in its place [*chez soi*].

It is uncanny, as he goes on to say: 'Such is the *Unheimlichkeit* of the *Geheimnis*' (p. 92). Rather than the Christian hypocrisy or 'the disavowal of a secret that is always *for me alone*' and that is therefore only ever a secret '*for the other*' (p. 92), Derrida foregrounds the experience of a secrecy 'incommensurable with knowing' (p. 93) or what he elsewhere refers to as 'the absolute solitude of a passion without martyrdom', a solitude that (he suggests) one might call 'life' or 'trace' as much as 'death'.[36] Against 'knowledge' he stresses the experience of bearing witness, an experience of solitude, in which 'one precisely cannot here trust any definite witness, nor even any guaranteed value to bearing witness' (P, p. 31). There is, he says, 'a solitude without any measure common to that of an isolated subject'. It is solitude as 'the other name of the secret', a solitude which is 'neither of consciousness, nor of the subject, nor of *Dasein*'. It is a solitude that 'does not answer', it is not 'captured or covered over by the relation to the other, by being-with or by any form of "social bond" ' (P, pp. 30–1). (

)

It may appear that I have been talking about 'the private parts of Jesus Christ' in a circumspect, even circumlocutory or periphrastic manner. 'Private parts' will perhaps have been understood to refer to the genitalia, the penis and prepuce of Jesus Christ. Why would this so-called 'sexual' reading be privileged over other readings of the phrase? As Leo Steinberg remarks, the sexuality of Jesus Christ is 'widely recognized as Christianity's greatest taboo'.[37] But as he makes clear at the start of the book that he wrote with a view to breaking it, the taboo needs to be seen from the outset in historical terms. *The Sexuality of Christ in Renaissance Art and Modern Oblivion* (1983) begins by noting that

> The first necessity is to admit a long-suppressed matter of fact … In many hundreds of pious, religious works, from before 1400 to past the mid–16th century, the ostensive unveiling of the [Christ] Child's sex, or the touching, protecting or presentation of it, is the main action … All of which has been tactfully overlooked for half a millennium.[38]

Close inspection of Leonardo's Madonna Litta will suggest that there is nothing unconventional at least in the picture's depiction of Christ's penis as uncircumcised. Assuming we know what a penis is, and where that uncanny event or idea called circumcision begins and ends.[39] Leo Steinberg's monumental tome on the sexuality of Christ offers only brief discussion of Jesus and circumcision, in a section entitled 'Resisting the physical evidence of circumcision'. He concludes that 'the refusal of Renaissance art to acknowledge [the] visual effect [of Christ's circumcision] remains an unexplained puzzle'.[40] (

)

Concerned with 'founding another religion' or 'refounding all of them ... playfully' (C, p. 222), Derrida's autobiothanatoheterographical 'Circumfession' is one of his most bizarre texts. Running along the lower part of the pages of a book called *Jacques Derrida*, the upper part of each page of which comprises Geoffrey Bennington's 'Derridabase', Derrida's contribution is subtitled 'Fifty-nine periods and periphrases [*périodes et périphrases*] *written in a sort of internal margin, between Geoffrey Bennington's book and work in preparation (January 1989–April 1990).*' '*Période*' in French suggests both 'period' and 'intermission'; 'periphrasis', in English as in French, means 'circumlocution' or 'round-about expression' (from the Greek *peri* around, *phrasis* speech). The title 'Circumfession' is itself at once period and periphrasis, a strange kind of intermission in itself, announcing the text without being part of it, anticipating the text to come. It is a promise. The title-word is a sort of portmanteau that combines 'circumcision' with 'confession' ('confession' in the Augustinian sense of 'praise' as well as 'acknowledgement of faults'). In a text internal to the internal margin, a notebook-entry dated 20 December 1976, quoted in 'Circumfession', Derrida declares: 'Circumcision, that's all I've ever talked about' (C, p. 70).[41] What is the relationship between 'circumcision' and 'confession' or, perhaps more generally, between circumcision and writing? How are the stakes of such a question made to reverberate in the singular case of Jesus' penis? (

)

Let me cut away, as carefully as I can, a few little pieces of 'Circumfession' together with one or two other excerpts from Derrida's writings, by way of conclusion, grafting them, without interposing any punctuation besides commas, the word 'comma' I note parenthetically from the Greek verb *koptein* to cut, to comma, write a church, without identifiable messiah, an almost secret sect, a new party, 'without party', 'untimely', 'barely public' (SM, p. 85), but also barely private, doing the truth of a new international, no more Derrida's than mine, I snip from section 22 as follows,

> one cannot *do* without truth but it's not the one they think they're confessing, they still haven't understood anything about it, especially those I see queuing up, *too late*, to get themselves circumcised and authorise themselves to speak for the 'Jews', this 'for' which makes you burst out laughing, obscene though it remains, either *in favour* or *in place* of the 'Jews', Jews 'themselves' knowing that they must not speak 'for' them, do I do that, (C, p. 114)

cut it there, do I do that, question without interrogation mark, trembling as does the I, circumcision and confession always *too late*, never on time, hatred here in Derrida's words, hatred for what is obscene, for a mystical or religious purity of ethnic or national identity, but this is also funny, it makes you burst out laughing at the same time, what is hateful and what is risible being themselves founded on a yes that would be the condition of every identity, every authority, every 'for', that's the truth, it is in the same sentence, (

)

the same lifedeath sentence, a little later on, Derrida grafts another passage, internal section, this time dated Christmas Eve, as one may care to call it, 24 December 1976, again extracted from one of the notebooks envisaged as 'The Book of Elijah' (see C, p. 89), addressing his 'dear reader' and 'himself' by his 'secret name' (C, p. 87), Elie, he invokes, and I quote,

> the only philosopher to my knowledge who, accepted – more or less – into the academic institution, author of more or less legitimate writings on Plato, Augustine, Descartes, Rousseau, Kant, Hegel, Husserl, Heidegger, Benjamin, Austin, will have dared describe his penis, as promised, in concise and detailed fashion, and as no one dared, in the Renaissance, paint the circumcised penis of Christ on the incredible pretext that there was no model for it, come off it, now if I do not invent a new language (through simplicity rediscovered), another fluid, a new SENTENCE [*une nouvelle PHRASE*], I will have failed in this book, which does not mean that that's the place to begin, on the contrary, you have to drag on in the old syntax, train oneself with you, dear reader, toward an idiom which in the end would be untranslatable in return into the language of the beginnings, learn an unknown language, (115–6/110–11, translation slightly modified)

how to read this sentence which is not a sentence, more the period (duration/ intermission) and periphrasis of a sentence that will have launched itself towards the experience of a new language, a new SENTENCE that would link this injunction 'learn an unknown language' to the injunction with which *Spectres of Marx* in some respects could be said to appear and vanish, namely 'learn to live' and this isn't separable, in the original French text, from 'teach to live', all recognizable models of pedagogy, mastery and discipleship dissolving in this injunction, but read this graft from 'Circumfession' to begin with perhaps in the light, as always in Derrida, of a double-motif, the first motif being that this passage just cited performs as well as states, performs stating, states performing, altering both, failing both, to paint in words Christ's circumcised penis, to paint what 'no one dared, in the Renaissance, paint', it implies in doing so or does so by implying that there is indeed a model for it, like any model, founded and structured on a logic of repetition and alterity, what Derrida platitudinously calls *différance*,[42] every circumcision is unique but this uniqueness is nevertheless *cut*, spiked, spooked, a resistance to what can be thought, as he observes at the start of the text entitled 'Shibboleth', I quote,

> One time alone: circumcision takes place but once.
>
> Such, at least, is the appearance we receive, and the tradition of the appearance, we do not say of the semblance [again then, as ever, a matter of ghosts, of the apprehension of an appearance or apparition].
>
> We will have to circle around this appearance. Not so much in order to circumscribe or circumvent some *truth* of circumcision – that must be given up for essential reasons. But rather to let ourselves be approached by the resistance which 'once' may offer to thought,[43]

once, one time, once upon a time, circumcision as 'what comes to mark itself as the one-and-only time: what one sometimes calls a *date*',[44] that is to say the spectrality of dates and of every story, concerning Derrida's proposition that 'circumcision takes place but once' Robert Smith notes that 'the uniqueness of its moment, never to be repeated, nevertheless gives onto further moments, generating a genre, a series of cases or a genus and race – the Jews, for example',[45] the exposure of Christ's circumcised penis would be a sort of phantomological revelation of the familiar-unfamiliar, an uncanny memento of the inscription of Christ's body within the logic of repetition and alterity that itself renders possible something like an ethnic or religious identity (Jew, Christian, Muslim or other), the second motif being that this passage from 'Circumfession' that I cited a few moments ago is a writing about other writings (for instance those of Augustine), a writing about itself and its so-called author (the 'philosopher' Jacques Derrida) and a writing about its incipient fault or failure as writing, a writing about the other as the untranslatable, as what precisely cannot be invented, even if it is just what calls to be affirmed, even if it is affirmation itself, the condition of every invention and every translation in the so-called traditional sense, (

)

interposing, posthuming, two 'memories of my childhood', for the love of Leonardo, first, once upon a time, being circumcised, I was three, my first night alone in a hospital, given a small tin toy-train and train-track, consigned to the general, and afterwards the bandaging, the pungent yellow ointment, the pain, the anguish and love of my mother and her sister, will I have been Jewish, who am I in secret, second, being expelled from my first school, a so-called 'Church of England primary school', I was five, for 'refusing to pray', publicly reprimanded during the Lord's prayer by a teacher who declared 'you're just moving your lips, you're not really praying', subvocally, will I ever have done anything else, (

)

cut back to it once more, 'now if I do not invent a new language (through simplicity rediscovered), another fluid, a new SENTENCE, I will have failed in this book', there is only period and periphrasis, there is no pure expression or idiom, there is no pure presentation, for example as the phrase 'stream of consciousness' might suggest, there perhaps being a naive temptation to describe Derrida's 'Circumfession' as 'stream of consciousness', as if nothing had happened (call it twentieth-century thought) to trouble or complicate the conception of language and consciousness, consciousness and the unconscious, better perhaps to think of the drift of a gift, yes, confession, adrift, as Derrida says 'like a gift confession must be from the unconscious, I know no other definition of the unconscious' (C, p. 233), 'Circumfession' apparently adrift, then, in a miming of the apparitions of spontaneity of Augustine's *Confessions*, and driven at the same time by an urgency without ground, an urgency whose force seems to come from a language of the future, 'pass[ing] over much because I am hurrying on to those things which especially urge me to make confession to you, and there is much that I do not remember',[46] failed phrase, the private parts of Jesus Christ carrying the secret of the promise as of a still unheard-of language, an absolute idiom,[47] circumcision alone, to be painted, Derrida's or mine, last of the Jews and last of the Christians.[48]

(*Good Friday* 2000)

NOTES

1 Jacques Derrida, 'Circumfession', in Geoffrey Bennington and Jacques Derrida, *Jacques Derrida*, trans. Bennington (Chicago: Chicago University Press, 1993), p. 48. Originally published in French as 'Circonfession' in *Jacques Derrida* (Paris: Seuil, 1991). Further page references to the English translation are given in the text, in parentheses, abbreviated 'C', followed by a slash and page reference to the original French text, where appropriate.

2 Hent de Vries, *Philosophy and the Turn to Religion* (Baltimore: Johns Hopkins University Press, 1999), p. 11.

3 Ibid.

4 Jacques Derrida, 'Back from Moscow, in the USSR', trans. Mary Quaintance, in *Politics,*

Theory, and Contemporary Culture, ed. Mark Poster (New York: Columbia University Press, 1993), pp. 197–235: here, p. 234.

5   Jacques Derrida, The Post Card: From Socrates to Freud and Beyond, trans. Alan Bass (Chicago: Chicago University Press, 1987), p. 114.

6   Jacques Derrida, Mémoires: For Paul de Man, trans. Cecile Lindsay, Jonathan Culler and Eduardo Cadava (New York: Columbia University Press, 1986), p. 115.

7   Mémoires: For Paul de Man, p. 94.

8   Jacques Derrida, Spectres of Marx: The State of the Debt, the Work of Mourning, and the New International, trans. Peggy Kamuf (London: Routledge, 1994), p. 143. Originally published in French as Spectres de Marx: L'État de la dette, le travail du deuil et la nouvelle Internationale (Paris: Galilée, 1993). Further page references to the English translation are given in the text, in parentheses, abbreviated 'SM', followed by a slash and page reference to the original French text, where appropriate.

9   Jacques Derrida, 'Faith and Knowledge: The Two Sources of "Religion" at the Limits of Reason Alone', trans. Samuel Weber, in Religion, eds Jacques Derrida and Gianni Vattimo (Cambridge: Polity Press, 1998), pp. 1–78: here, p. 61. Further page references are given in the text, in parentheses, abbreviated 'FK'.

10   Jacques Derrida, Monolingualism of the Other; or, The Prosthesis of Origin, trans. Patrick Mensah (Stanford: Stanford University Press, 1998), p. 85.

11   Jacques Derrida, 'Ulysses Gramophone: Hear Say Yes in Joyce', trans. Tina Kendall and Shari Benstock in Acts of Literature, ed. Derek Attridge (London and New York: Routledge, 1992), 256–309: here, p. 295.

12   Vries, Philosophy and the Turn to Religion, p. 161.

13   Friedrich Nietzsche, 'Attempt at a Self-criticism' (1886), in The Birth of Tragedy (London: Penguin, 1993), pp. 8–9.

14   Jacques Derrida, Politics of Friendship, trans. George Collins (London: Verso, 1997), p. 236.

15   Kenneth Clark, Leonardo da Vinci: An Account of His Development as an Artist (London: Penguin, 1958), p. 48.

16   Robert Payne, Leonardo (London: Robert Hale, 1979), p. 35.

17   Payne, Leonardo, p. 35.

18   See Walter Pater, The Renaissance (1873; New York: Modern Library, 1919), p. 102.

19   Cecil Gould, The Artist and the Non-artist (London: Weidenfeld and Nicolson, 1975), p. 65.

20   Martin Kemp, Leonardo da Vinci: The Marvellous Works of Nature and Man (London: Dent, 1981), p. 54.

21   Clark, Leonardo da Vinci, p. 48.

22   Payne, Leonardo, p. 35.

23   Leo Steinberg, The Sexuality of Christ in Renaissance Art and in Modern Oblivion, 2nd edn (Chicago: Chicago University Press, 1996), p. 293.

24   St Augustine observes that the human infant, 'although he is ignorant of where he is, what he is, by whom created, of what parents born, is already guilty of offense, incapable as yet of receiving a commandment ... He cannot be aroused out of his sleep, so as to recognize even these facts; but a time must be patiently awaited, until he can shake off this strange intoxication ... Infants are disturbed with irrational affections, and are restrained [only] by pains and penalties, or the terror of such.' See On the Merits and Remission of Sins and on the Baptism of Infants, in Saint Augustine: Anti-Pelagian Writings, Select Library of the Nicene and Post-Nicene Fathers, 5 (New York, 1908), I, 68, p. 42. (Quoted by Steinberg, p. 292.)

25   Leo Steinberg, The Sexuality of Christ, p. 293.

26 For Freud, Leonardo is in some respects the very embodiment of the uncanny. In his essay 'Leonardo da Vinci and a Memory of His Childhood' (*PFL*, 14: 143–231), Freud characterizes the artist in terms of precisely such uncanny childish play: 'Indeed, the great Leonardo remained like a child for the whole of his life in more than one way; it is said that all great men are bound to retain some infantile part. Even as an adult he continued to play, and this was another reason why he often appeared uncanny and incomprehensible to his contemporaries' (p. 220).

27 Jacques Derrida, *The Post Card*, p. 98.

28 Jacques Derrida, *The Gift of Death*, trans. David Wills (Chicago: Chicago University Press, 1995), p. 92, translation modified. The original French version was first given as a lecture in 1990 and published in *L'éthique du don: Jacques Derrida et la pensée du don*, eds Jean-Michel Rabaté and Michael Wetzel (Paris: Métailié-Transition, 1992), pp. 11–108: here, p. 88. A somewhat revised version has more recently appeared as *Donner la mort* (Paris: Galilée, 1999). Further references to Wills's translation are given in the text, in parentheses, abbreviated '*GD*', followed by a slash and page reference to the original 1992 French version, where appropriate.

29 Jacques Derrida, seminar ('Derrida's Arguments') at Queen Mary and Westfield College, University of London, 10 March 2000.

30 Cf. Hent de Vries's summary of this strange duplicity: 'Derrida adopts or, rather, lets himself be adopted by a *doubly heretical* tradition marked by a certain secrecy: one that is heterodox with respect to Judaism as well as with respect to Christianity, one that challenges, without ever blurring, the distinction between the Judaic and the Christian. In short, one that peregrinates between the inner conviction and the outer appearance or vice versa, partaking of both while belonging to no one strictly speaking. It is as if one carried a certain tradition along with oneself, as that which can be neither excluded nor included, that is neither totally alien nor intimately familiar, neither distant nor nearby, or both' (*Philosophy and the Turn to Religion*, p. 351). It is, we may say, uncanny: experience of the uncanny, experience as uncanny. While he does not quite put it in this way, it is clear that the notion of the uncanny is a consistent and indeed crucial motif in de Vries's admirable study: for further instances see, for example, pp. 4, 6, 9, 39, 155, n. 55, 219, 344–5.

31 This formulation alludes to Derrida's account of *différance* about which he remarks: 'This unnameable is not an ineffable Being which no name could approach: God, for example. This unnameable is the play which makes possible nominal effects.' See Jacques Derrida, 'Différance', in *Margins of Philosophy*, trans. Alan Bass (Chicago: Chicago University Press, 1982), p. 26. Cf. also the proposition that 'In every prayer there must be an address to the other as other; *for example* – I will say, at the risk of shocking – God'. See Derrida, 'How to Avoid Speaking: Denials', trans. Ken Frieden, in *Languages of the Unsayable: The Play of Negativity in Literature and Literary Theory*, ed. Stanford Budick and Wolfgang Iser (New York: Columbia University Press, 1989), p. 41. For a good elucidation of Derrida's work in this context, see Rodolphe Gasché, 'God, for Example', in his *Inventions of Difference: On Jacques Derrida* (Cambridge, Mass.: Harvard University Press, 1994), pp. 150–70.

32 Or, as Derrida calls it on one occasion in *The Post Card*, the 'PrePuce' (*le PréPuce*): see *The Post Card*, p. 221/237.

33 We might also consider here, for example, Matthew 12: 25; Luke 5: 22; 6: 8; 9: 47; and John 4: 29, 39.

34 See Jacques Derrida, 'Of an Apocalyptic Tone Newly Adopted in Philosophy', trans. John P. Leavey, Jr, in *Derrida and Negative Theology*, eds Harold Coward and Toby Foshay (Albany, NY: State University of New York Press, 1992), p. 57.

35   The convention, of course, has been to talk about the Bible in terms of omniscient narration. For a detailed account see Meir Sternberg, *The Poetics of Biblical Narrative: Ideological Literature and the Drama of Reading* (Bloomington: Indiana University Press, 1985), esp. Chapter 3 ('Ideology of Narration and Narration of Ideology'), pp. 84–128. In Chapter 19 above, I try to sketch a possible shift away from thinking in terms of omniscience towards a thinking of telepathic narration.

36   See Jacques Derrida, 'Passions: "An Oblique Offering"', trans. David Wood, in *On the Name*, ed. Thomas Dutoit (Stanford: Stanford University Press, 1995), pp. 3–31: here, p. 31. Further references are given in parentheses in the text, abbreviated 'P'.

37   Steinberg, *The Sexuality of Christ*, p. 219.

38   Steinberg, *The Sexuality of Christ*, p. 3.

39   In 'Moses and Monotheism' (1934–38; *PFL*, 13: 239–386), Freud discusses the 'disagreeable, uncanny impression' made by circumcision, linking this to the fear of castration and anti-semitism. The anti-semitism of Christians becomes uncannily reversed in Freud's account: '[t]heir hatred of Jews is at bottom a hatred of Christians'. See 'Moses and Monotheism', p. 336. On issues concerning the identity, divinity, humanity and, in a range of respects, the supple-mentarity of Christ's foreskin, including the theological problem of 'whether, in the interval between the Resurrection and the Ascension, Jesus' foreskin was resurrected along with his penis' (p. 349), see Marc Shell, 'The Holy Foreskin; or, Money, Relics, and Judeo-Christianity', in *Jews and Other Differences: The New Jewish Cultural Studies*, eds Jonathan Boyarin and Daniel Boyarin (Minneapolis: University of Minnesota Press, 1997), pp. 345–59: here, p. 349. Besides the inexhaustibly provoking infant Jesus in this Leonardo painting, the eerie serenity of the mother (if she is the mother), the maternity gown with laces loosened, the translucent veil, the numerous penile (circumcised?) fingers (especially the thumb of Jesus' left hand, holding the bird that symbolizes transience or the Passion) and the mountainous, even apocalyptic scene beyond the windows, we may ask ourselves a double question: What would Freud have made of this painting? (His essay 'Leonardo da Vinci and a Memory of His Childhood' makes no mention of the *Madonna Litta*.) And what might this painting make of Freud?

40   See Steinberg, pp. 165–7: here, p. 165.

41   If, as Jeffrey Mehlman has suggested, Derrida with *Glas* (1974) 'turned his work into a pro-tracted meditation on the institution of circumcision' (*Legacies of Anti-Semitism in France*, Minneapolis: University of Minnesota Press, 1983, p. 82), 'Circumfession' (1990) constitutes a significant supplementary turn in the meditation. On the crucially related but different question of 'female circumcision', see Chantal Zabus, 'Bouches cousues: L'autobiographie de l'excisée', in *L'animal autobiographique: Autour de Jacques Derrida*, ed. Marie-Louise Mallet (Paris: Galilée, 1999), pp. 331–52.

42   As Derrida observes regarding '*différance*' in the essay of that title: '"There is no name for it": a proposition to be read in its *platitude*. This unnameable [*différance*] is not an ineffable Being which no name could approach: God, for example.' See *Margins of Philosophy*, p. 26.

43   Jacques Derrida, 'Shibboleth', trans. Joshua Wilner, in *Acts of Literature*, ed. Derek Attridge (London: Routledge, 1992), pp. 373–413: here, p. 373.

44   'Shibboleth', p. 474.

45   See Robert Smith, *Derrida and Autobiography* (Cambridge: Cambridge University Press, 1995), p. 41.

46   St Augustine, *Confessions*, trans. Henry Chadwick (Oxford: Oxford University Press, 1991), p. 50.

47   Cf. Derrida, *Monolingualism of the Other*, p. 67.

48   On the undecidable force of Derrida as 'the last of the Jews' (C, p. 190), see de Vries, p. 30.

22

Book end: *déjà vu* (reprise)

In our procedure *everything*, so to speak, is perseveration. (Sigmund Freud)[1]

And yet did we not know that the closure of the book was not a simple closure among others? And that only in the book, coming back to it unceasingly, drawing all our resources from it, could we indefinitely designate the writing beyond the book? (Jacques Derrida)[2]

◀ In my case with a micro-loudspeaker in my head, telling me to fall, I feel as if I'm falling, I'm experiencing some kind of seizure, an episode, an attack, a fit. Freud's remarks on epileptic and similar fits in 'The Uncanny' are only reiterating what Jentsch had already seen and said, in his 1906 essay 'On the Psychology of the Uncanny': such cases (and everything has to do with the 'case' as the 'fall') can produce the dawning of a 'dark knowledge' that unsettles any sense of the 'human psyche' as 'unified'; witnessing epileptic or other kinds of fit can be uncanny because they reveal the human being 'as an immensely complicated and delicate mechanism'.[3]

◀ Fit, from Old English *fitt* 'a struggle': an attack of illness, *esp.* epilepsy; a convulsion or paroxysm; a temporary attack or outburst of anything, e.g. laughter; a sudden effort or motion; a mood or passing humour; but also, in a so-called obsolete sense (but obsoletion and obsolescence have to be rethought, any 'obsolete' sense is spectral, it can come back), a fit means a crisis, a painful experience, the approach of death. (See *Chambers*.) The sense of 'fit' as simply 'a spell' or 'short period' (*OED*, sense 2d), also allegedly 'obsolete', is still alive and kicking in the plural usage: 'fits' as 'irregular impulses or periods of action' (*OED*, sense 2c). And then 'fit' is already double, a homonym even in Old English, for there is *fitt* as 'song': a division of a poem, a canto; a strain of music. When Jacques Derrida announces, at the start of *Of Grammatology* (1967), that 'The idea of the book, which always refers to a natural totality, is profoundly alien to the sense of writing', he sets it off against what will always already have disrupted it, namely the 'aphoristic energy' of writing.[4] Writing as fitful: writing fits.

◀ In fits and starts. 'The unconscious does not know the difference between the virtual and the actual, the intention and the action ... We will never have finished, we have not in truth begun, drawing all the ... consequences from this', remarks Derrida. 'How can one not, and why not, take into account *unconscious*, and more generally *virtual* archives?'[5]

◀ In fits and starts we have to speak with ghosts, in order to begin to learn to live. The uncanny, interminable rewriting of psychoanalysis: transfer everything that Freud says about the psyche to reading and writing. Transfer everything, which will have included repression, substitution, displacement, condensation, negative hallucination, the death drive, the repetition compulsion, madness, ghosts, telepathy, delayed action or deferred effect, cannibalism, live burial, circumcision, the double, the return of the dead and, first of all perhaps, transference itself.[6]

◀ And *déjà vu*. It's as if this will have happened before. When did *déjà vu* begin? It is usually traced back to 1876, to a man called Boirac who wrote: 'It has happened that, seeing for the first time a monument, a landscape, a person, I have suddenly and despite myself arrived at this conviction: I have already seen [*déjà vu*] that which I am seeing.'[7]

◀ It was the day after a long journey back from the north, I was in the supermarket and knew that I had lost you, we had fallen together too quickly apart, scanning the shelves of the refrigerated goods, I thought of Wordsworth's phrase concerning the traveller who 'sees too clearly', I thought of scanning, a small bright light, irrational, in the corner of my vision, I'll have to look into this, bring it to an end, turn to see, hard to turn, I keep turning, exceptional force required, I'm having a fit, and smash my head, bite my tongue, pass out, in what order who will say, against the side of the fridge, I fall on the floor, it's several minutes before anyone notices me, and an ambulance is called, coming to I think how sweet this is, as if I have died.

◀ Hillel Schwartz, who cites the 1876 passage from Boirac in his book *The Culture of the Copy*, offers an earlier example, an American or perhaps we should say Anglish-American example, of *déjà vu* before *déjà vu*, the experience before the name. It is Nathaniel Hawthorne, reminiscing in 1856 about a visit to Stanton Harcourt, in Oxfordshire, that had taken place three years earlier: 'I had never before had so pertinacious an attack, as I could not but suppose it, of that odd state of mind wherein we fitfully and teazingly remember some previous scene or incident, of which the one now passing appears to be but the echo and reduplication.'[8] It is an 'attack', working 'fitfully' and 'teazingly'. Hawthorne puts his 'weird and ghostly sensation' down to the inadvertent remembering of some lines by Alexander Pope.[9]

◀ At a meeting at the Park Hotel in Munich on 24 November 1912, Ernest Jones recalls:

> as we were finishing luncheon (in the Park Hotel) [Freud] began reproaching the two Swiss, Jung and Riklin, for writing articles expounding psycho-analysis in Swiss periodicals without mentioning his name. Jung replied that it was unnecessary to do so, it being so well known, but Freud ... persisted, and I remember thinking he was taking the matter rather personally. Suddenly, to our consternation, he fell on the floor in a dead faint. The sturdy Jung carried him to a couch in the lounge, where he soon revived. His first words as he was coming to were strange: 'How sweet it must be to die' – another indication that the idea of death had some esoteric meaning for him.[10]

◀ Imagine the virtual scene of all this. I had no knowledge of Freud's 'death-like attacks' when I had mine in the supermarket in London (on my way back to Oxford), it was in March 1979 (at about the same time, likewise unbeknownst to me, that Derrida was writing his postcards about falling: for example, 'You substitute yourself for yourself all the time, I forget you in order to fall in love [*tomber amoreux*], with you, from the very next second ... and as soon as you called me, the first time, I forgot you, I lost consciousness' (9 March 1979)).[11] Now that fit and the extraordinary feeling on awakening is identified for me with a singular sense of uncanny repetition, as if I have died, in the voice of someone else, with a micro-loudspeaker in my head I will have heard Ernest Jones's translation of Freud's words: 'How sweet it must be to die'.

◀ The uncanniness of naming and anonymity: as if Freud, 'taking it rather personally ... falls on the floor in a dead faint', miming the words of Hamlet's Ghost: 'Adieu ... Remember me' (1.5.91). The documentation and interpretations of Freud's strange 'attacks' (for he experienced several of them, if 'experience' is the word) suggest some of the ways in which psychoanalysis might be said to figure 'the end of the book and the beginning of writing'.[12] How to analyse such a 'death-like attack' as the one in the Park Hotel in 1912? It is already caught up in repetition: Freud's words, on coming to, 'How sweet it must be to die', are for Ernest Jones '*another* indication that the idea of death had some esoteric meaning for him' (emphasis added). The 'meaning' is 'esoteric': to adopt Derrida's phrasing in *Archive Fever*, it 'can only be given over to the spectre'. It belongs to the space of 'the inviolable secret', '[b]eyond every possible and necessary enquiry', 'without a name, without the least symptom'.[13] Freud had already had such an attack in the presence of Jung, just before travelling to the United States together in 1909. On both occasions, Ernest Jones noted, there had been an argument about how much importance to attach to 'death wishes'; and on both occasions Freud had, according to Jones, 'won a little victory over Jung'.[14] In the case of the Munich incident, it had been foreseen, predicted, already inscribed within a kind of program of *déjà vu*. As Jones put it, 'Ferenczi was so far-seeing as to wonder himself beforehand whether Freud would not repeat this in Munich, a prediction that was confirmed by the event' (Jones, 2: 165). But then Freud had also *already* had a fainting attack in the same room in Munich. As he explains to Ernest Jones, in a letter of 8 December 1912:

> I cannot forget that six and four years ago I suffered from very similar though not such intense symptoms in the *same* room of the Park Hotel. I saw Munich first when I visited Fliess during his illness and this town seems to have acquired a strong connection with my relation to that man. There is some piece of unruly homosexual feeling at the root of the matter. (Jones, 1: 348)

Max Schur, who discusses Freud's 'fainting spells' at some length in *Freud: Living and Dying*, notes that 'he had had an attack resembling fainting during his visit to Fliess in Munich … in 1894 (16 years before this episode)'.[15]

◀ The next day, 9 December 1912, in another writing-fit, Freud writes to Ferenczi that 'All these attacks point to the significance of very early experiences with death (in my case a brother who died very young)'.[16] The following month he writes to Binswanger in apparently more frivolous terms: 'I am resigned to being declared a candidate for eternity on the basis of my attack in Munich.'[17] And at the start of the following year he writes to Binswanger once again on the subject, this time supplementing the explanations with a range of 'somatic reinforcements': in particular, 'a week of troubles, a sleepless night, the equivalent of a migraine', together with the effects of 'a bit of alcohol for which I have no tolerance'.[18] The proliferation of explanations and speculations recalls, or perhaps we should say anticipates or prefigures, Freud's attempt to classify, categorize and enumerate cases of the uncanny, in the great essay of 1919. This would be the uncanny as the interminably supplementary, opening on to the experience of the 'overrunning' of the book, as set out in what Derrida has called his 'starting-point': 'no meaning can be determined out of context, but no context permits saturation'.[19]

◀ Max Schur stresses that Freud, in his 'self-analysis' of these attacks, 'never neglected the aspect of overdetermination' (p. 266). But what is 'overdetermination', after Freud? Schur concludes, as if this could be a conclusion: 'In summary, the background information and most of all Freud's own analysis indicate the overdetermination of these fainting spells' (p. 271). Can there be a self-analysis of a fainting fit? Freud's account 'is based on his *memory* of a subjective experience', says Schur: some 'slight amnesia' in such a context is 'very frequent' (p. 268). So quite apart from the thought of what can only be given over to the spectre or complications arising from the aporetic self-analytical scenario of remembering 'loss of consciousness', permit me simply to record the prime suspects in an interminable hetero-thanato-analysis: homosexual feeling, whether in relation to Fliess or to a substitute such as the 'sturdy Jung'; death wishes; the repression or suppression of the proper name of Freud in so-called psychoanalytical publications; the effect of a 'small victory' or being 'wrecked by success' (Jones, 2: 165); the desire to be 'a candidate for eternity'; 'somatic' factors; and, finally, literature, starting perhaps with the case of Dostoevsky. Re-read (once again) Freud's essay on 'Dostoevsky and Parricide' (published in 1928) (PFL, 14: 441–60). It begins with an acknowledgement of his greatness as an artist: 'Dostoevsky's place is not far behind Shakespeare' (p. 441). Freud goes on to ruminate at some length on Dostoevsky's susceptibility to what he calls 'the uncanny disease' (p. 444) of epilepsy. Long before the epileptic attacks began, Freud remarks, Dostoevsky had suffered from other 'death-like attacks' (p. 447).[20] Indeed Freud is very sceptical about distinctions between these different kinds of attack. Thus he refers to 'our author's *so-called* epilepsy' (p. 449, emphasis added), while also observing that 'attacks' may be 'reduced to brief periods of *absence*, or rapidly passing fits of vertigo or may be replaced by short spaces of time during which the patient does something out of character, as though he were under the control of his unconscious' (p. 444). Imagine if Freud had admitted to his own 'death-like attacks' in the essay on Dostoevsky, or in the essay on the uncanny. But how can one be sure that he doesn't, in effect? Is it not necessary, indeed, to listen with another ear, to tune into the speech of the phantom in a virtual archive? Of Dostoevsky, Freud declares: 'We know the meaning and intention of such death-like attacks. They signify an identification with a dead person, either with someone who is really dead or with someone who is still alive and whom the subject wishes dead' (p. 447). I know about these death-like attacks because I have experienced quite a number of them myself, if 'experience' is the word. I have analysed them elsewhere, especially in so-called 'private correspondence': they are in the Freudian archive, ghosts from the future.

◀ Fitful, teasing, it is *déjà vu*, that 'peculiar feeling' that in The Psychopathology of Everyday Life Freud notes 'would merit the most exhaustive treatment', and about which he declared in 1907 that 'we must include [it] in the category of the miraculous or the uncanny' (*PFL*, 5: 328–9) but then, twelve years later, in the 'actual' text entitled 'The Uncanny', he seems to have forgotten all about it: the term as such never appears there. I can feel it all coming on again. How are you going to read all this? As 'tedious familiarity'?

◀ The *OED* defines *déjà vu* as: 'a. An illusory feeling of having previously experienced a present situation; a form of paramnesia ... b. occas. The correct impression that something has been previously experienced; tedious familiarity.' The first recorded usage of the term in English in sense (a) is 1903; in sense (b) 1960. We are living in the epoch of the double-sense of '*déjà vu*'. In *The Culture of the Copy*, Hillel Schwartz has remarked on this as follows:

> Attacks of *déjà vu*, however well met, are still inexplicable; what has changed since Hawthorne's visitation is the feeling about them. Once provocative of 'uneasiness and actual discomfort', today they stir a casual wonder; once symptomatic of psychosis or epileptic fit, today they point to metempsychosis or to the split-second lag between sensation and cognition. The immediacy and clarity of a *déjà vu* is readily assimilable to our habit of instant replay.[21]

Schwartz's treatment of the topic recalls Havelock Ellis's *The World of Dreams* (1911), where he refers to paramnesia (of which the best-known example is *déjà vu*) as a 'fatigue product'.[22] Fatigue product, perhaps, now in ways more resonant than Ellis envisaged, but *déjà vu* also demands a certain sharpness and clarity. Schwartz registers that 'attacks' are 'still inexplicable', but he seems a little too tired. *Déjà vu* is 'readily assimilable', he declares. I'm not so sure. Indeed I believe that the opposite remains the case, perhaps more than ever: the challenge and responsibility to think what is not 'assimilable', what is 'still inexplicable' under the heading of this figure.[23] No book end without an interminable suspicion and vigilance concerning *déjà vu*. Not least as regards psychoanalysis. Recall that *déjà vu* is put forward as apparently the most satisfactory figure for the end, the success, the goal and final achievement of psychoanalysis. At the end of his essay '*Fausse Reconnaissance* ("*déjà raconté*") in Psycho-analytic Treatment' (1914) Freud asserts:

> After [the analyst] has succeeded in forcing the repressed event (whether it was of a real or of a psychical nature) upon the patient's acceptance in the teeth of all resistances, and has succeeded, as it were, in rehabilitating it – the patient may say: '*Now I feel as though I had known it all the time.*'[24]

◀ *The Culture of the Copy* saves perhaps its most abyssal moment for the index. Half-a-dozen lines below the entry for '*déjà vu*' we discover: 'Derrida, Jacques, nary an appearance in the text'.[25] Never an appearance, not a single one anywhere in the whole of the book, claims the Index. Except here, at the very end, in the index, where the negation of the appearance of Jacques Derrida is of course an affirmation. The Index will thus have seized up. And fallen. Overflowing and dissemination of the book. Recalling on the one hand that, as Derrida has said, 'the discourse of deconstruction' is heterogeneous to 'the form of a concluded, closed, closed-off totality, a book' and on the other that '[a] nonmasterable dissemination is not even a polysemia, it belongs to what is outside language'.[26]

◀ In the context of a meditation about ends, about the end of history, the end of Marxism, the end of philosophy (but let's also add, the end of literature and the end of the book), near the start of *Spectres of Marx*, Derrida notes that all of these questions are linked, for him, to 'a troubling sense of "*déjà vu*", and even of a certain "*toujours déjà vu*"'.[27] *Déjà vu* is, by definition, in its definition, 'troubling'. He describes it as 'this malaise of perception, hallucination and time' [*ce malaise de la perception, de l'hallucination et du temps*].[28] It is a malaise, a feeling of uneasiness, disquiet, sickness, faintness. Out of joint, it is a malaise of time itself. He doesn't come back to this term, but the malaise of *déjà vu* could be said to provide the framework for the rest of the book, *Spectres of Marx*. To recall a remark he makes elsewhere: 'One text reads another ... Each "text" is a machine with multiple reading heads for other texts.'[29] '*Déjà vu*' will have initiated the program.

◀ Where does *déjà vu* begin? What would it mean to say that it begins in writing, even, perhaps, in a certain experience of literature? Some years prior to Hawthorne's Popeish reminiscence in *Our Old Home* comes *David Copperfield* (1849–50):

> 'If you had not assured us, my dear Copperfield, on the occasion of that agreeable afternoon we had the happiness of passing with you, that D was your favourite letter,' said Mr Micawber, 'I should unquestionably have supposed A had been so.'
> We have all some experience of a feeling, that comes over us occasionally, of what we are saying and doing having been said and done before, in a remote time – of our having been surrounded, dim ages ago, by the same faces, objects, and circumstances – of our knowing perfectly what will be said next, as if we suddenly remembered it! I never had this mysterious impression more strongly in my life, than before he had uttered those words.[30]

Dickens's novel offers perhaps the earliest definitive appearance in print of what, by prolepsis or anachrony, we now call *déjà vu*.

◀ Let's note the ordering of this Dickensian appearance: it embroils *déjà vu* in a scene of writing or reading. Mr Micawber's is an utterance concerned with letters, the love and ordering of letters. The text only describes the 'mysterious impression' *after* the initial presentation of the utterance that brings on the 'attack' (to use Hawthorne's word). We are apprised of the uncanny strangeness only after it has happened. The text, in effect, duplicates the *déjà vu*, generating a textual diplopia. The reader has to re-read, experience anew, in deferral, the utterance already read or *déjà lu*. Where does this begin? Again, already, earlier on in the novel, we have been invited to be a party to what the narrator calls 'the strange feeling (to which, perhaps, no one is quite a stranger) that all this had occurred before, at some indefinite time, and that I knew what he [Uriah Heep] was going to say next'.[31] As intimated earlier, what might seem a long time ago now: *déjà vu* is double.[32]

◀ What, then, is a 'definitive appearance'? Where does *David Copperfield* , or *déjà vu* in *David Copperfield*, begin? Serialization of the 'I am born'. Chapter 1 of *David Copperfield* is entitled '*I am born*'. A fitting start:

> Whether I shall turn out to be the hero of my own life, or whether that station will be held by anyone else, these pages must show. To begin my life with the beginning of my life, I record that I was born (as I have been informed and believe) on a Friday, at twelve o'clock at night.[33]

'These pages must show': everything will have worked back to front, end to start, already seen. 'I record that I was born': how many times is one born? Resonating like a negative hallucination of a translational hesitation in French (*je suis né*), the opening page (which like any autobiography or 'personal history' must always appear to play, madly, with coming from beyond, after the end of the *bio-* that is its subject) entitles itself, records and reiterates, 'I am born', 'I was born' and, finally, as if with a necessary supplement, a prosthetic membrane, 'I was born with a caul'.[34] Like a certain 'Wolf Man': a coincidence that may not have escaped Freud. Caul *déjà vu*.[35]

◀ A book is not published when it is published. *David Copperfield* appears in monthly instalments, between 1 May 1849 and 1 November 1850, and then as a single volume in November 1850. Serialization changes the nature of the institution of literature. *Déjà vu* acquires a new, unprecedented kind of explicitness, a cryptic visibility. Re-read Dickens, for example *Our Mutual Friend* and, especially, *The Mystery of Edwin Drood*, novels about *déjà vu* as a condition of narrative. The fact of a narrator with uncanny knowledge of the narrative as *déjà vu*, of what is going to happen next, of how it is going to end (or, in the case of *Drood*, not end, end in knots, suspending itself perhaps in the transfer of a *déjà vu*, a phantasmagoric readerly implant: you know the story, unendingly coming back to end at the beginning, 'The Dawn Again'),[36] this fact (which also governs the genres of detective fiction and psychoanalytic discourse, in particular the 'case history', though Freud immeasurably complicates and transforms things), this fact of uncanny knowledge broaches the end of literature. Henceforth literary writing cannot *not* take account, however tacitly or stereophonically, of this *déjà vu* effect. It is the very question of literature, as that which falls, fitfully perhaps, outside the program.

◀ In this respect it is perhaps not by chance that two recent novels that deal with *déjà vu*, Don DeLillo's *White Noise* (1984) and Janice Galloway's *The Trick Is to Keep Breathing* (1989), are at the same time deeply engaged with the uncanny all-pervasiveness of 'the program'.[37] I mean 'program' here in Christopher Johnson's sense, when he says that 'with the increasing relief of human motion, memory, calculation and communication, with the increasing delegation of the vital to the programmatic, it becomes increasingly impossible to locate the program'.[38] Janice Galloway's *The Trick Is to Keep Breathing* loses its marbles along with its margins. Right up against the spine of the book, or right off the outer margin, fragments such as these begin to appear:

sometime
that feeli
deja vu

The text consigns itself, perhaps too easily and thus troublingly, to a double-program: on the one hand, to a literary generic program that would graft the text on to innumerable others, from *Jane Eyre* and 'The Yellow Wallpaper' to *The Bell Jar* and *The Edible Woman*; on the other hand, to a socio-economico-tele-technologico-political program that determines the figure of the woman (the narrator ironically named 'Joy') as obliged to follow a life dictated by television and media, which means have a nervous breakdown and become a late twentieth-century version of the so-called 'madwoman in the attic' or the woman as buried alive. The script is already written, 'sometime that feelin deja vu'.[39]

◀ *White Noise* stages the narratological aporia of *déjà vu* in singularly 'eerie' terms.[40] There is an 'airborne toxic event' (p. 117), a massive leakage of a chemical called Nyodene D. that produces experiences of *déjà vu* (quickly followed by 'coma, convulsions, and miscarriage': p. 125). A loudspeaker is declaring, over and over: 'Abandon all domiciles. Now, now. Toxic event, chemical cloud' (p. 120). *White Noise* is *déjà vu*. The text contaminates itself, supplements, entertains and auto-immunizes itself with the figure of *déjà vu*. The narrator Jack Gladney wonders: 'Is it possible to have a false perception of an illusion? Is there a true *déjà vu* and a false *déjà vu*?' (p. 126). Everything that the novel tries to put forward on the question of what it calls 'modern death' (p. 150) is bound up with it: Gladney asks why so many people now are having 'episodes'; his colleague Murray replies: 'Because death is in the air' and then goes on to expound his 'theory of *déjà vu*': 'Maybe when we die, the first thing we'll say is, "I know this feeling, I was here before"' (p. 151). The text may appear thematically to relinquish the topic of *déjà vu*: 'The *déjà vu* crisis centers closed down. The hotline was quietly discontinued. People seemed on the verge of forgetting' (p. 221). But this in another sense only intensifies or redoubles it: however construed, *déjà vu* is at once the condition of the narrative (recounting the events, the narrator has a peculiar tacit knowledge of what is going to happen, it will have been from the start as if he knew it all along) and the novel's most decisive figure for its explorations of 'death' and of the effects of the simulacrum. SIMUVAC ('Short for simulated evacuation. A new state program': p. 139) uses the 'roiling' event of the 'immense toxic cloud' (p. 157) as 'a model', 'a chance to use the real event in order to rehearse the simulation' (p. 139). Everything is incorporated into the model ghost, the ghostly model of *déjà vu*.[41]

◀ I'm having another episode. Once again: can one truly speak of a first, 'definitive appearance' of *déjà vu*? A question of the 'virtual archive', here for example imprinted in the relation between *Spectres of Marx* or *Archive Fever* on the one hand and Shakespeare's *Hamlet* on the other. 'O my prophetic soul!' (1.5.40): the Ghost's revelation that his brother Claudius has murdered him comes to Hamlet, apparently, with the force of a *déjà vu*, as if he (or his soul) knew it in advance.[42] Derrida does not quote Hamlet's response to what the Ghost says, even if he makes the question of how to address the Ghost, or ghosts, the presiding question of *Spectres of Marx*, *Archive Fever*, and perhaps of all his so-called books. With the words 'Adieu ... Remember me' (1.5.91), the Ghost has already exited, but Hamlet addresses it as 'thee', as though the Ghost were listening.

> Remember thee?
> Ay, thou poor ghost, whiles memory holds a seat
> In this distracted globe. Remember thee?

Yea, from the table of my memory
I'll wipe away all trivial fond records,
All saws of books, all forms, all pressures past
That youth and observation copied there,
And thy commandment all alone shall live
Within the book and volume of my brain,
Unmix'd with baser matter ... [*Writes.*]
...

              ... Now to my word.
It is 'Adieu, adieu, remember me.'

                (1.5.92–111)

Despite his concern with the question of how to address the ghost, Derrida does not cite this passage anywhere in *Spectres of Marx*, or *Archive Fever*, or in the related shorter text entitled 'The Time Is Out of Joint'.[43] It makes 'nary an appearance'. Would this speech not constitute part of the virtual archive informing what Derrida describes as Freud's desire (in the *Gradiva* essay [*PFL*, 14: 33–118] and elsewhere) to 'exhume a more archaic *impression* ... to exhibit a more archaic *imprint* than the one the other archaeologists of all kinds bustle around'?[44] Feverishly to wipe out the archive, yes, wipe away all the records, all sayings of books, all wax imprints or impressions, so that the Ghost's commandment is able to 'live', absolutely pure and singular, 'all alone', 'Unmix'd with baser matter', 'Within the book and volume of my brain'.

◀ Let us try to attend to one word in the unfolding of this inexhaustible passage from *Hamlet*: it is 'and'. It is a question of the 'and' or 'ands' of which Derrida has recently proposed: 'Wondering what the *"and"* is, what *and* ... means and does not mean, does and does not do ... is perhaps ... the most constant task of any deconstruction.'[45] Why does Hamlet say 'Within the book and volume of my brain'? Trying to take account of the fact that, like Freud and like Derrida, Hamlet construes the mental apparatus as a kind of uncanny writing pad, we might ask: what is the meaning of the 'and' in this line, what is the sense in saying 'the book *and* volume of my brain'? The phrase is an example of a strange rhetorical figure known as hendiadys. From the Greek *hen dia dyoin*, literally 'one through two', hendiadys entails what George T. Wright has described as 'the use of two substantives, joined by a conjunction (*et, atque,* or *-que*, all signifying "and"), to express a single but complex idea'.[46] The most often quoted example is from the *Georgics* (II.192): *pateris libamus et auro* ('we drink from cups and gold', usually normalized in English translation as 'we drink from golden cups'). A more colloquial example from so-called everyday English would be 'house and home' or, perhaps, 'fits and starts'. Hendiadys, remarks Wright with admirable prudence, 'if there is such a thing' (p. 170, emphasis added). The very title of his essay, 'Hendiadys and *Hamlet*', poses the strangeness: is this title itself an example of hendiadys? How can one prove the *absence* of hendiadys? What are the limits of this figure?[47] Wright proposes that, at a conservative estimate, there are at least three hundred cases of hendiadys in Shakespeare's oeuvre, and 66 (yes, sixty-six) in *Hamlet*. As Wright sharply demonstrates, it becomes in certain respects impossible to disentangle 'hendiadys' and *Hamlet*. Suggesting that Shakespeare's style has perhaps still not yet been 'adequately explored' (p. 172), Wright sees hendiadys as a sort of signature effect. Shakespeare, he observes, 'appears to have taken this odd figure to his bosom and to have made it entirely his own' (p. 169).

◀ Hendiadys, Wright claims, 'has always struck English-speaking people as a disturbing and foreign device' (p. 170). In a footnote he refers, for example, to the linguist Geoffrey N. Leech who considers hendiadys an example of what 'we can value only as curiosities … It is so rare that I have found no certain instance of it in English literature'.[48] Hendiadys, says Wright, 'resists logical analysis' (p. 169): it is 'too confusing, too disorderly' (p. 172). It 'makes us do a double take' (p. 175), he says. Or rather, hendiadys 'is' a double-take. Like *déjà vu*. Hendiadys *and déjà vu*. Hendiadys and the uncanny *and* …

◀ Wright refers, in passing (p. 173), to an example from *All's Well That Ends Well*. Lafeu declares: 'They say miracles are past, and we have our philosophical persons to make modern and familiar things supernatural and causeless' (2.3.1–3). The Norton editors gloss this as meaning that philosophical persons 'make supernatural things, without apparent cause, seem commonplace and easily explained'.[49] Perhaps unintentionally, the Norton editors' syntax in fact preserves the resistance to univocality or 'clear sense' here. The hendiadys in 'supernatural and causeless' doubles the sense of a statement already to double business bound: 'to make modern and familiar things supernatural and causeless'. Hendiadys, in other words, does not merely do the work of 'intensification' or 'amplification' (as if with a micro-loudspeaker within): it involves what Wright calls 'an interweaving … of meanings, a deliberate violation of clear sense' (p. 172). Or as Frank Kermode has put it: hendiadys works 'by deviations, by doing something other than we expect from words joined by "and", by a sort of violation of the promise of simple parataxis'.[50] Hendiadys is out of joint: it fits.

◀ It is the language of the Ghost, language around the Ghost. It is almost as if cases of hendiadys, or of what Wright calls 'hendiadic transformations' (p. 183, n. 5), *summon up* the Ghost. The very witnessing of the Ghost is a matter of hendiadys, of what Horatio calls 'the sensible and true avouch / Of mine own eyes' (1.1.60) ('the sensorily accurate testimony' or 'accurate sensory testimony', as Wright glosses it (p. 174)). The time of the Ghost is hendiadic, 'In the dead waste and middle of the night' (1.2.198). Indeed, the Ghost himself, the Ghost itself, is hendiadic: neither exactly distinct from nor the same as Hamlet's father.[51] The Ghost's speech, and speech in the face (or visor) of the Ghost, is haunted with hendiadys. 'Angels and ministers of grace defend us!' (1.4.39) are the son's first words on seeing the Ghost. Come back up from the 'ponderous and marble jaws' (1.4.50) of the sepulchre, the Ghost tells Hamlet of 'sulph'rous and tormenting flames' (1.5.3), of the 'certain term' before his crimes are 'burnt and purg'd away' (1.5.10,13), of making the listener's 'knotted and combined locks to part' (1.5.18).[52] The 'wild and whirling words' (1.5.139) with which Hamlet responds to the Ghost would include the hendiadys ('wild and whirling words') that encapsulates them: not only destroying the archive in a kind of fit of madness, wiping away everything 'That youth and observation copied there', but substituting this hendiadys for another, 'Within the book and volume of my brain'). A matter, in each case, of the 'and'.

◀ George Wright comments on this phrase, 'the book and volume of my brain': 'Two competing senses of *volume* are felt here: (1) tome, (2) "Size, bulk or dimensions (of a book)" (*OED*). At first glance, the two words seem nearly synonymous, but the phrase also seems to mean "within the book and largeness of my brain", i.e., "within the spacious book of my brain" ' (p. 186). The end of the book is inscribed here, in the 'and'. 'At first glance', says Wright, 'book' and 'volume' 'seem nearly synonymous' – as if there is a 'second glance', after a lucid interval, by which time things will have been cleared up. But the first glance is *déjà vu*: 'book' is and is not 'volume'; 'volume' is and is not 'book'; the hendiadic 'and' undoes the specificity, internal coherence and integrity of each alike.[53]

◀ 'And' figures the supplement that makes it possible to say, as Derrida does at the start of *Dissemination* (1972): 'This (therefore) will not have been a book.'[54] Or as he has more recently formulated it: 'in the beginning, there is the *and*'.[55] It is an uncanny 'and', as in 'the distance [*l'écart*, the space, gap, discrepancy, difference] between the book and the book' [*l'écart entre le livre et le livre*] that he speaks of at the end of *Writing and Difference*.[56] The end of the book: the uncanny. In telling us at the end of *Spectres of Marx* that his text could have been subtitled 'Marx – *das*

Unheimliche', Derrida inscribes a logic of uncanny subtitling that may let itself be read across all his texts.[57] For Derrida, in the end, the uncanny is always 'set in place elsewhere' *and* 'to be continued'.[58]

◀ Witnessing Ophelia disseminating her anthology of flowers ('There's rosemary, that's for remembrance – pray you, love, remember. And there is pansies, that's for thoughts'), Laertes declares: 'A document in madness: thoughts and remembrance fitted' (4.5.173–6). 'Document' here carries the so-called obsolete sense of teaching (from the Latin *docere*). A seminar in madness: the fitting of present (thoughts) and past (remembrance). 'Fitted' is supposedly to be understood in the sense of 'bestowed where they fit or belong' (Harold Jenkins's gloss on the word): isn't this in its turn a sort of mad reading? How could one not also hear the 'madding', 'distracting' play on this word ('fitted') that constitutes what Stephen Booth has called 'so gross a stumbling block to understanding' in Sonnet 119? 'How have mine eyes out of their spheres been fitted / In the distraction of this madding fever!'[59] 'Fitted' and 'fitted'.

◀ Wittgenstein remarks:

> The feeling of the uncanny [*Das Gefühl des Unheimlichen*]. How is it manifested? The *duration* of such a 'feeling'. What is it like, e.g., for it to be interrupted? Would it be possible, for example, to have it and not have it every other second? Don't its marks include a characteristic kind of course (beginning and ending), distinguishing it from, e.g., a sense perception?[60]

This endearing proliferation of questions recalls his characterization of Freud as 'charming'.[61] Recall *déjà vu*: How long will it last? Is this an event? To whom is it happening? There is a beauty in questioning. The fitful beauty of Wittgenstein's 'remark' or 'remarks' comports with Wallace Stevens's suggestion that 'questions are remarks'.[62] Wittgenstein, it may seem, wants to do what Freud wanted to do: fix the uncanny, analyse *the* uncanny, distinguish, define and categorize *the* feeling of the uncanny. Commenting on Wittgenstein and the uncanny, Gordon C. F. Bearn writes:

> If the world comes to seem uncanny, this will not happen gradually, reasonable doubt by reasonable doubt; it will come all of a sudden. It will be prepared of course, like an avalanche, but when it comes, it comes all at once. The uncanniness comes as a revelation.[63]

A feeling of the uncanny entails revelatory suddenness. It happens, it arises, it comes as if out of the blue. Correspondingly, we speak of having *had* an uncanny feeling or experience, as something that came to an end, something now past. But if a feeling of uncanniness compels Freud and so many others (including myself) to want to tell its story, to give it a story with (in Wittgenstein's words) 'a characteristic kind of course (beginning and ending)', it also figures as radical interruption or fitting. When Wittgenstein wonders what it is like for a feeling or feelings [*des Gefühls*] of the uncanny to be interrupted, he is perhaps feeling for the impossible that the uncanny nevertheless 'is'. As Derrida has remarked: 'Without interruption – between letters, words, sentences, books – no significa-tion could be awakened … Death strolls between letters.'[64] For 'interruption' read 'death', 'ghosts' 'haunting'. I began: 'The uncanny entails another thinking of beginning: the beginning is already haunted. The uncanny is ghostly.' Like a book, the uncanny would neither begin nor end.

◀ Final episode in this series. Have we really even begun to draw the con-sequences of Freud's reading of *Hamlet*? Perhaps the most haunting *term* for any notion of a book end, an end of the book, a book's ending (or beginning), Freud's discovery of delayed action or deferred effect (*Nachträglichkeit*) is delayed and deferred not least in its articulation, displaying and displacing itself, for example, in all the footnotes and other additions he makes to texts he has already published. In the 1900 text of *The Interpretation of Dreams*, he asserts that 'it can of course only be the poet's own mind which confronts us in Hamlet'. His reading is concerned with the death of Shakespeare's father John in 1601.[65] *Hamlet* is considered to have been written 'under the immediate impact of his bereave-ment and … while his childhood feelings about his father had been freshly revived'. Freud's Oedipal interpretation thus attempts 'to interpret the deepest layers of impulses in the mind of the creative writer' (*PFL*, 4: 368). It is only later, as a deferred effect, in the 1908 Preface to the Second Edition, that Freud acknowledges the extent to which the 'self-analysis' called *The Interpretation of Dreams* constituted '[his] reaction to [his own] father's death' (*PFL* 4: 47). Under what may be called the immediate impact of his bereavement, in November 1896, Freud had written to Fliess that 'the occasion of his death has re-awakened all my early feelings'.[66] In a footnote to his celebrated so-called Oedipal reading of *Hamlet*, added to the text of *The Interpretation of Dreams* in 1930, Freud writes: 'Incidentally, I have in the meantime ceased to believe that the author of Shakespeare's works was the man from Stratford' (p. 368, n. 1). 'Incidentally': by the by, it so befalls. So the astonishing English translation has it. Or as the German more literally says, without any indication that the footnote has been added some thirty years afterwards: 'The above assumption that the author of

Shakespeare's works was the man from Stratford has since then driven me mad [*An der oben gemachten Voraussetzung, dass der Autor der Werke Shakespeares der Mann aus Stratford war, bin ich seither irre geworden*].[67] Remember me, remember my theory of the Oedipus or in truth, more precisely, the Hamlet complex, after all I'm not denying that psychoanalysis is inextricably bound up with Shakespeare, but incidentally I have gone mad, there is no need in future to mention Shakespeare's name. Expound psychoanalysis without it. Wipe away all remembrance of Shakespeare. This is my document for the archive. '*Now I feel as though I had known it all the time*': Shakespeare and psychoanalysis fitted.[68]

NOTES

1   Sigmund Freud, 'Psychoanalysis and the Establishment of the Facts in Legal Proceedings' (1906), in *SE*, XI: 111. A little earlier in the same text (p. 107), he proposes as an alternative to 'perseveration' [*Perseveration*] the term 'after-effect' [*Nachwirkung*]. For the original German text see 'Tatbestandsdiagnostik und Psychoanalyse', in Sigmund Freud, *Gesammelte Werke*, 7 (London: Imago, 1941), p. 7.

2   Jacques Derrida, 'Ellipsis', in *Writing and Difference*, trans. Alan Bass (London: Routledge and Kegan Paul, 1978), p. 294.

3   Ernst Jentsch, 'On the Psychology of the Uncanny', trans. Roy Sellars, *Angelaki* vol. 2, no. 1 (1995), ed. Sarah Wood, p. 14.

4   Jacques Derrida, *Of Grammatology*, trans. Gayatri Chakravorty Spivak (Baltimore: Johns Hopkins University Press, 1976), p. 18.

5   See Jacques Derrida, *Archive Fever: A Freudian Impression*, trans. Eric Prenowitz (Chicago: Chicago University Press, 1996), pp. 64–6.

6   To quote Derrida once again: 'a text can stand in a relationship of transference (primarily in the psychoanalytical sense) to another text! … [O]ne text loves another.' See 'Living on/ Border Lines', trans. James Hulbert, in Harold Bloom et al., *Deconstruction and Criticism* (New York: Seabury Press, 1979), 75–176: here, 'Border Lines', p. 147.

7   E. Boirac, 'Correspondance', *Revue philosophique*, vol. 1 (1876), 430–1; qoted in W. H. Burnham, 'Memory, Historically and Experimentally Considered', *American Journal of Psychology*, vol. 2 (1889), 441–2.

8   Nathaniel Hawthorne, *Our Old Home: A Series of English Sketches*, Centenary Edition of the Works of Hawthorne, 5, ed. Fredson Bowers et al. (Columbus: Ohio State University Press, 1970), p. 183; cited, and partly mis-cited, in Hillel Schwartz, *The Culture of the Copy: Striking Likenesses, Unreasonable Facsimiles* (New York: Zone Books, 1996), p. 298. (Schwartz omits the 'not' in 'as I could not but suppose it', and adds a 'the' before 'reduplication': laws of citation will perhaps not have escaped the disorientations of a certain *déjà vu* effect.)

9   Hawthorne, *Our Old Home*, p. 184.

10   Ernest Jones, *Sigmund Freud: Life and Work*, 3 vols (London: Hogarth Press, 1953–57). Here, 1: 348. Further references to Jones will be incorporated into the main body of the text, giving volume and page number, abbreviated 'Jones'.

11   Jacques Derrida, *The Post Card: From Socrates to Freud and Beyond*, trans. Alan Bass (Chicago: Chicago University Press, 1987), p. 180; *La carte postale: de Socrate à Freud et au-delà* (Paris:

Flammarion, 1980), p. 195. The present chapter will thus have sought to sketch a preliminary and almost silent reading of that 'almost silent reading of the word *"tombe"* (tomb) or *"tomber"* (to fall)', as Derrida describes the essay entitled 'My Chances / *Mes Chances*: A Rendezvous with Some Epicurean Stereophonies', trans. Irene Harvey and Avital Ronell, in *Taking Chances: Derrida, Psychoanalysis, and Literature*, eds Joseph H. Smith and William Kerrigan (Baltimore and London: Johns Hopkins University Press, 1984), pp. 1–32: see p. 31, n. 1. A brilliantly fitful and strange 'case'-study on chance and falling, Derrida's essay explores the ways in which 'An implacable program takes shape ... accelerating a rhythm that merely gives the *feeling* of randomness to those who do not know the prescription – which, incidentally, is also my case' (p. 14).

12 I borrow this phrase, of course, from the opening chapter of Derrida's *Of Grammatology*, pp. 6–26.

13 See Derrida, *Archive Fever*, pp. 100–1.

14 See Jones, *Sigmund Freud*, 2: 61, 165–6. He writes: 'Confirmatory of Freud's interpretation of his fainting attacks is the fact that on both occasions there had just been an argumentative discussion on the topic of *death wishes*, and on both occasions Jung had reproached him for attaching too much importance to them. In Bremen Jung had been descanting at length on the significance of some prehistoric cemeteries that had been discovered in the neighbourhood. Freud became restive and finally suggested that Jung's continuing with the theme must indicate the operation of some unconscious death wishes. Jung warmly repudiated this and asserted that Freud was too ready to make such interpretations' (pp. 165–6).

15 See Max Schur, 'Fainting Spells and Their Meaning', in his *Freud: Living and Dying* (London: Hogarth Press and Institute of Psycho-Analysis, 1972), pp. 264–72: here, p. 269. Further page references to Schur are given in the main body of the text.

16 Letter to Ferenczi, 9 December 1912, quoted in Schur, pp. 267–8.

17 Letter to Binswanger, 16 December 1912, quoted in Schur, p. 271. This letter goes on to refer to Stekel's characterization of Freud's having a 'hypocritical streak' and quotes Mark Twain: 'Reports of my death grossly exaggerated.' See Schur, pp. 271–2.

18 Letter to Binswanger, 1 January 1913, quoted in Schur, p. 268.

19 Derrida, 'Living on', p. 81.

20 On epilepsy and the death drive see also Sándor Ferenczi, 'The Unwelcome Child and his Death Drive' (1929), in his *Selected Writings*, ed. Julia Borossa (Harmondsworth: Penguin, 1999), pp. 269–74. Ferenczi here seeks to corroborate Freud's view that 'the symptoms of epilepsy express the frenzy of a tendency to self-destruction that is almost free from the inhibitions of the wish to live' (p. 269).

21 Schwartz, *The Culture of the Copy*, pp. 298–9.

22 Havelock Ellis, *The World of Dreams* (London: Constable, 1911), p. 247.

23 Schwartz's tiredness is also evident in his later formulation that 'Boredom is perpetual *déjà vu*' (p. 316). Again, this seems too readily assimilating, too quick to set aside what remains uncertain or indeed perhaps 'inexplicable' about the nature of *déjà vu*.

24 Sigmund Freud, '*Fausse Reconnaissance ("déjà raconté")* in Psycho-analytic Treatment', trans. James Strachey, *SE*, XIII: 207. Schwartz (p. 300) also makes reference to this extraordinary moment (which I discuss in more detail in Chapter 11, above) in Freud's text.

25 Schwartz, *The Culture of the Copy*, p. 543.

26 See Jacques Derrida, 'Afterw.rds: or, at least, less than a letter about a letter less', trans. Geoffrey Bennington, in *Afterwords*, ed. Nicholas Royle (Tampere, Finland: Outside Books, 1992), pp. 199; and 'White Mythology', in *Margins of Philosophy*, trans. Alan Bass (Chicago: Chicago University Press, 1982), p. 248.

27 Jacques Derrida, *Spectres of Marx: The State of the Debt, the Work of Mourning, and the New International*, trans. Peggy Kamuf (London: Routledge, 1994), p. 14. Originally published in French as *Spectres de Marx: L'État de la dette, le travail du deuil et la nouvells Internationale* (Paris: Galilée, 1993).

28 Derrida, *Spectres of Marx*, p. 14; French text, p. 36.

29 Jacques Derrida, 'Living on', p. 107. Or as Timothy Clark puts it: '[Derrida's work] is experimenting with the novel psychic and noetic effects of new forms of textual machine ... Derrida's writing employs, in a non-calculating way, the unforeseeable effects of novel technics of signification, setting up mini-machines as originary prostheses to his "own" act of inscription.' See Timothy Clark, 'Deconstruction and Technology', in *Deconstructions: A User's Guide*, ed. Nicholas Royle (Basingstoke and New York: Palgrave, 2000), pp. 238–57: here, p. 252.

30 Charles Dickens, *David Copperfield* (1849–50), ed. Jeremy Tambling (Harmondsworth: Penguin, 1996), p. 523.

31 Dickens, *David Copperfield*, p. 356.

32 The link between the double and *déjà vu* can be 'already seen', for example, in Poe's 'William Wilson' (1839): 'I discovered, or fancied I discovered, in his accent, his air, and general appearance, a something which first startled, and then deeply interested me, by bringing to mind various dim visions of my earliest infancy – wild, confused and thronging memories of a time when memory herself was yet unborn. I cannot better describe the sensation which oppressed me, than by saying that I would with difficulty shake off the belief of my having been acquainted with the being who stood before me, at some epoch very long ago – some point of the past even infinitely remote. The delusion, however, faded rapidly as it came.' It is striking here, too, that Poe's text evokes a sort of double-birth for memory itself: the narrator recalls 'memories of a time when memory herself was yet unborn'. See 'William Wilson', in *Collected Works of Edgar Allan Poe, vol. 2, Tales and Sketches 1831–1842*, ed. Thomas Ollive Mabbott (Cambridge, Mass.: Belknap Press, 1978), p. 436. If *déjà vu avant la lettre* can be sensed in a number of mid-nineteenth-century literary texts, these include poetry as well as narrative fiction. Recall the first two fits of D. G. Rossetti's 'Sudden Light' (written in 1854, published in 1863):

> I have been here before,
>> But when or how I cannot tell:
> I know the grass beyond the door,
>> The sweet keen smell,
> The sighing sound, the lights around the shore.

> You have been mine before, –
>> How long ago I may not know:
> But just when at that swallow's soar
>> Your neck turned so,
> Some veil did fall, – I knew it all of yore.

See *The Poetical Works of Dante Gabriel Rossetti*, ed. William M. Rossetti (London: Ellis and Elvey, 1905), p. 295.

33 Dickens, *David Copperfield*, p. 11.

34 Dickens, *David Copperfield*, p. 11. Regarding the French phrase (*je suis né*: both 'I am born' and 'I was born'), Jacques Derrida speaks of the need for 'an interminable analysis of the phrase "je, je suis, je suis né" in which the tense is not given. Anxiety will never be dispelled on this subject, for the event that is hereby designated can herald itself in me only in the future: "I am (not yet) born", but the future has the form of a past which I will never have witnessed and

which for this reason remains always promised – and moreover also multiple.' See *Points …*
Interviews, 1974–1994, ed. Elisabeth Weber, trans. Peggy Kamuf et al. (London: Routledge, 1995), p. 339.

35   The Wolf Man too was 'born with a caul'. As Freud describes this strange prosthesis: 'the caul was the veil which hid him from the world and hid the world from him' (*PFL*, 9: 340). For a fascinating account of the uncanny relations between Dickens and Freud see Ned Lukacher, 'Dialectical Images: Benjamin/Dickens/Freud' in his *Primal Scenes: Literature, Philosophy, Psychoanalysis* (Ithaca: Cornell University Press, 1986), pp. 275–336. Arguing that 'In the culture of psychoanalysis, Dickens has always been the figure of both its prehistory and its future' (p. 336), Lukacher generates a provoking sense of what we are referring to here, after Derrida, as the virtual archive of psychoanalysis.

36   *The Mystery of Edwin Drood* (Harmondsworth: Penguin, 1974) begins *and* ends (without ending) with 'the dawn', with a chapter called 'The Dawn' and another called 'The Dawn Again'. See 'The "telepathy effect"' (Chapter 19, above) for further discussion of Dickens's final, unfinished novel.

37   Don DeLillo, *White Noise* (1984; London: Picador, 1999); Janice Galloway, *The Trick Is to Keep Breathing* (1989; London: Minerva, 1991). Further page references to these novels will be given in the main body of the text.

38   Christopher Johnson, 'Ambient Technologies, Uncanny Signs', *Oxford Literary Review*, vol.21 (1999), 131.

39   The book's margins begin to dissolve, explicitly giving way to *déjà vu* effects, from p. 64; but one of the effects of such '*déjà vu*' is of course to estrange any straightforward sense of 'the beginning'. For further examples see pp. 110–11, 163, 174–5, 186, 194–5.

40   DeLillo's novel is an interesting example of a text that may seem quite studiously to avoid deploying the word – and thus explicitly remarking itself as – 'uncanny'. The text's preferred, but inevitably linked term is 'eerie': see, for example, pp. 122, 236, 238, 242, 244, 258. I discuss the 'non-appearance' of the word 'uncanny' in Chapter 1, n. 60, above.

41   On the uncanniness of 'the model' as 'the dreamed-of ghost' see Jacques Derrida, *The Truth in Painting*, trans. Geoff Bennington and Ian McLeod (Chicago: University of Chicago Press, 1987), p. 217.

42   Intriguingly, perhaps, a similar effect might be noted in relation to Sophocles. The revelation of what Freud would call the Oedipus complex happens at the uncanny crossroads of a kind of *déjà vu*, in the shadowy world of dreams. As Jocasta tries to comfort her increasingly fear-filled, filial husband: 'Many a man before you, / In his dreams, has shared his mother's bed. / Take such things for shadows, nothing at all.' See Sophocles, *Oedipus the King*, ll. 1074–6, in *The Three Theban Plays: Antigone, Oedipus the King, Oedipus at Colonus*, trans. Robert Fagles (Harmondsworth: Penguin, 1984), p. 215. Freud quotes this passage in *The Interpretation of Dreams*: see *PFL*, 4: 366.

43   Jacques Derrida, 'The Time Is Out of Joint', trans. Peggy Kamuf, in *Deconstruction is/in America: A New Sense of the Political*, ed. Anselm Haverkamp (New York: New York University Press, 1995), pp. 14–38.

44   See Derrida, *Archive Fever*, p. 97.

45   Jacques Derrida, 'Et Cetera … (and so on, und so weiter, and so forth, et ainsi de suite, und so überall, etc.)', trans. Geoffrey Bennington, in *Deconstructions: A User's Guide*, ed. Nicholas Royle (Basingstoke and New York: Palgrave, 2000), p. 285.

46   George T. Wright, 'Hendiadys and *Hamlet*', *PMLA*, vol. 96 (1981), 168–90: here, p. 168. Further page references are given in the main body of the text.

47   This is not to suggest that hendiadys lacks specificity, only that it has singularly 'estranging effects' (to echo Wright's term: p. 173). Wright thus distinguishes it from zeugma (Alexander Pope's 'Dost sometimes counsel take – and sometimes tea', for example), for with zeugma 'each of [the] phrases binds in a syntactically parallel structure two disparate ideas ["counsel" and "tea"], not two related ones' (p. 170).

48   Geoffrey N. Leech, *A Linguistic Guide to English Poetry* (London: Longman, 1969), p. 4; quoted by Wright, 'Hendiadys and *Hamlet*', p. 183, n.1.

49   *The Norton Shakespeare: Based on the Oxford Edition*, ed. Stephen Greenblatt et al. (New York: W. W. Norton, 1997), p. 2201, n. 1.

50   Frank Kermode, *Forms of Attention* (Chicago: Chicago University Press, 1985), p. 50.

51   George Wright's essay elaborates the case for thinking about hendiadys in relation to the analysis of character in Shakespeare's play: see pp. 178 ff. In particular he considers 'the extent to which characters act *through* others', noting that 'When at any given moment on the stage two persons appear to be in conference, we are likely to understand them better as one character working through the other ... Again, this situation is exactly that of hendiadys' (pp. 179–80). Here, perhaps more than ever, hendiadys would be the figure of the Ghost, a ghostly figure.

52   The Ghost is, to anticipate the hendiadic words that usher in his second 'talking part' in the play, 'A king of shreds and patches' (3.4.102) – a phrase ostensibly referring to the present king ('A cutpurse of the empire and the rule', as Hamlet has just hendiadically described him (3.4.99)), but in truth strangely duplicitous, antithetical, ghostly, conjurious.

53   Can one move away from hendiadys? Freudian perseveration must give us pause. Frank Kermode, who was preoccupied with (or by) it in his 1985 book *Forms of Attention*, comes back to it in his most recent work, *Shakespeare's Language* (London: Allen Lane The Penguin Press, 2000). Having devoted some detailed attention to this rhetorical figure (if it is one), he tries to move on: 'So doubling is a principal characteristic of the language of *Hamlet*. Once alerted to it, and to its extreme form of hendiadys, one hears it throughout; it takes its part in a greater complex of linguistic devices, and serves more than one purpose. Of course I am not suggesting that it is the only characteristic that distinguishes this play. Much more celebrated is delay' (p. 102). As should be clear from our reading of *Hamlet* here, hendiadys is just as much a question of the nature of 'delay' as it is of 'doubling'.

54   Jacques Derrida, *Dissemination*, trans. Barbara Johnson (Chicago: Chicago University Press, 1981), p. 3.

55   Derrida, 'Et Cetera', p. 282.

56   Derrida ends the book with a previously unpublished essay which ends with a discussion of 'the deferral within the now of writing, the distance between the book and the book': see Jacques Derrida, 'Ellipsis', in *Writing and Difference*, trans. Alan Bass (London: Routledge and Kegan Paul, 1978), p. 300; *L'écriture et la différence* (Paris: Éditions du Seuil, 1967), p. 436.

57   Derrida, *Spectres of Marx*, p. 174.

58   In *The Post Card* (1979) he will say of the uncanny: 'I cannot take up again what was set in place elsewhere' (p. 342). Then in a footnote we are referred back to 'The Double Session', in *Dissemination*. In 'The Double Session' we find two detailed footnotes concerning the uncanny, both ending with the parenthetical words: '(to be continued)' [*à suivre*]. See *Dissemination*, pp. 220, n. 32 and 268, n. 67, and *La dissémination* (Paris: Éditions du Seuil, 1972), pp. 249, n. 25 and 300, n. 56. Derrida has been criticized for this apparent avoidance of an 'in depth' sustained analysis of Freud's essay, 'The Uncanny'. Mark Wigley, for example, declares, rather tetchily: 'despite, or perhaps because of the unique attraction of [Freud's essay] or, more likely, its subject [the uncanny], it is never explicitly analyzed in ["The Double

Session"] ... Nor is it read in depth anywhere else in Derrida's writings. Like the figure of the house to which it is bound, it is a theme that can be traced throughout Derrida's work without it ever becoming a discrete subject, as if it is itself repressed, returning only occasionally to surface in very isolated and what seem, at first, isolated points. But precisely for this reason it can be argued that its effects actually pervade all the texts that are unable or unwilling to speak about it.' See Mark Wigley, *The Architecture of Deconstruction: Derrida's Haunt* (Cambridge, Mass.: MIT Press, 1993), p. 108. I think Wigley fails to appreciate the canniness of Derrida's thinking on the uncanny and the wiliness, meticulousness and consistency of his engagement with it in his writings. As I hope the present study will have made apparent, it would be quite misguided to characterize the uncanny as a 'repressed' topic in Derrida's work or to suppose that it is something he is 'unable or unwilling to speak about'. At the same time, however, Wigley has a point: to the extent that the 'to be continued' suggests the promise of a 'full', 'in depth' reading of Freud's essay, this remains unfulfilled.

59   See *Shakespeare's Sonnets*, ed. with analytic commentary by Stephen Booth (New Haven: Yale University Press, 1977), pp. 103, 401–2. Recalling the hendiadic 'fits and starts', we may note here the appearance of 'spheres' (as 'eye-sockets') in *Hamlet* itself, once again in the words of the Ghost: 'I could a tale unfold whose lightest word / Would harrow up thy soul, freeze thy young blood, / Make thy two eyes like stars *start* from their spheres' (1.5.15–17).

60   Ludwig Wittgenstein, *Remarks on the Philosophy of Psychology*, 1, eds G. E. M. Anscombe and G. H. von Wright, trans. Anscombe (Oxford: Blackwell, 1980), section 887.

61   See Ludwig Wittgenstein, *Lectures and Conversations on Aesthetics, Psychology and Religious Belief*, Compiled from Notes taken by Yorick Smythies, Rush Rhees and James Taylor, ed. Cyril Barrett (Oxford: Basil Blackwell, 1966), pp. 24–5.

62   This is the title of a poem. See 'Questions Are Remarks' in *The Collected Poems of Wallace Stevens* (New York: Alfred A. Knopf, 1954), pp. 462–3.

63   Gordon C. F. Bearn, 'Wittgenstein and the Uncanny', *Soundings: An Interdisciplinary Journal*, vol.76, no. 1 (1993), 37.

64   Jacques Derrida, 'Edmond Jabès and the Question of the Book', in *Writing and Difference*, p. 71. On Derrida as someone who 'practises an art of interruption' see Geoffrey Bennington, *Interrupting Derrida* (London: Routledge, 2000), p. 3 and passim. At issue here is a notion of interruption that, in Bennington's phrase, 'does not come along to interrupt something that was there *before* interruption' (p. 196).

65   It is now generally reckoned that the death of Shakespeare's father, in 1601, occurred after *Hamlet* was written, or at least in the year after it was begun (1600). Less noticed in Freud's celebrated 'Oedipal' interpretation, perhaps, is his passing acknowledgement of the possible significance of the death in 1596 of Shakespeare's only son Hamnet, a name (as Freud says) 'which is identical with Hamlet'. Freud focuses on how Shakespeare deals with 'the relation of a son to his parents', however, and not, as his observation about the dead Hamnet might have led us to suppose, the relations of parents to their son.

66   Letter to Fliess, 2 November 1896, in *The Origins of Psychoanalysis: Letters to Wilhelm Fliess, Drafts and Notes: 1887–1902*, ed. Marie Bonaparte, Anna Freud, Ernst Kris, trans. Eric Mosbacher and James Strachey (London: Imago, 1954), p. 170; quoted here in the English translation given in Jones, 1, 356. He had also a few days earlier (26 October) written to Fliess about the event of his father's death itself, with all its 'stuporous attacks and inexplicable temperatures, hyperaesthesia and muscular spasms': see *The Origins of Psychoanalysis*, p. 170.

67   See Sigmund Freud, *Die Traumdeutung über Traum, Gesammelte Werke*, 2–3 (London: Imago, 1942), p. 273 n. 1.

68   Cf. Harold Bloom's provoking remarks in *The Western Canon: The Books and School of the Ages* (London: Macmillan, 1995): 'Hamlet did not have an Oedipus complex, but Freud certainly had a Hamlet complex, and perhaps psychoanalysis is a Shakespeare complex! ... Shakespearean criticism of Freud will have a hard birth, but it will come, since Freud as a writer will survive the death of psychoanalysis' (p. 376). I have explored in more detail elsewhere the question of Freud's 'distraction' concerning the authorship of the works attributed to Shakespeare: see *After Derrida* (Manchester: Manchester University Press, 1995), pp. 85–123.

The uncanny: a bibliography

Note: This bibliography comprises only essays and books focused specifically or extensively on 'the uncanny'. For more localized or passing references in other writings, especially in the work of Nietzsche, Freud, Heidegger, Bloom and Derrida, the reader is encouraged to consult the main index.

Aichele, George. 1997. 'Postmodern Fantasy, Ideology, and the Uncanny', in *The Return of the Uncanny*, special issue of *Paradoxa: Studies in World Literary Genres*, vol. 3, no. 3–4: 498–514.

Apter, Terry E. 1982. *Fantasy Literature: An Approach to Reality*. London: Macmillan. (See esp. Chapter 3, 'The Uncanny: Freud, E.T.A. Hoffmann, Edgar Allan Poe', 32–47.)

Armitt, Lucie. 2000. 'The Magical Realism of the Contemporary Gothic', in *A Companion to the Gothic*, ed. David Punter (Oxford: Blackwell), pp. 305–16.

Armstrong, Philip. 1994. 'Uncanny Spectacles: Psychoanalysis and the Texts of *King Lear*', *Textual Practice*, vol. 8, no. 2: 414–34.

Arnzen, Michael, ed. and intro. 1997. *The Return of the Uncanny*, special issue of *Paradoxa: Studies in World Literary Genres*, vol. 3, no. 3–4.

Arnzen, Michael. 1997. 'Supermarketing the Uncanny: Anxiety at the Point-of-sale', in *The Return of the Uncanny*, special issue of *Paradoxa: Studies in World Literary Genres*, vol. 3, no. 3–4: 571–93.

Batty, Nancy. 1997. 'America's Worst Nightmare ... Roseanne!', in *The Return of the Uncanny*, special issue of *Paradoxa: Studies in World Literary Genres*, vol. 3, no. 3–4: 539–55.

Bearn, Gordon C. F. 1993. 'Wittgenstein and the Uncanny', *Soundings: An Interdisciplinary Journal*, vol. 76, no. 1: 29–58.

Belsey, Catherine. 1999. 'English Studies in the Postmodern Condition: Towards a Place for the Signifier', in *Post-theory: New Directions in Criticism*, eds Martin McQuillan, Graeme MacDonald, Robin Purves and Stephen Thomson (Edinburgh: Edinburgh University Press), pp. 123–38.

Bennett, Andrew, and Nicholas Royle. 1999. *An Introduction to Literature, Criticism and Theory*, 2nd edn (London: Prentice Hall). (See esp. Chapter 5, 'The Uncanny', 36–43.)

Bloom, Harold. 1982. 'Freud and the Sublime: A Catastrophe Theory of Creativity', in *Agon: Towards a Theory of Revisionism* (Oxford: Oxford University Press).

Bresnick, Adam. 1996. 'Prosopoetic Compulsion: Reading the Uncanny in Freud and Hoffmann', *Germanic Review* , vol. 71, no. 2: 114–32.

Bronfen, Elisabeth. 1992. *Over Her Dead Body: Death, Femininity and the Aesthetic* (Manchester: Manchester University Press).

Bronfen, Elisabeth. 1992. 'The Death Drive (Freud)', in *Feminism and Psychoanalysis: A Critical Dictionary*, ed. Elizabeth Wright (Cambridge, Mass. and Oxford: Blackwell), pp. 52–7.

Castle, Terry. 1995. *The Female Thermometer: Eighteenth-century Culture and the Invention of the Uncanny* (Oxford: Oxford University Press).

Castle, Terry. 1997. 'Interview with Terry Castle', conducted by Michael Arnzen, in *The Return of the Uncanny*, special issue of *Paradoxa: Studies in World Literary Genres*, vol. 3, no. 3–4: 521–6.

Cavell, Stanley. 1988. *In Quest of the Ordinary: Lines of Skepticism and Romanticism* (Chicago: Chicago University Press). (See esp. Chapter 6, 'The Uncanniness of the Ordinary'.)

Chisholm, Dianne. 1992. 'The Uncanny', in *Feminism and Psychoanalysis: A Critical Dictionary*, ed. Elizabeth Wright (Cambridge, Mass. and Oxford: Blackwell), pp. 436–40.

Cixous, Hélène. 1976. 'Fiction and Its Phantoms: A Reading of Freud's *Das Unheimliche* (The "uncanny")', *New Literary History*, vol. 7, no. 3: 525–48.

Coats, Karen. 1997. 'Underwriting the Uncanny: The Role of Children's Literature in the Economy of the Subject', in *The Return of the Uncanny*, special issue of *Paradoxa: Studies in World Literary Genres*, vol. 3, no. 3–4: 489–97.

Coffman, Elizabeth. 1997. 'Uncanny Performances in Colonial Narratives: Josephine Baker in *Princess Tam Tam*', in *The Return of the Uncanny*, special issue of *Paradoxa: Studies in World Literary Genres*, vol. 3, no. 3–4: 379–94.

Derrida, Jacques. 1994. *Spectres of Marx: The State of the Debt, the Work of Mourning, and the New International*, trans. Peggy Kamuf (London: Routledge).

Dolar, Mladen. 1991. ' "I Shall Be with You on Your Wedding-night": Lacan and the Uncanny', *October*, vol. 58: 5–23.

Ferrall, Charles. 2001. ' "Neither Living nor Dead": T. S. Eliot and the Uncanny', in *Modernist Writing and Reactionary Politics* (Cambridge: Cambridge University Press), pp. 71–114.

Ferreira, Maria Aline. 1997. 'The Uncanny (M)other: Angela Carter's *The Passion of the New Eve*', in *The Return of the Uncanny*, special issue of *Paradoxa: Studies in World Literary Genres*, vol. 3, no. 3–4: 471–88.

Foster, Hal. 1993. *Compulsive Beauty* (Cambridge, Mass.: MIT Press).

Freud, Sigmund. 1985. 'The Uncanny' (1919), in *Pelican Freud Library*, 14, trans. James Strachey (Harmondsworth: Penguin), pp. 335–76.

Garber, Marjorie. 1987. *Shakespeare's Ghost Writers: Literature as Uncanny Causality* (London: Routledge).

Gelder, Ken. 1994. 'Vampires and the Uncanny: Le Fanu's "Carmilla"', in *Reading the Vampire* (London: Routledge), pp. 42–64.

Gelder, Ken, and Jane M. Jacobs. 1998. *Uncanny Australia: Sacredness and Identity in a Postcolonial Nation* (Melbourne: Melbourne University Press).

Germer, Stephan. 1999. 'Pleasurable Fear: Géricault and Uncanny Trends at the Opening of the Nineteenth Century', *Art History*, vol. 22, no. 2: 159–83.

Ginsburg, Ruth. 1992. 'A Primal Scene of Reading: Freud and Hoffmann', *Literature and Psychology*, vol. 38, no. 3: 24–46.

Grant, Barry. 1997. 'Interview with Barry Keith Grant', in *The Return of the Uncanny*, special issue of *Paradoxa: Studies in World Literary Genres*, vol. 3, no. 3–4: 429–37.

Guenther, Irene. 1995. 'Magic Realism, New Objectivity, and the Arts during the Weimar Republic', in *Magical Realism: Theory, History, Community*, eds Lois Parkinson Zamora and Wendy B. Faris (Durham, NC: Duke University Press), pp. 35–73.

Gunning, Tom. 1995. 'Phantom Images and Modern Manifestations: Spirit Photography, Magic Theater, Trick Films, and Photography's Uncanny', in *Fugitive Images: From Photography to Video*, ed. Patrice Petro (Bloomington: Indiana University Press), pp. 42–71.

Hertz, Neil. 1985. 'Freud and the Sandman', in *The End of the Line: Essays on Psychoanalysis and the Sublime* (New York: Columbia University Press), pp. 97–121.

Hopkins, Brooke. 1989. 'Keats and the Uncanny: "This living hand"', *The Kenyon Review*, vol. 11, no. 4 (1989), 28–40.

Hutch, Richard A. 1990. 'Uncanny Update and Henry James', *Psychoanalytic Review*, vol. 77, no. 3: 375–90.

Iverson, Margaret. 1998. 'In the Blind Field: Hopper and the Uncanny', *Art History*, vol. 21, no. 3: 409–29.

Jackson, Rosemary. 1981. *Fantasy: The Literature of Subversion* (London: Methuen). (On the uncanny, see esp. pp. 63–72.)

Jentsch, Ernst. 1995. 'On the Psychology of the Uncanny' (1906), trans. Roy Sellars, *Angelaki* vol. 2, no. 1: 7–16.

Johnson, Christopher. 1999. 'Ambient Technologies, Uncanny Signs', *Oxford Literary Review*, vol. 21: 117–34.

Kauppinen, Asko. 2000. *The Doll: The Figure of the Doll in Culture and Theory*. PhD diss., University of Stirling.

Kelso, Sylvia. 1997. 'The Postmodern Uncanny: or Establishing Uncertainty', in *The Return of the Uncanny*, special issue of *Paradoxa: Studies in World Literary Genres*, vol. 3, no. 3–4: 456–70.

Kittler, Friedrich A. 1997. 'Romanticism – Psychoanalysis – Film: A History of the Double', in *Literature, Media, Information Systems*, ed. John Johnston (Amsterdam: G+B Arts International), pp. 85–100.

Kofman, Sarah. 1984. 'Un philosophe "unheimlich"', in *Lectures de Derrida* (Paris: Galilée), pp. 11–114.

Kofman, Sarah. 1991. *Freud and Fiction*, trans. Sarah Wykes (Cambridge: Polity Press).

Krell, David Farrell. 1992. '*Das Unheimliche*: Architectural Sections of Heidegger and Freud', *Research in Phenomenology*, vol. 22: 43–61.

Kristeva, Julia. 1991. *Strangers to Ourselves*, trans. Leon C. Roudiez. (New York: Columbia University Press).

Kunkle, Sheila. 1997. 'The Uncanny Effects of Cruelty', in *The Return of the Uncanny*, special issue of *Paradoxa: Studies in World Literary Genres*, vol. 3, no. 3–4: 556–70.

Lloyd Smith, Allan. 1989. *Uncanny American Fiction: Medusa's Face* (Basingstoke: Macmillan).

Lloyd Smith, Allan. 1992. 'The Phantoms of *Drood* and *Rebecca*: The Uncanny Reencountered through Abraham and Torok's "Cryptonymy"', *Poetics Today*, vol. 13, no. 2 (Summer), 285–308.

Longenbach, James. 1990. 'Uncanny Eliot', in *T.S. Eliot: Man and Poet*, 1, ed. Laura Cowan (Orono, Maine: National Poetry Foundation), pp. 47–69.

Lydenberg, Robin. 1997. 'Freud's Uncanny Narratives', *PMLA*, 112: 1072–86.

Mackenthun, Gesa. 1997. 'Haunted Real Estate', in *The Return of the Uncanny*, special issue of *Paradoxa: Studies in World Literary Genres*, vol. 3, no. 3–4: 438–55.

Marks, W. S. 1965–66. 'The Psychology of the Uncanny in Lawrence's "The Rocking-Horse Winner', *Modern Fiction Studies*, vol. 11, no. 4 (Winter), 381–92.

Masschelein, Anneleen. 1997. 'Double Reading/Reading Double: Psychoanalytic Poetics at Work', in *The Return of the Uncanny*, special issue of *Paradoxa: Studies in World Literary Genres*, vol. 3, no. 3–4: 395–406.

McCaffrey, Phillip. 1994. 'Freud's Uncanny Woman', in *Reading Freud's Reading*, eds Sander L. Gilman, Jutta Birmele, Jay Geller and Valerie D. Greenberg (New York: New York University Press), pp. 91–108.

McQuire, Scott. 1997. 'The Uncanny Home: Television, Transparency and Overexposure', in *The Return of the Uncanny*, special issue of *Paradoxa: Studies in World Literary Genres*, vol. 3, no. 3–4: 527–38.

Mellencamp, Patricia. 1986. 'Uncanny Feminism: The Exquisite Corpses of Cecelia Condit', *Framework*, vol. 32, no. 3: 104–22. (Reprinted in *Fantasy and the Cinema*, ed. James Donald (London: British Film Institute, 1989), pp. 269–85.)

Miller, J. Hillis. 1979. 'The Critic as Host', in *Deconstruction and Criticism*, ed. Harold Bloom et al. (New York: Seabury Press), pp. 217-53.

Miller, J. Hillis. 1982. '*Wuthering Heights*: Repetition and the "Uncanny"', in *Fiction and Repetition: Seven English Novels* (Oxford: Basil Blackwell).

Møller, Lis. 1991. '"The Sandman": The Uncanny as Problem of Reading', in *The Freudian Reading: Analytical and Fictional Constructions* (Philadelphia: University of Pennsylvania Press).

Monleón, José B. 1990. *A Specter is Haunting Europe: A Sociohistorical Approach to the Fantastic* (Princeton, NJ: Princeton University Press).

Morlock, Forbes. 1995. 'Doubly Uncanny', in *Home and Family*, ed. Sarah Wood, special issue of *Angelaki*, vol. 2, no. 1: 17–21. (Includes bibliography of critical and theoretical material on the uncanny.)

Morris, David B. 1985. 'Gothic Sublimity', *New Literary History*, vol. 16: 299–319.

Mueller, Roswitha. 1983. 'The Uncanny in the Eyes of a Woman: Valie Export's *Invisible Adversaries*', *SubStance*, vol. 37/38: 129–39.

Norden, Martin. 1997. 'The Uncanny Film Image of the Obsessive Avenger', in *The Return of the Uncanny*, special issue of *Paradoxa: Studies in World Literary Genres*, vol. 3, no. 3–4: 367–78.

Parkin-Gounelas, Ruth. 2001. *Literature and Psychoanalysis: Intertextual Readings* (Basingstoke and New York: Palgrave). (See esp. Chapter 5, 'The Uncanny Text'.)

Paul, William. 1997. 'Uncanny Theater: The Twin Inheritances of the Movies', in *The Return of the Uncanny*, special issue of *Paradoxa: Studies in World Literary Genres*, vol. 3, no. 3–4: 321–47.

Pinedo, Isabel. 1997. 'Wet Death and the Uncanny', in *The Return of the Uncanny*, special issue of *Paradoxa: Studies in World Literary Genres*, vol. 3, no. 3–4: 407–16.

Punter, David. 1999. 'Revising the Uncanny, or, Coleridge Forgets Freud', *European Romantic Review*, vol. 10, no. 2: 254-64.

Punter, David. 2000. 'Shape and Shadow: On Poetry and the Uncanny', in *A Companion to the Gothic*, ed. David Punter (Oxford: Blackwell), pp. 193–205.

Rand, Nicholas, and Maria Torok. 1994. '*The Sandman* Looks at "The Uncanny": The Return of the Repressed or of the Secret; Hoffmann's Question to Freud', in *Speculations after Freud: Psychoanalysis, Philosophy and Culture*, eds Sonu Shamdasani and Michael Munchow (London: Routledge), pp. 185–203.

Rank, Otto. 1971. *The Double: A Psychoanalytic Study* (1914), trans. Harry Tucker, Jr (Chapel Hill, NC: University of North Carolina Press).

Royle, Nicholas. 1991. *Telepathy and Literature: Essays on the Reading Mind* (Oxford: Basil Blackwell) (See esp. Chapter 4, pp. 63–83.)

Schneider, Stephen. 1997. 'Uncanny Realism and the Decline of the Modern Horror Film', in *The Return of the Uncanny*, special issue of *Paradoxa: Studies in World Literary Genres*, vol. 3, no. 3–4: 417–28.

Schwenger, Peter. 1995. 'Uncanny Reading', *English Studies in Canada*, vol. 21, no. 3: 333–45.

Simms, Eva-Maria. 1996. 'Uncanny Dolls: Images of Death in Rilke and Freud', *New Literary History*, vol. 27: 663–77.

Sprigg, C. St John (aka Christopher Caudwell), ed. and intro. 1936. *Uncanny Stories* (London: Thomas Nelson).

Stern, Lesley. 1997. 'I Think Sebastian, Therefore I … Somersault: Film and the Uncanny', in *The Return of the Uncanny*, special issue of *Paradoxa: Studies in World Literary Genres*, vol. 3, no. 3–4: 348–66.

Thomas, Sophie. 2001. 'The Return of the Fragment: "Christabel" and the Uncanny', *Bucknell Review*, vol. 25, no. 2.

Todd, Jane Marie. 1986. 'The Veiled Woman in Freud's "Das Unheimliche"', *Signs* vol. 2, no. 3: 519–28.

Todorov, Tzvetan. 1975 (orig. 1970). *The Fantastic: A Structural Approach to a Literary Genre*, trans. Richard Howard (Ithaca: Cornell University Press). (See esp. Chapter 3, 'The Uncanny and the Marvellous', pp. 41–57.)

Vidler, A. 1992. *The Architectural Uncanny: Essays in the Modern Unhomely* (Cambridge, Mass.: MIT Press).

Weber, Samuel. 1973. 'The Sideshow, or: Remarks on a Canny Moment', *Modern Language Notes*, vol. 88: 1102–33.

Wigley, Mark, 1993. *The Architecture of Deconstruction: Derrida's Haunt* (Cambridge, Mass.: MIT Press).

Williams, Linda Ruth. 1995. *Critical Desire: Psychoanalysis and the Literary Subject* (London: Edward Arnold). (See esp. 'Home is Where the Uncanny Is', pp. 177–82.)

Winchell, James. 1997. 'Century of the Uncanny: The Modest Terror of Theory', in *The Return of the Uncanny*, special issue of *Paradoxa: Studies in World Literary Genres*, vol. 3, no. 3–4: 515–20.

Wolfreys, Julian. 2002. *Victorian Hauntings: Spectrality, Gothic, the Uncanny and Literature* (Basingstoke and New York: Palgrave).

Wood, Sarah, ed. 1995. *Home and Family*, special issue of *Angelaki*, vol. 2, no. 1.

Wright, Elizabeth. 1989. 'The uncanny and surrealism', in *Modernism and the European Unconscious*, eds. Peter Collier and Judith Davies. London: Polity Press.

Wright, Elizabeth. 1998. *Psychoanalytic Criticism: A Reappraisal*. 2nd edn (Cambridge: Polity Press). (See esp. 124–34, 'The Return of Freud: Jokes and the Uncanny'.)

Wright, Elizabeth. 1999. *Speaking Desires Can Be Dangerous: The Poetics of the Unconscious*. (Cambridge: Polity Press). (See esp. pp. 18–30, 'The Uncanny and its Poetics'.)

Yingling, Thomas E. 1997. 'Homosexuality and the Uncanny: What's Fishy in Lacan', in *The Gay Nineties*, ed. Thomas Foster, Carol Siegel and Ellen Berry (New York: New York University Press).

Young, Robert. 1984. 'Psychoanalytic Criticism: Has It Got Beyond a Joke?', *Paragraph*, vol. 4: 87–114.

Index

Note: The idea of an index to a study of 'the uncanny' is perhaps manifestly insane. This is especially clear in the case of an 'index of topics', which is bound to be violently selective, arbitrary and misleading. It is nevertheless hoped that it may be of some help to readers wishing to orient themselves in relation to 'the uncanny'. Both indexes in this book were prepared by Jinan Joudeh, to whom the author hereby expresses his deep gratitude.

INDEX OF NAMES

INDEX OF TOPICS